ASIAN DEVELOPMENT OUTLOOK 2021 UPDATE

TRANSFORMING AGRICULTURE IN ASIA

SEPTEMBER 2021

ADB

ASIAN DEVELOPMENT BANK

© 2021 Asian Development Bank
6 ADB Avenue, Mandaluyong City, 1550 Metro Manila, Philippines
Tel +63 2 8632 4444; Fax +63 2 8636 2444
www.adb.org

Some rights reserved. Published in 2021.

ISBN 978-92-9269-054-0 (print); 978-92-9269-055-7 (electronic); 978-92-9269-056-4 (ebook)
ISSN 1655-4809 (print)
Publication Stock No. FLS210352-3
DOI: http://dx.doi.org/10.22617/FLS210352-3

The views expressed in this publication are those of the authors and do not necessarily reflect the views and policies of the Asian Development Bank (ADB) or its Board of Governors or the governments they represent.

ADB does not guarantee the accuracy of the data included in this publication and accepts no responsibility for any consequence of their use. The mention of specific companies or products of manufacturers does not imply that they are endorsed or recommended by ADB in preference to others of a similar nature that are not mentioned.

By making any designation of or reference to a particular territory or geographic area, or by using the term "country" in this document, ADB does not intend to make any judgments as to the legal or other status of any territory or area.

Corrigenda to ADB publications may be found at http://www.adb.org/publications/corrigenda.

Notes:
In this publication, "$" refers to US dollars.
ADB recognizes "Hong Kong" as Hong Kong, China; "China" as the People's Republic of China; "Korea" and "South Korea" as the Republic of Korea; and "Vietnam" as Viet Nam.

Cover design by Anthony Victoria.

Contents

Foreword

The growth trajectories of developing Asia's economies are heading in different directions. Stronger growth is expected in economies that are coping well with the COVID-19 pandemic, as they can take advantage of the strengthening recovery in global demand. But those that are struggling with the pandemic cannot, and are falling behind. With more contagious variants emerging, making good progress on national vaccination programs and taking effective measures to keep COVID-19 at bay have played a role in determining which economies are making stronger recoveries.

In this mutable landscape, *Asian Development Outlook 2021 Update* expects somewhat slower regional growth, which is now forecast at 7.1% in 2021 and 5.4% in 2022 in an uneven recovery caused by divergent growth paths. Growth forecasts are revised up for East Asia and Central Asia, but down for South Asia, Southeast Asia, and the Pacific from the projections made in April. This reflects not just the differences in vaccine progress and control of domestic outbreaks but also other factors, including rising commodity prices which are helping Central Asia, and depressed tourism which continues to weigh on tourism-dependent economies in the Pacific and elsewhere.

The pandemic notwithstanding, developing Asia must continue to address its other, longer-term development goals. Our theme chapter tackles one of the most basic of them—building sustainable food production and agriculture systems. Both the public and private sectors have important roles to play to increase agricultural productivity while ensuring long-term environmental sustainability and resilient livelihoods. The theme chapter aligns with one of the seven operational priorities of the Asian Development Bank (ADB)—promoting rural development and food security.

Through the *Asian Development Outlook 2021 Update*, ADB continues to generate useful economic analysis, forecasts, and policy advice to our members. The *Asian Development Outlook* reports are a prime example of ADB's push to strengthen its role as a knowledge provider. Our role as a knowledge bank becomes even more important during periods of high uncertainty, such as the present, when past experience provides little guidance and our ability to learn from each other can mean the difference between moving ahead or falling behind. The *Asian Development Outlook* reports and ADB's other knowledge products and services are all aimed at providing the region's policy makers with the insights they need to help them chart the development journey of their economies through this pandemic and beyond.

MASATSUGU ASAKAWA
President
Asian Development Bank

Acknowledgments

Asian Development Outlook 2021 Update was prepared by staff of the regional departments and resident missions of the Asian Development Bank (ADB) under the guidance of the Economic Research and Regional Cooperation Department (ERCD). Representatives of these departments met regularly as the Regional Economic Outlook Task Force to coordinate and develop consistent forecasts for developing Asia.

ERCD economists, led by Abdul Abiad, director of the Macroeconomics Research Division, coordinated the production of this report, assisted by Edith Laviña. Shiela Camingue-Romance, Cindy Castillejos-Petalcorin, David Keith De Padua, Rhea Manguiat Molato, Nedelyn Magtibay-Ramos, Pilipinas Quising, Dennis Sorino, and Priscille Villanueva provided technical and research support. Emmanuel Alano, Kristina Baris, Jesson Pagaduan, Reizle Jade Platitas, Rene Cris Rivera, and Michael Timbang did additional research. Joseph Bulan, Arturo Martinez, Jr., and Orlee Velarde provided valuable support. Economic editorial advisors Robert Boumphrey, Eric Clifton, Joshua Greene, Srinivasa Madhur, Richard Niebuhr, and Reza Vaez-Zadeh made substantial contributions to the chapters on ADB's developing members and the regional outlook. Josef Yap and Tuesday Soriano gave editorial advice on the theme chapter and Margarita Debuque-Gonzales on the regional outlook.

The support and guidance of former ADB Chief Economist Yasuyuki Sawada and Acting Chief Economist Joseph E. Zveglich Jr. throughout this *Update's* production is gratefully acknowledged.

Authors who contributed the sections are bylined in each chapter. The subregional coordinators were Kenji Takamiya, Lilia Aleksanyan, and Fatima Catacutan for Central Asia; Akiko Terada-Hagiwara for East Asia; Rana Hasan and Lani Garnace for South Asia; James Villafuerte and Dulce Zara for Southeast Asia; and Rommel Rabanal, Cara Tinio, and Remrick Patagan for the Pacific.

Peter Fredenburg and Alastair McIndoe advised on ADB style and English usage. Alvin Tubio did the typesetting and graphics, assisted by Heili Ann Bravo, Elenita Pura, and Angel Love Roque. Anthony Victoria did the cover art. Kevin Nellies designed the landing page for this *Update*. Fermirelyn Cruz and Rhia Bautista-Piamonte provided administrative and secretarial support. A team from the Department of Communications, led by David Kruger and Terje Langeland, planned and coordinated the dissemination of this *Update*.

Definitions and assumptions

The economies discussed in *Asian Development Outlook 2021 Update* are classified by major analytic or geographic group. For the purposes of this report, the following apply:

- **Association of Southeast Asian Nations** (ASEAN) comprises Brunei Darussalam, Cambodia, Indonesia, the Lao People's Democratic Republic, Malaysia, Myanmar, the Philippines, Singapore, Thailand, and Viet Nam. The ASEAN-5 are Indonesia, Malaysia, the Philippines, Thailand, and Viet Nam.
- **Developing Asia** comprises the 46 members of the Asian Development Bank listed below by geographic group.
- **Central Asia** comprises Armenia, Azerbaijan, Georgia, Kazakhstan, the Kyrgyz Republic, Tajikistan, Turkmenistan, and Uzbekistan.
- **East Asia** comprises Hong Kong, China; Mongolia; the People's Republic of China; the Republic of Korea; and Taipei,China.
- **South Asia** comprises Afghanistan, Bangladesh, Bhutan, India, Maldives, Nepal, Pakistan, and Sri Lanka.
- **Southeast Asia** comprises Brunei Darussalam, Cambodia, Indonesia, the Lao People's Democratic Republic, Malaysia, Myanmar, the Philippines, Singapore, Thailand, Timor-Leste, and Viet Nam.
- **The Pacific** comprises the Cook Islands, the Federated States of Micronesia, Fiji, Kiribati, the Marshall Islands, Nauru, Niue, Palau, Papua New Guinea, Samoa, Solomon Islands, Tonga, Tuvalu, and Vanuatu.

Unless otherwise specified, the symbol "$" and the word "dollar" refer to US dollars.

A number of assumptions have been made for the projections in *Asian Development Outlook 2021 Update*: The policies of national authorities are maintained. Real effective exchange rates remain constant at their average from 5 August to 3 September 2021. The average price of oil is $69/barrel in 2021 and $67/barrel in 2022. The 6-month London interbank offered rate for US dollar deposits averages 0.1% in 2021 and 0.3% in 2022, the European Central Bank refinancing rate averages 0% in both years, and the Bank of Japan's overnight call rate averages −0.1% in both years.

The forecasts and analysis in this *Update* are based on information available to 3 September 2021.

Abbreviations

ADB	Asian Development Bank
ADO	Asian Development Outlook
ASEAN	Association of Southeast Asian Nations
BPO	business process outsourcing
bps	basis points
CAB	current account balance
COVID-19	Coronavirus Disease 2019
FAO	Food and Agriculture Organization
FSM	Federated States of Micronesia
FY	fiscal year
GDP	gross domestic product
GHG	greenhouse gas
H	half
ha	hectare
ICT	information and communication technology
IMF	International Monetary Fund
IPM	integrated pest management
IT	information technology
kCal	kilocalorie
Lao PDR	Lao People's Democratic Republic
Libor	London interbank offered rate
M2	broad money that includes cash and highly liquid accounts
M3	broad money that adds time accounts to M2
m^2	square meter
m^3	cubic meter
MSME	micro, small, or medium-sized enterprise
N_2O	nitrous oxide
NIE	newly industrialized economy
NPL	nonperforming loan
OECD	Organisation for Economic Co-operation and Development
OPEC	Organization of the Petroleum Exporting Countries
PMI	purchasing managers' index
PNG	Papua New Guinea
PRC	People's Republic of China
Q	quarter
R&D	research and development
RCP	representative concentration pathway
ROK	Republic of Korea
RSE	recognized seasonal employer
SDG	Sustainable Development Goal
SME	small or medium-sized enterprise
SOE	state-owned enterprise
SOFAZ	State Oil Fund of Azerbaijan
tCO_2e	ton of carbon dioxide equivalent
US, USA	United States

ADO 2021 Update—Highlights

Developing Asia continues to grapple with the COVID-19 pandemic. Renewed outbreaks are a cause for concern, amid uneven progress on vaccination. The region's output is forecast to expand by 7.1% in 2021 and 5.4% in 2022, supported by a broad recovery in exports. Regional growth paths are diverging, with economies that have successfully contained the pandemic or are making good progress on vaccination programs forging ahead. Price pressures are expected to remain in check, with headline inflation forecast at 2.2% in 2021 and 2.7% in 2022.

Several risks cloud developing Asia's outlook. The main threats come from the COVID-19 pandemic, including the emergence of new variants, slower-than-expected vaccine rollouts, and waning vaccine effectiveness. Geopolitical tensions, financial turmoil, and disruptions to global supply chains may also undermine the region's growth prospects. As economies recover from the pandemic, medium-term risks will take center stage again, led by the natural disasters and extreme weather events related to climate change, which are becoming more frequent.

Sustainable food production and agricultural systems that are resilient to climate change will be crucial for developing Asia. To transform agriculture, regional economies must tackle challenges from three ongoing shifts— in consumer demand, demographics, and a changing and more fragile environment. Innovative solutions are required to increase the productivity of developing Asia's smallholder farmers and sustainably meet changing demand. Early warning systems and insurance programs will help mitigate the impact of extreme weather shocks on farmers and build resilience. Agricultural policy across the region should support the transformation of agriculture through innovation and markets, and promote food security and improved nutrition.

Joseph E. Zveglich, Jr.
Acting Chief Economist
Asian Development Bank

Vaccines, variants, and Asia's uneven recovery

■ **The COVID-19 pandemic continues to besiege developing Asia.**
New daily cases peaked at 105 per million in May and declined to 25 per million in June, only to rise again to 43 per million in July, driven by more infectious variants. The new wave of infections started flattening in August across the region. Developing Asia's progress on vaccination remains uneven and lags behind the rollout in advanced economies. As of 31 August 2021, 28.7% of the region's population had been fully vaccinated, compared with 51.8% in the United States (US) and 58.0% in the European Union.

■ **Vaccines are gradually changing policy responses to the pandemic.**
While unable to completely stop the spread of the virus, successful vaccine rollouts are turning COVID-19 into a less deadly disease—and this is changing the nature of the pandemic. Governments across the world and in developing Asia are adapting their containment approaches to this changing landscape, so that the link between the severity of an outbreak and the stringency of public health restrictions is being gradually broken by increased vaccination coverage.

■ **The uneven progress of vaccinations is contributing to the divergence of growth paths in developing Asia.** In the first half of 2021, growth in the region's largest economies was higher than in the second half of 2020, including in Hong Kong, China; the People's Republic of China (PRC); Singapore; and Taipei,China. These economies quickly rolled out vaccines and successfully contained outbreaks, thereby avoiding tighter restrictions and allowing them to capitalize on strengthening global demand. In Indonesia, the Philippines, and Thailand, however, recovery was held back by new waves of infections and slower progress on vaccination. Leading business indicators suggest economic growth is set to slow across the region.

■ **Inflation has accelerated across developing Asia but remains in check.**
After declining continuously in 2020, the region's headline inflation rate rose from 0.8% in January to 2.3% in June on rising energy and food prices in some economies and because of increased economic activity as containment measures eased. Inflation remains benign and close to the targets of most central banks across the region, but some Central Asian economies are notable exceptions.

■ **Developing Asia's exports are levelling off above prepandemic levels.**
Exports continued to rise in the first quarter of 2021 on recovering external demand, and they were 19% above prepandemic volumes in June. Since early 2021, exports have been characterized by a wider range of products, including mechanical machinery and mineral fuels, than was the case early in the pandemic. The increased demand for a broader product base has boosted exports from more developing Asian economies, including India, Kazakhstan, and Pakistan. Meanwhile, Hong Kong, China; Malaysia; the PRC; the Republic of Korea; and Viet Nam continued to benefit from strong global demand for goods and electronics related to the pandemic.

■ **Remittances picked up in the first quarter of 2021 in most developing Asian economies; international tourism remains depressed.** Even where remittances did not increase in the first quarter, they declined by less than they did in 2020. International tourism remains generally depressed, although a gradual rebound is ongoing in Georgia and Maldives.

■ **Fiscal and monetary policies continue to be supportive of economic recovery in developing Asia.** Fiscal policy will remain accommodative in several economies this year, with a general shift toward consolidation expected for 2022 and beyond. The monetary stance is also largely expansionary, as most central banks refrained from raising policy rates after cutting them in 2020, leading to low or negative real interest rates in many economies.

■ **Most regional currencies weakened in the first 8 months of 2021; buoyant liquidity supported financial conditions.** Most regional exchange rates depreciated, and foreign portfolio outflows resulted from the strong economic recovery in the US, the possibility of early monetary normalization by the US Federal Reserve, and uncertainty over the region's recovery due to rising COVID-19 cases. But accommodative monetary stances in developing Asia and around the world have supported liquidity and financial conditions. Regional equity markets remained robust and were above their prepandemic levels. Average risk premiums narrowed marginally.

■ **Recovery paths will continue to diverge in developing Asia.** This *Update* expects the regional economy to expand at a slower rate than projected in *Asian Development Outlook 2021* in April. While growth forecasts are raised for East Asia and Central Asia, downward revisions for the rest of the region weigh on the outlook. The recovery in global demand for exports from developing Asia, supported by robust growth in advanced economies, will continue to benefit the region's export-oriented economies. But the recovery momentum has weakened in economies battling renewed waves of COVID-19.

■ **Inflation remains benign but is expected to pick up in some developing Asian economies.** Regional inflation is forecast to remain moderate at 2.2% this year before accelerating to 2.7% in 2022. Tepid inflation will be shaped by declining food prices in the PRC and weaker demand in economies hit by new waves of COVID-19. The continuing trend of rising international commodity prices in the first half of 2021 could stoke inflation in economies where pass-through effects on domestic prices are significant.

■ **A resurgence in the COVID-19 pandemic remains the main risk to the outlook.** Renewed pandemic waves, possibly driven by the emergence of more infectious and vaccine-resistant variants, the waning effectiveness of vaccines already administered, and slower-than-expected vaccine rollouts could derail developing Asia's recovery—and further sharpen the divergence between the region's economies. But policy makers must also pay heed to other risks, including those arising from climate change, geopolitical tensions, and tightening financial conditions.

Transforming agriculture in Asia

Summary

❖ **Asia must transform agriculture to tackle three emerging challenges: changing demand, changing demographics, and a changing and fragile environment.** *Food demand is increasing and shifting toward animal products, requiring more resource-intensive agriculture. Meanwhile, Asia struggles to improve agricultural productivity as rural populations shrink and age. Further, agriculture is exposed to risks from a changing climate and from farm practices that are not environmentally sustainable.*

❖ **Innovation can improve productivity and sustainably meet shifting demand.** *New approaches have emerged to help Asia's smallholder farmers avail of agricultural machine services and thus enhance their labor productivity. Improved technologies and practices help farmers produce more food without overusing chemical inputs or water. Recent rapid expansion in aquaculture can, if properly regulated, sustainably provide to Asian consumers animal protein from healthy seafood products.*

❖ **Asia's farmers need better and more comprehensive support systems.** *As extreme weather shocks worsen and become more frequent, early warning systems and affordable insurance can mitigate impacts on farmers and rural communities. Expanding value chains allow farmers to diversify their production into high-value crops. Digital technologies can help farmers and traders reach new markets, just as they have served urban consumers during the COVID-19 pandemic. Government policies should focus less on traditional production support and, instead, encourage market-oriented innovation.*

Evolving demand even as food insecurity persists

■ **Rising incomes and urbanization are transforming food consumption.**
Daily energy consumption per capita in the region is expected to increase from
2,612 kilocalories in 2012 to 2,844 by 2030. Meanwhile, demand for food
in Asia has shifted away from basic staples toward more resource-intensive
animal products. Notably, Asians are the biggest consumers of fish per capita in
the world. Agriculture in Asia must be productive enough to meet demand as it
expands and evolves.

■ **Despite the region's growing prosperity, malnourishment persists.**
In the past 2 decades, developing Asia has achieved remarkable
progress in reducing undernourishment and micronutrient deficiency.
Despite these gains, 86.8 million children in Asia under age 5 still suffer
stunting. Whereas insufficient agricultural production used to be a primary
cause of undernourishment in Asia, today the larger problem is economic
access to nutritious food. Even in economies that have achieved high average
calorie intake per capita, malnutrition persists as micronutrient deficiency.
Another consequence is the incidence of obesity and related noncommunicable
diseases rising steeply as healthy traditional diets yield to convenient processed
food, often imported.

Shifting demographics that challenge agricultural development

■ **Asia's rural communities are rapidly shrinking, feminizing, and aging.**
A predictable feature of modern economic development is a population
shift away from agriculture. Higher-paying manufacturing and service jobs
in cities draw workers out of rural areas, steadily eroding the share of rural
population in Asia from 80% in 1970 to 52% in 2020 and a projected 38%
by 2050. With many men migrating to cities, agriculture relies increasingly on
female workers, who often have less access to finance and other resources.
The share of older farmworkers has similarly increased, with farmers aged 50 or
older becoming the majority in Sri Lanka and Thailand.

Stiff environmental challenges facing agriculture in Asia

■ **Climate change poses ever greater challenges to agriculture in Asia.**
Crop growth and yields are highly sensitive to significant changes in
temperature and rainfall. Extreme weather such as storms, floods, and
droughts have frequently battered Asian agriculture in the recent past.
In 2013, Typhoon Haiyan dealt Philippine agriculture over $1.4 billion in losses.
With climate change, the frequency and scale of such events is escalating,
as is the damage they cause. In South Asia, monsoon rains are likely to increase
by 6.4% even as droughts lengthen and occur 5–10 times more frequently.

■ **Agriculture faces environmental challenges of its own making.** The green revolution succeeded in part through its heavy use of chemical fertilizers and pesticides. Fertilizer subsidies lowered prices for chemical inputs and encouraged their overuse, causing environmental pollution. At the same time, water scarcity worsened. Asia has developed and expanded irrigation systems such that it has 70% of the world's irrigated farmland, but farmers' collective management of irrigation has weakened in recent decades. As aquaculture expands rapidly in Asia, sustainability issues revolve around mangrove destruction, land salinization, groundwater depletion, and health issues concerning residual chemicals in fish cultured for human consumption.

Innovation to boost productivity, and regulation for sustainability

■ **Smallholder farmers' access to machines can be improved.** Small and fragmented landholding inhibits farm mechanization in much of Asia. Innovative arrangements have emerged that enable some of Asia's 350 million smallholder farmers to hire machine services to work on fields consolidated by farmer groups. These innovative approaches would better realize their potential if outdated laws and regulations governing land and other agriculture factors were modernized.

■ **With improved practices, farmers can safeguard the environment.** Chemical inputs can be optimized and reduced by promoting such innovative techniques as site-specific nutrient management and environmentally sensitive integrated pest management. When improved modern irrigation systems use volumetric water tariffs, lined canals, and remote water sensing and control facilities, farmers can use water more efficiently. Potential exists for the private sector to play an important role in providing the farm extension and advisory services that are critical to making agriculture more sustainable.

■ **Well-regulated aquaculture can meet Asian consumer demand for seafood.** With many marine fisheries around the world already overfished, satisfying Asian consumers' robust and growing appetite for seafood will depend on increased aquaculture production. Aquaculture currently provides 52% of fishery production worldwide, and Asia dominates global aquaculture with an 88% share. When seafood is more readily available and affordable, consumer nutrition improves.

Better and more comprehensive support systems for Asian farmers

■ **Early warning systems offer efficient protection from weather risks.** In 2019, timely information on monsoon floods in northern Bangladesh helped communities and the government prepare and secure necessary supplies, slashing economic losses by two-thirds. Advanced spatial information systems are critically important in developing early warning systems able to mitigate farmers' exposure to climate risks and protect their livelihoods— as is strengthened national and local capacity to integrate these systems. Farmers can improve their climate resilience by adopting crop varieties that cope well with weather shocks.

- **Innovative crop insurance builds resilience in Asian farm communities.** Crop insurance schemes exist in over three-fourths of the economies in developing Asia but are fully operational nationally in only four: India, the PRC, the Philippines, and Sri Lanka. Insurance programs use spatial information systems to speed crop damage assessments and expedite claim settlement. Enhanced spatial information systems can expand the coverage of insurance programs.

- **Value chains evolve as farmers diversify into high-value crops.** With high-value crops providing 32% of agriculture production value, surpassing that of cereal crops at only 26%, contract farming is now widely used to facilitate production and procurement. Although contract disputes often arise because of unclear agreements and weak contract enforcement, contract farming can benefit farmers in Asia with advanced agreement on output prices and the technical assistance they need to compete in high-value food markets.

- **Digital technologies can expand inclusive growth to farmers in remote areas.** In recent years, digital technology has improved supply chains and helped farmers acquire technical and market information, connecting farmers in remote areas with traders and consumers. Under the COVID-19 pandemic, expanded e-commerce facilitated sales of agricultural products and home delivery of prepared food, which mitigated food service disruption and losses.

- **Agricultural policy should support innovation, markets, and better nutrition.** Traditional agricultural policies have directly supported agricultural production to achieve and maintain self-sufficiency. However, such policies can induce overproduction and distort markets. A better approach decouples rural welfare support from agricultural policy, which properly invests in research and development, encourages innovation, and pursues market-oriented development. Finally, food policies should promote a balanced and nutritious diet for all.

GDP growth rate, % per year

	2020	2021		2022	
		April ADO 2021	*September Update*	*April ADO 2021*	*September Update*
Developing Asia	**-0.1**	**7.3**	**7.1**	**5.3**	**5.4**
Central Asia	**-1.9**	**3.4**	**4.1**	**4.0**	**4.2**
Armenia	-7.4	1.8	5.2	3.0	3.5
Azerbaijan	-4.3	1.9	2.2	2.5	2.5
Georgia	-6.2	3.5	8.5	6.0	6.5
Kazakhstan	-2.6	3.2	3.4	3.5	3.7
Kyrgyz Republic	-8.6	3.5	3.5	5.0	5.0
Tajikistan	4.5	5.0	5.0	5.5	5.5
Turkmenistan	1.6	4.8	4.8	4.9	4.9
Uzbekistan	1.6	4.0	5.0	5.0	5.5
East Asia	**1.8**	**7.4**	**7.6**	**5.1**	**5.1**
Hong Kong, China	-6.1	4.6	6.2	4.5	3.4
Mongolia	-5.3	4.8	4.6	5.7	6.0
People's Republic of China	2.3	8.1	8.1	5.5	5.5
Republic of Korea	-0.9	3.5	4.0	3.1	3.1
Taipei,China	3.1	4.6	6.2	3.0	3.0
South Asia	**-5.6**	**9.5**	**8.8**	**6.6**	**7.0**
Afghanistan	-1.9	3.0	..	4.0	..
Bangladesh	3.5	6.8	5.5	7.2	6.8
Bhutan	0.9	-3.4	-3.4	3.7	3.7
India	-7.3	11.0	10.0	7.0	7.5
Maldives	-32.0	13.1	18.0	14.0	15.0
Nepal	-2.1	3.1	2.3	5.1	4.1
Pakistan	-0.5	2.0	3.9	4.0	4.0
Sri Lanka	-3.6	4.1	3.4	3.6	3.4
Southeast Asia	**-4.0**	**4.4**	**3.1**	**5.1**	**5.0**
Brunei Darussalam	1.2	2.5	1.8	3.0	3.5
Cambodia	-3.1	4.0	1.9	5.5	5.5
Indonesia	-2.1	4.5	3.5	5.0	4.8
Lao People's Democratic Republic	-0.5	4.0	2.3	4.5	4.0
Malaysia	-5.6	6.0	4.7	5.7	6.1
Myanmar	3.3	-9.8	-18.4	...	...
Philippines	-9.6	4.5	4.5	5.5	5.5
Singapore	-5.4	6.0	6.5	4.1	4.1
Thailand	-6.1	3.0	0.8	4.5	3.9
Timor-Leste	-8.5	3.4	2.2	4.3	4.0
Viet Nam	2.9	6.7	3.8	7.0	6.5
The Pacific	**-5.3**	**1.4**	**-0.6**	**3.8**	**4.8**
Cook Islands	-5.9	-26.0	-26.0	6.0	7.1
Federated States of Micronesia	-3.9	-1.8	-1.1	2.0	2.0
Fiji	-15.7	2.0	-5.0	7.3	8.8
Kiribati	0.6	-0.2	0.3	2.3	2.3
Marshall Islands	-2.6	-1.4	-3.3	2.5	4.0
Nauru	0.8	1.5	1.5	1.0	1.0
Niue	...	...	...	...	...
Palau	-10.3	-7.8	-10.8	10.4	8.8
Papua New Guinea	-3.3	2.5	1.3	3.0	4.1
Samoa	-3.2	-9.2	-9.2	3.1	3.1
Solomon Islands	-4.5	1.0	1.0	4.5	4.5
Tonga	-0.8	-5.3	-5.3	1.8	1.8
Tuvalu	1.0	2.5	2.5	3.0	3.0
Vanuatu	-8.5	2.0	-3.0	4.0	5.0

... = not available, *ADO = Asian Development Outlook*, GDP = gross domestic product.

Note: Because of the uncertain situation, no forecasts are provided for 2021 and 2022 in Afghanistan, and for fiscal year 2022 in Myanmar.

Inflation, % per year

	2020	2021		2022	
		April ADO 2021	*September Update*	*April ADO 2021*	*September Update*
Developing Asia	**2.8**	**2.3**	**2.2**	**2.7**	**2.7**
Central Asia	**7.5**	**6.8**	**7.7**	**6.3**	**6.7**
Armenia	1.2	3.8	5.5	2.5	3.0
Azerbaijan	2.8	3.5	4.5	3.0	3.0
Georgia	5.2	5.0	9.5	3.5	4.0
Kazakhstan	6.8	6.5	6.9	6.2	6.4
Kyrgyz Republic	6.3	7.0	10.0	7.0	7.0
Tajikistan	9.4	9.0	9.5	8.0	9.0
Turkmenistan	10.0	8.0	10.0	8.0	10.0
Uzbekistan	12.9	10.0	10.0	9.0	9.0
East Asia	**2.2**	**1.5**	**1.4**	**2.2**	**2.2**
Hong Kong, China	0.3	1.3	1.5	2.0	2.0
Mongolia	3.7	6.9	6.9	8.5	8.5
People's Republic of China	2.5	1.5	1.3	2.3	2.3
Republic of Korea	0.5	1.3	2.0	1.5	1.6
Taipei,China	-0.2	1.1	1.5	1.1	1.1
South Asia	**6.5**	**5.5**	**5.8**	**5.1**	**5.1**
Afghanistan	5.6	5.0	...	4.0	..
Bangladesh	5.7	5.8	5.6	5.8	5.8
Bhutan	3.0	6.4	8.2	5.3	6.2
India	6.2	5.2	5.5	4.8	4.8
Maldives	-1.4	3.0	2.5	2.5	2.0
Nepal	6.2	5.0	3.6	6.0	5.2
Pakistan	10.7	8.7	8.9	7.5	7.5
Sri Lanka	4.6	4.5	5.1	5.0	5.3
Southeast Asia	**1.2**	**2.4**	**2.2**	**2.4**	**2.4**
Brunei Darussalam	1.9	0.7	1.3	0.7	0.7
Cambodia	2.9	3.1	2.9	3.0	2.7
Indonesia	2.0	2.4	1.7	2.8	2.7
Lao People's Democratic Republic	5.1	4.5	3.7	5.0	4.5
Malaysia	-1.1	1.8	2.5	2.0	2.3
Myanmar	5.7	6.2	6.2	...	...
Philippines	2.6	4.1	4.1	3.5	3.5
Singapore	-0.2	1.0	1.6	1.2	1.4
Thailand	-0.8	1.1	1.1	1.0	1.0
Timor-Leste	0.5	2.0	2.3	2.0	2.0
Viet Nam	3.2	3.8	2.8	4.0	3.5
The Pacific	**3.4**	**3.7**	**3.6**	**3.9**	**4.1**
Cook Islands	0.7	1.0	1.0	0.7	0.7
Federated States of Micronesia	1.6	1.9	1.9	2.0	2.0
Fiji	-2.6	3.5	1.0	3.0	3.0
Kiribati	1.0	1.1	1.1	1.5	1.5
Marshall Islands	0.3	1.0	1.0	1.5	1.7
Nauru	0.9	1.1	1.1	2.0	2.0
Niue	2.7	...	...	...	...
Palau	0.7	0.0	-0.3	1.0	1.0
Papua New Guinea	4.9	4.3	4.6	4.4	4.6
Samoa	1.5	-2.5	-3.0	2.7	3.2
Solomon Islands	3.0	2.5	2.5	3.5	3.5
Tonga	0.2	0.8	1.3	2.5	2.5
Tuvalu	1.6	3.3	4.0	3.5	2.5
Vanuatu	5.3	3.5	5.0	3.7	3.7

... = not available, *ADO = Asian Development Outlook.*

Note: Because of the uncertain situation, no forecasts are provided for 2021 and 2022 in Afghanistan, and for fiscal year 2022 in Myanmar.

1

VACCINES, VARIANTS, AND ASIA'S UNEVEN RECOVERY

Vaccines, variants, and Asia's uneven recovery

The COVID-19 pandemic continues to besiege developing Asia and is furthering economic divergence in the region. The export rebound has become more broad-based, encompassing more sectors, but not all regional economies are benefiting from this. Because of successful COVID-19 pandemic containment measures and rapid vaccine rollouts, some are forging ahead on the global economic recovery. But others are unable to capitalize on strong external demand, due partly to insufficient progress on vaccination and renewed outbreaks bringing tighter restrictions. The regional recovery remains fragile, with leading indicators in August pointing to a general slowdown in manufacturing. Remittances to the region remain resilient, but international tourism continues to be depressed. Inflation has ticked up in some economies on rising energy and food prices, and exchange rate depreciations. But it nevertheless remains close to the targets of central banks across the region, excluding Central Asia. Against this backdrop, fiscal and monetary policies continue to be accommodative and financial conditions remain robust.

Developing Asia's economic prospects in 2021 and 2022 hinge on the progress of the pandemic and vaccination programs. Buoyed by healthy demand for exports and accelerating growth in East Asia and Central Asia, the regional economy is set to expand by 7.1% in 2021—0.2 percentage points less than forecast in Asian Development Outlook 2021. The growth projection for 2022 is marginally revised up, from 5.3% to 5.4%. Inflation should remain under control, at 2.2% in 2021 and 2.7% in 2022. The region's current account surplus will narrow slightly in both years mainly on rising imports in recovering economies. The main threats to the outlook are associated with COVID-19, including delayed vaccine rollouts, the emergence of new variants, and waning vaccine effectiveness. Additional downside risks come from geopolitical tensions, possible financial market turbulence, and global supply chain disruptions. As economies recover from the pandemic, medium-term risks will return to center stage, including rising threats from extreme weather events linked to climate change.

This section was written by Abdul Abiad, Shiela Camingue-Romance, David Keith De Padua, Jules Hugot, Matteo Lanzafame (lead), Nedelyn Magtibay-Ramos, Irfan Qureshi (co-lead), Arief Ramayandi, Marcel Schroder, Dennis Sorino, and Shu Tian of the Economic Research and Regional Cooperation Department (ERCD), Asian Development Bank (ADB) , Manila, and Kristina Barris, Jesson Pagaduan, Reizle Jade Platitas, and Michael Timbang, ERCD consultants.

Recent developments— gaps widen as the fight against COVID-19 carries on

The COVID-19 pandemic continues to beleaguer developing Asia, as the region faces renewed outbreaks and more infectious variants. Daily new cases in the region peaked at 105 per million in May, and then declined to 25 per million in June, before surging again to 43 per million in July, with sharp rises in Southeast Asia, Central Asia, and the Pacific (Figure 1.1.1). The region's latest wave of outbreaks plateaued in August. By the end of that month, the cut-off date for this report, daily new cases were at 40 per million. The pandemic, however, continues to wreak havoc across the world, with cases rising since late June and bringing the number of daily new cases to 83 per million in August.

Figure 1.1.1 Daily new COVID-19 cases in developing Asia

New and more infectious variants are driving outbreaks across the region.

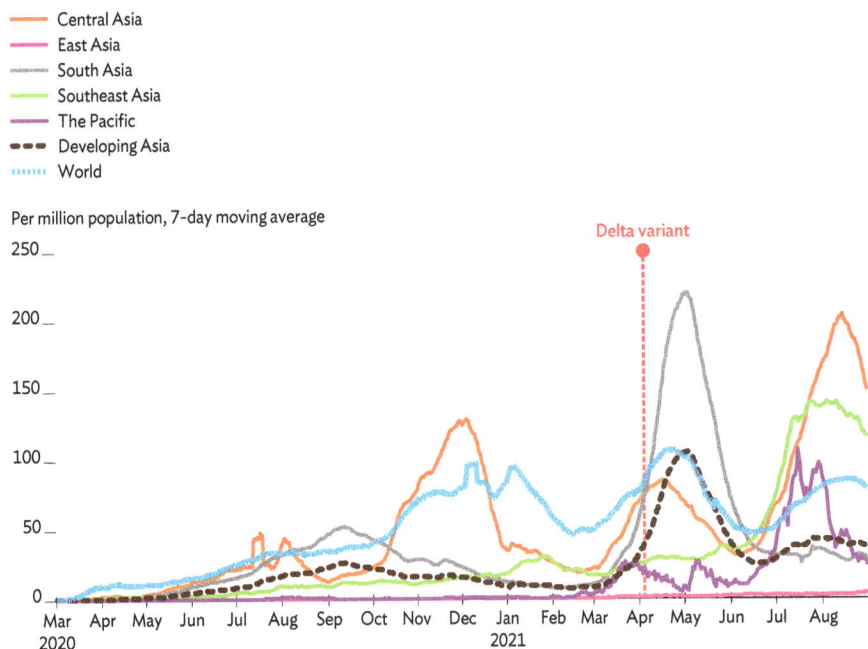

Per million population, 7-day moving average

Sources: CEIC Data Company (accessed 6 September 2021); Ministry of Healthcare (Kazakhstan). https://www.coronavirus2020.kz/ (accessed 8 September 2021).

Vaccination coverage has progressed unevenly, as developing Asia continues to lag behind advanced economies. As of 31 August 2021, 28.7% of the region's population had full vaccine protection, roughly half of the 51.8% coverage in the United States and 58.0% in the European Union (Figure 1.1.2). Progress on vaccination in developing Asia remains uneven and, except for the People's Republic of China (PRC), higher inoculation rates are skewed in favor of economies with relatively small populations, such as Bhutan, Maldives, Mongolia, and Singapore. In two-thirds of the region's economies, the share of the population that has been fully vaccinated is 30% or lower, with inadequate supplies of vaccines often the primary constraint to more rapid progress.

Vaccines are making COVID-19 a much less deadly disease. Although unable to completely stop the spread of the virus, evidence shows that vaccines are highly protective against severe cases of COVID-19. Because of this, the number of hospitalizations and deaths per case have declined significantly on the increasing share of vaccinated people (Figure 1.1.3). Widespread vaccination makes it possible to live with the virus, allowing economies to remain relatively open and breaking the trade-off between lives and livelihoods.

As vaccinations move ahead, governments across developing Asia are adapting to the changing environment through calibrated containment strategies. With rising vaccination coverage, indicators other than daily new cases, such as deaths or the hospital occupancy rate, are starting to be given more weight as guidelines for tightening or relaxing restrictions. So, as an increasing share of an economy's population is vaccinated, the relationship between containment stringency and daily new infections becomes weaker (Box 1.1.1). Indeed, declines in mobility and economic activity have not been as sharp this year despite the reimposition of containment measures. This not only reflects the more targeted and time-bound restrictions governments have been imposing but also businesses and households learning to function within those restrictions.

Partly due to uneven vaccination progress, recovery in developing Asia diverged in the first half of 2021. Growth was positive in all of the region's 10 largest economies and higher than in the second half of 2020 (Figure 1.1.4). Growth tended to be stronger in economies that had progressed the most in controlling the pandemic. The recovery was particularly strong in Hong Kong, China; the PRC; and Singapore, where governments successfully contained virus outbreaks and quickly rolled out vaccines.

Figure 1.1.2 Vaccinated against COVID-19

Developing Asia's vaccination progress remains uneven and lags behind advanced economies.

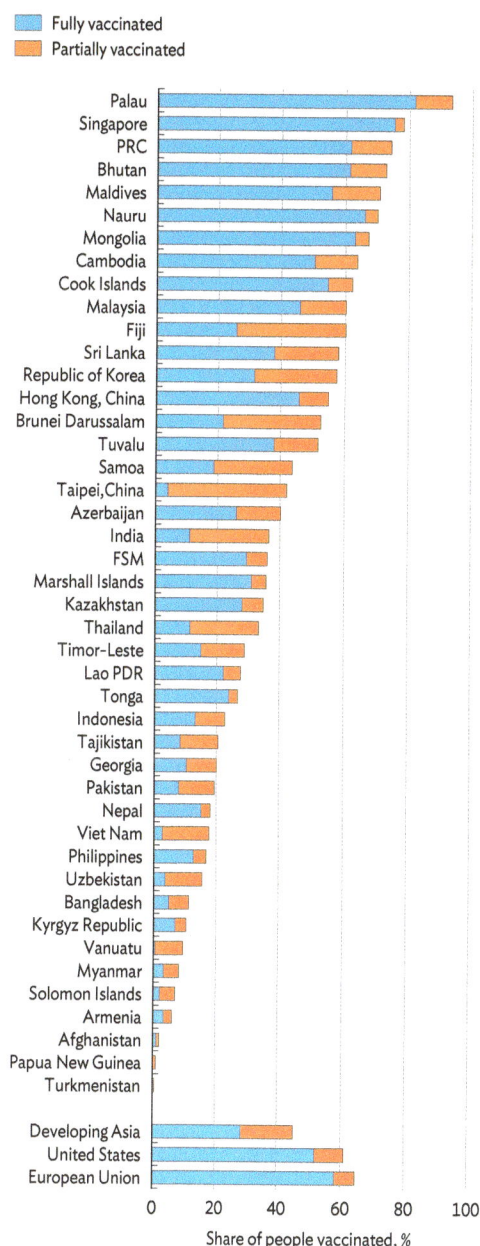

FSM = Federated States of Micronesia, Lao PDR = Lao People's Democratic Republic, PRC = People's Republic of China.

Note: Data are latest available for August for all economies except Turkmenistan (April).

Sources: CEIC Data Company (accessed 6 September 2021); Our World in Data. https://ourworldindata.org/coronavirus (accessed 3 September 2021).

Figure 1.1.3 COVID-19 death rate and vaccination coverage, March–August 2021

Higher vaccination rates are associated with fewer deaths per case.

- Developing Asia
- Comparators
- ···· Linear (developing Asia)

Deaths per 100 cases, 14-day lagged cases

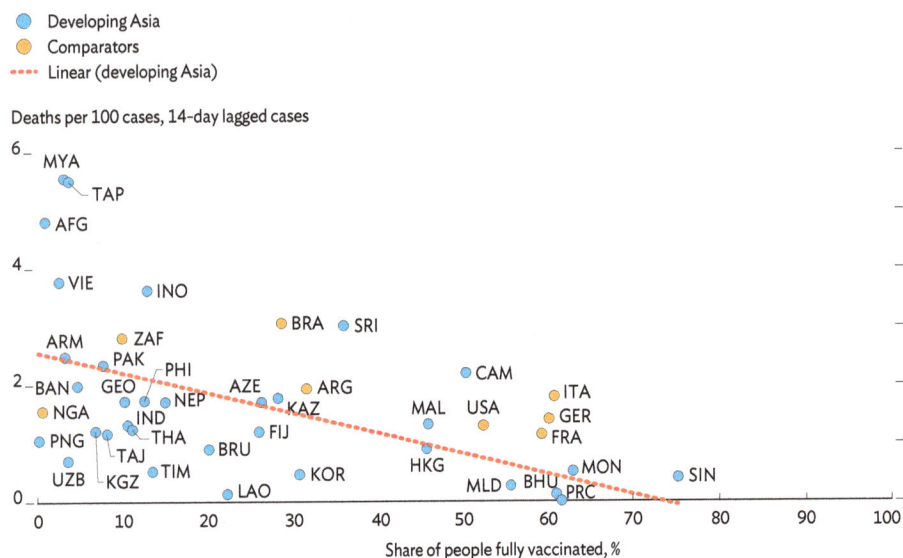

AFG = Afghanistan, ARG = Argentina, ARM = Armenia, AZE = Azerbaijan, BAN = Bangladesh, BHU = Bhutan, BRA = Brazil, BRU = Brunei Darussalam, CAM = Cambodia, COVID-19 = Coronavirus Disease 2019 FIJ = Fiji, FRA = France, GEO = Georgia, GER = Germany, HKG = Hong Kong, China, IND = India, INO = Indonesia, ITA = Italy, KAZ = Kazakhstan, KGZ = Kyrgyz Republic, KOR = Republic of Korea, LAO = Lao People's Democratic Republic, MAL = Malaysia, MLD = Maldives, MON = Mongolia, MYA = Myanmar, NEP = Nepal, NGA = Nigeria, PAK = Pakistan, PHI = Philippines, PNG = Papua New Guinea, PRC = People's Republic of China, SIN = Singapore, SRI = Sri Lanka, TAJ = Tajikistan, TAP = Taipei,China, THA = Thailand, TIM = Timor-Leste, USA = United States, UZB = Uzbekistan, VIE = Viet Nam, ZAF = South Africa.

Notes: Number of deaths per 100 cases is based on the total confirmed deaths and total confirmed cases since March. It is calculated as the ratio between total confirmed deaths and total confirmed cases 14 days prior to account for the lag between the onset of illness and death.

Source: Our World in Data. https://ourworldindata.org/coronavirus (accessed 2 September 2021).

Figure 1.1.4 Demand-side contributions to growth in developing Asia

Economies that did better with COVID-19 vaccination and pandemic control tended to perform better.

- Net exports
- Investment
- Consumption
- H2 2020 GDP growth, yoy
- H1 2021 GDP growth, yoy

Percentage points

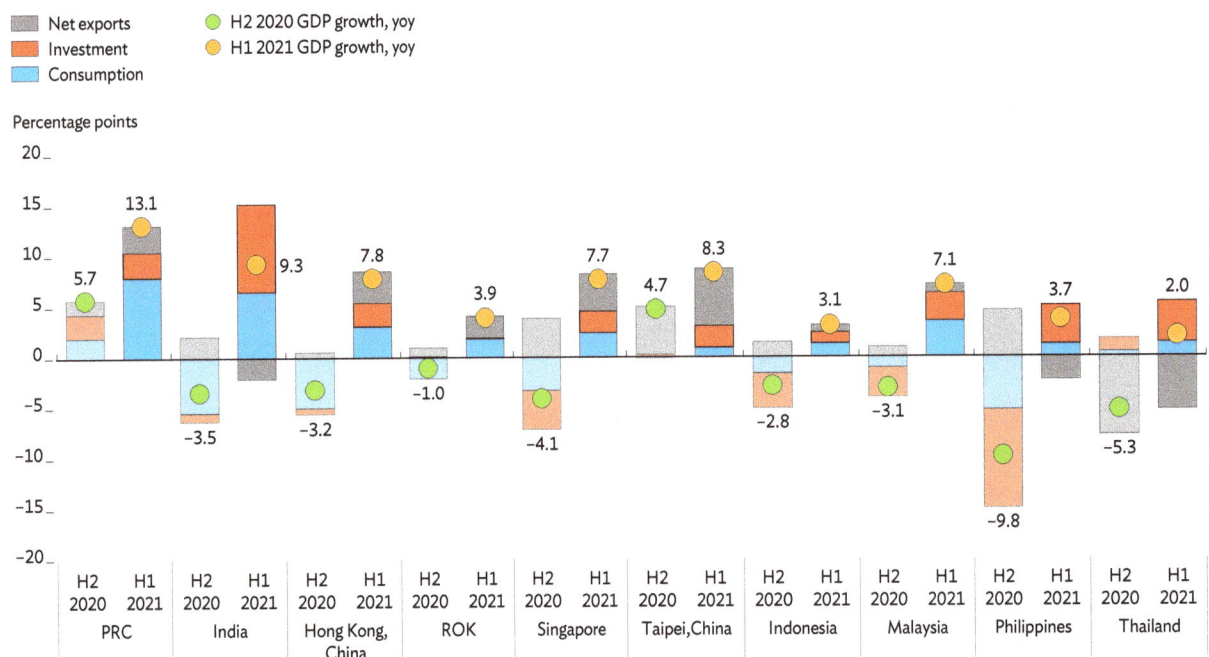

COVID-19 = Coronavirus Disease 2019, GDP = gross domestic product, H = half, PRC = People's Republic of China, ROK = Republic of Korea, yoy = year on year.

Note: Data refers to calendar half years. Consumption and investment includes both the private and public sector. Statistical discrepancy is excluded from the bars.

Source: CEIC Data Company (accessed 8 September 2021).

Economic expansion was modest in Indonesia, Thailand, and the Philippines, which grappled with new COVID-19 infection waves and lagging vaccination programs. The contribution of consumption to growth improved in all the 10 economies shown in Figure 1.1.4, and the contribution of investment rose in nine. Net exports also contributed positively to growth in most of these economies on robust external demand, but this was not the case in tourism-dependent Thailand.

Readings of the manufacturing purchasing managers' index have declined since March on a resurgence in COVID-19 cases and supply chain disruptions. The index, after peaking earlier this year has fallen below the 50-mark that separates improvement from deterioration in Indonesia, Malaysia, the Philippines, the PRC, Thailand, and Viet Nam (Figure 1.1.5). Readings rose sharply to 55.3 in India in July and have remained above 50 in the Republic of Korea and Taipei,China. The index has generally performed better in economies with high vaccination rates in recent months (Figure 1.1.6). One exception is Malaysia, where the vaccine rollout that accelerated from mid-July was too late to stop the variant-driven wave that started earlier in that month, and which prompted the government to impose tight restrictions even as the vaccine rollout continued.

Figure 1.1.5 Manufacturing purchasing managers' index in developing Asia, Q1–Q3 2021

Falling indexes in Q3 show the recovery's fragility in the region.

Manufacturing purchasing managers' index, seasonally adjusted

	2021							
	Q1			Q2			Q3	
Economy	Jan	Feb	Mar	Apr	May	Jun	Jul	Aug
PRC	51.5	50.9	50.6	51.9	52.0	51.3	50.3	49.2
India	57.7	57.5	55.4	55.5	50.8	48.1	55.3	52.3
Indonesia	52.2	50.9	53.2	54.6	55.3	53.5	40.1	43.7
Malaysiaª	51.9	50.7	52.9	56.9	54.3	42.9	43.1	46.4
Philippines	52.5	52.5	52.2	49.0	49.9	50.8	50.4	46.4
Republic of Korea	53.2	55.3	55.3	54.6	53.7	53.9	53.0	51.2
Taipei,China	60.2	60.4	60.8	62.4	62.0	57.6	59.7	58.5
Thailand	49.0	47.2	48.8	50.7	47.8	49.5	48.7	48.3
Viet Nam	51.3	51.6	53.6	54.7	53.1	44.1	45.1	40.2

Services purchasing managers' index, seasonally adjusted

PRC	52.0	51.5	54.3	56.3	55.1	50.3	54.9	46.7
India	52.8	55.3	54.6	54.0	46.4	41.2	45.4	56.7

PRC = People's Republic of China, Q = quarter.

ª For Malaysia, the series is adjusted by adding 3 points, as historical experience suggests that an index value above 47 is consistent with expansion. Pink to red indicates contraction (<50), and white to green indicates expansion (>50).

Source: CEIC Data Company (accessed 6 September 2021).

Figure 1.1.6 Manufacturing output growth and COVID-19 vaccinations

Manufacturing performance has been better in economies with higher vaccination rates.

- ▣ Central Asia
- ▲ East Asia
- ● South Asia
- ◆ Southeast Asia
- ● Advanced economies

Manufacturing PMI

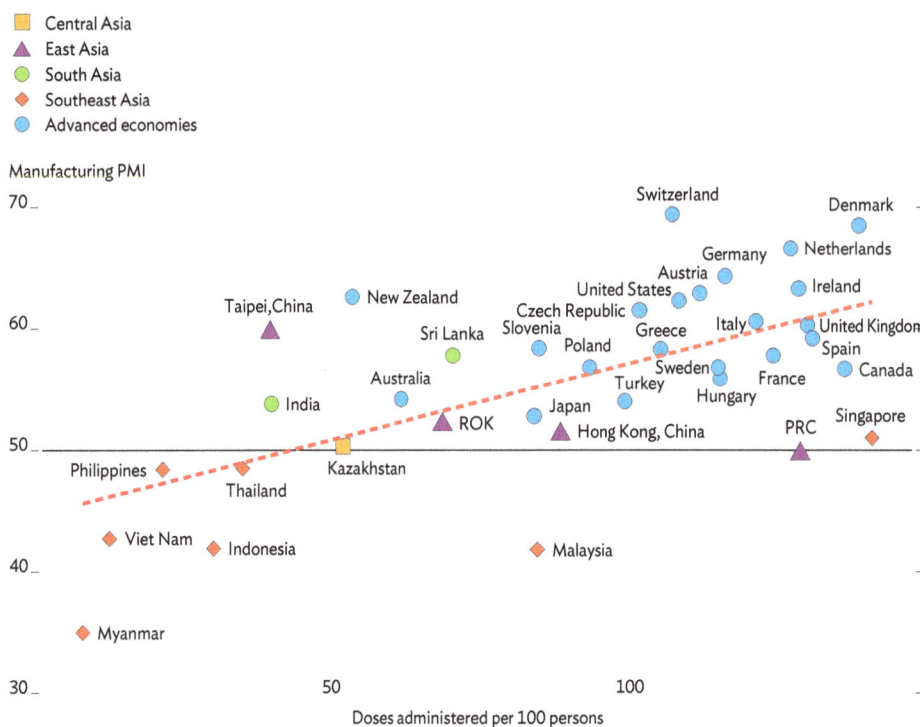

COVID-19 = Coronavirus Disease 2019, PMI = purchasing managers' index, PRC = People's Republic of China, ROK = Republic of Korea.
Note: The manufacturing PMI and doses administered per 100 persons are the average of July and August 2021.
Sources: Bloomberg. Covid-19 Vaccine Tracker. https://www.bloomberg.com/graphics/covid-vaccine-tracker-global-distribution/; Haver Analytics; IHS Markit (all accessed 1 September 2021).

The services purchasing managers' index in developing Asia's two largest economies moved in opposite directions in August. In India, it surged to 56.7, up from 45.4 in July, on improved access to vaccines and the easing of containment measures. In the PRC, it fell to 46.7 amid travel restrictions and localized lockdowns.

Regional inflation edged up in the first half of 2021 but remains in check. Headline inflation rose from 0.8% in January to 2.3% in June, as governments across developing Asia eased containment measures and business activity picked up (Figure 1.1.7). The regional aggregate, however, hides significant differences in the inflation dynamics across subregions. Inflation rates remained highest in Central Asia, at 8.3% in June, on currency depreciations in some economies, followed by South Asia, at 6.5%. The rate in Southeast Asia was 2.2% in June and 1.3% in East Asia. Rising global commodity prices this year are reflected in regional inflationary dynamics to varying degrees across the subregions (Figure 1.1.8). Food prices have been rising this year in Central Asia and South Asia, but remained stable in Southeast Asia.

Figure 1.1.7 Headline inflation in developing Asia

After a continual decline in 2020, headline inflation edged up in the first half of 2021.

Central Asia
East Asia
South Asia
Southeast Asia
Developing Asia

% year on year

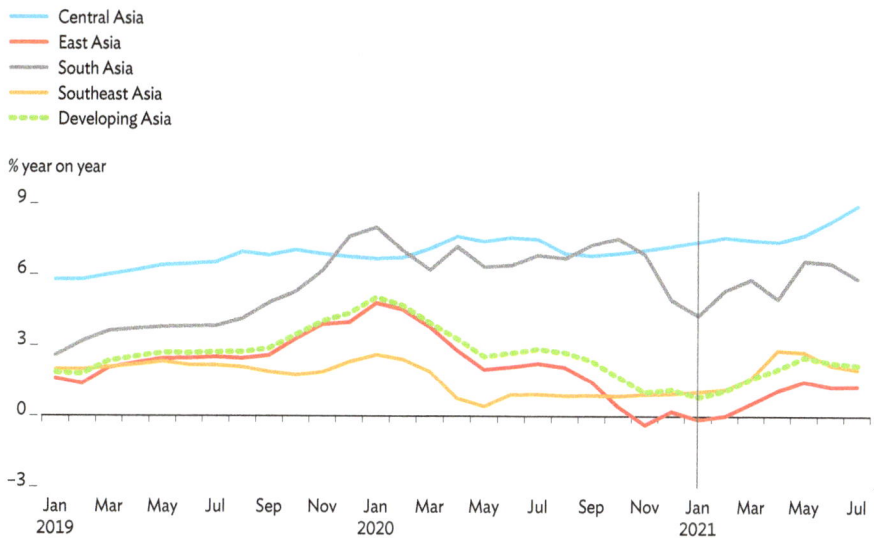

Note: The Pacific is excluded due to data unavailability.
Source: CEIC Data Company (accessed 6 September 2021).

Figure 1.1.8 Global commodity prices

Prices surged since the second half of 2020.

Food
Brent crude oil price
Copper
Gold

$, December 2019 = 100

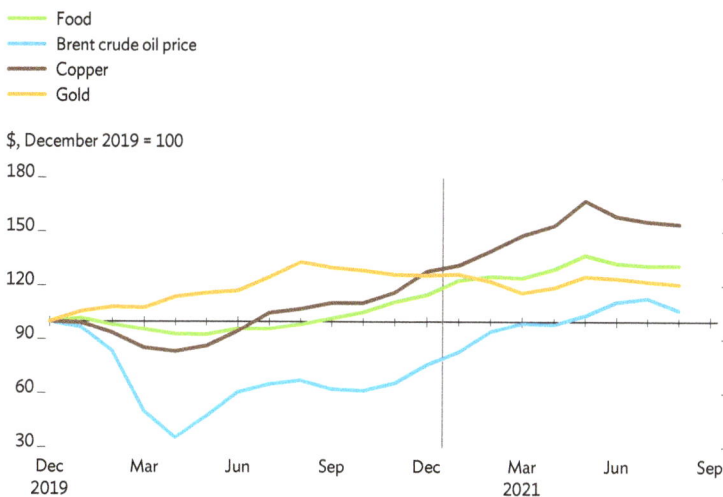

Source: World Bank. Commodity Markets, Pink Sheet data. https://www.worldbank.org/en/research/commodity-markets (accessed 7 September 2021).

In East Asia, food price inflation has decelerated since early 2021, reflecting falling pork prices in the PRC following an outbreak of African swine fever in 2019 and 2020 (Figure 1.1.9, panel A). Energy costs have remained subdued in East Asia and Southeast Asia, but have been increasing in Central Asia and South Asia (panel B). Inflation rates remain close to or below the inflation targets of many central banks in the region, with the exception of some Central Asian economies (Figure 1.1.10).

Figure 1.1.9 Food and energy prices in developing Asia

Domestic prices rose in Central Asia and South Asia in the first 7 months of 2021, but were stable or declining in the rest of the region.

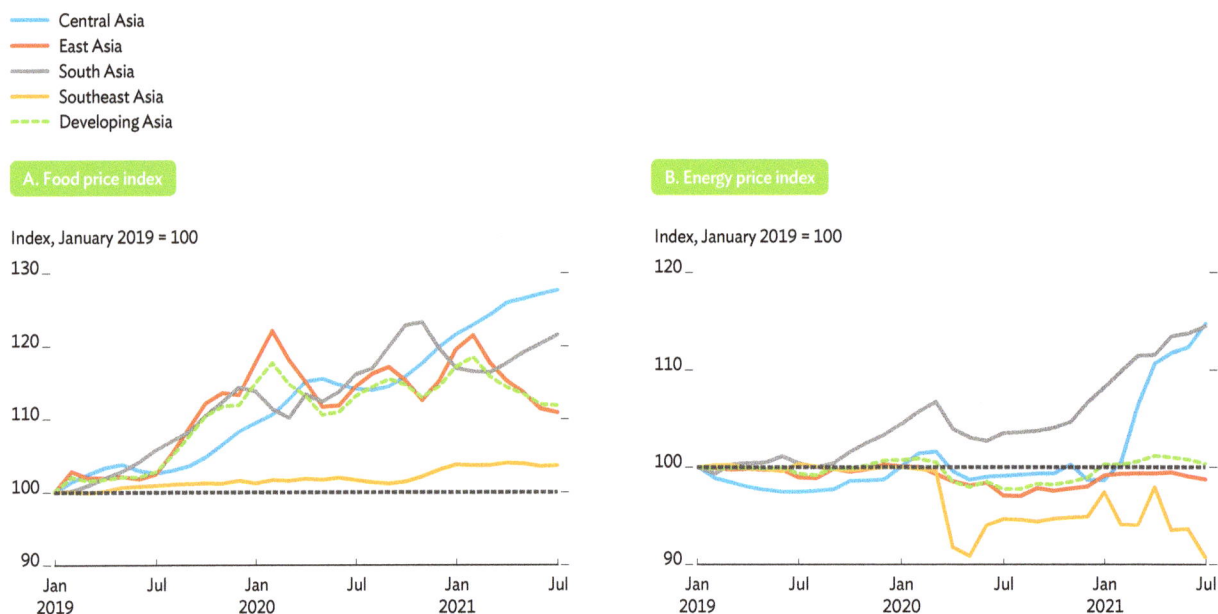

- Central Asia
- East Asia
- South Asia
- Southeast Asia
- Developing Asia

A. Food price index

Index, January 2019 = 100

B. Energy price index

Index, January 2019 = 100

Sources: CEIC Data Company (accessed 27 August 2021); Asian Development Bank estimates.

Figure 1.1.10 Headline, core inflation, and inflation targets in developing Asia

Outside Central Asia, core inflation remains within or below central bank targets.

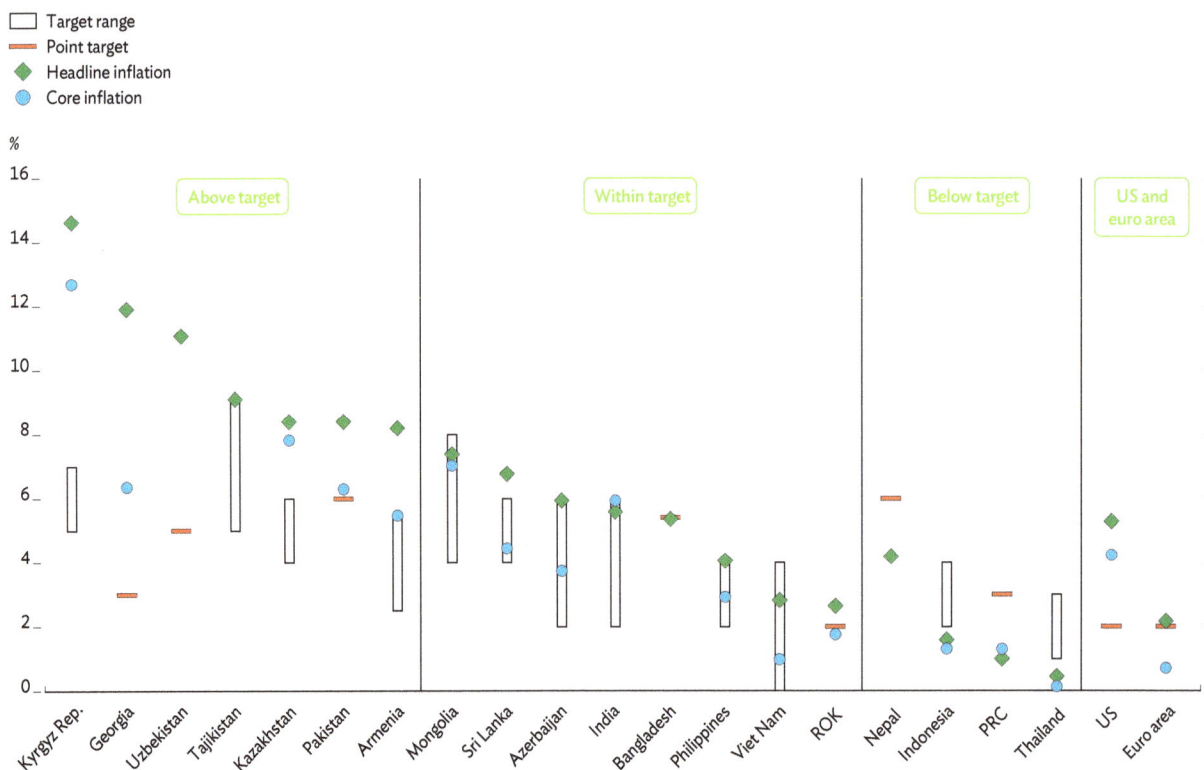

- ☐ Target range
- ▬ Point target
- ◆ Headline inflation
- ● Core inflation

%

Above target | Within target | Below target | US and euro area

Kyrgyz Rep., Georgia, Uzbekistan, Tajikistan, Kazakhstan, Pakistan, Armenia, Mongolia, Sri Lanka, Azerbaijan, India, Bangladesh, Philippines, Viet Nam, ROK, Nepal, Indonesia, PRC, Thailand, US, Euro area

PRC = People's Republic of China, ROK = Republic of Korea, US = United States.

Notes: Headline and core inflation are the latest available for each economy. Viet Nam's target is inflation of less than 4%. Inflation data refer to July 2021 for all economies except Indonesia, Pakistan, the ROK, and Viet Nam (August). Core inflation is unavailable for Bangladesh, Nepal, Tajikistan, and Uzbekistan.

Sources: CEIC Data Company (accessed 3 September 2021); Central Bank News. http://www.centralbanknews.info/p/inflation-targets.html (accessed 29 July 2021).

Developing Asia's exports are levelling off above prepandemic levels

World trade continued to rise in the first quarter of 2021, before stabilizing above pre-COVID-19 levels. Global merchandise exports have continued their strong rebound since April 2020, rising in the first quarter of 2021 on the recovery in advanced economies (Figure 1.1.11). World trade then stabilized during March–June at about 4.5% above 2019's average volumes. Global demand for manufactured goods, however, seems to be plateauing. Consumers in advanced economies are shifting expenditure back to services, as indicated by accelerating growth for services consumption and decelerating growth for goods consumption in the US. This rebalancing is already visible in August data from the Republic of Korea, where exports were still high but decreasing to the European Union and the US. Constraints to further export growth include disruptions to factories and ports due to the COVID-19 Delta variant, shipping bottlenecks, and the effect of semiconductor shortages on manufacturing (Box 1.1.2).

Rebounding global demand has boosted developing Asia's exports, first from the PRC and then from other regional economies. In June, export volumes from the PRC were 22.5% above prepandemic levels, after they peaked in January and February. Export volumes from the rest of the region followed a similar pattern as the PRC, but with a lag, reflecting the later arrival of and recovery from the pandemic. These export volumes have stabilized since April and were 16.2% above prepandemic levels in June.

Figure 1.1.11 Real export volume in developing Asia

Exports are stabilizing at close to 20% above prepandemic levels.

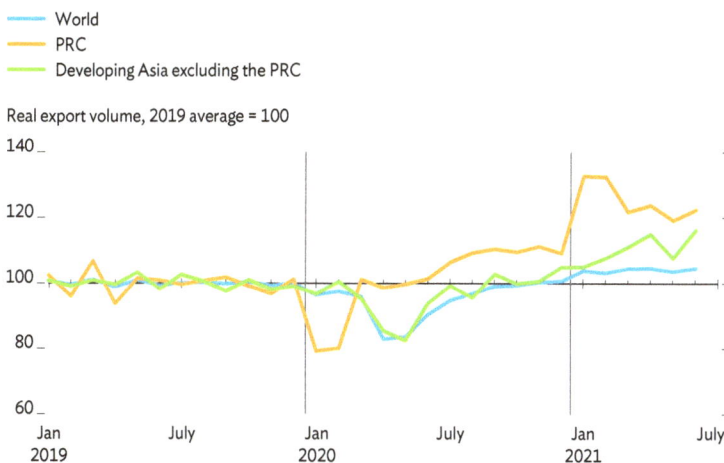

Real export volume, 2019 average = 100

PRC = People's Republic of China.

Note: Developing Asia excluding the PRC comprises Hong Kong, China, India, Indonesia, the Republic of Korea, Malaysia, Pakistan, the Philippines, Singapore, Taipei,China, Thailand, and Viet Nam.

Source: CPB World Trade Monitor. https://www.cpb.nl/en (accessed 23 August 2021).

Figure 1.1.12 Sector contributions to nominal export growth in developing Asia

Electronics, mechanical machinery, and vehicles have become the main drivers of the regions's exports rebound.

- Pandemic-related goods
- Mechanical machinery and vehicles
- Textiles and footwear
- Other
- Electronics
- Metals and jewelry
- Mineral fuels
- Overall change

% change from the same month in 2019

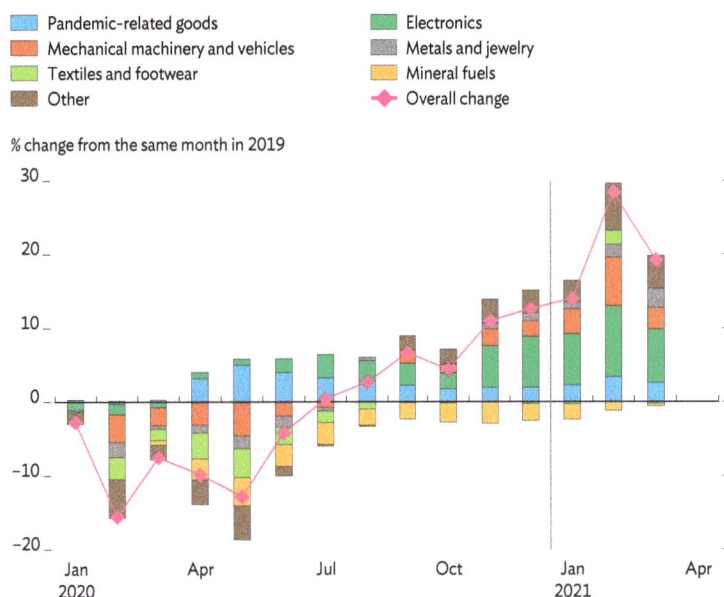

Note: The sample includes 15 economies accounting for 86% of developing Asia's exports: Armenia, Azerbaijan, Cambodia, Georgia, India, Kazakhstan, Malaysia, Pakistan, the People's Republic of China, the Philippines, the Republic of Korea, Singapore, Taipei,China, Thailand, and Uzbekistan.
Sources: International Trade Centre. Trade Map. https://www.trademap.org/ (accessed 27 July 2021); Observatory of Economic Complexity. https://oec.world/; United Nations Comtrade Database. https://comtrade.un.org/ (both accessed 27 August 2021).

Rising demand for electronics, mechanical machinery, and vehicles strengthened the rebound in developing Asia's exports. The first phase of the export recovery was driven by surging demand for goods to tackle the pandemic, such as face masks and COVID-19 test kits (Figure 1.1.12). An upturn in exports of electronics, mechanical machinery, and vehicles has also contributed to the overall rebound since the last quarter of 2020.

Growing demand for a broader range of products has supported exports from all parts of developing Asia. Exports from East Asia and Southeast Asia stabilized in the second quarter of 2021, exceeding their value in 2019 by about 25% (Figure 1.1.13), mostly due to the surge in electronics exports (Figure 1.1.14, panels A and B). By December, South Asia's exports had fully recovered from the collapse in the second quarter of 2020, aided by the rebound in food, textiles and footwear, and base metal exports (panel C). The disruptions associated with the Delta COVID-19 variant, however, hit India's exports during April–May. Central Asia's exports, after remaining depressed through 2020, turned the corner in March 2021 as rising oil and gas prices boosted nominal exports, notably from Azerbaijan and Kazakhstan.

Figure 1.1.13 Nominal export growth in developing Asia

Exports exceed 2019 levels for Central Asia, East Asia, and Southeast Asia.

- Central Asia
- East Asia
- South Asia
- Southeast Asia

$, same month in 2019 = 100

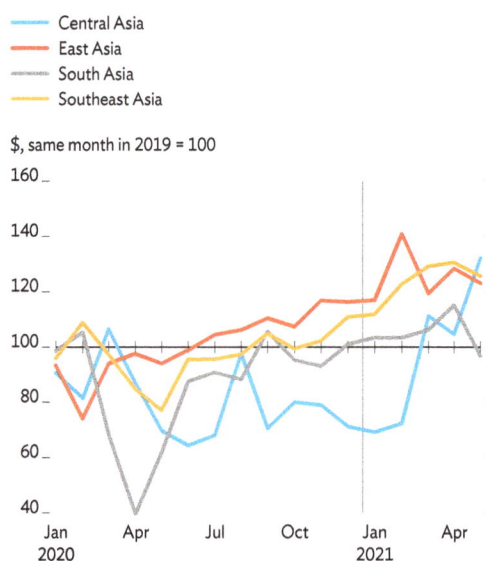

Note: East Asia excludes Taipei,China.
Source: International Monetary Fund. Direction of Trade Statistics. https://data.imf.org/?sk=9d6028d4-f14a-464c-a2f2-59b2cd424b85 (accessed 27 August 2021).

Figure 1.1.14 Sector contributions to nominal export growth by developing Asia subregion

- Pandemic-related goods
- Electronics
- Mechanical machinery and vehicles
- Metals and jewelry
- Textiles and footwear
- Mineral fuels
- Other
- Overall change

A. East Asia[a]

Pandemic-related goods no longer drive East Asia's exports rebound.

% change from the same month in 2019

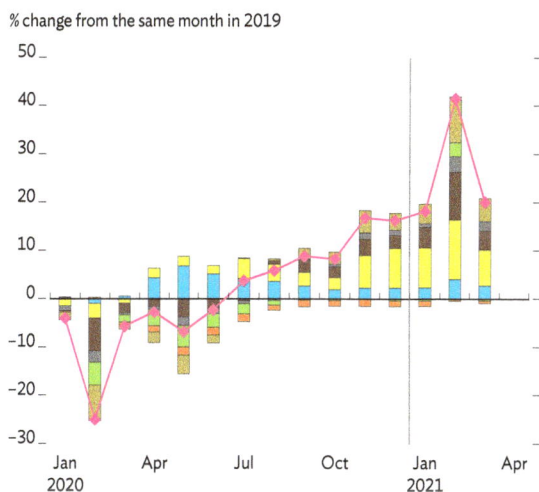

B. Southeast Asia[b]

Electronics led Southeast Asia's export rebound.

% change from the same month in 2019

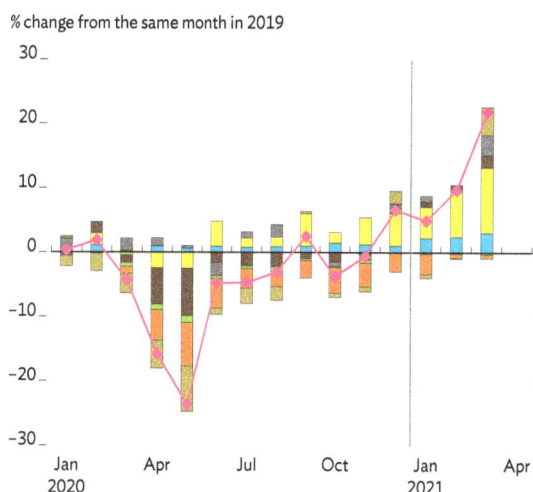

C. South Asia[c]

Rebounding demand for textiles and metals drove South Asia's export recovery.

% change from the same month in 2019

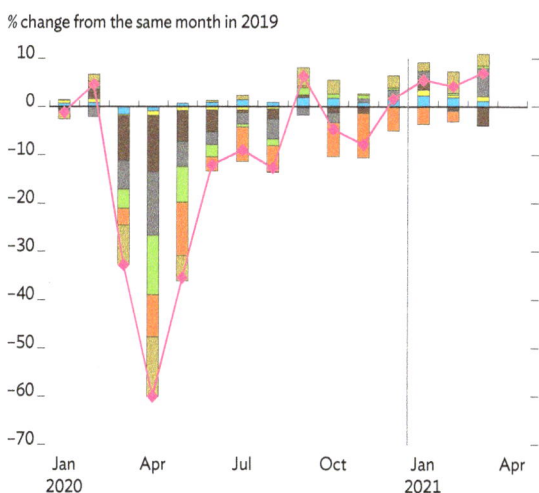

D. Central Asia[d]

Rebounding oil and gas prices reversed Central Asia's fall in exports.

% change from the same month in 2019

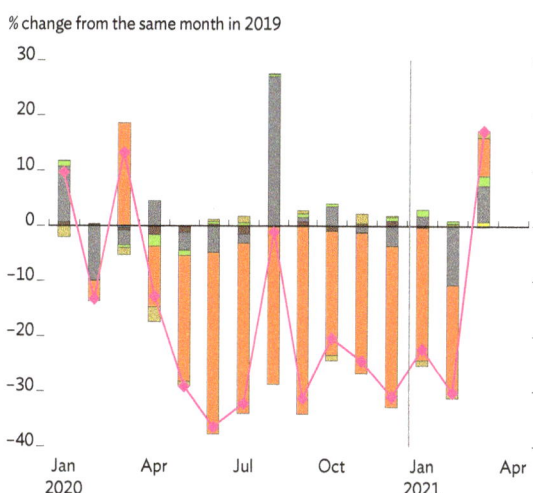

[a] Comprises the People's Republic of China, the Republic of Korea, and Taipei,China.
[b] Comprises Cambodia, Malaysia, the Philippines, Singapore, and Thailand.
[c] Comprises India and Pakistan.
[d] Comprises Armenia, Azerbaijan, Georgia, Kazakhstan, and Uzbekistan.

Sources: International Trade Centre. Trade Map. https://www.trademap.org/ (accessed 27 July 2021); Observatory of Economic Complexity. https://oec.world/; United Nations Comtrade Database. https://comtrade.un.org/ (both accessed 27 August 2021).

Copper and other base-metal exporters in the subregion, including Armenia, Georgia, and Tajikistan, also benefited from rising global demand (panel D).

The trade rebound has bolstered shipping demand, but COVID-19 disrupted global shipping. With global trade exceeding prepandemic levels since January, freight rates have risen steeply and are now more than eight times higher than average rates in 2019 (Figure 1.1.15). Shipping costs from the PRC to the US West Coast have increased 14 times, pushed up by the widening US trade deficit with the PRC. Delivery times also sharply increased before stabilizing since July, far exceeding levels over the last 2 decades. Shipping bottlenecks are partly due to supply-side rigidities since shipping capacity is fixed in the short-term. Disruptions to shipping were worsened by the closure of the Suez Canal in March and the partial closure of several PRC ports during June–August as COVID-19 cases affected workers and a typhoon hit the east coast of the PRC. Port congestion continues to constrain capacity as ships wait to be unloaded. The impact of the recent rally in shipping costs on inflation is expected to be temporary and small since international shipping accounts on average for less than 1% of the final cost of goods— and imported goods account for a small portion of consumer spending (about 11% in the US, for example). Demand for shipping should ease as COVID-19 vaccination becomes widespread and consumers rebalance their spending toward services.

Figure 1.1.15 Container freight rates

Shipping costs from the PRC have increased by up to 14 times since 2019.

- From the PRC to the US West Coast
- From the PRC to Europe
- From the PRC to the Mediterranean
- From the PRC to the US East Coast
- FBX Global container index

Same week in 2019 = 100

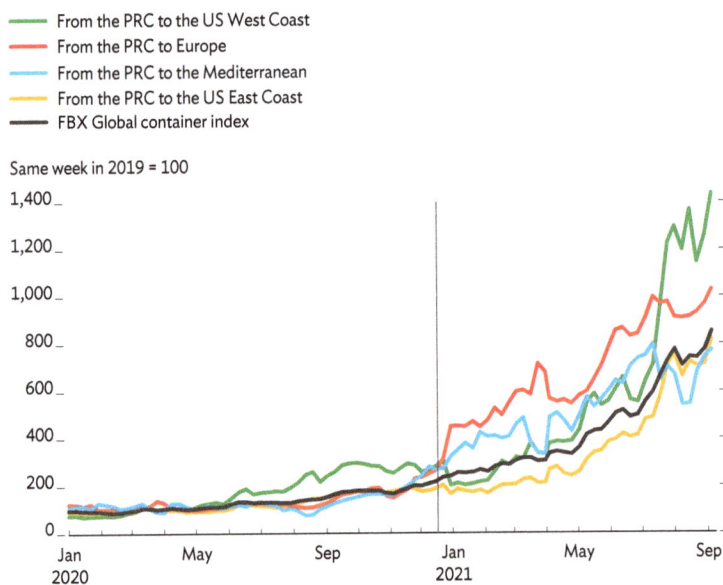

FBX = Freightos Baltic Index, PRC = People's Republic of China, US = United States.
Source: Freightos Baltic Index. https://fbx.freightos.com/ (accessed 14 September 2021).

Still, replenishing inventories will take time even after final demand cools. And because ships ordered since early 2021 will not be delivered before 2023, relief from the supply side will be unlikely in 2022.

Remittances increased in most economies across developing Asia in early 2021. For the Asian Development Bank's 19 developing members for which data are available for the first quarter of 2021, remittances rose by 14.6% on average compared with the first quarter of 2019. The good performance this year follows a 1.6% increase in 2020 (Figure 1.1.16). For four of the five economies where remittances account for the largest share of gross domestic product (GDP)—Armenia, Georgia, Nepal, and the Philippines—remittances were higher in the first quarter of 2021 than before the pandemic, a reversal from declines in 2020. For Uzbekistan—where remittances accounted for 14.8% of GDP in 2019—they were 7.0% below their prepandemic level in the first quarter of this year, improving from an 18.3% decline in 2020. The reopening of the Russian Federation to migrant workers supported the improvement in remittances for Central Asia.

Figure 1.1.16 Changes in remittances in developing Asia, 2020 and Q1 2021

Remittances picked up in most of the region's economies in Q1 2021; where they declined, they did so by less than in 2020.

- Further improvement
- Rebound
- Still down compared to 2019

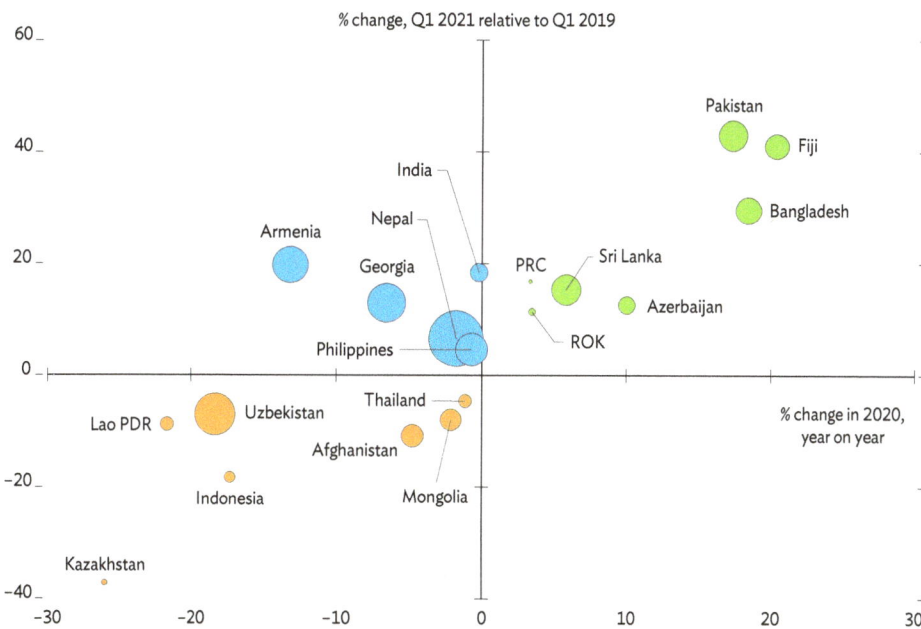

Lao PDR = Lao People's Democratic Republic, PRC = People's Republic of China, Q = quarter, ROK = Republic of Korea.

Notes: The sample is for 19 economies for which data are available. Bubble sizes are proportional to the share of remittances in 2019 gross domestic product.

Sources: International Monetary Fund. Balance of Payments and International Investment Position Statistics. https://data.imf.org/; World Bank. World Development Indicators database. http://wdi.worldbank.org/ (both accessed 14 September 2021).

Remittances to Bangladesh continued to exceed prepandemic levels, by 29.5% in the first quarter; this was largely due to relaxed documentation requirements and a 2% cash bonus added by the government to incoming remittances. Pakistan's remittances also exceeded prepandemic levels, by 42.9%, supported by strong inflows from Saudi Arabia and the United Arab Emirates. Interestingly, no economy falls in the bottom right quadrant of Figure 1.1.16, which seems to refute one of the possible explanations for the strong remittance performance in 2020—that many migrant workers had lost their jobs and so moved most of their savings home.

International tourism remains depressed, but a rebound is in sight for some developing Asian economies. Arrivals are still down by 90%–100% in most economies, but Maldives is seeing a gradual revival, with arrivals in July down just 28% compared with the annual average in 2019. Tourism is also recovering in Georgia, although arrivals were still down 59% in August (Figure 1.1.17). Both countries adopted deliberate policies to attract foreign tourists despite the COVID-19 pandemic, notably by reopening their borders in July 2020 without quarantine requirements. Georgia and Maldives are among the developing Asian economies where visitors from Europe account for the largest share of foreign tourists, at 31% and 41% in 2019, respectively. This suggests that Europe's high vaccination rates might be contributing to the revival of tourism. More generally, as vaccination rates continue to rise in Europe and North America, tourism in economies where arrivals are largely from these areas may recover earlier, including Armenia, Azerbaijan, Bhutan, India, Nepal, and Sri Lanka.

Figure 1.1.17 International tourist arrivals in developing Asia

Tourism mostly remains depressed, but a few bright spots are slowly emerging.

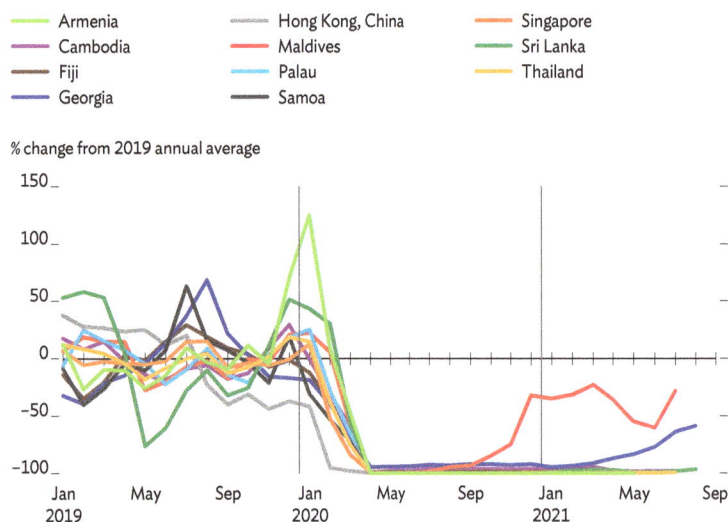

Note: The sample is restricted to economies where tourism accounted for at least 5% of gross domestic product in the latest year for available data during 2017–2019.

Sources: CEIC Data Company; national sources (both accessed 14 September 2021).

Fiscal and monetary policies remain accommodative

Macroeconomic policies continue to support developing Asia's economic recovery. The proactive response last year by fiscal and monetary authorities to the COVID-19 crisis has been followed by a cautious approach in 2021, reflecting the continued fragility of the recovery in most economies, as well as concerns over the potential costs of prematurely withdrawing policy support.

Fiscal policy is set to remain accommodative this year in many regional economies, with most tightening expected in 2022 and beyond. In many economies, budget balances are forecast to further decline or increase only slightly this year, thereby avoiding a substantial withdrawal of fiscal support in a still uncertain landscape (Figure 1.1.18). A general shift to fiscal consolidation is expected in 2022. The main exceptions to this are those economies that put in place the largest fiscal stimulus packages in 2020, and which are forecast to bring their fiscal balances closer to normal already in 2021. Among them are Singapore and Hong Kong, China, where strong recoveries will be reflected in improved fiscal balances; Brunei Darussalam, where government revenue should benefit from healthy commodity prices; and Mongolia, where the fiscal deficit is expected to narrow on rising tax receipts and the gradual withdrawal of stimulus measures.

Figure 1.1.18 Fiscal impulses in developing Asia, 2020–2022

Fiscal policy will remain accommodative in much of the region in 2021; consolidation is expected for 2022 or beyond.

- 2020
- 2021
- 2022

Fiscal balance as % of GDP, change from the previous year

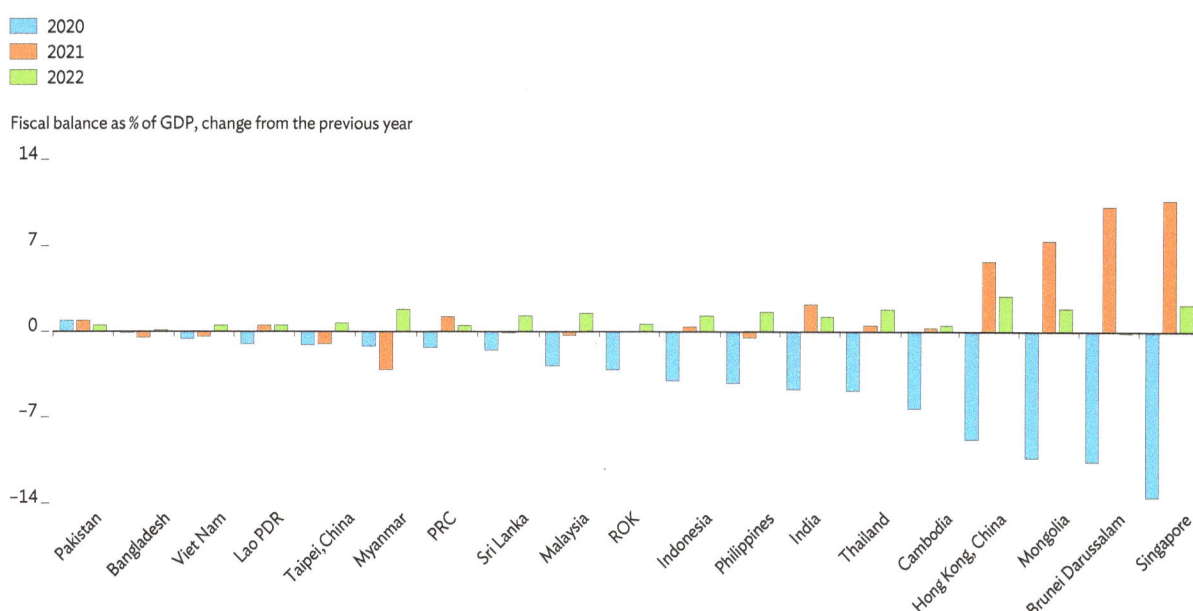

GDP = gross domestic product, Lao PDR = Lao People's Democratic Republic, PRC = People's Republic of China, ROK = Republic of Korea.

Notes: Fiscal impulse is defined as the change in the fiscal balance, expressed as percentage of GDP, from the previous year. Positive changes in the fiscal balance indicate fiscal consolidation; negative changes indicate fiscal expansion. Data for 2021 and 2022 are forecasts.

Sources: FocusEconomics. 2021. FocusEconomics Consensus Forecast reports, September; Asian Development Bank estimates.

Figure 1.1.19 Gross public debt in developing Asian economies

Public debt rose almost everywhere in the region last year, but remained below 60% of GDP in most economies.

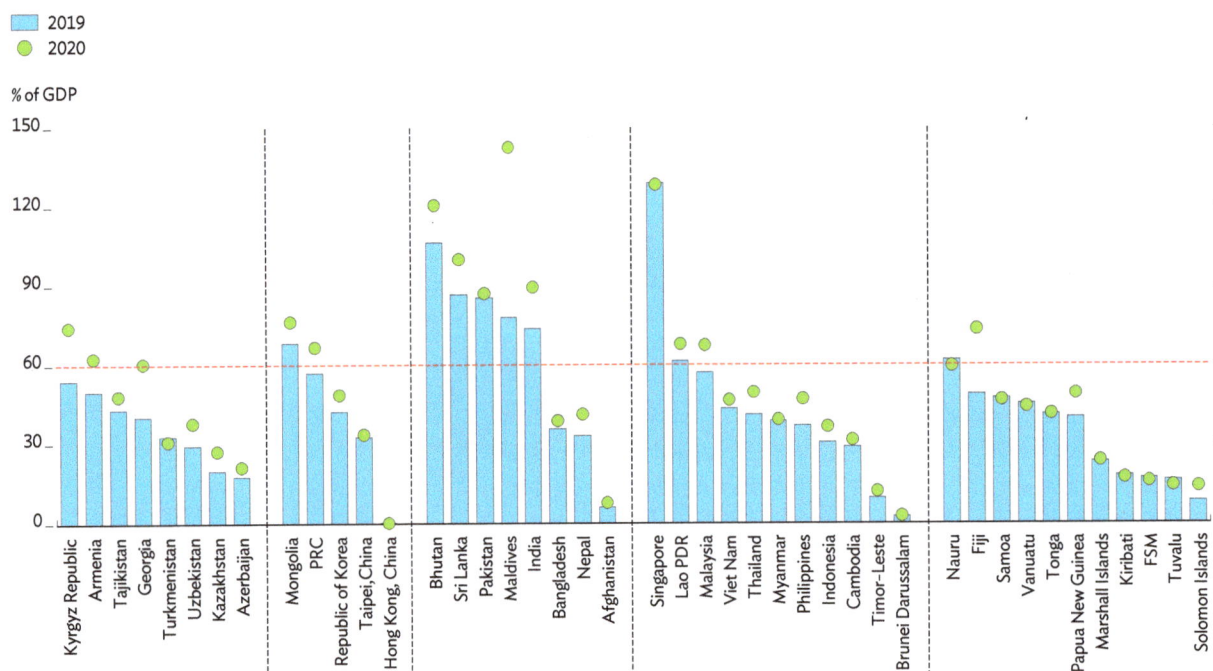

FSM = Federated States of Micronesia, GDP = gross domestic product, Lao PDR = Lao People's Democratic Republic, PRC = People's Republic of China.
Note: The Pacific excludes the Cook Island, Niue, and Palau, as no data are available for these economies.
Source: International Monetary Fund. World Economic Outlook April 2021 Database. https://www.imf.org/en/Publications/WEO/weo-database/2021/April.

Public debt increased substantially in 2020 but remains manageable for most developing Asian economies. Ratios of public debt to GDP across the region increased significantly in 2020 as governments delivered strong fiscal support to cushion the impact of the pandemic, with only the Pacific bucking this trend (Figure 1.1.19). Still, in two-thirds of the region's economies, public debt remained below 60% of GDP.

After cutting interest rates in 2020, central banks in developing Asia continue to maintain an accommodative monetary policy. Following several policy rate cuts from March to July 2020 in response to the initial impact of COVID-19, central banks have largely refrained from further loosening, but also from reversing course (Figure 1.1.20, panel A). As of 3 September, almost no changes to policy rates were made in major economies in 2021 except for a cut of 25 basis points (bps) in Indonesia in February, an increase of 25 bps in Kazakhstan in July, and increases of 50 bps in Sri Lanka and 25 bps in the Republic of Korea in August. Monetary policy remains broadly expansionary across most economies in developing Asia, with real interest rates below or close to zero. Positive real interest rates bucked this trend in Indonesia, the PRC, and some Central Asia economies, including Azerbaijan, Kazakhstan, and Uzbekistan (Figure 1.1.20, panel B).

Currencies and foreign portfolio investment weaken, but financial conditions remain robust

Currencies across developing Asian economies weakened amid softening regional growth prospects and the strong US economic recovery. Almost 70% of exchange rates in the region depreciated against the US dollar from 1 April to 3 September 2021 as renewed COVID-19 outbreaks clouded regional recovery prospects (Figure 1.1.21). Expectations of a tightening monetary stance by the US Federal Reserve on a strong US recovery also contributed to the depreciation of regional currencies against the US dollar. From 1 April to 3 September, regional currencies depreciated against the US dollar by 1.0% on average, reversing an appreciation of 0.1% in the first quarter of 2021. The weakening in regional currencies interrupted the appreciation momentum from the third quarter of 2020 to the first quarter 2021, when nearly two-thirds of regional currencies strengthened against the US dollar (Figure 1.1.22).

Foreign portfolio flows declined in many developing Asian markets on the US's strong recovery and possible early monetary policy normalization there. Foreign portfolio flows to Asian and non-Asian emerging markets show co-movement in their exposure to common global shocks related to global monetary stances and COVID-19 containment measures. Developing Asia's financial markets, with the exception of the PRC, experienced portfolio outflows during February–March and in May over news on possible early monetary policy tightening and a strong US recovery, as well as in July and August as the regional economic outlook deteriorated over renewed COVID-19 outbreaks (Figure 1.1.23). Portfolio outflows in the first 8 months of 2021 were, however, much smaller than in the first half of 2020. Foreign portfolio flows to the PRC remained largely positive, buoyed by the country's recovery prospects .

Other capital flows remained robust in the first quarter of 2021. Although foreign portfolio investments in the first quarter fell to $18.2 billion from $141.2 billion in the fourth quarter of 2020, other capital flows remained robust amid the global recovery.

Net foreign direct investment (FDI) to developing Asia has risen steadily since the third quarter of 2020, with FDI inflows rising from $65.4 billion in the second quarter of 2020 to $150.5 billion in the first quarter of 2021. Bank loans and other flows turned to inflows in the first quarter, reversing a net outflow during the second half of 2020 (Figure 1.1.24).

Figure 1.1.20 Monthly changes in policy interest rates in developing Asia

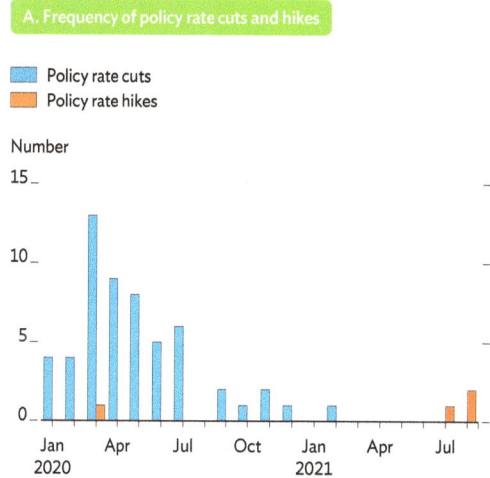

A. Frequency of policy rate cuts and hikes

Note: The figure covers policy interest rate changes in 18 developing Asian economies: Azerbaijan, Bangladesh, Fiji, Hong Kong, China, India, Indonesia, Kazakhstan, Malaysia, Pakistan, Papua New Guinea, the People's Republic of China, the Philippines, the Republic of Korea, Sri Lanka, Taipei,China, Thailand, Uzbekistan, and Viet Nam.

Source: Haver Analytics (accessed 3 September 2021).

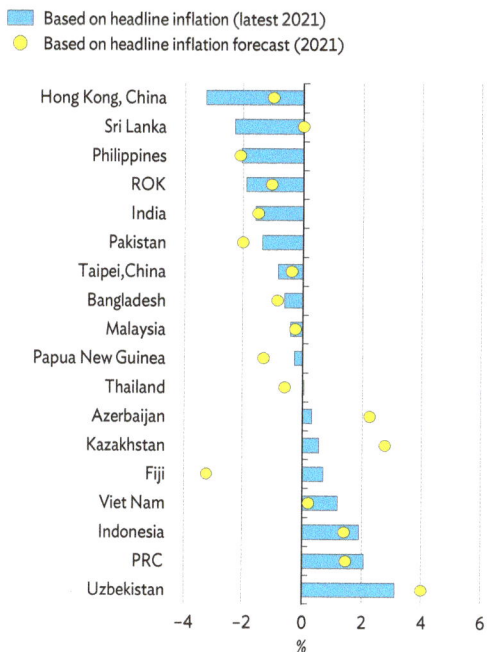

B. Real interest rates

PRC = People's Republic of China, ROK = Republic of Korea.

Notes: The real interest rate is the difference between the latest policy rate and headline inflation (blue bars) and the forecast inflation for 2021 in the July *Asian Development Outlook 2021 Supplement* (yellow dots). Latest data for Indonesia, Kazakhstan, Pakistan, the ROK, Uzbekistan, and Viet Nam as of August 2021. Azerbaijan, Bangladesh, Fiji, Hong Kong, China, India, Malaysia, the Philippines, the PRC, Sri Lanka, Taipei,China, and Thailand as of July 2021. Papua New Guinea as of June 2021.

Source: CEIC Data Company; Haver Analytics (both accessed 3 September 2021).

Figure 1.1.21 Exchange rate changes in developing Asian economies

Nearly 70% of currencies in the region weakened against the US dollar since April 2021.

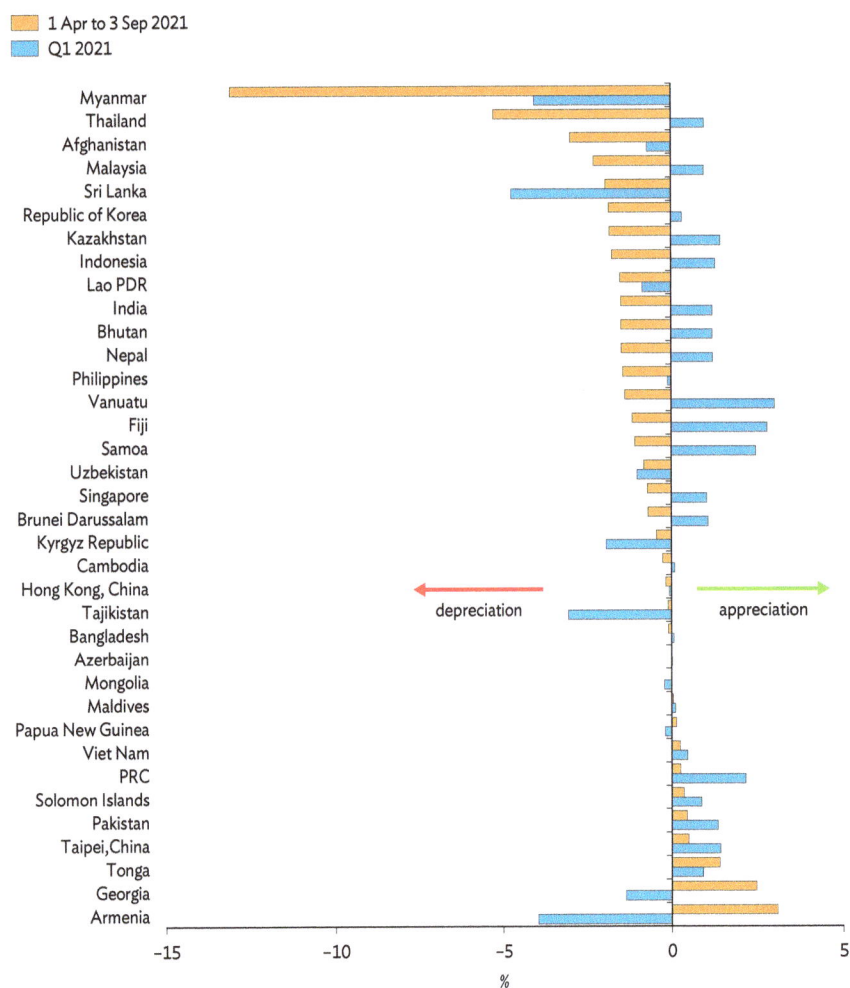

■ 1 Apr to 3 Sep 2021
■ Q1 2021

Myanmar
Thailand
Afghanistan
Malaysia
Sri Lanka
Republic of Korea
Kazakhstan
Indonesia
Lao PDR
India
Bhutan
Nepal
Philippines
Vanuatu
Fiji
Samoa
Uzbekistan
Singapore
Brunei Darussalam
Kyrgyz Republic
Cambodia
Hong Kong, China
Tajikistan
Bangladesh
Azerbaijan
Mongolia
Maldives
Papua New Guinea
Viet Nam
PRC
Solomon Islands
Pakistan
Taipei,China
Tonga
Georgia
Armenia

← depreciation   appreciation →

%

Lao PDR = Lao People's Democratic Republic, PRC = People's Republic of China, Q = quarter.
Source: Asian Development Bank estimates using Bloomberg (accessed 4 September 2021).

Figure 1.1.22 Currency depreciations and appreciations in developing Asian economies

Currency depreciations reversed the appreciation momentum from Q3 2020 to Q1 2021.

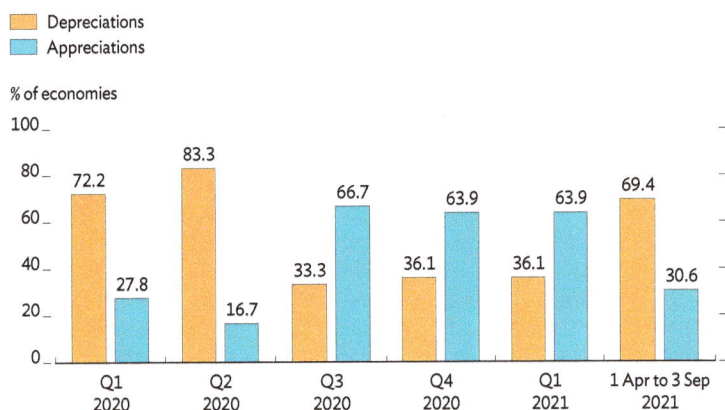

■ Depreciations
■ Appreciations

% of economies

	Q1 2020	Q2 2020	Q3 2020	Q4 2020	Q1 2021	1 Apr to 3 Sep 2021
Depreciations	72.2	83.3	33.3	36.1	36.1	69.4
Appreciations	27.8	16.7	66.7	63.9	63.9	30.6

Q = quarter.
Note: Numbers above bars indicate the percentage of economies with exchange rate depreciations or appreciations.
Source: Asian Development Bank calculations using Bloomberg (accessed 4 September 2021).

Figure 1.1.23 Foreign portfolio flows into developing Asia

Outflows in many markets on the US's economic rebound, expectations of US monetary tightening, and a fragile regional recovery.

— Developing Asia excluding the PRC
— PRC
— Non-Asia emerging markets

$ billion, 28-day moving average

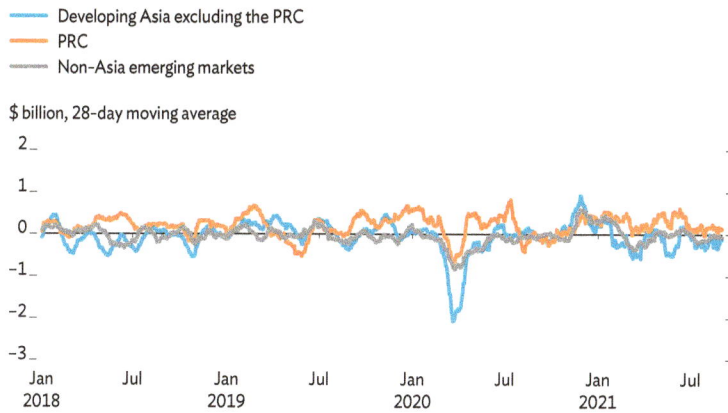

PRC = People's Republic of China, US = United States.

Notes: Developing Asia in this figure comprises India, Indonesia, Malaysia, Pakistan, the PRC, the Philippines, the Republic of Korea, Sri Lanka, Taipei,China, Thailand, and Viet Nam. Non-Asia emerging markets comprise Brazil, Colombia, Hungary, Mexico, Poland, Qatar, Saudi Arabia, South Africa, Turkey, and Ukraine.

Source: Institute of International Finance Capital flow tracker database. https://www.iif.com (accessed 4 September 2021).

Figure 1.1.24 Foreign investment flows into developing Asia

Robust net inflows of FDI, loans, and other flows continued in Q1 2021.

▨ Foreign direct investment   ▨ Portfolio equity
▨ Portfolio debt   ▨ Financial derivatives
▨ Loans   ▨ Trade credit and advances
▨ Other flows   — Nonresident Flows

$ billion

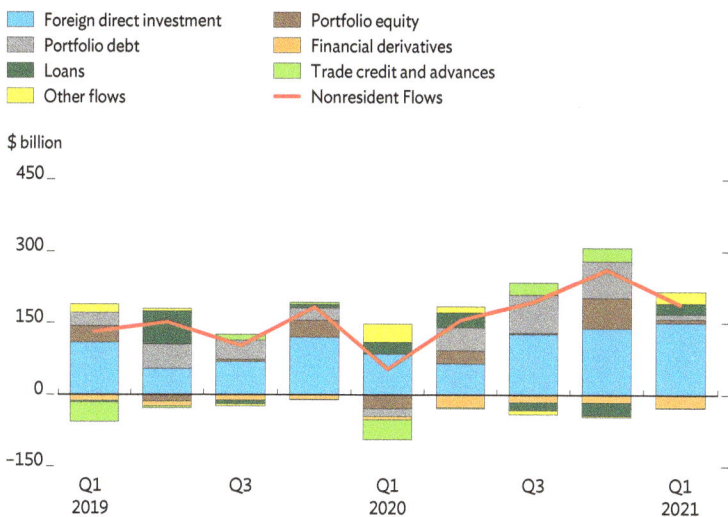

FDI = foreign direct investment, Q = quarter.

Notes: Data cover 13 economies: Afghanistan, Azerbaijan, Bangladesh, Georgia, Hong Kong, China, India, Indonesia, Kazakhstan, Malaysia, the People's Republic China, the Philippines, Tajikistan, and Thailand.

Source: Haver Analytics (accessed 4 September 2021).

Developing Asia's equity markets continued to rise and risk premiums narrowed marginally. Both developments have been supported by accommodative monetary policy stances and healthy liquidity conditions. From 1 January to 3 September 2021, South Asia's equity markets gained an average 21.7%, followed by Central Asia (20.2%), Southeast Asia (6.2%) and East Asia (3.6%). Equity markets in all four subregions are above prepandemic levels, with a weighted average return of 23% as of 3 September 2021 compared with 1 January 2020 (Figure 1.1.25). Bond markets have been similarly robust. Risk premiums, as measured by the J. P. Morgan Emerging Markets Bond Index's stripped spread, remained largely stable in major regional markets, with an average marginal decline from 216.2 basis points on 1 January to 207.7 on 3 September. Nevertheless, average risk premiums were 38.1 basis points higher on 3 September than they were on 1 January 2020 (Figure 1.1.26).

Figure 1.1.25 Equity indices in developing Asian markets

The region's equity markets rose in the first 8 months of 2021 on accommodative liquidity conditions and monetary stance.

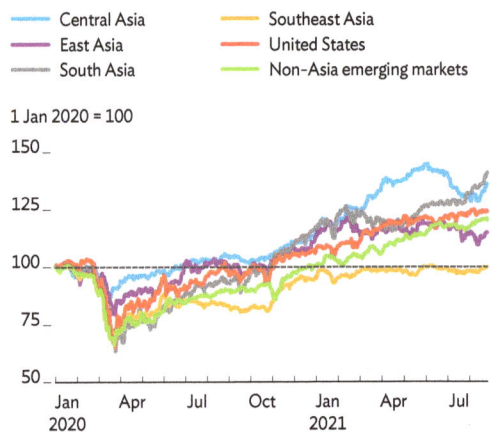

Note: Central Asia in this figure comprises Kazakhstan; East Asia comprises Hong Kong, China, the People's Republic of China, the Republic of Korea, and Taipei,China; South Asia comprises Bangladesh, India, and Sri Lanka; Southeast Asia comprises Indonesia, Malaysia, the Philippines, Singapore, Thailand, and Viet Nam; non-Asia emerging markets comprise Brazil, Colombia, Hungary, Mexico, Poland, Qatar, Saudi Arabia, South Africa, Turkey, and Ukraine.

Source: CEIC Data Company (accessed 4 September 2021).

Figure 1.1.26 J. P. Morgan Emerging Markets Bond Index stripped spreads in developing Asia

Regional risk premiums remain stable, but are still higher than levels before COVID-19.

Source: Bloomberg (accessed 4 September 2021).

COVID-19 resurgence complicates developing Asia's outlook

The pandemic is clouding developing Asia's economic prospects. Despite the rebound in demand for exports and the revival in global demand, renewed COVID-19 outbreaks since July are slowing the growth momentum in some parts of the region. The recovery has been weaker in economies hit by domestic outbreaks and those facing weak demand for their key industries, such as tourism-dependent economies. Overall, the region's vaccination coverage is still low and uneven. Raising this and strengthening health care preparedness in handling COVID-19 would substantially improve the prospects for a faster economic recovery.

Strong growth in advanced economies will continue supporting the recovery in global trade. Rapid vaccine rollouts in these economies have reduced the incidence of severe cases, hospitalizations, and deaths during the resurgence of COVID-19 infections (Figure 1.1.27). As of 31 August, the ratio between COVID-19 deaths and infection cases has declined to 1.0% in the US, 0.6% in the euro area, and 0.3% in Japan. Because of this, containment measures were not significantly tightened, despite increasing daily COVID-19 cases. GDP in the three economies is forecast to grow strongly at 5.0% in 2021, a slight downward adjustment from the 5.3% expansion projected in *ADO 2021* (Table A1.1 in the Annex) due to slower-than-expected second-quarter growth in the US. Growth in the US, euro area, and Japan will remain robust in 2022, with GDP projected to expand by 3.9% on average. The Annex gives a more detailed discussion on the outlook in these economies.

The rebound in developing Asia is expected to be a bit weaker than *ADO 2021*'s forecast. Regional GDP is expected to expand by 7.1% this year, a marginal downward revision from the earlier projection of 7.3% (Figure 1.1.28). Regional growth this year will be characterized by slower-than-expected expansions in South Asia and Southeast Asia, a slight contraction in the Pacific, and faster recoveries in East Asia and Central Asia. Marginally higher growth than earlier projected is forecast for 2022. An upward revision in South Asia's growth forecast for next year brightens the region's growth prospects in 2022.

Differing growth trajectories are shaping the regional recovery. GDP growth forecasts are revised up in East Asia and Central Asia, and down in the rest of developing Asia. Robust growth in advanced economies will continue to benefit developing Asia's export-oriented economies.

Figure 1.1.27 COVID-19 cases and deaths in the United States, euro area, and Japan

High vaccination coverage helped contain deaths during the latest pandemic wave.

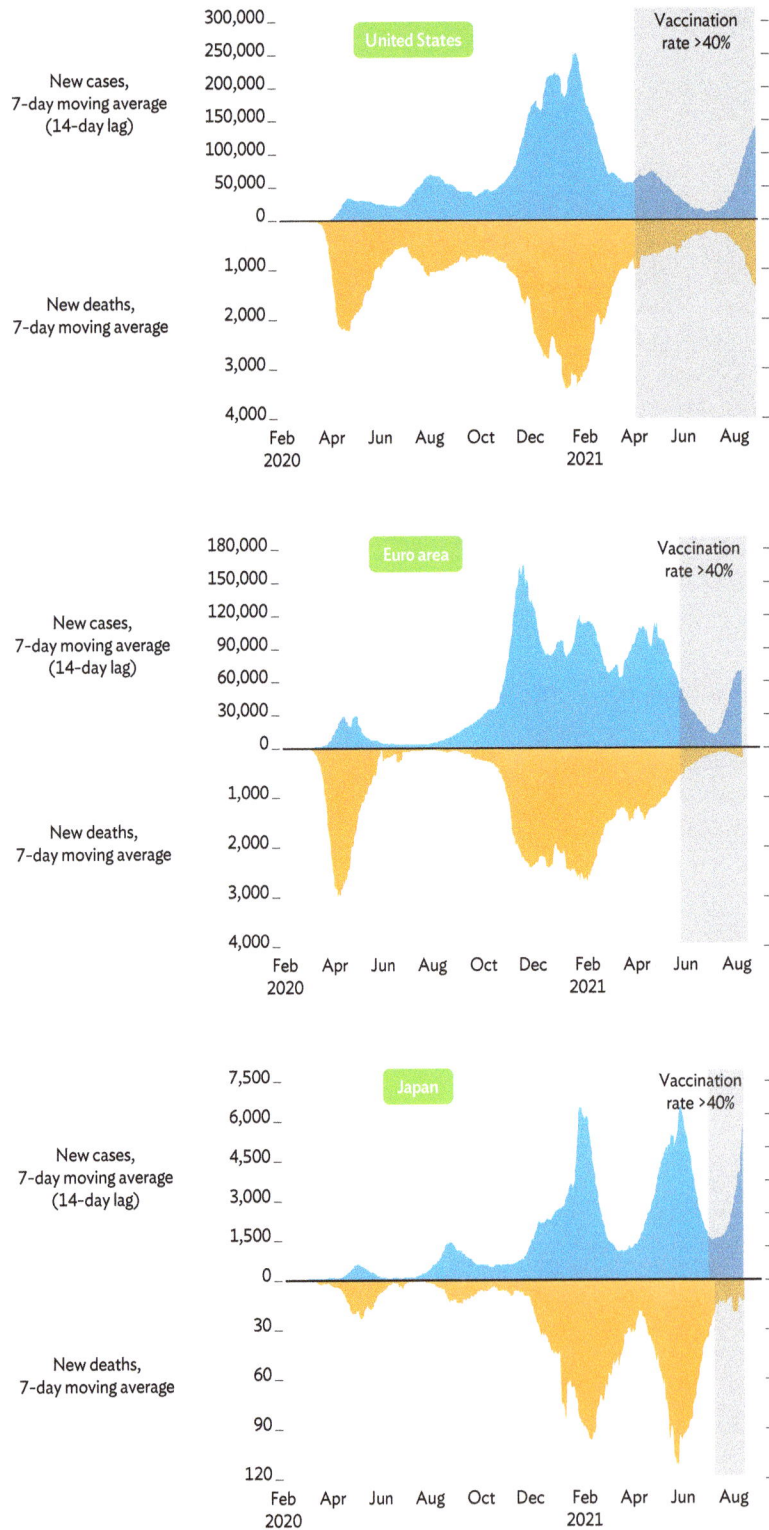

COVID-19 = Coronavirus Disease 2019.
Source: Our World in Data. https://ourworldindata.org (accessed 3 September 2021).

Within this group, growth forecasts have been revised up for those economies that have managed to contain COVID-19 (Figure 1.1.29). For example, strong export orders in the Republic of Korea, Singapore, Taipei,China, and—for most of this year—the PRC suggest that exports from these economies will remain high for the coming months, supporting overall growth (Figure 1.1.30). In contrast, forecasts are revised down for economies where the new wave of infections spiked after the first quarter of this year—many of which are making slow progress in vaccination campaigns. Weak export orders in Southeast Asia—Singapore excluded—during July–August, suggest that exports from the subregion will remain moderate. For India, the forecast is revised down as the economy suffered another wave of COVID-19, but healthy export orders point to strong external demand cushioning the impact.

Regional output will be below the prepandemic trend in 2021 and 2022 despite the rebound in growth. Overall GDP in developing Asia will still be 2.5% lower than implied by its prepandemic trend by the end of next year (Figure 1.1.31). The gap, however, varies substantially across subregions and economies. With the strong recovery in the PRC and newly industrialized economies, East Asia's GDP is forecast to be only 0.7% below its prepandemic trend by the end of 2022. The gaps are wider for the other subregions, with the largest in Southeast Asia, at 8.6%. This subregion's recovery continues to be curtailed by recurring spikes of COVID-19 cases, resulting in the reimposition of stringent containment measures in some economies, including the Philippines.

Figure 1.1.28 Growth outlook in developing Asia

A slightly weaker rebound is now expected in 2021.

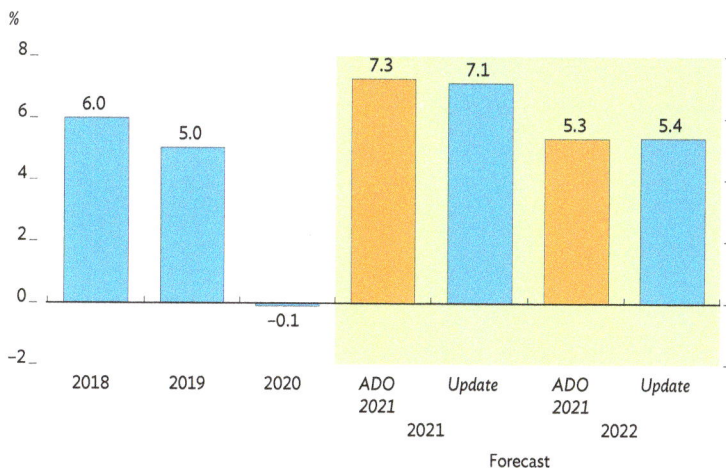

ADO = Asian Development Outlook.
Source: ADO database.

Figure 1.1.29 Revisions in growth forecasts for developing Asian economies

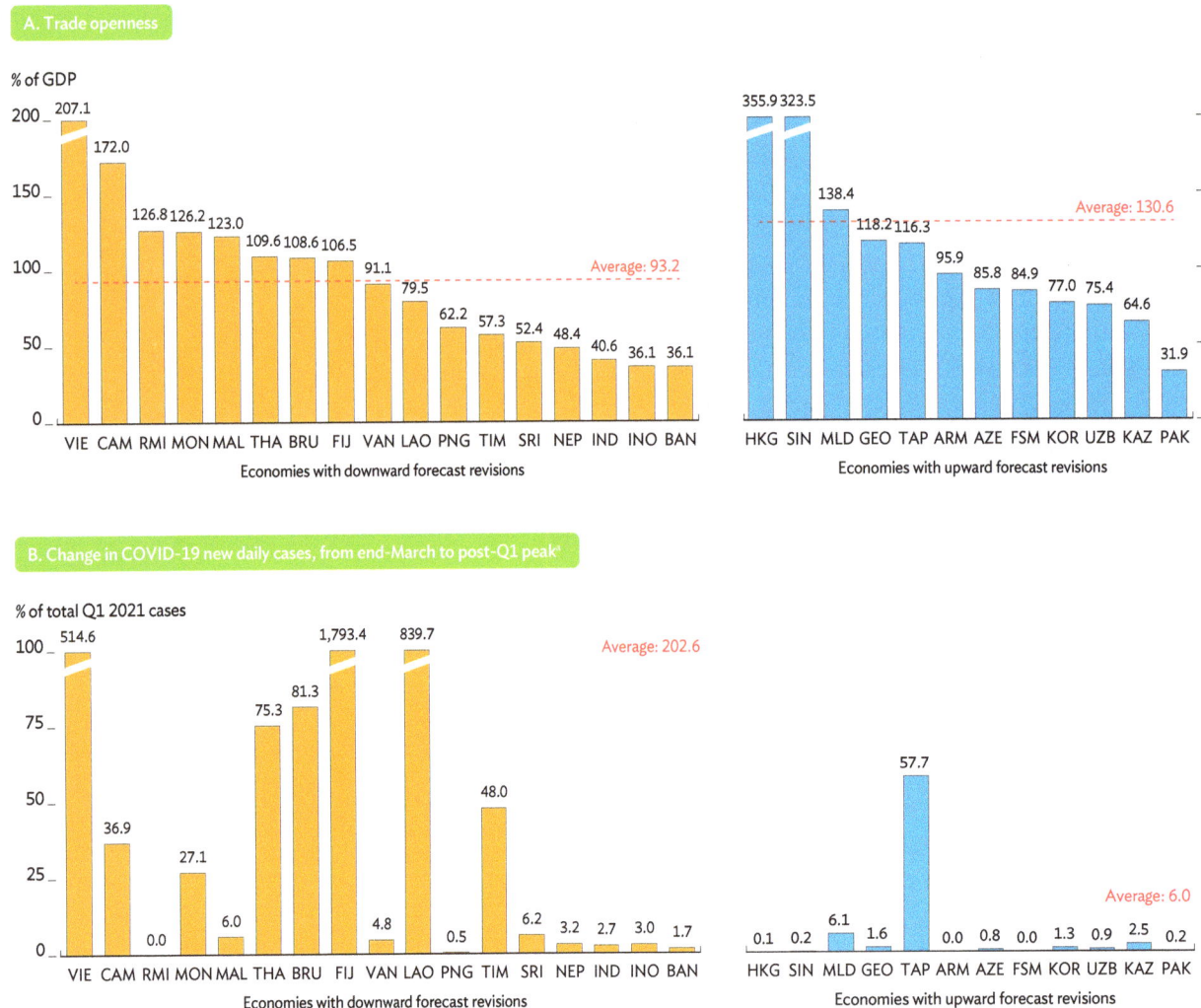

A. Trade openness

% of GDP

Economies with downward forecast revisions

VIE 207.1, CAM 172.0, RMI 126.8, MON 126.2, MAL 123.0, THA 109.6, BRU 108.6, FIJ 106.5, VAN 91.1, LAO 79.5, PNG 62.2, TIM 57.3, SRI 52.4, NEP 48.4, IND 40.6, INO 36.1, BAN 36.1

Average: 93.2

Economies with upward forecast revisions

HKG 355.9, SIN 323.5, MLD 138.4, GEO 118.2, TAP 116.3, ARM 95.9, AZE 85.8, FSM 84.9, KOR 77.0, UZB 75.4, KAZ 64.6, PAK 31.9

Average: 130.6

B. Change in COVID-19 new daily cases, from end-March to post-Q1 peak[a]

% of total Q1 2021 cases

Economies with downward forecast revisions

VIE 514.6, CAM 36.9, RMI 0.0, MON 27.1, MAL 6.0, THA 75.3, BRU 81.3, FIJ 1,793.4, VAN 4.8, LAO 839.7, PNG 0.5, TIM 48.0, SRI 6.2, NEP 3.2, IND 2.7, INO 3.0, BAN 1.7

Average: 202.6

Economies with upward forecast revisions

HKG 0.1, SIN 0.2, MLD 6.1, GEO 1.6, TAP 57.7, ARM 0.0, AZE 0.8, FSM 0.0, KOR 1.3, UZB 0.9, KAZ 2.5, PAK 0.2

Average: 6.0

ARM = Armenia, AZE = Azerbaijan, BAN = Bangladesh, BRU = Brunei Darussalam, CAM = Cambodia, COVID-19 = Coronavirus Disease 2019, FIJ = Fiji, FSM = Federated States of Micronesia, GDP = gross domestic product, GEO = Georgia, HKG = Hong Kong, China, IND = India, INO = Indonesia, KAZ = Kazakhstan, KOR = Republic of Korea, LAO = Lao People's Democratic Republic, MAL = Malaysia, MLD = Maldives, MON = Mongolia, NEP = Nepal, PAK = Pakistan, PNG = Papua New Guinea, Q = quarter, RMI = Marshall Islands, SIN = Singapore, SRI = Sri Lanka, TAP = Taipei,China, THA = Thailand, TIM = Timor-Leste, UZB = Uzbekistan, VAN = Vanuatu, VIE = Viet Nam.

[a] The bars measure the percentage difference between the peak of daily new COVID-19 cases after Q1 2021 and the daily new cases at the end of Q1, relative to the total cumulative cases at the end of Q1.

Note: The charts only include economies with revisions from forecasts made in April's *Asian Development Outlook 2021*.

Sources: *Asian Development Outlook* database; Haver Analytics (accessed 7 September 2021); World Bank. World Development Indicators database. https://databank.worldbank.org/source/world-development-indicators (accessed 7 September 2021).

Figure 1.1.30 New manufacturing export orders index for developing Asia

Export orders from the region remain strong, except in most of Southeast Asia.

Legend:
- World
- Southeast Asia
- Singapore
- India
- People's Republic of China
- Republic of Korea
- Taipei,China

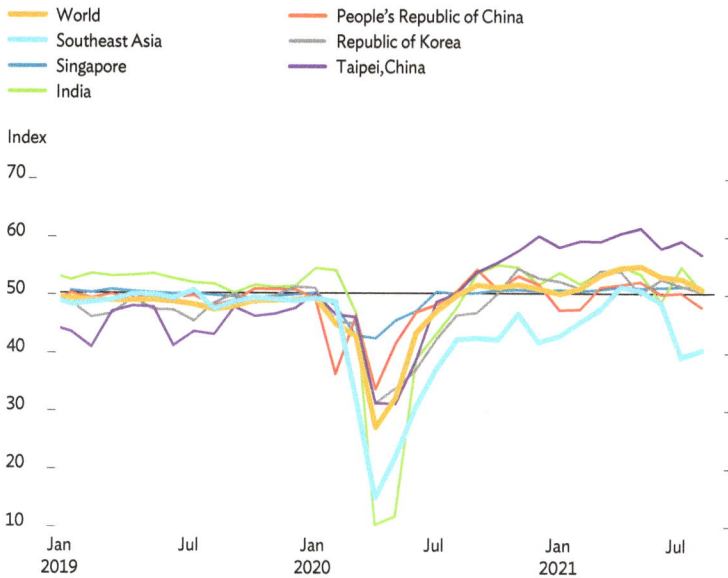

COVID-19 = Coronavirus Disease 2019.

Note: Index over 50 indicates higher new manufacturing export orders relative to previous month. Southeast Asia in this figure comprises Indonesia, Malaysia, Singapore, Thailand, the Philippines, and Viet Nam.

Sources: IHS Markit; Singapore Institute of Purchasing and Materials Management; Haver Analytics (all accessed 15 September 2021).

Figure 1.1.31 Gap between GDP forecasts and their COVID-19 prepandemic trend in developing Asia, 2022

Regional output will be below the prepandemic trend by the end of 2022.

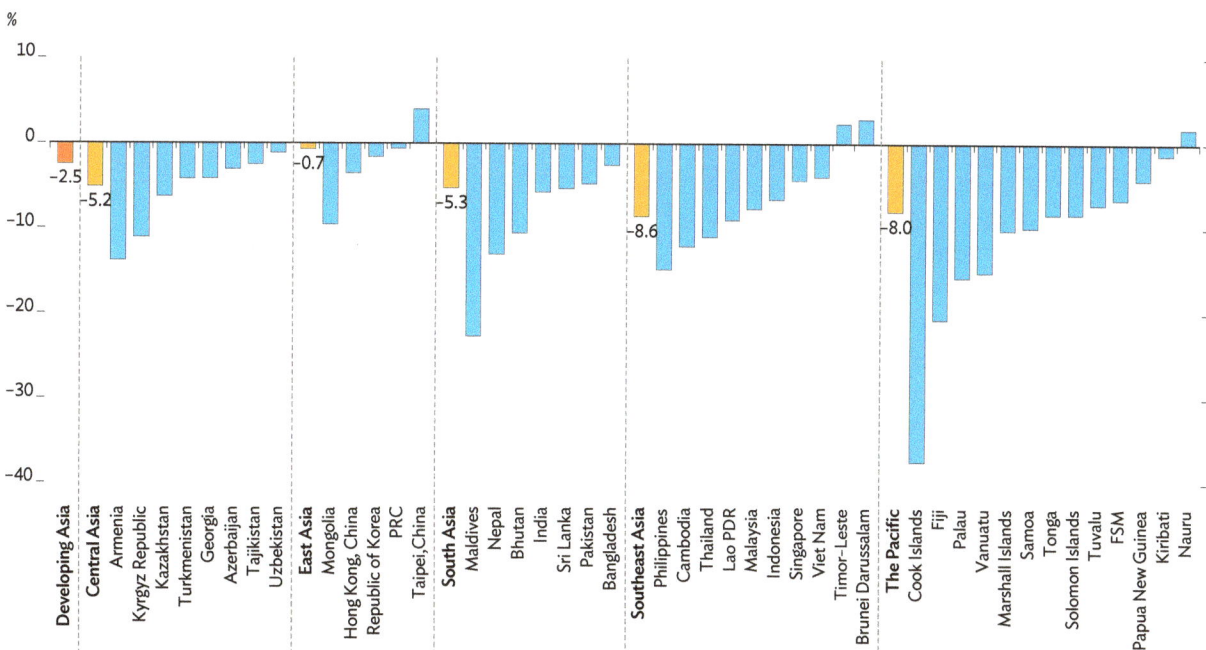

COVID-19 = Coronavirus Disease 2019, FSM = Federated States of Micronesia, GDP = gross domestic product, Lao PDR = Lao People's Democratic Republic, PRC = People's Republic of China.

Note: The 2022 prepandemic GDP level is measured based on its trend in the 5 years before the pandemic begins.

Source: *Asian Development Outlook* database.

Recovery patterns across developing Asia remain qualitatively similar to *ADO 2021*'s forecast. Moderate expansions are forecast for Central Asia and Southeast Asia in 2021, but growth will accelerate in 2022 (Table 1.1.1). The rebound in East Asia this year will be stronger than earlier forecast, while recovery in South Asia, reflecting a less optimistic outlook for India, is expected to be somewhat slower than earlier forecast. Growth in these subregions will decelerate next year. The Pacific will return to a positive growth rate only in 2022, as output in this subregion is now projected to contract again this year.

The rapid economic recovery will continue across East Asia. The subregion is forecast to grow by 7.6% in 2021 and 5.1% in 2022. Growth this year will be supported mainly by the recovery in global demand and effective COVD-19 containment. Strong export performances have bolstered growth in Hong Kong, China; the Republic of Korea; and Taipei,China and this trend is expected to continue over the rest of this year. In Mongolia, a strong recovery in mining will underpin the projected rebound. Rapid vaccine rollouts in some economies in the subregion have helped contain the new wave of COVID-19 infections, providing room for economic activity to normalize.

Growth in the PRC will remain strong, despite a protracted recovery in household consumption. The GDP growth forecast remains unchanged at 8.1% in 2021 and 5.5% in 2022, as a solid export performance and higher fiscal support in the second half of 2021 keep growth on track. Despite an increase in new COVID-19 cases, the gradual recovery in consumption is expected to continue, buttressed by improvements in the job market and consumer confidence. The contributions of net exports and investment to the PRC's growth, supported by healthy trade dynamics, are also expected to increase this year, before moderating in 2022.

The growth forecast for India in fiscal year 2021 (FY2021, ending 30 September 2021) is revised down, as May's spike in COVID-19 dented the recovery. The outbreak, however, dissipated faster than anticipated, resulting in several states easing lockdown measures and returning to more normal travel patterns. The economy is expected to rebound strongly in the remaining three quarters of FY2021, and grow by 10.0% in the full fiscal year before moderating to 7.5% in FY2022. Because consumption will recover only gradually, government spending and exports will contribute more to FY2021's growth than they did in the previous fiscal year.

The outlook varies across South Asia. The subregion is projected to expand more slowly this year than earlier projected, but faster next year. While India's drives the forecast, growth rates will vary across economies. As well as for India, this *Update* revises down 2021's forecasts for Bangladesh and Nepal, both grappling with another

Table 1.1.1 GDP growth rate in developing Asia, % per year

The region is set to recover in 2021, except for the Pacific.

	2018	2019	2020	2021		2022	
				ADO 2021	Update	ADO 2021	Update
Developing Asia	6.0	5.0	−0.1	7.3	7.1	5.3	5.4
Central Asia	4.5	4.9	−1.9	3.4	4.1	4.0	4.2
Armenia	5.2	7.6	−7.4	1.8	5.2	3.0	3.5
Azerbaijan	1.5	2.5	−4.3	1.9	2.2	2.5	2.5
Georgia	4.8	5.0	−6.2	3.5	8.5	6.0	6.5
Kazakhstan	4.1	4.5	−2.6	3.2	3.4	3.5	3.7
Kyrgyz Republic	3.8	4.6	−8.6	3.5	3.5	5.0	5.0
Tajikistan	7.3	7.5	4.5	5.0	5.0	5.5	5.5
Turkmenistan	6.2	6.3	1.6	4.8	4.8	4.9	4.9
Uzbekistan	5.4	5.8	1.6	4.0	5.0	5.0	5.5
East Asia	6.1	5.3	1.8	7.4	7.6	5.1	5.1
Hong Kong, China	2.8	−1.7	−6.1	4.6	6.2	4.5	3.4
Mongolia	7.2	5.2	−5.3	4.8	4.6	5.7	6.0
People's Republic of China	6.7	6.0	2.3	8.1	8.1	5.5	5.5
Republic of Korea	2.9	2.2	−0.9	3.5	4.0	3.1	3.1
Taipei,China	2.8	3.0	3.1	4.6	6.2	3.0	3.0
South Asia	6.4	4.2	−5.6	9.5	8.8	6.6	7.0
Afghanistan	1.2	3.9	−1.9	3.0	...	4.0	...
Bangladesh	7.9	8.2	3.5	6.8	5.5	7.2	6.8
Bhutan	3.8	4.3	0.9	−3.4	−3.4	3.7	3.7
India	6.5	4.0	−7.3	11.0	10.0	7.0	7.5
Maldives	8.1	7.0	−32.0	13.1	18.0	14.0	15.0
Nepal	7.6	6.7	−2.1	3.1	2.3	5.1	4.1
Pakistan	5.5	2.1	−0.5	2.0	3.9	4.0	4.0
Sri Lanka	3.3	2.3	−3.6	4.1	3.4	3.6	3.4
Southeast Asia	5.1	4.5	−4.0	4.4	3.1	5.1	5.0
Brunei Darussalam	0.1	3.9	1.2	2.5	1.8	3.0	3.5
Cambodia	7.5	7.1	−3.1	4.0	1.9	5.5	5.5
Indonesia	5.2	5.0	−2.1	4.5	3.5	5.0	4.8
Lao PDR	6.2	4.7	−0.5	4.0	2.3	4.5	4.0
Malaysia	4.8	4.4	−5.6	6.0	4.7	5.7	6.1
Myanmar	6.4	6.8	3.3	−9.8	−18.4	...	...
Philippines	6.3	6.1	−9.6	4.5	4.5	5.5	5.5
Singapore	3.5	1.3	−5.4	6.0	6.5	4.1	4.1
Thailand	4.2	2.3	−6.1	3.0	0.8	4.5	3.9
Timor-Leste	−1.1	1.8	−8.5	3.4	2.2	4.3	4.0
Viet Nam	7.1	7.0	2.9	6.7	3.8	7.0	6.5
The Pacific	0.8	4.3	−5.3	1.4	−0.6	3.8	4.8
Cook Islands	8.9	5.3	−5.9	−26.0	−26.0	6.0	7.1
Federated States of Micronesia	0.2	1.2	−3.9	−1.8	−1.1	2.0	2.0
Fiji	3.8	−0.4	−15.7	2.0	−5.0	7.3	8.8
Kiribati	2.3	2.4	0.6	−0.2	0.3	2.3	2.3
Marshall Islands	3.6	0.7	−2.6	−1.4	−3.3	2.5	4.0
Nauru	5.7	1.0	0.8	1.5	1.5	1.0	1.0
Niue	6.5	5.6	...	...	...	...	...
Palau	5.8	−1.8	−10.3	−7.8	−10.8	10.4	8.8
Papua New Guinea	−0.3	5.9	−3.3	2.5	1.3	3.0	4.1
Samoa	−2.1	3.6	−3.2	−9.2	−9.2	3.1	3.1
Solomon Islands	3.0	1.2	−4.5	1.0	1.0	4.5	4.5
Tonga	0.3	0.7	−0.8	−5.3	−5.3	1.8	1.8
Tuvalu	4.3	13.9	1.0	2.5	2.5	3.0	3.0
Vanuatu	2.9	3.5	−8.5	2.0	−3.0	4.0	5.0

... = not available, ADO = *Asian Development Outlook*, Lao PDR = Lao People's Democratic Republic.

Source: *ADO database*.

resurgence in COVID-19 cases. Maldives is revised up on more favorable prospects for international tourism, as is Pakistan on the better handling of the pandemic and last year's government stimulus. The subregion's other economies are on track to achieving *ADO 2021*'s forecasts.

Southeast Asia will recover at a much slower pace than earlier projected. Weaker growth rates are expected in 9 out of the subregion's 11 economies, bringing the forecast for growth in 2021 down to 3.1% from the earlier projection of 4.4% and to 5.0% from 5.1% for 2022. Recurring waves of COVID-19 have caused stringent mobility restrictions in Cambodia, Indonesia, the Lao People's Democratic Republic, Malaysia, Thailand, Timor-Leste, and Viet Nam—all of which have downgraded growth forecasts compared with *ADO 2021*. Growth in Myanmar will slow across all sectors. Projections for growth are unchanged for the Philippines and upgraded for Singapore, where high vaccination coverage will continue allowing the economy to benefit from the rise in global demand.

A better-than-expected recovery is anticipated in Central Asia. The subregion turned in a strong economic performance in the first half, amid the continued recovery in commodity prices. Because of this, the growth forecast is revised up to 4.1% from the earlier projection of 3.4% for 2021 and to 4.2% from 4.0% for 2022. The growth outlook has improved in five out of the subregion's eight economies— Armenia, Azerbaijan, Georgia, Kazakhstan, and Uzbekistan. Nevertheless, several economies have been hit by a new wave of COVID-19 and reimposed lockdowns, and other restrictions. These developments, along with slow vaccine rollouts, pose a risk to Central Asia's growth prospects.

The Pacific will continue contracting for the second consecutive year and by 0.6% in 2021, a downward revision from *ADO 2021*'s projection of 1.4% growth. The contraction reflects the severe constraints that COVID-19 containment measures, particularly, border restrictions, continue to have on business activity and tourism in the Cook Islands, Fiji, Palau, Samoa, Tonga, and Vanuatu. Weak mining and petroleum output in Papua New Guinea will weigh on its growth this year, but improvements in this sector should boost GDP next year. The subregion's economy is expected to rebound in 2022 on wider vaccination coverage and the continued reopening of borders, which are expected to boost trade and tourism, particularly in the Cook Islands, Fiji, and Vanuatu. This *Update* revises up 2022's GDP growth for the Pacific to 4.8% from the earlier projection of 3.8%.

Regional inflation will remain benign, but accelerate in some economies

The protracted recovery will result in lower inflation in developing Asia this year. The region's average inflation is forecast to fall from 2.8% in 2020 to 2.2% in 2021, slightly lower than *ADO 2021*'s forecasts of 2.3% and 2.7%, respectively (Figure 1.1.32). The region's tepid inflation this year is mainly because of price dynamics in the PRC and India, its two largest economies. The PRC's inflation rate is expected to decline to 1.3% in 2021 from 2.5% last year due to the effect of pork-price deflation on food prices. Inflation in India is expected to decelerate to 5.5% this year from 6.2% in 2020.

Excluding the PRC and India, average inflation is forecast to rise from 1.9% in 2020 to 2.9% this year. Inflation accelerated in the first half in the newly industrialized economies of Hong Kong, China, the Republic of Korea, Taipei,China, and Singapore; some economies in Central Asia (Armenia and Georgia); and some economies in Southeast Asia (Malaysia, the Philippines, and Thailand). Inflation this year is expected to be higher in Central Asia and South Asia, and slower in East Asia, Southeast Asia, and the Pacific than *ADO 2021*'s forecasts (Figure 1.1.33).

Figure 1.1.32 Inflation forecasts for developing Asia

Economic slack due to the COVID-19 pandemic will dampen inflation in 2021.

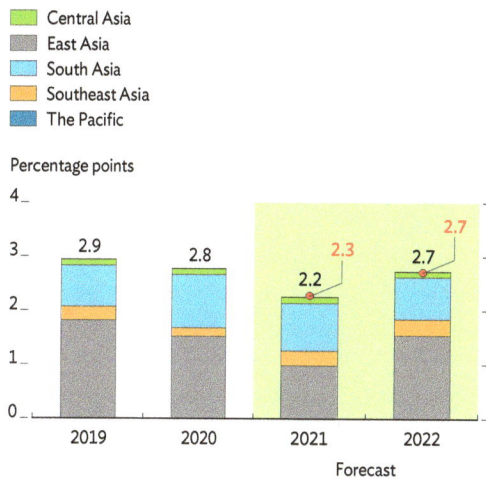

ADO = Asian Development Outlook, COVID-19 = Coronavirus Disease 2019.

Note: The red dots represent the 2021 and 2022 inflation forecasts from the projections in *ADO 2021*, released in April 2021.

Source: *ADO* database.

Figure 1.1.33 Changes to inflation forecasts for subregions in developing Asia, 2021

Inflation dynamics vary across the region.

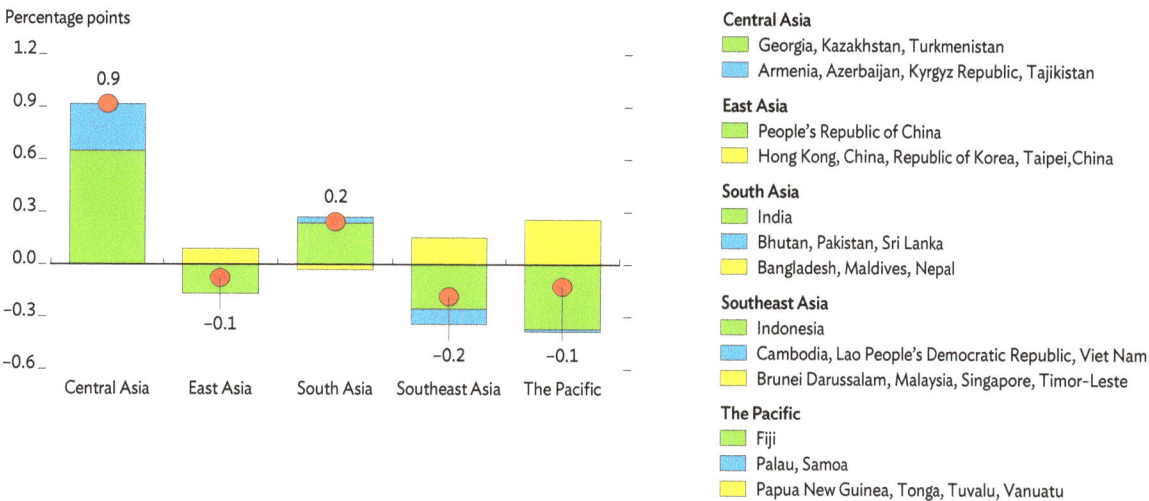

Central Asia
- Georgia, Kazakhstan, Turkmenistan
- Armenia, Azerbaijan, Kyrgyz Republic, Tajikistan

East Asia
- People's Republic of China
- Hong Kong, China, Republic of Korea, Taipei,China

South Asia
- India
- Bhutan, Pakistan, Sri Lanka
- Bangladesh, Maldives, Nepal

Southeast Asia
- Indonesia
- Cambodia, Lao People's Democratic Republic, Viet Nam
- Brunei Darussalam, Malaysia, Singapore, Timor-Leste

The Pacific
- Fiji
- Palau, Samoa
- Papua New Guinea, Tonga, Tuvalu, Vanuatu

Note: The red dots represent changes in inflation forecasts for 2021 from the projections in *Asian Development Outlook 2021*, released in April 2021. Green bars represent the main drivers for changes in subregional forecasts. Blue bars represent the economies with the same directional changes. Yellow bars represent economies with opposite directional changes.

Source: *Asian Development Outlook* database.

The forecast for Central Asia's inflation this year is revised up to 7.7% from *ADO 2021*'s 6.8%. After higher-than-expected price increases in the first 6 months, inflation projections for 2021 are raised in seven subregional economies—Armenia, Azerbaijan, Georgia, Kazakhstan, the Kyrgyz Republic, Tajikistan, and Turkmenistan. The revisions are largest in Georgia, Kazakhstan, and Turkmenistan, contributing 0.6 percentage points to the subregional average. Factors driving the acceleration vary across economies, but they are generally caused by higher food and other commodity prices, currency depreciation, and a stronger-than-expected recovery in aggregate demand.

Inflation in South Asia has risen faster than expected on rising food prices. This *Update* revises up the subregion's 2021 inflation forecast to 5.8% from the earlier projection of 5.5%, with the increase mainly due to the India's FY2021 inflation forecast being increased from 5.2% to 5.5%. Rising global oil and commodity prices, and soaring food prices due to delayed crop sowing, will continue to put upward pressure on India's inflation. The inflation rates of Bhutan, Pakistan, and Sri Lanka this year are expected to rise on higher food prices. But their effect on the subregional inflation forecast is offset by muted price dynamics in Bangladesh and Nepal, where inflation is projected to slow on weaker demand, and in Maldives due to changes in administered prices.

Inflation in Southeast Asia will be muted due to weakening growth. The inflation forecast for 2021 is revised down to 2.2% from 2.4% in *ADO 2021* due largely to the subregion's worsening economic outlook following recent COVID-19 outbreaks. Indonesia's downward adjustment is the largest contributor to the revision to the subregional inflation forecast, followed by downward adjustments in Viet Nam, the the Lao People's Democratic Republic, and Cambodia. These declines are partly offset by upward revisions to the inflation forecasts for Brunei Darussalam, Malaysia, Singapore, and Timor-Leste, as higher global oil and commodity prices fueled inflationary pressures in these economies.

Weaker-than-expected inflation in the PRC will keep prices in check in East Asia. Inflation will accelerate in Hong Kong, China; the Republic of Korea; and Taipei,China this year on stronger domestic demand and the pass-through from higher international commodity prices. These upward adjustments, however, are outweighed by a lower inflation forecast for the PRC, resulting in subregional inflation projected at 1.4% in 2021—a tad lower than *ADO 2021*'s forecast. Mongolia's inflation rate remains high compared with other economies in the subregion.

Inflation in the Pacific should remain at its *ADO 2021* forecast. Prices are rising slower than expected in Fiji, Palau, and Samoa. Weaker economic activity because of COVID-19 slowed inflation in Fiji, despite higher international commodity prices.

Subsidies on utilities contributed to slowing price increases in Palau and Samoa. But inflation in Papua New Guinea is expected to accelerate this year on rising food, fuel, and education costs.

Rising imports will narrow the regional current account surplus

Developing Asia's current account balances will deteriorate, except in Central Asia. The regional surplus is forecast to continue declining, from the equivalent of 2.4% of GDP in 2020 to 1.9% in 2021 and to 1.5% in 2022 (Figure 1.1.34). This is mostly because of a rebound in imports on recovering GDP growth after the contraction in 2020. Current account surpluses in 2021 will narrow in East Asia, Southeast Asia and the Pacific, and South Asia will turn a deficit, relative to last year. The rise in global commodity prices will benefit commodity-exporting economies, including Azerbaijan, Brunei Darussalam, Georgia, Kazakhstan, and Papua New Guinea. Bangladesh and Pakistan are expected to have higher earnings from remittances, and Maldives and Fiji should benefit from the gradual reopening of their tourism sectors.

Figure 1.1.34 Current account dynamics in developing Asia

Surpluses will narrow except in Central Asia; South Asia will turn a deficit.

- 2020
- 2021 forecast
- 2022 forecast

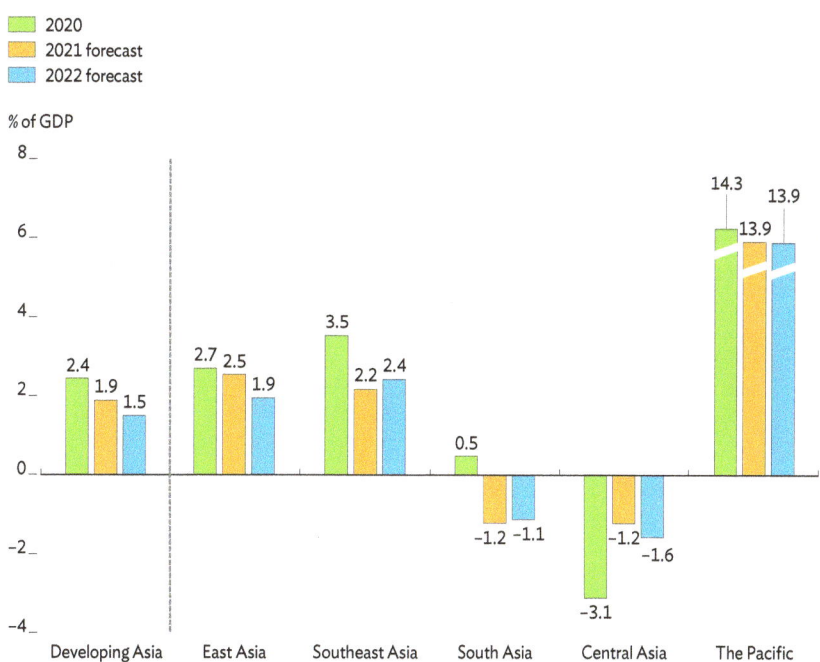

% of GDP

Source: *Asian Development Outlook* database.

Risks to the outlook are tilted to the downside

COVID-19 remains the main threat to the outlook in developing Asia. The new, more infectious variants, such as the increasingly dominant Delta variant, amplify the risks from a slower-than-expected vaccine rollout. Renewed and rapidly expanding outbreaks may reverse the trend toward more selective containment measures, and lead to the reimposition of stringent lockdowns. Emerging evidence on the waning effects of COVID-19 vaccines suggests that supply constraints—which are currently slowing down vaccination programs in developing Asia—may worsen. This is because the need for booster shots could increase global and regional demand for vaccines, even before most economies have achieved widespread vaccination.

Other issues associated with the economic impact of the pandemic are turning into medium-term policy concerns. The income losses caused by the pandemic in particular threaten to leave lasting scars and have a multidimensional effect on regional economies. According to estimates in the Asian Development Bank's *Key Indicators for Asia and the Pacific 2021*, COVID-19 pushed 75 million to 80 million more people into extreme poverty in developing Asia last year, compared with a scenario without COVID-19. The economic growth projected for this year and next will only bring poverty in 2022 down to what it would have been in 2020 had the pandemic not happened. So, progress on reducing poverty has been set back at least 2 years. The extended school closures due to the persistence of COVID-19 imply that learning and earning losses are bound to be higher than those estimated in *ADO 2021*. And prolonged business closures and unemployment increase the risk of substantial labor market scarring.

Additional risks to the outlook are associated with geopolitical tensions, developments in financial markets, and global supply disruptions. Relations between the US and the PRC remain strained on trade, technology, and several other fronts. Turbulence in financial markets remains a threat, particularly on rising expectations of a forthcoming monetary policy tightening in the US. For economies with higher external debt levels and weaker macroeconomic fundamentals, rising US interest rates could lead to increasing debt-repayment burdens, capital outflows, and currency depreciations. The persistence of supply bottlenecks, including in semiconductors, also casts a shadow on the short-term outlook of some exporters in the region (Box 1.1.2).

Risks that have been overshadowed by the pandemic may also return to center stage. Even as economies gradually recover from the COVID-19 crisis, other threats, led by climate change, loom large. Disasters triggered by extreme weather events are becoming more severe and more frequent. Climate change could have a big impact on the region's economic potential, and the risks are particularly serious for the poor and vulnerable groups, which could suffer increased food insecurity and malnutrition (Box 1.1.3). Sustainable food production and agricultural systems that can cope with the effects of climate change will be crucial for developing Asia, as discussed in the theme chapter of this report.

Box 1.1.1 Vaccines are breaking the link between containment stringency and COVID-19

Vaccines help protect against severe cases of COVID-19. Increasing vaccination leads to a declining number of deaths and hospitalizations per case even with new outbreaks. This in turn means that governments can implement containment measures that are less stringent and more targeted. This box presents empirical evidence that this has been occurring.

To test whether progress in vaccination programs has altered the relationship between containment stringency and new COVID-19 cases in developing Asia, the following panel regression specification is adopted:

$$stringency_{it} = \beta\, cases_{it} + \gamma\, vaccines_{it} + \delta\, cases_{it} \times vaccines_{it} + \mu_i + \lambda_t + \varepsilon_{it}.$$

In this equation, the dependent variable $stringency_{it}$ is Oxford University's COVID-19 Government Response Stringency Index, a measure from 0 (lowest) to 100 (highest) that indicates the tightness of COVID-19 containment measures in economy i on day t. The variable $cases_{it}$ is the number of daily COVID-19 cases per million, and $vaccines_{it}$ measures progress on vaccination. Two different indicators are explored: the share of partially and fully vaccinated individuals in the population and the share of fully vaccinated individuals in the population. Country fixed effects (μ_i) capture time-invariant factors, and the term λ_t controls for common factors affecting stringency over time. The sample includes 30 developing Asian economies from 1 April 2020 to 31 August 2021.

The hypothesis is that governments increase stringency when cases rise, but to a lesser extent as a greater share of the population becomes vaccinated.

How vaccinations change government responses to COVID-19

Increased vaccination breaks down the link between daily new cases and stringency of restrictions.

Independent variables	(1)	(2)
	Dependent variable: Government response stringency index	
Cases (per million)	0.0273***	0.0240***
	(0.00936)	(0.00625)
Share of partially and fully vaccinated	0.0106	
	(0.0806)	
Cases × partially and fully vaccinated	−0.000520**	
	(0.000218)	
Share of fully vaccinated		−0.0823
		(0.112)
Cases × fully vaccinated		−0.000677***
		(0.000171)
Number of observations	15,216	15,216
R-squared	0.275	0.281
Number of economies	30	30
Country fixed effects	Yes	Yes
Time fixed effects	Yes	Yes

COVID-19 = Coronavirus Disease 2019.

Notes: *** p<0.01, ** p<0.05, * p<0.1. Robust standard errors in parentheses. Sample period is 1 April 2020 to 31 August 2021.
Source: Authors.

continued on next page

Box 1.1.1 *Continued*

Therefore, β is expected to be positively signed, while δ is expected to be negative.

Regression results reported in the box table support the idea that vaccines have weakened the link between containment stringency and new COVID-19 cases as coefficients bear the expected signs. The box figure illustrates the effect of an increase in daily new COVID-19 cases per million by 100, depending on either the share of partially and fully vaccinated (blue bars) or fully vaccinated (orange bars) in the population.

For the blue bars, the results suggest that an economy that has not yet commenced its vaccination program will tighten containment measures to the equivalent of 2.7 points on average. When 20% and 30% of the population are either partially or fully vaccinated, the effect on the stringency index decreases to 1.7 points and 1.2 points, respectively. At 40% partial or full vaccination coverage, the increase in stringency is 0.6 points and is statistically not significantly different from zero. For the orange bars, the estimated increase in stringency is smaller when conditioned on the share of fully vaccinated individuals in the population, all else equal. This outcome is not surprising, since full vaccination offers better protection against COVID-19 than partial vaccination and governments are aware of this. For example, at 20% fully vaccinated, the increase in stringency in response to a rise in cases is 1.0 points on average. At 30% it is 0.4 and insignificant.

Estimated effect of COVID-19 vaccines on containment stringency

Stringency increases when cases rise, but by less as vaccination progresses.

■ Partially and fully vaccinated
■ Fully vaccinated

Change in stringency in response to rise in COVID-19 cases

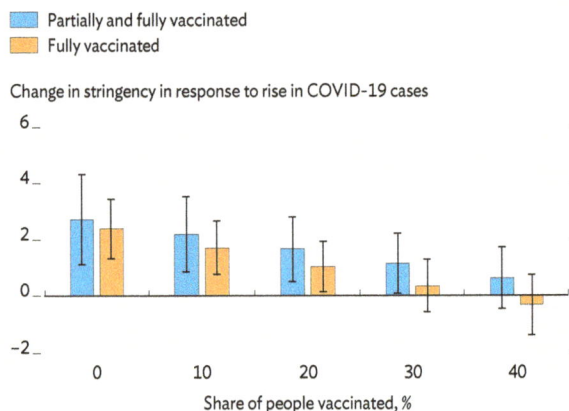

Share of people vaccinated, %

COVID 19 = Coronavirus Disease 2019.
Note: Whiskers denote the 90% confidence interval.
Sources: T. Hale et al. 2020. Oxford COVID-19 Government Response Tracker. Blavatnik School of Government. https://www.bsg.ox.ac.uk/research/research-projects/covid-19-government-response-tracker; Our World in Data. https://ourworldindata.org/coronavirus; Asian Development Bank estimates.

This box was written by Matteo Lanzafame, Irfan Qureshi, and Marcel Schroder of the Economic Research and Regional Cooperation Department, Asian Development Bank, Manila.

Box 1.1.2 Developing Asia's electronics and automobile exporters at risk from the shortage of semiconductor chips

With the global economy recovering from the deep recession caused by COVID-19 in 2020, mismatches between supply and demand for semiconductor chips arose in early 2021. These frictions have resulted in shortages in the production of chips, which are used intensively in many industries, including the electronics and automotive industries. Chips shortages are a particular concern for developing Asian economies since these two industries account for a large share of regional exports.

The chips industry has been disrupted by the COVID-19 pandemic. Recurring waves of the pandemic have caused staff shortages and supply-chain disruptions. For example, most semiconductor factories in Malaysia were only allowed to operate at 60% of staff capacity when the country was under a strict lockdown from 1 June to 16 August (*Malay Mail* 2021; Ruehl and Hille 2021).

Disasters triggered by natural hazards in early 2021 hit the supply of chips. In February, a cold snap in Texas and an earthquake in Japan disrupted the production of several chip manufacturers. And Taipei,China's worst drought in 56 years affected supplies from the world's largest exporter of chips because their production requires large amounts of water for cooling manufacturing equipment.

Tensions between the United States and the People's Republic of China (PRC) have also affected the production of chips. The Government of the United States restricted exports of software and semiconductor manufacturing equipment to several entities in the PRC in 2018 and 2019. This made it harder for PRC manufacturers to upgrade their production facilities to make the more sophisticated chips that are in high demand.

continued on next page

Box 1.1.2 *Continued*

The US expanded the restrictions in August 2020 by banning the export of chips manufactured using US technology—regardless of where they were produced—to certain PRC companies. This effectively forced Samsung and TSMC to stop supplying some of their largest PRC clients. Because these two companies hold a combined 71% share of the global chips market—and even more for higher-end chips—the US restrictions cannot easily be circumvented by sourcing from other producers (box figure 1).

The COVID-19 pandemic has further boosted demand for chips. Sales of electronic goods for work-from-home, home schooling, and leisure soared after social distancing measures were imposed from January 2020. Supply chain disruptions caused by the pandemic, US–PRC tensions, and widespread expectations of a prolonged period of high prices have pushed manufacturers relying on chips to increase their precautionary inventories, further fueling demand. Recurrent surges in the price of Bitcoin, which rose 456% from October 2020 to April 2021, and other cryptocurrencies have also contributed to drying out the market for chips, particularly for graphics processing units that are vital for mining cryptocurrencies.

The imbalance between supply and demand has triggered higher chip prices this year, reversing a trend of declining prices (box figure 2). Average delivery times have also risen, from about 13 weeks in 2019 and 2020 to more than 20 weeks as of July 2021 (box figure 3).

In the first half of 2020, heavy demand for chips from the electronics industry was mitigated by reduced demand from automakers, which also heavily rely on chips. But increased demand for automobiles since the second half of 2020—and notably for electric cars, which rely even more heavily on electronics—exacerbated the shortage. Because automakers often rely on just-in-time supply chains, chip inventories were drawn down when sales rebounded. As a result, automakers have reduced or paused the production of certain vehicles since early 2021 (Browne 2021). Ford cut its production by 50% in the second quarter because of the chip shortage (Wayland 2021). Nissan and Ram Trucks, among others, have left out some electronic equipment that require chips from the vehicles they produce. Since the second quarter, the shortage has spilled over to electronics and household appliances (Shead 2021).

The chip shortage is a concern for exporters of automobiles and electronics in developing Asia. The shortage poses a risk to the outlook for economies where vehicles account for significant shares of exports, as they do in the Republic of Korea and

1 Market shares of major semiconductor chip manufacturers, %

The four leading manufacturers account for 83% of the global chip market.

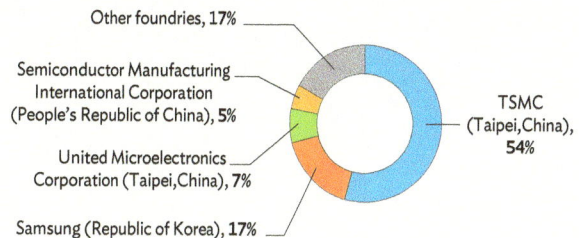

- Other foundries, 17%
- Semiconductor Manufacturing International Corporation (People's Republic of China), 5%
- United Microelectronics Corporation (Taipei, China), 7%
- Samsung (Republic of Korea), 17%
- TSMC (Taipei, China), 54%

Source: TrendForce. www.trendforce.com (accessed 3 September 2021).

2 US producer price index for semiconductor chips and other electronics components

The chip shortage has reversed the long-term trend of falling semiconductor prices.

Index, December 1984 = 100

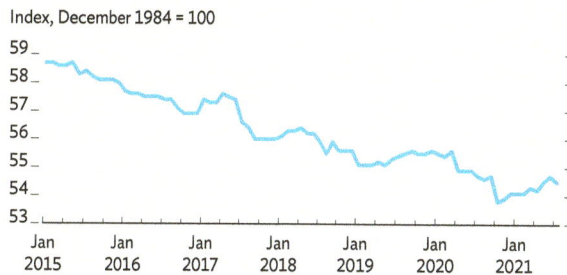

US = United States.
Source: Federal Reserve Economic Data. https://fred.stlouisfed.org (accessed 3 September 2021).

3 Average duration between orders and delivery of semiconductor chips

The gap between orders and delivery rose sharply in 2021.

Weeks

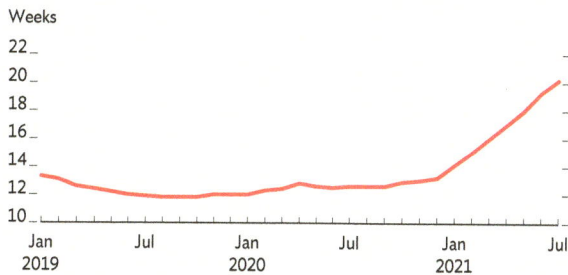

Sources: Bloomberg; Economist Intelligence Unit; Susquehanna Financial Group. www.sig.com (all accessed 3 September 2021).

Thailand (box figure 4). The shortage is also a challenge for economies in the region that heavily depend on electronics exports (excluding chips), as do Viet Nam, the PRC, Hong Kong, China, and the Philippines, where electronics account for more than 20% of exports.

continued on next page

Box 1.1.2 *Continued*

4 Share of vehicles and electronics excluding chips, 2019

Vehicles and electronics, which critically rely on chips, jointly account for more than 15% of exports in nine developing Asian economies.

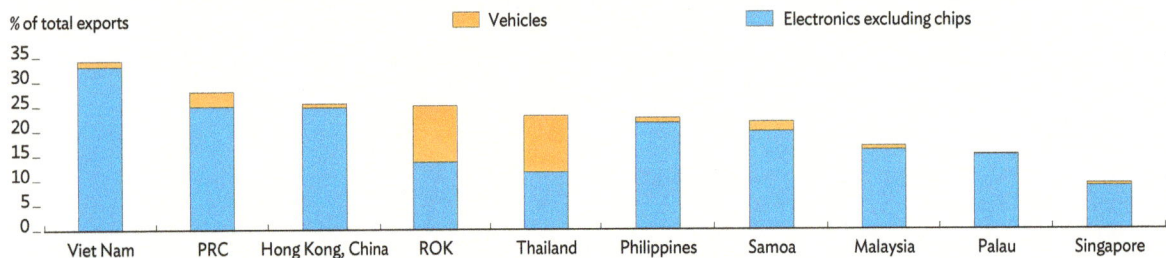

PRC = People's Republic of China, ROK = Republic of Korea.

Note: The sample is restricted to developing Asian economies for which "electronics excluding chips" under the Harmonized System product classification and "road vehicles" accounted for at least 10% of exports in 2019.

Source: Observatory of Economic Complexity. https://oec.world/ (accessed 5 August 2021).

The chip shortage was initially expected to be over by the end of 2021 (Gartenberg 2021). However, it has continued due to semiconductor manufacturing in Southeast Asia being disrupted by COVID-19 outbreaks. The industry consensus is that the shortage will last at least until mid-2022 (Shead 2021). Some analysts expect that replacing higher-end chips with less powerful ones—for which the shortage is less severe—will bring some relief toward the end of 2021. Efforts by some chip manufacturers to prevent hoarding through greater scrutiny of customer orders could also help (Jeong and Strumpf 2021). Among the more pessimistic forecasts for the shortage is one by Intel's chief executive, Pat Gelsinger, who fears it could last into 2023 since only new plants will bring durable relief (Fitch 2021).

Large investments in chip manufacturing should ease the shortage in the longer term. Motivated by the current shortage and rising geopolitical tensions, the European Commission and the Government of the United States have announced ambitious plans to boost domestic chip production, supported by generous subsidies. Intel's chief executive is seeking an €8 billion subsidy to increase chip manufacturing capacity in the European Union (Cerulus 2021). In the US, Samsung has sought tax incentives to support a $17 billion investment in a new chip plant, and TSMC is building a $12 billion factory in Arizona (Park 2021). In the long term, these initiatives could improve the resilience of the global semiconductor market by diversifying production locations, but this could also threaten Asia's preeminence in the sector.

References:

Browne, R. 2021. The Global Chip Shortage Is Starting to Hit the Smartphone Industry. CNBC. 29 July. https://www.cnbc.com/2021/07/29/the-global-chip-shortage-is-starting-to-hit-the-smartphone-industry.html.

Cerulus, L. 2021. Too Big, Too Bold? EU "Moonshot" Microchip Plant Faces Doubts. Politico. 28 April. https://www.politico.eu/article/europe-microchip-conundrum-go-big-or-go-home/.

Fitch, A. 2021. Intel CEO Says Chip Shortage Could Stretch into 2023. *Wall Street Journal*. 22 July. https://www.wsj.com/articles/intel-intc-2q-earnings-report-2021-11626899296.

Gartenberg, C. 2021. The Chip Shortage Will Likely Get Worse before It Gets Better. The Verge. 23 June. https://www.theverge.com/2021/6/23/22547826/chip-shortage-cars-playstation-5-gpus-semiconductors-time-foundaries-tsmc.

Jeong, E-Y., and D. Strumpf. 2021. Why the Chip Shortage Is So Hard to Overcome. *Wall Street Journal*. 19 April. https://www.wsj.com/articles/why-the-chip-shortage-is-so-hard-to-overcome-11618844905.

Malay Mail. 2021. Perodua Sales Surge in Aug as Operations Resume after Lockdown. 3 Sept. https://www.malaymail.com/news/malaysia/2021/09/03/perodua-sold-6988-vehicles-in-august-as-production-increases/2002637.

Park, E-J. 2021. Samsung Does Texas Two-Step while Competitor Builds. *Korea JoongAng Daily*. 19 July. https://koreajoongangdaily.joins.com/2021/07/19/business/tech/Samsung-Electronics-TSMC-Intel/20210719195500493.html.

Ruehl, M., and K. Hille. 2021 South-east Asia's Covid Surge Poses Latest Blow to Global Chip Supply. *Financial Times*. 21 July.

Shead, S. 2021. The Global Chip Shortage Is Starting to Have Major Real-World Consequences. CNBC. 17 May. https://www.cnbc.com/2021/05/07/chip-shortage-is-starting-to-have-major-real-world-consequences.html.

Wayland, M. 2021. Ford to Cut F-150 Pickup Truck Production Due to Chip Shortage. CNBC, 16 August. https://www.cnbc.com/2021/08/26/ford-to-cut-f-150-pickup-truck-production-due-to-chip-shortage.html.

This box was written by Jules Hugot, economist, and Jesson Pagaduan, consultant, Economic Research and Regional Cooperation Department, Asian Development Bank, Manila.

Box 1.1.3 COVID-19's impact on food security

The COVID-19 pandemic has disrupted food supply chains in developing Asia, heightening challenges to food security. Lockdowns and mobility restrictions to contain COVID-19 have disrupted food supply chains, estimated to provide about 80% of all food consumed in the region (Reardon et al. 2019). Initial estimates suggest a sharp increase in food insecurity, with women and children being disproportionately affected.

The disruption in food supply chains is working through several channels. Uncertainty during the initial days of COVID-19 lockdowns across the region induced panic buying, temporary shortages, and price spikes. Disruptions to domestic and international food supply chains—which emerged as rising health risks led to major travel restrictions—undermined food availability and accessibility (Kim et al. 2020). Exports of perishables fell on steep declines in global air cargo capacity (FAO 2020a and 2020b). Domestic transport of food was similarly disrupted by lockdowns. Micro, small, and medium-sized enterprises have been battered by lost sales, higher production costs to ensure safe working environments, and difficulty accessing inputs, equipment, and services (Nordhagen et al. 2021; FAO 2020b; MSU and IFPRI 2020). Notable among these enterprises are the family-owned stores and informal food vendors that dominate food distribution systems in developing Asia's low- and middle-income economies.

The impact of COVID-19 on food insecurity is still unfolding, but initial estimates suggest a sharp increase in food insecurity—defined by the Food and Agriculture Organization of the United Nations as "lacking regular access to enough safe and nutritious food for normal growth and development and an active and healthy life." Globally, the number of people experiencing severe food insecurity rose by 148 million in 2020 to 928 million—12% of the global population.[a] To put this in perspective, last year's increase equals that of the previous 5 years combined (FAO et al. 2021). Global hunger is expected to affect an additional 291 million people in 2021 of which 72% will be in developing Asia, particularly in Bangladesh, India, Indonesia, and Pakistan (Baquedano et al. 2021). The COVID-19 crisis will therefore substantially reverse progress made in reducing hunger and malnutrition in the region and set developing Asia back from achieving its target of zero hunger by 2030. At the peak of the crisis, food insecurity hit some economies severely, particularly Afghanistan, Pakistan, and Tajikistan, as the figure shows.

Population shares in developing Asia with insufficient food consumption, April 2021

COVID-19 has worsened hunger, with some economies experiencing very high food insecurity.

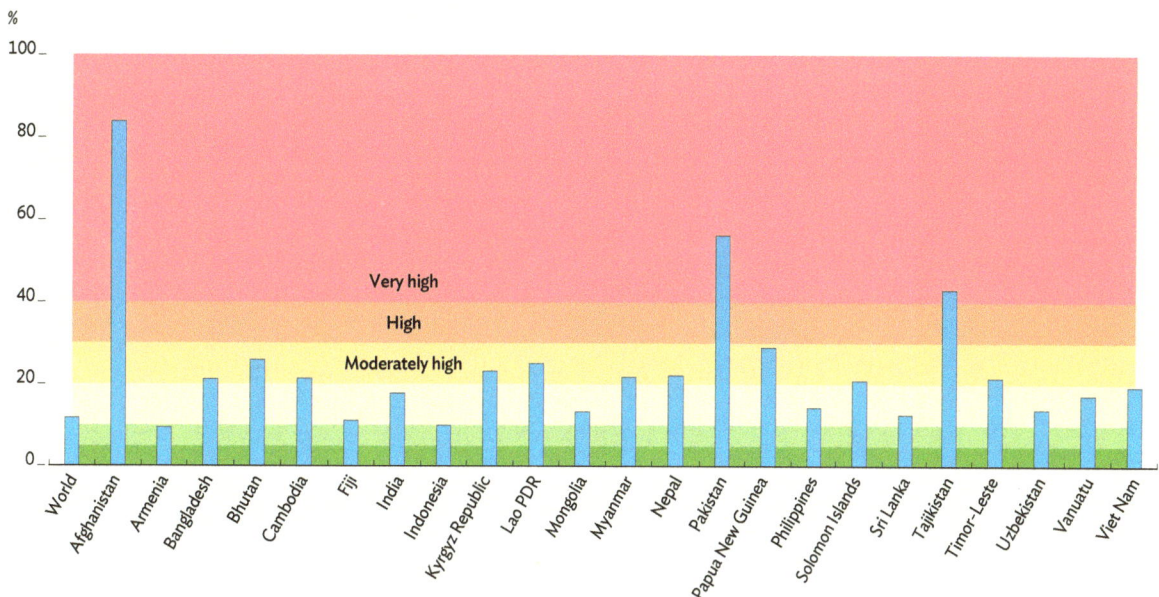

COVID-19 = Coronavirus Disease 2019, Lao PDR = Lao People's Democratic Republic.

Note: Prevalence of insufficient food consumption: very low = 0%–5%, low = 5%–10%, moderately low = 10%–20%, moderately high = 20%–30%, high = 30%–40%, very high = above 40%.

Source: World Food Programme. Hunger Map Live. https://hungermap.wfp.org (accessed 28 April 2021).

continued on next page

Box 1.1.3 *Continued*

Several other economies faced moderately high food insecurity, including Bhutan, the Kyrgyz Republic, the Lao People's Democratic Republic, and Papua New Guinea. As the pandemic continues to affect the regional economy, further income losses will worsen food security across the region.

The impact of the pandemic on food security is uneven within economies. Urban centers have been more severely affected because of higher population density, a disproportionately larger share of COVID-19 cases and outbreaks, and stricter restrictions on movement. Among the worst affected are the urban poor, who largely rely on insecure jobs in the informal sector, which accounts for 70% of total employment in the region (Kim, Kim, and Park 2020), and spend a substantial portion of their income on food (Anand et al. 2019). FAO (2020c) highlights the major channels that affected urban food supply systems, including the closure of schools, which resulted in the suspension of school meals; the closure of restaurants, canteens, and street food outlets; restrictions on selling food in public spaces, such as parks, squares, and streets; and restrictions on public transport. Rural areas were found to be more resilient due to their proximity to agricultural production areas and their shorter food supply and distribution chains. Evidence from India, suggests that mothers are much more likely to be affected by food insecurity and inadequate dietary diversity in urban centers, despite greater poverty in rural areas (Headey et al. 2020).

Women and children will be disproportionally affected by the COVID-19 crisis. The pandemic has intensified gender inequality in access to food. For the prevalence of moderate and severe food insecurity, the disparity between men and women increased from 6% to 10% from 2019 to 2020 (FAO et al. 2021). Women are also more likely to consume reduced portions at meals or skip meals entirely. One third of female respondents to a survey in Bangladesh said they had reduced their food consumption for the benefit of others in their households, and in Afghanistan, women reported skipping more meals than did male respondents (CARE 2020). Early evidence from India shows a similar gender gap in food insecurity (Agarwal 2021). Income losses, along with the availability of nutritious food and disrupted health and nutrition services, could expose an additional 9.3 million children worldwide to wasting by 2022, 2.6 million to stunting, and 168,000 to death, and induce 2.1 million maternal anemia cases (Osendarp et al. 2021).

[a]   Food insecurity is measured using the Food and Agriculture Organization of the United Nations' Food Insecurity Experience Scale. This is a survey of eight questions on people's access to adequate food. See http://www.fao.org/hunger/en/ for more details.

References:

Agarwal, B. 2021. Livelihoods in COVID Times: Gendered Perils and New Pathways in India. *World Development* 139. https://doi.org/10.1016/j.worlddev.2020.105312.

Anand S., et al. 2019. Urban Food Insecurity and its Determinants: A Baseline Study of Bengaluru. *Environment and Urbanization* 31(2).

Baquedano, F. et al. 2021. *International Food Security Assessment*. No. 2021–31. United States Department of Agriculture, Economic Research Service. https://www.ers.usda.gov/webdocs/outlooks/101733/gfa-32.pdf?v=2059.3.

CARE. 2020. *Left Out and Left Behind: Ignoring Women Will Prevent Us from Solving the Hunger Crisis: Policy Report*. Cooperative for Assistance and Relief Everywhere.

FAO. 2020a. *Second Rapid Assessment of Food and Nutrition Security in the Context of COVID-19 in Bangladesh: May–July 2020*. Food and Agriculture Organization of the United Nations. https://doi.org/10.4060/cb1018en.

———. 2020b. *Food Outlook: Biannual Report on Global Food Markets*. Food and Agriculture Organization of the United Nations.

———. 2020c. *Impacts of COVID-19 on Food Security and Nutrition: Developing Effective Policy Responses to Address the Hunger and Malnutrition Pandemic*. Rome.

FAO et al. 2021. *The State of Food Security and Nutrition in the World: Transforming Food Systems for Food Security, Improved Nutrition, and Affordable Healthy Diets for All*. Food and Agriculture Organization of the United Nations.

Headey, D., et al. 2020. Poverty and Food Insecurity during Covid-19: Telephone Survey Evidence from Mothers in Rural and Urban Myanmar. *Strategy Support Program Working Paper* No. 3. International Food Policy Research Institute.

Kim, K., S. Kim, and C-Y. Park. 2020. Food Security in Asia and the Pacific amid the COVID-19 Pandemic. *ADB Briefs* No. 139. Asian Development Bank.

MSU and IFPRI. 2020. *Impacts of COVID-19 on Myanmar's Agri-food System: Evidence Base and Policy Implications*. Michigan State University and International Food Policy Research Institute.

Nordhagen, S., et al. 2021. COVID-19 and Small Enterprises in the Food Supply Chain: Early Impacts and Implications for Longer-Term Food System Resilience in Low- and Middle-Income Countries. *World Development* 141. https://doi.org/10.1016/j.worlddev.2021.105405.

Osendarp, S., et al. 2021. *The Potential Impacts of the COVID-19 Crisis on Maternal and Child Undernutrition in Low and Middle Income Countries*. Unpublished.

Reardon, T., et al. 2019. Rapid Transformation of Food Systems in Developing Regions: Highlighting the Role of Agricultural Research & Innovations. *Agricultural Systems* 172.

This box was written by Manisha Pradhananga and Takashi Yamano of the Economic Research and Regional Cooperation Department, Asian Development Bank, Manila.

Annex: Global recovery steadies despite renewed COVID-19 outbreaks

The aggregate growth forecast for the major industrial economies of the United States, the euro area, and Japan are lowered from the projection made in April to 5.0% for 2021 and 3.9% for 2022. (Table A1.1). The strong rebound—yet weaker-than-expected growth—in the first half of this year in the United States, combined with delayed recovery in Japan due to a renewed COVID-19 outbreak, weigh on growth prospects. But on balance, the outlook is positive and a particularly bright spot is the euro area's rapid vaccine rollout.

Table A1.1 Baseline assumptions on the international economy

	2020	2021		2022	
		April ADO 2021	*September Update*	*April ADO 2021*	*September Update*
GDP growth, %					
Major industrial economies[a]	−4.6	5.3	5.0	4.1	3.9
United States	−3.4	6.5	6.0	4.4	4.0
Euro area	−6.5	4.3	4.6	4.2	4.2
Japan	−4.7	2.9	2.2	2.4	2.9
Prices and inflation					
Brent crude spot prices, average, $/barrel	42.35	64.00	69.00	61.00	67.00
Consumer price index inflation, major industrial economies' average, %	0.7	1.9	2.6	2.0	1.9
Interest rates					
United States federal funds rate, average, %	0.4	0.1	0.1	0.8	0.3
European Central Bank refinancing rate, average, %	0.0	0.0	0.0	0.0	0.0
Bank of Japan overnight call rate, average, %	0.0	−0.1	−0.1	−0.1	−0.1
$ Libor,[b] %	0.5	0.1	0.1	0.8	0.3

ADO = Asian Development Outlook, GDP = gross domestic product.
[a] Average growth rates are weighted by gross national income, Atlas method.
[b] Average London interbank offered rate quotations on 1-month loans.
Sources: Bloomberg; CEIC Data Company; Haver Analytics (all accessed 3 September 2021); Asian Development Bank estimates.

This annex was written by David De Padua, Jules Hugot, Matteo Lanzafame, Nedelyn Magtibay-Ramos, Yuho Myoda, Pilipinas Quising, Arief Ramayandi, Marcel Schroder, and Dennis Sorino of the Economic Research and Regional Cooperation Department (ERCD), ADB, Manila, and by ERCD consultants Michael Timbang and Jesson Pagaduan.

Recent developments in the major advanced economies

United States

The economic recovery continued strongly in the first half of 2021. The economy grew by 6.3% in the first quarter (Q1) in seasonally adjusted annualized terms (as assumed for all growth rates in this annex) and by 6.6% in Q2 (Figure A1.1), pushing the gross domestic product (GDP) back to its prepandemic level by midyear. GDP growth was mainly driven by strong consumption, as economic activity accelerated on rapid progress with COVID-19 vaccination. But falling inventories and residential investment, weaker government spending, and negative net exports, as imports outpaced exports, dampened growth in Q2.

Consumption grew by 11.4% in Q1 as spending soared on goods, including motor vehicles, household equipment, recreational goods, and food and beverages. Household spending on goods and services picked up in Q2, pushing consumption growth to 11.9%, underpinned mainly by increased spending on recreation, food services, and accommodation as activity normalized. Even so, the increase in Q2 consumption fell short of expectations given March's large fiscal stimulus payments. The positive effect of the stimulus was evident in the jump in retail sales in March, which steadied in April and have remained flat since then. Consumer confidence improved significantly after a large spike of 20.7% in March and a 7.4% rise in June as consumers spent more on services at the start of summer (Figure A1.2). The June rise is consistent with expectations of strong consumption holding up economic growth in Q3.

Falling investment was a drag on GDP growth over the first half of this year, with investment contracting by 2.3% in Q1 and 4.0% in Q2. This is primarily a reflection of falling inventories, mainly in retail trade. Nonresidential investment has been strong, growing by 12.9% in Q1 and 9.3% in Q2. This is consistent with the momentum for investment getting stronger. The industrial production index increased from March to June, and the purchasing managers' index (PMI)—up 14.1% in March—has remained above 60, well over the threshold of 50 that indicates an expansion (Figure A1.2). Together with the strength on the consumer side, these trends support the view for the US economy's strong expansion continuing. Improvements in the labor market are also evident. The unemployment rate fell to 5.4% in July after moving below 6.0% since May despite slight increases in the labor participation rate.

Stronger economic activity has been accompanied by accelerating inflation. The headline inflation rate rose to 4.2%

Figure A1.1 Demand-side contributions to growth, United States

Robust consumption supports the recovery in H1 2021.

- Private expenditure
- Private investment
- Government expenditure & investment
- Net exports
- Gross domestic product

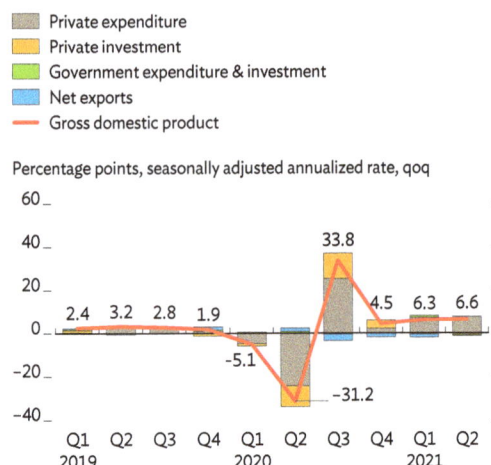

Percentage points, seasonally adjusted annualized rate, qoq

H = half, Q = quarter, qoq = quarter on quarter.
Sources: US Department of Commerce. Bureau of Economic Analysis. http://www.bea.gov; Haver Analytics (both accessed 3 September 2021).

Figure A1.2 Business activity, United States

Fiscal stimulus jump starts private business activity in March 2021.

- Consumer confidence
- Retail sales
- Composite purchasing managers' index

Note: A purchasing managers' index reading <50 signals deterioration, >50 improvement.
Source: Haver Analytics (accessed 3 September 2021).

in April and 5.4% in July. Core inflation, which excludes volatile food and energy components, rose to 3.0% in April and 4.3% in July 2021 (Figure A1.3). Inflation this year is likely to overshoot the Federal Reserve's target of 2.0%. Ultra-loose monetary policy, the rebound in economic activity, and ample fiscal support may have played some role in stoking inflation, but the increase in core inflation is mainly due to transitory factors that should subside. The Federal Reserve has indicated that it remains committed to maintaining its loose monetary policy stance and that it is willing to accommodate temporarily high inflation to guarantee a return to lower unemployment.

The US's mass vaccination program had led to a continual decline in new COVID-19 cases since early January, but this has been interrupted by another resurgence of cases. As of the first week of August, close to 70% of adults (ages 18 and over) had been vaccinated and 60% fully vaccinated. The resurgence in new daily COVID-19 cases was observed since the first week of July, due mainly to the spread of the highly infectious Delta variant, especially in less-vaccinated parts of the country. Even so, the high vaccination rate seems to have helped to contain the more severe consequences of the recent outbreak, with daily COVID-19 deaths rising at a slower pace than the rise in new infections (Figure 1.1.27 on page 24). With mask-wearing again being mandated, businesses and consumers are now better adapted to the pandemic, and the baseline does not assume a return to substantial restrictions on economic activity.

This *Update* revises down the GDP forecast in *Asian Development Outlook 2021* to a still-strong 6% in 2021 and moderating to 4% in 2022 given the weaker-than-expected Q2 2021 growth rate. Growth is expected to return to its prepandemic trend by the end of next year. The inflation forecast is revised up to 3.8% in 2021 before slowing to 2.7% in 2022. The federal funds rate is expected to remain at 0.1% over 2021, but some gradual monetary policy tightening is expected in 2022 in an indication that the Federal Reserve will not let inflation get out of hand. A variant-driven worsening of COVID-19 outbreaks is a downside risk to these forecasts.

Euro area

The euro area's GDP fell by 1.1% at a seasonally adjusted annualized rate (saar) (–1.2% year on year) in Q1 2021, stifled by the reimposition of tighter COVID-19 containment measures throughout the currency bloc (Figure A1.4). With consumer sentiment still downbeat, private consumption expenditure suffered its largest decline, dropping by 8.2% saar (–5.4% year on year).

Figure A1.3 Inflation and federal funds rate, United States

High inflation in 2021 due largely to transitory factors.

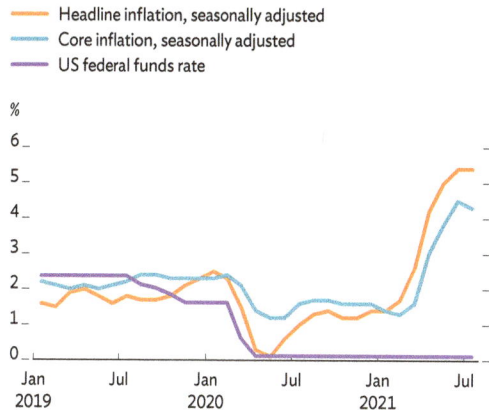

— Headline inflation, seasonally adjusted
— Core inflation, seasonally adjusted
— US federal funds rate

Source: Haver Analytics (accessed 3 September 2021).

Figure A1.4 Demand-side contributions to growth, euro area

Growth recovered in Q2 on easing COVID-19 restrictions and rapid vaccination.

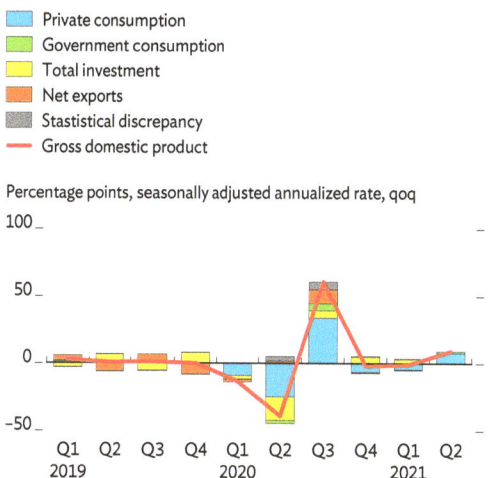

■ Private consumption
■ Government consumption
■ Total investment
■ Net exports
■ Stastistical discrepancy
— Gross domestic product

Percentage points, seasonally adjusted annualized rate, qoq

COVID-19 = Coronavirus Disease 2019, Q = quarter, qoq = quarter on quarter.
Source: Haver Analytics (accessed 8 September 2021).

Fixed-investment growth in Q1 cooled by 0.8% (–6.2% year on year) on worsening business conditions and an uncertain outlook. Net trade added 0.5 percentage points to growth, as exports strengthened alongside falling imports. Among the euro area's major economies, GDP fell by 7.8% saar (–3.1% year on year) in Germany and 1.7% (–4.2% year on year) in Spain, while growth in France rose to 0.2% (1.5% year on year) and in Italy to 0.9% saar (–0.7% year on year).

After Q1's weak start, the euro area economy bounced back in Q2, growing by 9.2% saar (14.3% year on year) as rising COVID-19 vaccination rates and easing containment measures benefited domestic demand. Strong growth in retail sales, rising consumer confidence, better services PMI readings, and falling unemployment all indicate that private consumption likely supported growth in Q2. Investment activity is also expected to have recovered in Q2, supported by the continual improvement in economic sentiment and strong growth in manufacturing. Across the euro area's major economies, France's GDP in Q2 rose by 4.5% saar (18.7% year on year), Germany's by 6.7% (9.4%), Italy's by 11.2% (17.3%), and Spain's by 11.5% (19.8%).

Leading indicators suggest the euro area's healthy growth continued in Q3. With economies reopening further, the composite PMI rose from 59.5 in June to 60.6 in July—the highest in 21 years (Figure A1.5). The services PMI reached a 15-year high of 60.4 in July from 58.3 in June, as eased travel restrictions boosted services exports. The manufacturing PMI was only marginally lower in July at 62.6 from 63.4 in June, despite protracted shortages of inputs and a hit to business confidence from rising concerns over COVID-19's Delta variant. The economic sentiment indicator rose steadily from 117.9 in June to 119.0 in July, the highest since 1995, reflecting improving expectations in services, industry, retail, and construction.

In light of these developments, the growth forecast for the euro area is revised up to 4.6% in 2021 and maintained at 4.2% for 2022. The COVID-19 vaccine rollout is proceeding rapidly. As of 7 September, 76.9% of the European Union's population had received at least one dose and 69.4% was fully vaccinated. The goal of widespread vaccination by the end of summer 2021 is within reach. This means that, even if there are renewed COVID-19 outbreaks, most euro area countries are expected to either continue easing restrictions or maintain lighter containment measures, thus supporting household spending and investment. Growth may also benefit from pent-up demand, while being supported by highly accommodative monetary policy and the disbursement of funds from the NextGenerationEU program. The contribution of exports should also be positive this year and next, reflecting strong global merchandise trade and an expected recovery in tourism. Even so, euro area GDP will return to its precrisis level only in 2022.

Figure A1.5 Economic sentiment and purchasing managers' indexes, euro area

Economic activity continued to improve in Q3.

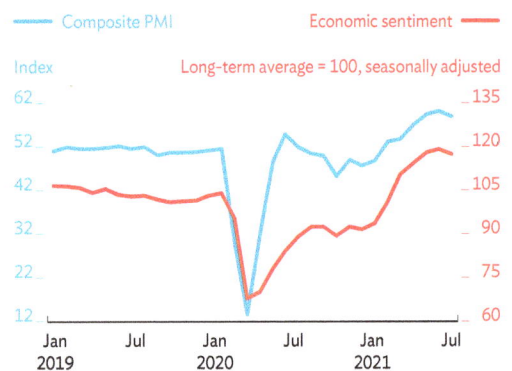

PMI = purchasing managers' index, Q = quarter.
Sources: CEIC Data Company; Haver Analytics (both accessed 3 September 2021).

The headline inflation rate rose to 2.2% in July and to 3.0% in August on increases in food, energy, and services prices. Core inflation rose to 1.6% in August and consumer price inflation averaged 1.7% over the first 8 months of 2021 (Figure A1.6). The European Central Bank left interest rates unchanged at record lows and maintained an ultra-loose monetary stance in July, in line with the new strategy adopted the same month and centered on a symmetric 2% inflation target over the medium term. Recovering economic activity and global supply disruptions will likely cause price pressures to linger in some sectors, but the large output gap should keep inflation at bay. Inflation is forecast averaging 1.6% in 2021 and 1.2% in 2022.

The main risk to the outlook is the spread of COVID-19's Delta variant, which could trigger a new wave of infections and damage growth prospects if it results in the reimposition of stricter containment measures and travel restrictions. Rising public debt stocks and banks' bad loans pose additional downside risks. To mitigate them, the European Central Bank has continued to deliver ample stimulus to improve liquidity and financial conditions by increasing the size of the Pandemic Emergency Purchase Programme and extending it until the end of 2023.

Japan

Renewed COVID-19 outbreaks and increased restrictions dampened private consumption in the first half of 2021 and slowed the recovery. The economy grew by only 1.9% in Q2 after a considerable 4.2% contraction in Q1. Because mobility restrictions were imposed multiple times in metropolitan areas, private consumption remained below the prepandemic level. Net exports were negative in Q1 (–0.9%) and Q2 (–1.3%) as import growth outpaced export growth (Figure A1.8). Private nonresidential investment has been picking up since hitting a trough in Q3 2020, partly supported by an early recovery of goods exports.

Private consumption came to a virtual standstill in the first half, contracting by 4.9% in Q1 and growing by a mere 3.8% in Q2. Reduced mobility caused by surges in new COVID-19 cases affected both retail and services sales, with particularly large impacts on apparel and accessories, motor vehicles, and services sales (Figure A1.7). Although the negative link between the number of COVID-19 cases and mobility seems to have weakened in the first half, mobility started declining after mid-August as government restrictions extended to wider regions (Figure A1.8). The services PMI remained contractionary and consumer confidence worsened after hitting a peak in June. The surge in COVID-19 cases undermined consumer sentiment and constrained consumption in the vacation season.

Figure A1.6 Headline and core inflation, euro area

Inflation is rising on the back of supply disruptions and economic recovery.

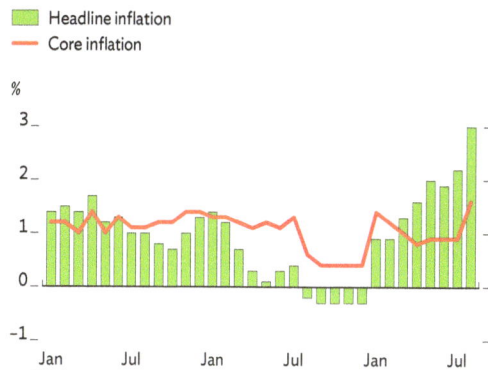

Source: Haver Analytics (accessed 3 September 2021).

Figure A1.7 Demand-side contributions to growth, Japan

After a contraction in Q1, the economy grew in Q2 driven largely by consumption.

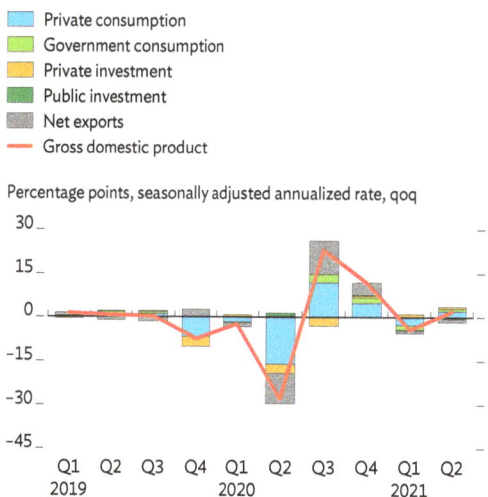

Q = quarter, qoq = quarter on quarter.
Source: Economics and Social Research Institute, Cabinet Office, Government of Japan. https://www.esri.cao.go.jp/en/sna/data/sokuhou/files/2021/qe212/gdemenuea.html (accessed 8 September 2021).

Because mobility restrictions are likely to be extended until late September, private consumption is expected to recover only from Q4 when, according to the government, all residents who want to be are fully vaccinated.

Industrial production has remained slightly below prepandemic levels, except for a drop in May due to reduced automobile production because of shortages of semiconductor chips. Despite supply chain disruptions caused by the COVID-19 pandemic in Southeast Asia, the manufacturing PMI has been expansionary since February, and was at 52.7 in August (Figure A1.9). The expansionary PMI readings, buoyed by strong goods exports suggests that improving global demand has benefited the operating environment for manufacturing. Core machinery orders have also continued to pick up and manufacturing enterprises reported better business conditions in the June Tankan survey. Both support a positive outlook for manufacturing and investment. The downside risks are further disruptions to the automobile industry's supply chain and rising input costs due to material shortages.

Inflation remains muted. The monthly readings for the overall and core consumer price indexes in the first 7 months of 2021 contracted year on year, with the overall index at –0.3% and the core index –0.6% in July. This mainly reflects a considerable decline in telecommunication prices. Without the telecommunication effect, the core inflation rate remained a touch above zero in the first 7 months, with the overall inflation rate starting the year at –0.7% and rising to 0.8% in July on soaring global material and energy prices. Strong inflationary pressures are unlikely to emerge this year since unemployment is still slightly higher than its prepandemic level of 2.9% and month-on-month real wage growth remaining flat in the first half of 2021. With inflation lower than the target of a stable 2.0%, the Bank of Japan is expected to maintain its accommodative monetary policy through 2021 and into 2022.

The economy is forecast to grow by 2.2% in 2021 and 2.9% in 2022. Growth is expected to reach a record level in the second half of 2022. This is a delayed recovery compared with the forecast in *ADO 2021*. The recovery's key driver is an expected rebound in private consumption in Q4 2021, by which time most of the population should be fully vaccinated against COVID-19. Investment and manufacturing will become a growth tailwind as temporary supply constraints subside. Zero inflation is forecast in 2021 and 0.5% in 2022 as the negative temporary effect from the decline in telecommunication prices fades. The additional fiscal stimulus expected in the coming months remains an upside risk. The major downside risks include a slower vaccine rollout and new waves of more potent COVID-19 variants stalling economic activity again.

Figure A1.8 COVID-19 indicators, Japan

More recent state of emergencies had a smaller impact on mobility because of accelerated vaccinations.

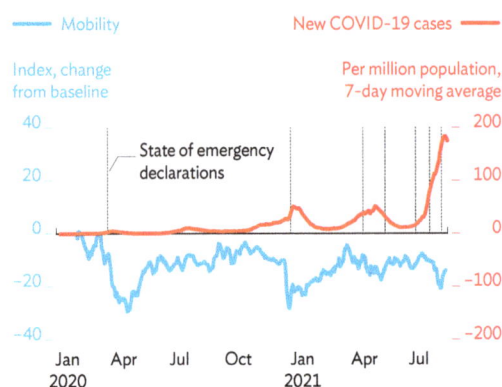

COVID-19 = Coronavirus Disease 2019.
Sources: Our World in Data. https://ourworldindata.org/coronavirus; Google COVID-19 Community Mobility Reports. https://www.google.com/covid19/mobility/ (both accessed 31 August 2021).

Figure A1.9 Consumption and business indicators, Japan

Industrial production and retail sales growth were volatile, but leading indicators remain strong.

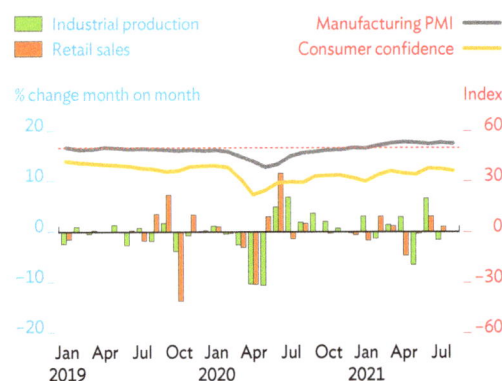

PMI = purchasing managers' index.
Notes: A PMI reading <50 signals deterioration, >50 improvement. A consumer confidence reading >50 signals better condition.
Source: CEIC Data Company (accessed 31 August 2021).

Recent developments and outlook in nearby economies

Australia

Economic recovery moderated in Q2 2021 as GDP expanded by 2.7% saar (Figure A1.10). Fixed capital investment, up 13.5%, and consumption, up 4.8%, were the biggest contributors to growth. Exports contracted by 12.1% in Q2; imports rose by 6.2%. Seasonally adjusted retail sales in Q2 expanded by 11.1%. The performance of manufacturing index rose to a record high of 63.2 in June, and the consumer sentiment index decreased to 104.1 in August, still above the 100-threshold indicating consumer optimism. The unemployment rate declined to 4.6% in July, the lowest in 10 years. Inflation surged to 3.8% in Q2, the highest in almost 13 years.

The Reserve Bank of Australia retained the cash target rate at 0.10% in August. In July, it decided to continue the purchase of government bonds at a rate of A$4 billion a week until at least mid-November. Renewed COVID-19 outbreaks and hard lockdowns mar the outlook. Australia's vaccination program has progressed slowly, with 28% of residents fully vaccinated as of 31 August 2021. This lags behind Europe and the US. But it is expected that vaccine supplies will be sufficient for all adults to be inoculated by the end of 2021. Consensus Forecasts, as of 9 August 2021, had GDP growing by 4.2% in 2021 and 3.4% in 2022.

Figure A1.10 Demand-side growth, Australia

Fixed investment led Q1 growth in 2021.

- Consumption
- Gross fixed capital formation
- Exports
- Imports
- Gross domestic product

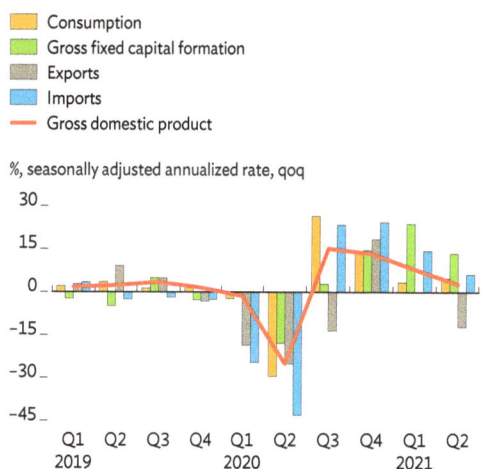

%, seasonally adjusted annualized rate, qoq

Q = quarter, qoq = quarter on quarter.
Source: CEIC Data Company (accessed 6 September 2021).

New Zealand

The economy continued its recovery in Q1 2021, with output rising by 5.7% saar (Figure A1.11). The expansion was on the back of robust domestic demand due to a 19% rise in Q1 consumption. Fixed investment expanded by 28% in the same quarter. Exports dragged down growth, which declined by 28.4% in Q1 on disruptions caused by the COVID-19 pandemic. Retail sales increased by 37.1% in Q2, up from 6.2% in the previous quarter. In June, the consumer confidence index rose to 107.1 on optimism over the economic outlook. In July, the performance of manufacturing index rose to 62.6, indicating expansion in the sector; the business confidence index fell to –14.2 in August, indicating ongoing pessimism. The labor market improved on the unemployment rate declining to 4.0% in Q2. Inflation, at 3.3% in Q2, was the highest since Q4 2011 and surpassed the inflation-target band of 1%–3%.

In August, the Monetary Policy Committee retained the official cash rate at 0.25%. Amid diminishing risks of deflation and unemployment, the Large Scale Asset

Figure A1.11 Demand-side growth, New Zealand

Consumption and investment supported Q1 2021 growth, but not exports.

- Consumption
- Gross fixed capital formation
- Exports
- Imports
- Gross domestic product

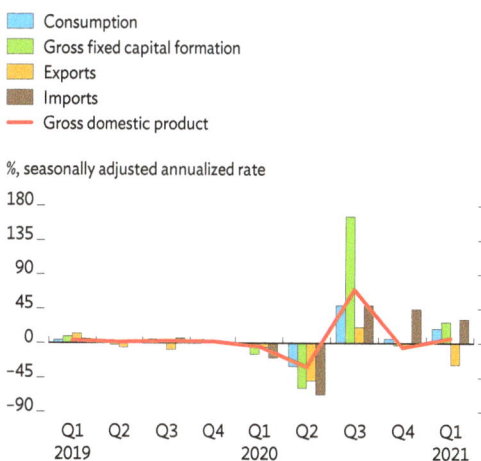

%, seasonally adjusted annualized rate

Q = quarter, qoq = quarter on quarter.
Source: CEIC Data Company (accessed 31 July 2021).

Purchase program was stopped on 23 July. On 17 August, the government announced nationwide Alert Level 4 (the highest alert level) restrictions following a renewed COVID-19 outbreak. The free vaccination program has been extended to everyone in New Zealand aged 12 years and over, regardless of visa or citizenship status. As of 1 September, 29% were fully vaccinated. Consensus Forecasts, as of 9 August 2021, had GDP growing by 5.6% in 2021 and 2.8% in 2022.

Russian Federation

The Russian Federation's economy contracted by 0.7% year on year in Q1 2021—an improvement on the 1.8% decline in Q4 2020 (Figure A1.12). Eased COVID-19 containment measures resulted in milder decreases in household consumption and gross fixed capital formation. A less pronounced fall in exports amid stronger global demand also contributed to the better performance. Because of lower stimulus expenses, government consumption grew by only 0.3% in Q1 after 4.1% growth in Q4 2020, which weighed on the overall improvement.

GDP growth accelerated sharply at 10.3% year on year in Q2, bolstered by expansions in mining and manufacturing. This strong rebound, however, is likely to lose steam in Q3 as the Russian Federation was hit by a third wave of COVID-19 infections. For example, industrial production grew by 6.7% year on year in July following a 10.3% increase in June, while retail sales growth decelerated to 4.7% from 10.9%.

Accelerating inflation caused the Central Bank of the Russian Federation to raise interest rates. Inflation overshot both market expectations and the central bank's 4.0% target, with the inflation rate rising to 6.5% in June, its highest since late 2016. Because of this, the central bank, at its meeting on 23 July, raised the key interest rate by 100 basis points to 6.5%—the fourth consecutive and largest hike since 2014. This tightening is expected to ease price pressures by the end of the year, although supply constraints and a strong recovery in demand are risks.

GDP is expected to rebound in the second half of 2021 as the Russian Federation's COVID-19 vaccination program further strengthens domestic demand. Global vaccination campaigns, coupled with higher energy prices, should bolster foreign demand. The main downside risks to the outlook are a slow domestic vaccination campaign (only 25% of the population was fully vaccinated as of 31 August), new COVID-19 variants, and geopolitical tensions. Consensus Forecasts, as of 7 September 2021, had GDP growing by 3.8% in 2021 and 2.8% in 2022.

Figure A1.12 Demand-side growth, Russian Federation

The economy recovered in Q1 2021.

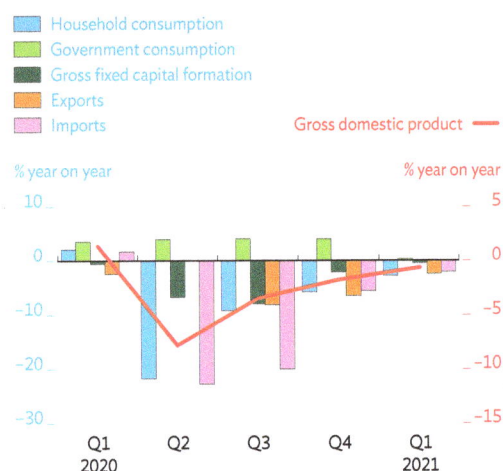

Q = quarter, yoy = year on year.
Source: Haver Analytics (accessed 28 July 2021).

Oil prices

Brent crude prices have maintained their strength, averaging $74.38/barrel in July 2021, up by $1.31/barrel from the previous month's average (Figure A1.13). June was the first month Brent crude averaged more than $70/barrel since May 2019. Oil prices surged to multiyear highs in early July following a deadlock in OPEC+ negotiations to ease supply restrictions. But crude oil prices have since eased after the group agreed on 18 July to increase production by 400,000 barrels per day, starting in August, until the adjustment of 5.8 million barrels per day is reached. Brent crude averaged $70.02 per barrel in August, down $4.37 per barrel from July but up $27.21 per barrel from August 2020.

High oil prices reflect continued market expectations of near-term tightness in global oil markets, as evidenced by the declines in global oil inventories. Increasing oil consumption, combined with production restraints from OPEC+ and relatively flat crude oil output in the US, have kept global oil consumption above global oil supply. This has drained inventories. The US Energy Information Administration estimates the global oil inventory declined by 1.8 million barrels per day in the first half of 2021. Crude oil prices got additional support from the global increase in economic activity and the declining rate of confirmed COVID-19 cases. The global manufacturing PMI was firmly expansionary in August, suggesting sustained increases in economic activity. Similarly, prices of non-energy commodities have continued rising since August last year in response to rising demand.

The positive outlook for a global economic recovery will continue to support oil prices this year and next. The International Energy Agency in August forecast global oil consumption rising by 5.3 million barrels per day in 2021 and 3.2 million in 2022. The decision of OPEC+ to raise production and the continued increase in US oil production will help meet the expected increase in global oil demand. Because of this, moderate downward oil price pressures will emerge as global oil production rises and cause inventories to be drawn down at a slower pace. This, coupled with the forecast deceleration in the growth of global oil demand and the negative sentiment on the effectiveness of vaccines to control new COVID-19 variants, will limit upward pressure on oil prices.

Given these developments and the recent strengthening of crude oil prices, the forecast price of Brent crude is revised up to average $69 per barrel in 2021 and $67 in 2022 (Figure A1.14). The oil market remains volatile and highly dependent on the success of vaccine rollouts and the easing of travel restrictions in the world's major economies. New COVID-19 variants, geopolitical tensions, and volatility in the supply of oil are key risks to the outlook.

Figure A1.13 Brent crude spot price

Oil prices remain high, although some steam lost in June–July rally.

Source: Bloomberg (accessed 3 September 2021).

Figure A1.14 Oil price forecast path

Price to decline but still above $60 per barrel by the end of 2022.

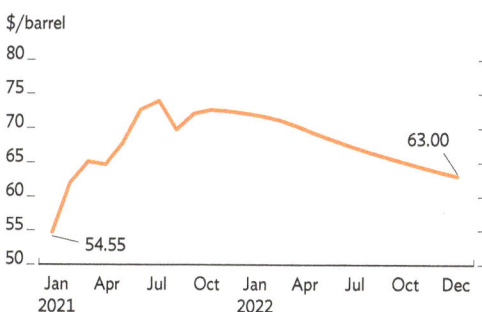

Sources: Bloomberg (accessed 3 September 2021); Asian Development Bank estimates.

2

TRANSFORMING AGRICULTURE IN ASIA

Transforming agriculture in Asia

In the last 50 years, agriculture has played a critical role in Asia and the Pacific's development and structural transformation. In the 1960s, most economies in the region were low-income, primarily agrarian, and struggling to feed their growing populations. The green revolution technologies that were adopted from the 1960s onward led to a sharp rise in yields and incomes, and helped to greatly reduce hunger and malnutrition in the region (ADB 2020a). By raising agricultural productivity, it also freed up labor, which enabled the rapid structural transformation of many economies and facilitated the emergence of the region's vibrant manufacturing and services sectors.

Even today, Asian agriculture is crucial to the region's development. One-third of developing Asia's workers are still employed in agriculture. But the sector is beset by low productivity and incomes. As a result, an estimated four of five people living below the international poverty line live in rural areas. This means that raising productivity in the sector is critical to making further inroads into poverty reduction and advancing the region's economic transformation. Agriculture also plays a central role in safeguarding the region's food supply and achieving the second Sustainable Development Goal of ending hunger, achieving food security and improved nutrition, and promoting sustainable agriculture.

But agriculture in developing Asia faces challenges from three ongoing shifts—in consumer demand, demographics, and a changing and fragile environment. As Asian economies become richer and more urbanized, food demand is increasing and shifting in composition, including toward animal products that are much more resource intensive. And despite the region's growing prosperity, malnourishment persists in various forms. Meanwhile, agricultural production is challenged by rural populations that are shrinking, as many people migrate to cities, leaving older workers and women on the farm. And agriculture is exposed to risks from a changing climate and from farm practices that are not environmentally sustainable.

This chapter was written by Takashi Yamano (lead), Manisha Pradhananga (co-lead), Jindra Samson, Ruth Francisco, Reneli Gloria, and Daryll Naval. It draws on the background papers listed at the end of the chapter. Inputs from Shingo Kimura and Aiko Kikkawa Takenaka are gratefully acknowledged. Other contributions are listed in the Acknowledgments section.

This chapter takes stock of the various challenges currently facing agriculture in developing Asia and examines possible solutions. The next section lays out the challenges in detail. Some challenges like changing consumer demand come from outside the sector; others such as unsustainable farming practices come from within. Many of the challenges and their possible solutions are interrelated. For example, one response to consumers' increased demand for seafood products—increased aquaculture production—comes with environmental challenges of its own. And some solutions, such as diversification into high-value crops, address more than one challenge. It is thus not easy to compartmentalize the various ways that policy makers and the private sector can respond. This chapter categorizes solutions into two groups, although the split is by no means clean. Section 2.2 lays out solutions whose impact is primarily at the place of production itself. These include innovations that help smallholder farmers benefit from greater mechanization; practices like organic farming and volumetric water pricing that help farmers produce more without overusing chemicals or water; and regulations that ensure sustainable agriculture and aquaculture practices. Section 2.3 then looks at support systems that help farmers beyond the place of production, some of which need to be implemented at the macro level. These include early warning systems and crop insurance schemes; the expansion of agriculture value chains and use of contract farming; and the adoption of digital technologies to help farmers and traders reach new markets. Section 2.4 concludes by discussing how government policies toward agriculture should focus less on traditional production support and, instead, encourage market-oriented innovation.

2.1 Agriculture in Asia faces multiple challenges

Agriculture in developing Asia is at a critical juncture, facing several challenges in its ability to provide nutritious and diverse food, while ensuring a sustainable and resilient future. On the consumption side, rising income and urbanization have shifted food preferences toward meat, fish, eggs, dairy, fruit, and vegetables. This change in food preference requires more resource-intensive production, which has implications for land and water use, as well as for climate change. Improved access to nutritious food has allowed developing Asia to make significant progress in the past 2 decades in its fight against hunger, lifting more than 200 million people from undernourishment. Despite this progress, undernourishment persists while the prevalence of obesity is rising in many parts of the region. On the production side, agriculture in the region faces multiple challenges. As higher-paying jobs in urban areas draw out workers, population in rural areas is shrinking and aging. Extreme weather events, which are increasing in frequency and intensity, expose many people and vast agricultural areas in Asia and the Pacific to climate-related disasters. And overuse of chemical inputs and water threatens long-term sustainability of agriculture.

2.1.1 Rising incomes and urbanization are transforming food consumption

Food consumption in developing Asia continues to grow, alongside changes in dietary preferences that reflect rising household income and rapid urbanization. The region is currently home to more than half of the world population, which is projected to reach 8.5 billion in 2030. While a slowdown is forecast for global population growth, two regions—Africa and South Asia—are expected to persist in showing significant increases. By 2030, the population of developing Asia is expected to reach 4.3 billion, while gross domestic product (GDP) per capita is forecast to reach $14,000 in purchasing power parity terms, more than double its value in 2015 (ADB 2019a). The number of people living in urban areas in developing Asia increased from 375 million in 1970 to 1.84 billion in 2017. By 2030, some 55% of the population in the region will dwell in urban areas (ADB 2019a).

These demographic changes are expected to increase food demand and shift food preferences away from food staples toward more diverse diets with higher shares of animal-sourced meat, seafood, eggs, and dairy products, as well as more fruit and vegetables.

Caloric intake in developing Asia has been increasing quickly but remains below that of high-income economies. The increase in income has helped developing economies put more food on the table and reach or even surpass the recommended daily dietary intake of 2,000 kilocalories (kCal) in 1961 to 3,206 kCal in 2018 (Figure 2.1.1a).

Meat consumption in the region is increasing but remains significantly lower than in advanced economies outside of Asia. In 2018, protein intake in developing Asia from meat stood at 10.0 grams per capita per day, and in Japan at 17.3 grams, both well below the 34.6 grams average in advanced economies outside of the region. In the People's Republic of China (PRC), daily protein intake per capita from meat increased almost twentyfold from 1.1 grams in 1961 to 19.7 grams in 2018. In India, meanwhile, meat consumption was stagnant at 1.4 grams over the same period, despite a sixfold increase in income (Figure 2.1.1b).

Figure 2.1.1 Income and food preference

Rising income levels in Asia and the Pacific have been accompanied by higher caloric intake and higher consumption of meat and seafood.

● IND   ● SAM
○ KAZ   □ JPN
● NEP   ■ ROK
● PHI   ▨ Advanced economies outside of Asia
● PRC

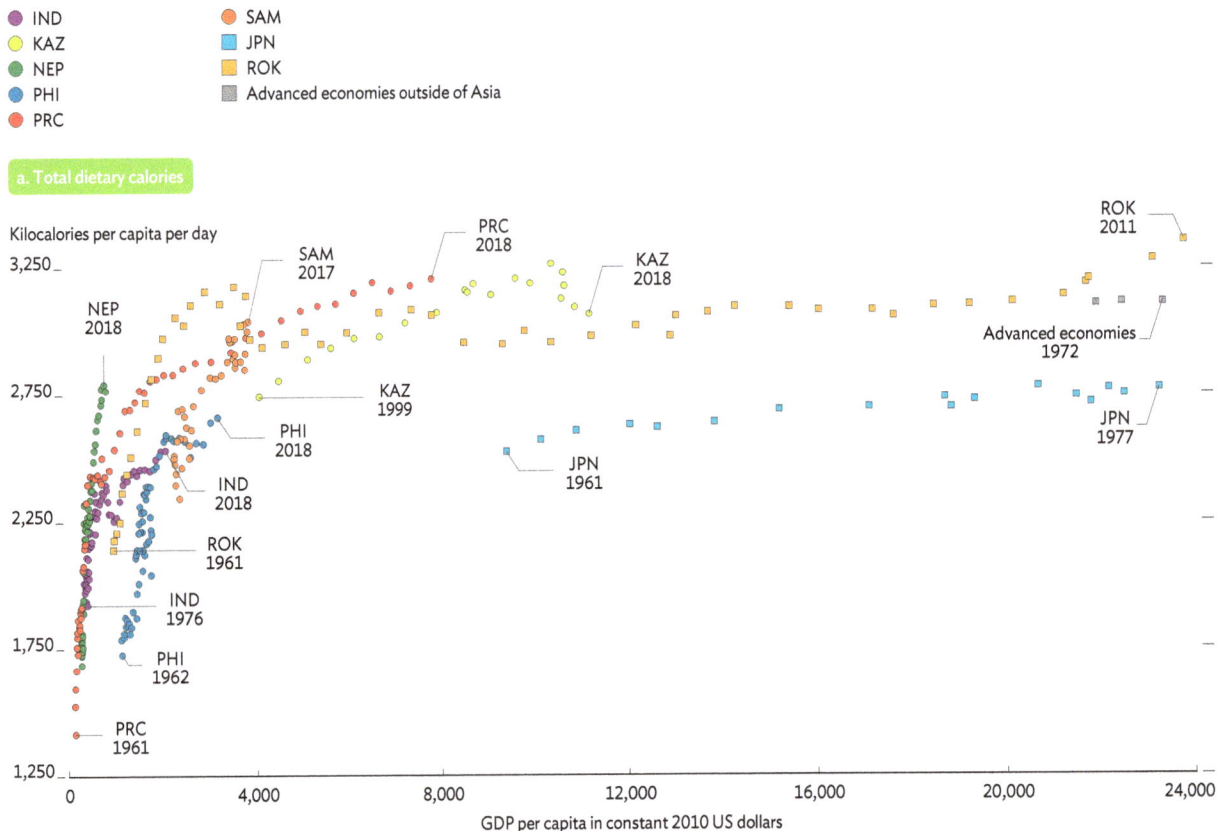

a. Total dietary calories

continued on next page

Figure 2.1.1 *Continued*

b. Animal meat[a]

Grams per capita per day

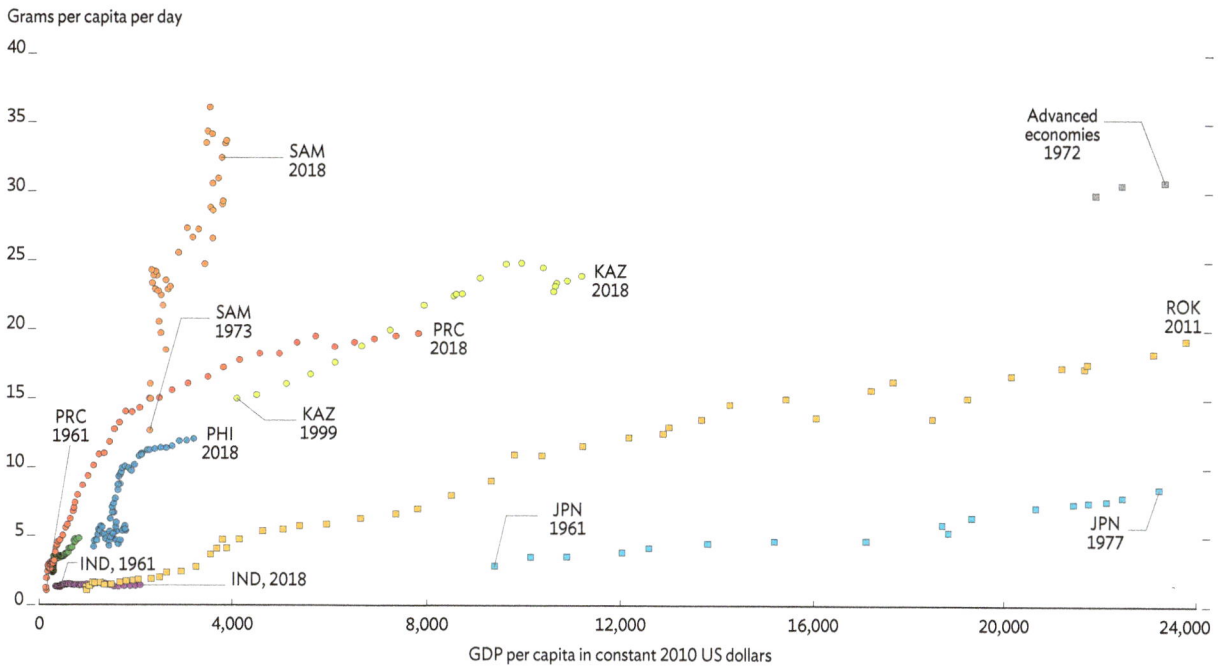

GDP per capita in constant 2010 US dollars

c. Seafood[b]

Grams per capita per day

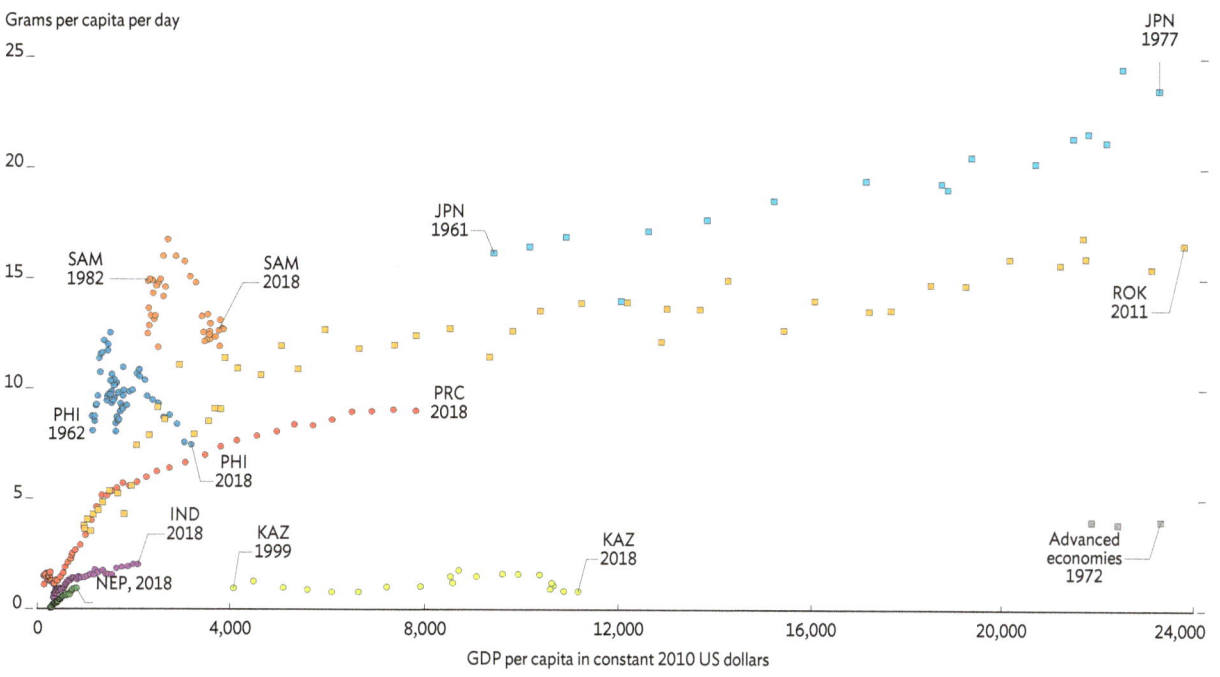

GDP per capita in constant 2010 US dollars

GDP = gross domestic product, IND = India, JPN = Japan, KAZ = Kazakhstan, NEP = Nepal, PHI = Philippines, PRC = People's Republic of China, ROK = Republic of Korea, SAM = Samoa.

Notes: Consumption per capita is deduced from country average consumption as derived from FAOSTAT food balance sheets. Advanced economies outside of Asia and the Pacific are Australia, Austria, Canada, Denmark, Finland, France, Germany, Ireland, the Netherlands, Norway, Sweden, the United Kingdom, and the United States.

[a] Animal meat comes from pigs, sheep, goats, poultry, and other land livestock.

[b] Seafood fish includes freshwater fish, demersal fish, pelagic fish, marine fish, crustaceans, cephalopods, and mollusks.

Sources: Dietary calories from FAO. FAOSTAT Food Balance Sheets. http://www.fao.org/faostat/en/#data/FBS (accessed 12 April 2021); GDP per capita from World Bank. World Development Indicators. https://databank.worldbank.org/source/world-development-indicators (accessed 12 April 2021).

In contrast, daily protein intake from fish in developing Asia slightly has surpassed the average in advanced economies outside of the region. Fish consumption is increasing in India, but not as quickly as elsewhere in the region (Figure 2.1.1c). Aquaculture in Asia has responded to the increase in fish demand and has witnessed rapid growth. Asia now accounts for 88% of world aquaculture production.

These trends are expected to continue in the future, with daily energy supply from food intake expected to increase until 2030 in all regions (FAO 2018a).[1] High-income economies will reach saturation at 3,400 kCal/day early, beyond which no further food consumption is regarded as necessary or desirable, while low-income economies will reach 2,860 kCal/day by 2030. In developing Asia, daily energy consumption per capita is expected to reach 2,844 kCal by 2030. Over the same period, the share of cereals in food intake will decrease by 2.7 percentage points, while the share of animal products will increase by 1.0 percentage point, and of fruit and vegetables by 0.5 percentage point. Figure 2.1.2 shows that these trends are more pronounced in East and Southeast Asia.

Figure 2.1.2 Difference in daily energy supply by food group, from 2012 to 2030

Asian consumption is shifting away from cereals toward animal products, fruit, and vegetables.

- Cereals
- Animal products
- Fruit and vegetables
- Vegetable oil
- Other food

Difference, percentage points

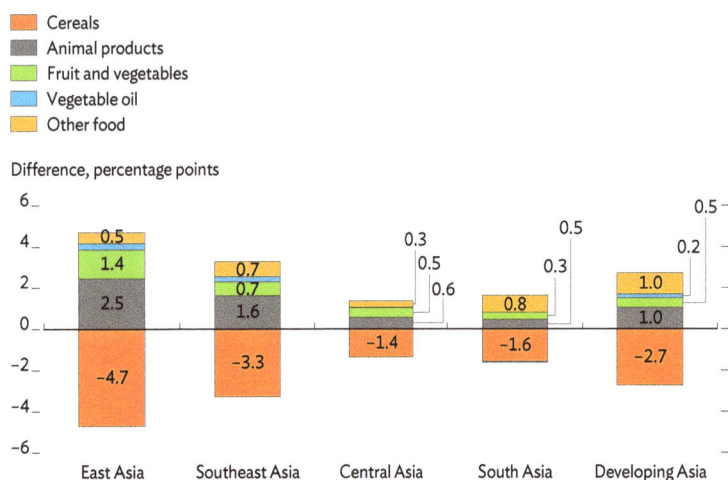

Note: East Asia is represented by Mongolia and the People's Republic of China; Central Asia by Armenia, Azerbaijan, Georgia, Kazakhstan, the Kyrgyz Republic, Tajikistan, Turkmenistan, and Uzbekistan; South Asia by Afghanistan, Bangladesh, India, Nepal, Pakistan, and Sri Lanka; and Southeast Asia by Cambodia, Indonesia, the Lao People's Democratic Republic, Malaysia, Myanmar, the Philippines, Thailand, and Viet Nam.

Source: ADB estimates using data from FAO. 2018. *The Future of Food and Agriculture—Alternative Pathways to 2050.* Food and Agriculture Organization of the United Nations.

---

[1]   Estimates assume a business-as-usual scenario in which the global community fails to address many challenges of food access and sustainable food production.

This shift in food preference away from staples toward animal-based products requires more resource-intensive production. As shown in Figure 2.1.3a, animal-based products consume more resources and produce higher emissions than plant-based products. This has significant implications for the environment.

Figure 2.1.3 Resource use and environmental impacts from plant-based versus animal-based products

Animal-based products consume more land and water resources than do plant-based products, and they generate more greenhouse gas emissions.

- Cropland
- Water use
- Greenhouse gas emissions

a. Per million kilocalories consumed

Hectares of land or 1,000 cubic meters of water

Tons of carbon dioxide equivalent

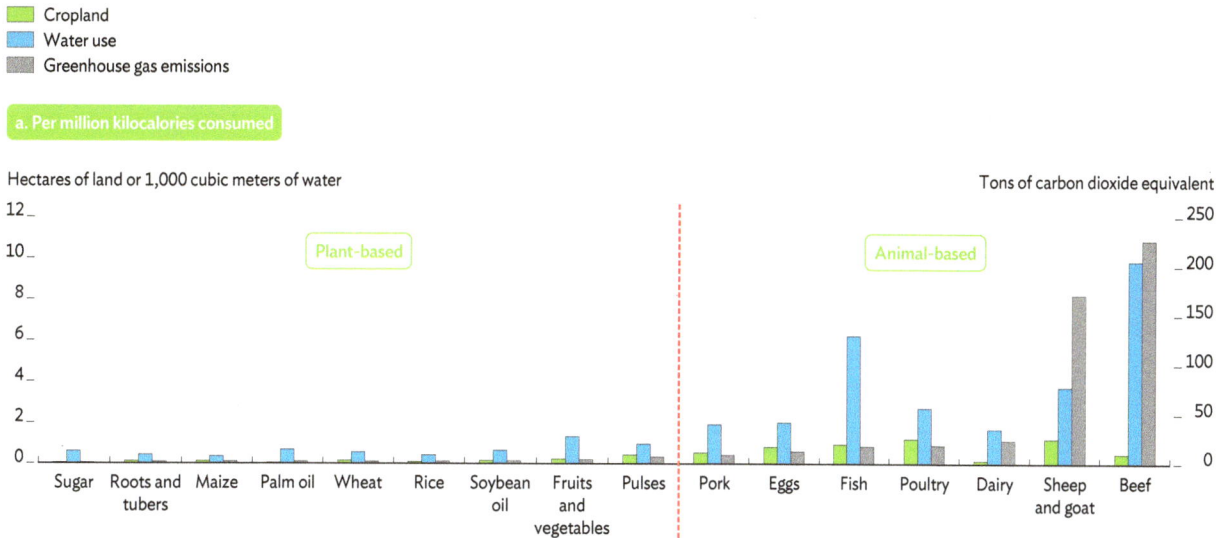

Plant-based: Sugar, Roots and tubers, Maize, Palm oil, Wheat, Rice, Soybean oil, Fruits and vegetables, Pulses

Animal-based: Pork, Eggs, Fish, Poultry, Dairy, Sheep and goat, Beef

Notes: Data presented are global means. Plant entries are ordered left to right by the amount of land used. Indicators for animal-based foods include resources used to produce feed, including pasture. Tons of harvested products were converted to quantities of calories and protein using the global average edible calorie and protein contents of food types. Fish include all aquatic animal products. Freshwater use for farmed fish products is shown as rainwater and irrigation combined. Estimates of land use and greenhouse gas emissions are based on marginal analysis, calculating additional agricultural land use and emissions per additional million calories or tons of protein consumed. In line with the approach taken by the European Union for estimating emissions from land-use change for biofuels, land-use change impacts are amortized over a period of 20 years and then shown as annual impacts. Land use and greenhouse gas emission estimates for beef production are based on dedicated beef production, not beef that is a coproduct of dairy. Dairy figures are lower in GlobAgri than some other models because GlobAgri assumes that beef produced by dairy systems displaces beef produced by dedicated beef-production systems.

Source: T. Searchinger et al. 2019. *World Resources Report: Creating a Sustainable Food Future (Final Report)*. World Resources Institute.

b. Average per capita consumption in developing Asia

Square meters of land or cubic meters of water

Tons of carbon dioxide equivalent

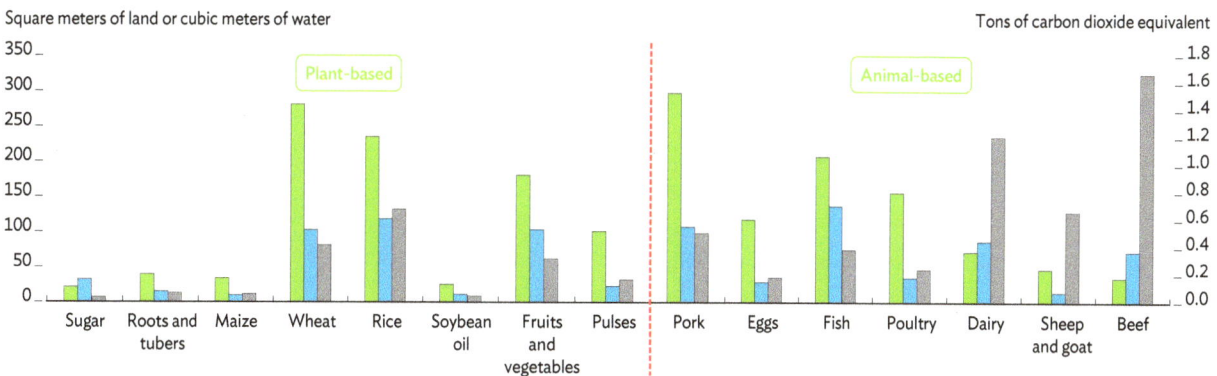

Plant-based: Sugar, Roots and tubers, Maize, Wheat, Rice, Soybean oil, Fruits and vegetables, Pulses

Animal-based: Pork, Eggs, Fish, Poultry, Dairy, Sheep and goat, Beef

Notes: The figure was created by multiplying data on global means for cropland use, water use, and greenhouse gas emissions by data on average daily consumption per capita in developing Asia. The resulting product was then multiplied by 365 days to yield annual data. See Searchinger et al. (2019) for more information about the assumptions used to generate the original calculations. Consumption is deduced from country average consumption as derived from FAOSTAT food balance sheets. The countries covered are Afghanistan, Armenia, Azerbaijan, Bangladesh, Cambodia, the People's Republic of China, Fiji, Georgia, India, Indonesia, Kazakhstan, the Kyrgyz Republic, the Lao People's Democratic Republic, Malaysia, Maldives, Mongolia, Myanmar, Nepal, Pakistan, the Philippines, Samoa, Solomon Islands, Sri Lanka, Tajikistan, Thailand, Uzbekistan, Vanuatu, and Viet Nam.

Sources: Cropland use, water use, and greenhouse gas emissions from T. Searchinger et al. 2019. *Creating a Sustainable Food Future (Final Report)*. World Resources Institute; dietary consumption from FAO. FAOSTAT Food Balance. http://www.fao.org/faostat/en/#data/FBS (accessed 12 August 2021).

Beef generates the most greenhouse gas (GHG) emissions per million kilocalories consumed, at 226.5 tons of carbon dioxide equivalent (tCO$_2$e), and has the biggest water footprint, at 9,850 cubic meters (m^3), compared with plant-based GHG emissions at 7 tCO$_2$e and water use at 1,300 m^3. A slightly different picture emerges from calculating resource use and environmental impacts based on current average consumption per capita in developing Asia (Figure 2.1.3b). Beef still dominates in terms of GHG emissions, at 1.67 tCO$_2$e per capita, followed by dairy at 1.2 tCO$_2$e. However, higher average consumption of rice per capita in the region makes GHG emissions per capita from rice significant at 0.68 tCO$_2$e. Rice and wheat also use a lot of water per capita, closely following fish. In terms of land footprint, pork has the highest utilization per capita, at 297 m^2, followed by wheat and rice.

It is important to move toward sustainable and healthy diets that are also socially acceptable and economically accessible for all. Searchinger et al. (2019) estimate that a 30% shift from meat derived from ruminants such as cows, sheep, and goats, to plant-based proteins by 2050 could close half of the GHG mitigation gap and nearly all of the combined land-use gap.[2] Some ways to achieve this are to promote mostly plant-based diets, reduce red meat consumption, promote fish obtained from sustainable stocks, and reduce food loss and waste throughout the supply chain.

Reducing food loss and waste provides another way to reduce the environmental impact.[3] Food loss and waste contribute 8% of annual GHG emissions and consume a quarter of all water used in agriculture (World Resources Institute 2019). The Food and Agriculture Organization of the United Nations (FAO) food loss index for 2019 showed 14% of the world's food lost in postharvest and wholesale. A further 17% of global food production, 931 million tons, is wasted further down the supply chain (UNEP 2021). Households are the primary wasters of food at 61%, followed by food service at 26% and retail at 13%. According to some estimates, the COVID-19 pandemic has worsened consumer food waste by 12% (Aldaco et al. 2020).

---

[2]   Land-use gap is the difference between the projected area of land needed to produce all the food the world will need at a specified future time and the amount of agricultural land in use in a given reference year. The GHG mitigation gap is the difference between agriculture-related GHG emissions projected at a specified future time and a target for emissions from agriculture and related land-use change for that future time that is deemed necessary to arrest global warming at an acceptable temperature difference.

[3]   Food loss is the quantity or quality diminished because of decisions and actions in postharvest and food wholesaling, and food waste in food retailing, food service provision, and consumption.

2.1.2 Despite the region's growing prosperity, malnourishment persists

In the past 2 decades, developing Asia has made significant progress in its fight against hunger, lifting more than 200 million people from undernourishment. Table 2.1.1 shows that, from 2001 to 2019, the prevalence of undernourishment in the region fell steadily from 15.3% to 8.7% (FAO 2021a).[4] Similarly, the region has reduced the prevalence of stunting in children under 5 years from 38.7% in 2000 to 23.2% in 2020.[5] East Asia achieved the steepest reduction, pushing the prevalence of stunting down to 4.6%, and Central Asia followed at 10.4%.

Table 2.1.1 Malnutrition in Developing Asia

Developing Asia has made progress against its fight against malnutrition, but significant challenges remain.

Subregion	Number of Undernourished (million)		Prevalence of Undernourishment (%)		Prevalence of Stunting in Children under 5 Years (%)		Prevalence of Wasting in Children under 5 Years (%)	Prevalence of Obesity in Children and Adolescents 5–19 Years (%)	
	2001	2019	2001	2019	2000	2020	2019	2000	2016
Central Asia	9.1	1.1	13.9	3.3	27.7	10.4	2.8	1.8	4.6
East Asia	134.1	0.9	9.7	2.5	19.5	4.6	1.9	2.2	11.6
South Asia	269.0	264.9	19.0	14.5	49.4	31.8	15.4	0.4	2.2
Southeast Asia	106.3	46.7	20.1	7.1	38.0	27.4	9.1	1.5	5.7
The Pacific	2.1	2.7	22.0	21.6	36.3	42.1	4.2	3.9	10.2
Developing Asia	**520.6**	**316.3**	**15.3**	**8.7**	**38.7**	**23.2**	**10.3**	**1.2**	**5.4**
World	817.8	650.3	13.1	8.4	33.1	22.0	6.8	2.9	6.7

Note: Small samples in the Pacific mean that stunting figures for this subregion should be viewed with caution.

Sources: For prevalence of undernourishment and the number of undernourished from FAO. FAOSTAT Suite of Food Security Indicators. http://www.fao.org/faostat/en/#data/FS (accessed 10 August 2021); for prevalence of obesity in children and adolescents from WHO. The Global Health Observatory. https://www.who.int/data/gho/data/indicators (accessed 10 August 2021); for prevalence of stunting and wasting from UNICEF, WHO, and World Bank. 2021. Joint Child Malnutrition Estimates. https://data.unicef.org/topic/nutrition/malnutrition (accessed 12 July 2021).

Despite this progress, the number of children in the region under age 5 who still suffer stunting remained significant at 74.7 million in 2020. South Asia accounted for a majority of them at 53.8 million followed by Southeast Asia at 15.3 million. In the past, child stunting was more prevalent in rural areas. With a rise in urban poverty, however, child stunting is no longer just a rural phenomenon.

---

[4]   Hunger is caused by insufficient consumption of dietary energy. It becomes chronic when a person does not consume sufficient calories regularly to have a normal, active, and healthy life. FAO uses the prevalence of undernourishment as an indicator to monitor hunger globally and regionally.

[5]   Stunting is defined as low height-for-age. It is a result of chronic or recurrent undernutrition, usually associated with poverty, poor maternal health and nutrition, frequent illness, and/or inappropriate feeding and care in early life.

Figure 2.1.4 Stunting among children under 5 years in developing Asia, 2019

Child stunting persists in developing Asia, as more than half of the countries in the region still suffer prevalence above 20%, with significant shares in both rural areas and urban centers.

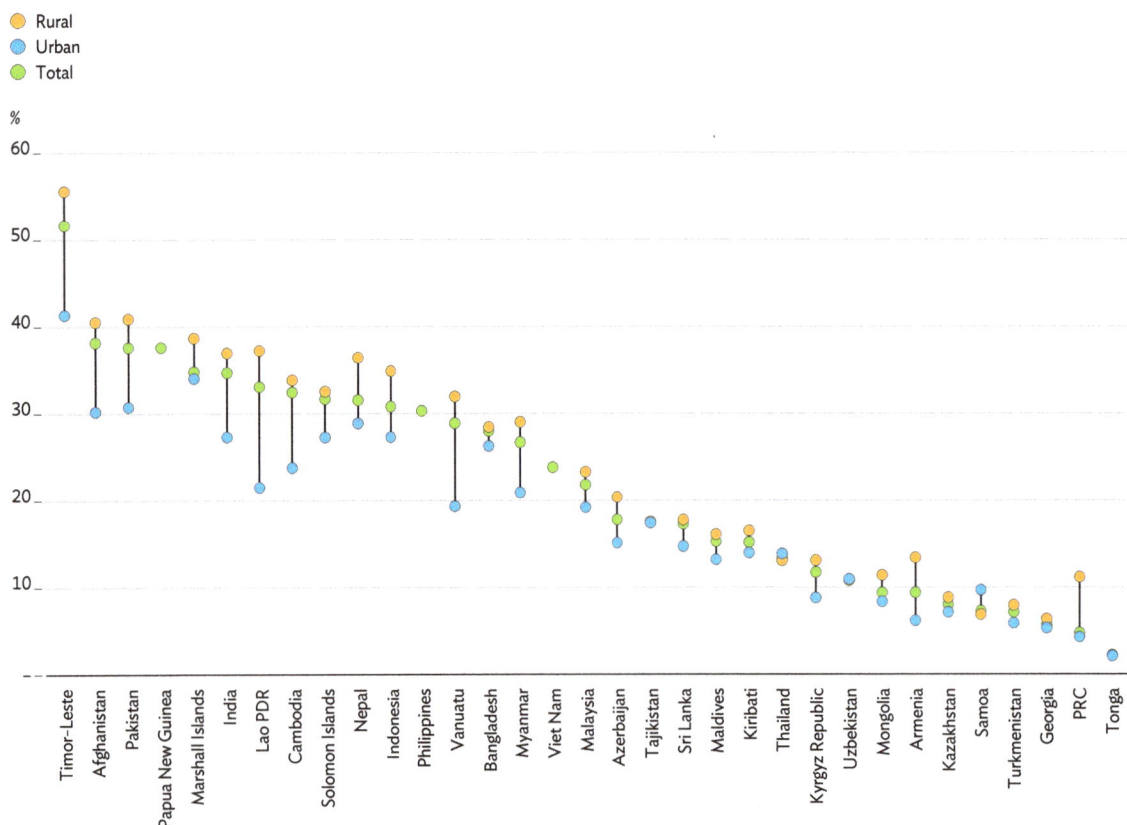

Lao PDR = Lao People's Democratic Republic, PRC = People's Republic of China.

Notes: Stunting is defined as low height for age, affecting those falling 2 standard deviations or more below the median in the child growth standards of the World Health Organization. Stunting figures here are the latest year available from 2013 to 2019. Urban–rural stunting estimates are based on an earlier year than overall stunting prevalence where the latest estimate does not disaggregate urban–rural: in Malaysia 2016 for urban–rural, 2019 for stunting overall, and in the PRC 2013 for urban–rural, 2017 for stunting overall. Papua New Guinea, the Philippines, and Viet Nam lack disaggregated urban–rural stunting estimates.

Sources: UNICEF, WHO, and World Bank. 2021. *UNICEF-WHO-World Bank Joint Child Malnutrition Estimates.* United Nations Children's Fund, World Health Organization, and World Bank; UNICEF. 2021. Malnutrition in Children. https://data.unicef.org/topic/nutrition/malnutrition/ (accessed 7 May 2021).

Figure 2.1.4 shows that more than half of the economies in developing Asia still suffered stunting prevalence above 20% in 2019, with significant shares of stunted children in both rural areas and urban centers.

Child wasting is another condition of undernutrition that can cause prolonged illness and higher risk of death when left untreated. Wasting is defined as low weight for height and occurs when a child has not had food of adequate quality and quantity. In developing Asia, child wasting prevalence in 2019 was 10.3%, much higher than the world average of 6.8% and the Sustainable Development Goal target of less than 5% by 2025. Progress has been slow and mixed. Laggard subregions in meeting this target are South Asia at 15.4% and Southeast Asia at 9.1%, while Central Asia has reduced child wasting to 2.8% and East Asia to 1.9%.

Figure 2.1.5 Prevalence of anemia in children under 5 and women aged 15–49, 2000 and 2019

The prevalence of anemia among women and children remains high, especially in South Asia.

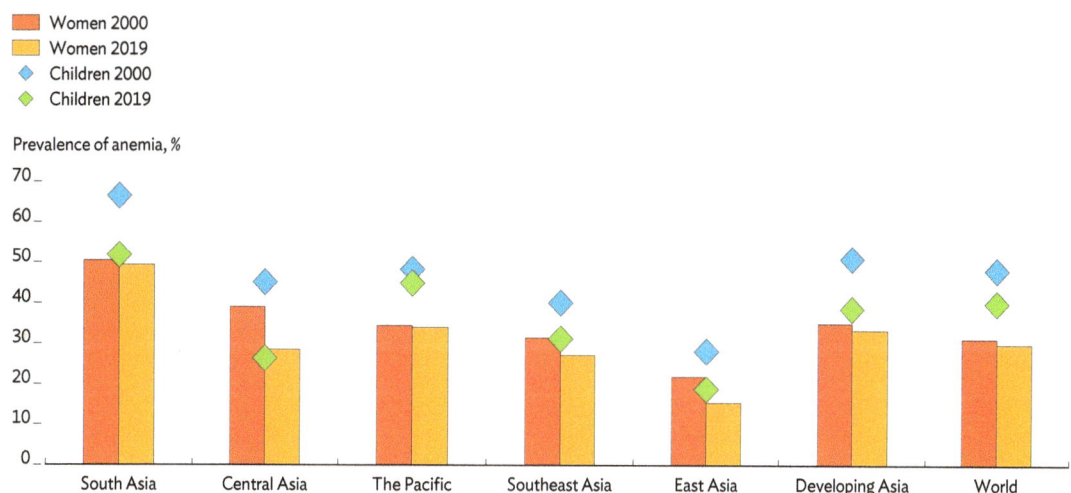

Sources: Data on country prevalence from the World Health Organization. The Global Health Observatory. https://www.who.int/data/gho/data/indicators (accessed 12 August 2021); for population weighting, United Nations. 2019 Revision of World Population Prospects. https://population.un.org/wpp/ (accessed 31 August 2021).

Developing Asia has made some progress in reducing the prevalence of anemia, though rates are still high. Iron deficiency is the most common micronutrient deficiency in the world, affecting 570.8 million women aged 15–49 and 269.4 million children under the age of 5 (WHO 2021). As its health impacts are not always visible, micronutrient deficiency is sometimes called "hidden hunger" and may persist even in economies that have achieved high calorie intake per capita. Figure 2.1.5 shows that the prevalence of anemia among children under 5 is still high at 51.7% in South Asia and 44.8% in the Pacific. More than one in three women in the region aged 15–49 faces anemia, with the prevalence in South Asia stubbornly high at 49.4%. Poor maternal nutrition has direct and lasting effects on child development, as chronic malnutrition in early childhood can affect physical and cognitive development (Grantham-McGregor et al. 2007). This can reduce an individual's potential for economic productivity and, in the long run, diminish the quality of human capital (Hickson and Julian 2018; Madjdian et al. 2018).

The prevalence of obesity is a growing problem in the region. In 2016, over 163 million adults in developing Asia were obese, almost 3.2 times higher than in 2000. Adult obesity prevalence averages 5.8% in the whole region but reaches 23.5% in the Pacific and 18.3% in Central Asia. Obesity can cause noncommunicable diseases such as diabetes and cardiovascular diseases. Ten Pacific economies have rates of adult obesity among the highest in the world, and the Pacific has 4 of the 10 economies in the world with the highest prevalence of diabetes among those aged 20–79 (International Diabetes Federation 2019).

Figure 2.1.6 Obesity in children 5–19 years old and GDP per capita, 2016

The prevalence of obesity among children and adolescents is high in several Pacific countries.

- 🟠 Pacific island economies
- 🔵 Other developing Asian economies
- 🔺 Regional and global averages

Prevalence of obesity in children 5–19 years old

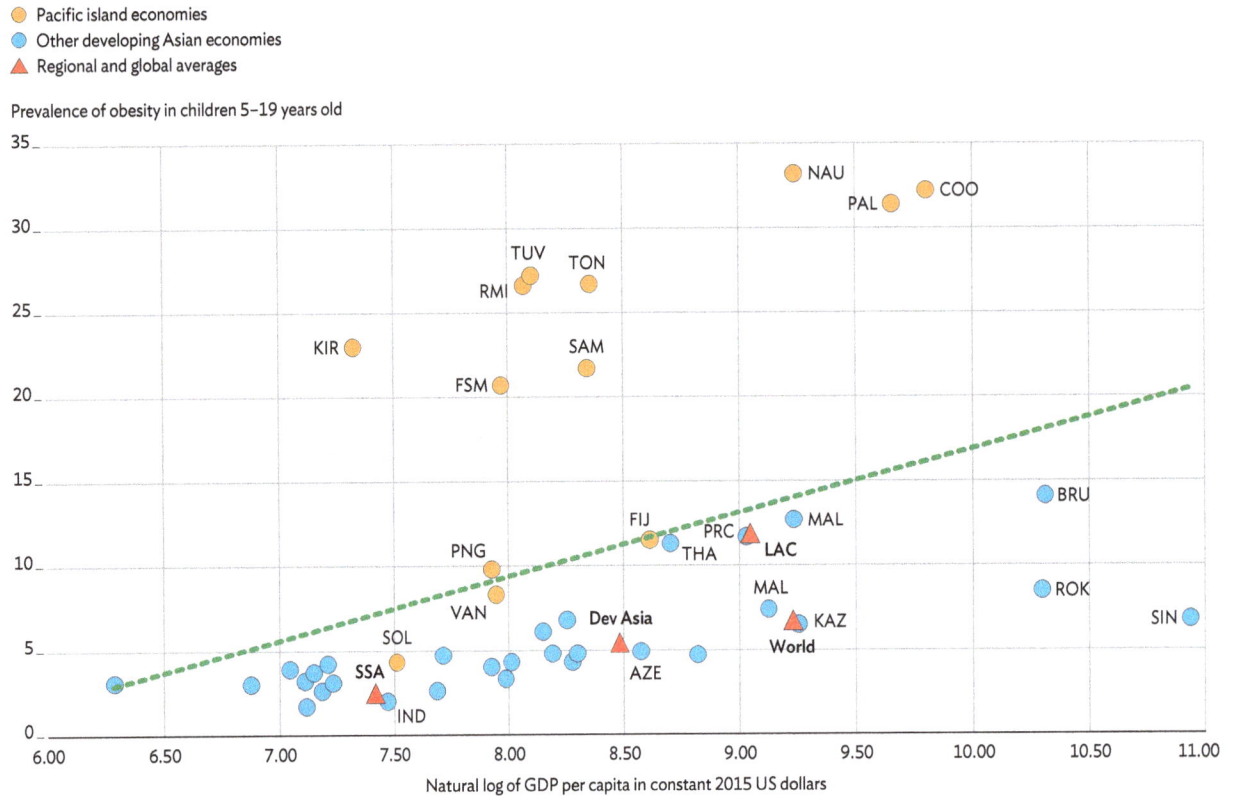

Natural log of GDP per capita in constant 2015 US dollars

AZE = Azerbaijan, BRU = Brunei Darussalam, COO = Cook Islands, FIJ = Fiji, FSM = Federated States of Micronesia, GDP = gross domestic product, IND = India, KAZ = Kazakhstan, KIR = Kiribati, LAC = Latin America and the Caribbean, MAL = Malaysia, NAU = Nauru, PAL = Palau, PNG = Papua New Guinea, PRC = People's Republic of China, RMI = Marshall Islands, ROK = Republic of Korea, SAM = Samoa, SIN = Singapore, SOL = Solomon Islands, SSA = Sub-Saharan Africa, THA = Thailand, TON = Tonga, TUV = Tuvalu, VAN = Vanuatu.

Note: Computation of regional, developing Asia, and world GDP per capita averages includes only countries with data on obesity prevalence for children and adolescents aged 5–19 years.

Sources: For country obesity prevalence, World Health Organization. The Global Health Observatory. https://www.who.int/data/gho/data/indicators (accessed 10 August 2021); for population 5–19 years old, UN DESA. World Population Prospects 2019. https://population.un.org/wpp/Download/Standard/Interpolated (accessed 10 August 2021); for constant 2015 US dollars, United Nations. UNdata. http://data.un.org/Explorer.aspx (accessed 10 August 2021).

Figure 2.1.6 shows a trend for child obesity. Obesity prevalence among children and adolescents in the Pacific is at 10.2%, and in East Asia, at 11.6%, double the regional average of 5.4%. Though Southeast Asia has lower obesity prevalence at 5.7%, Brunei Darussalam, Malaysia, and Thailand registered the largest increases from 2000 to 2016, by about 8 percentage points. According to WHO (2014), obesity in childhood is linked to higher risk of incurring noncommunicable diseases in adulthood such as type 2 diabetes, asthma and other respiratory problems, high blood pressure, and liver disease, which can cause disability and premature death.

Increased physical inactivity and consumption of processed food are contributing to developing Asia's obesity problem. While urbanization correlates with economic growth and improved standards of living, it is also associated with lifestyle changes that often reduce physical activity and encourage poor food preferences.

About 25% of developing Asia's population is physically inactive, which is defined as not doing weekly at least 150 minutes of moderately intense physical activity, 75 minutes of vigorous activity, or an equivalent combination of the two. Partly because time-poor urban dwellers work longer hours, they have shifted to ultra-processed food that is convenient but often higher in salt, fat, and sugar (Popkin 2001). Poverty and inequality in urban and peri-urban areas also impede access to healthy food. In the Pacific, sharp increases in obesity associated with noncommunicable diseases are attributed to heavy reliance on imported processed foods high in sugar, salt, and animal fat—and to increasingly sedentary lifestyles (World Bank 2016). More importantly, the region has been moving away from the production of healthy agricultural produce, a development strongly linked to a lack of arable land (Taylor, McGregor, and Dawson 2016). Recommendations to reduce the prevalence of obesity aim to change consumer behavior and promote healthy diets by imposing mandatory labeling of trans fat, raising taxes on sugar-sweetened beverages, and restricting the marketing to children of food high in calories and low in nutrients (FAO 2021a).

2.1.3　Asia's rural communities are rapidly shrinking, feminizing, and aging

Rapid structural transformation has led to a steady decline in the share of rural population. A rapid and enormous structural transformation has characterized Asian development since the 1970s (ADB 2020a). This has dramatically reduced the economic share of agriculture in terms of both output and employment. The decline in agriculture's share of GDP has been especially steep in the PRC, where it dropped from 32% in the 1970s to 7% in 2019, and in India, where the decline was from 40% to 16%. Although agriculture remains a major employer in many developing economies in Asia, the overall share has declined over the years. Higher-paying jobs in manufacturing and services in urban areas have attracted workers out of rural areas, causing a steady decline in the share of the rural population of developing Asia from 80% in 1970 to 52% in 2020. The rural population started to shrink in the 2000s, despite a steady increase in total population. The rural share is expected to decline further to 38% by 2050, and the absolute number to drop below 600 million (Figure 2.1.7). In East Asia, the rural population share is already below 40% and is expected to sink to less than 25% by 2050. In Southeast Asia, the rural population share is seen contracting from about 50% in 2021 to below 40% by 2050. South Asia currently has over 60% of its population in rural areas, but this share is likewise declining rapidly.

Figure 2.1.7 Urban and rural population in developing Asia, 1970–2050

The share of rural population has declined as people moved to cities in search of better economic opportunities.

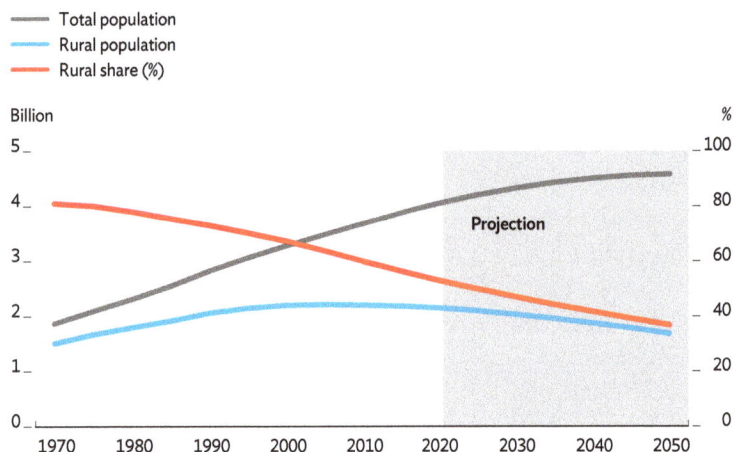

Source: United Nations. World Urbanization Prospects 2018. https://population.un.org/wup/Download/ (accessed 18 August 2021).

As the outmigration of male workers continues, Asia's agriculture is increasingly reliant on women and elderly to provide labor. This trend is particularly pronounced in Bangladesh, Cambodia, and Nepal, three economies with high labor migration (Figure 2.1.8). Bangladesh saw the share of female workers in agriculture rise by 9.3 percentage points from 2010 to 2019, and Nepal by 7.7 points.

Figure 2.1.8 Share of women in agricultural employment, 2010 and 2019

Asian agriculture relies increasingly on women...

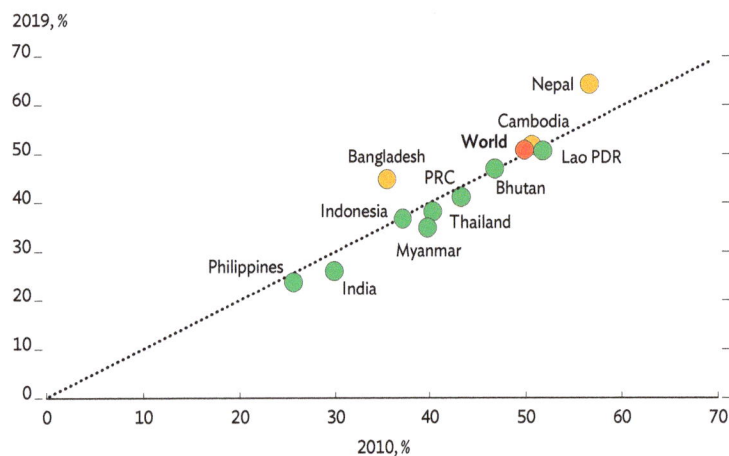

Lao PDR = Lao People's Democratic Republic, PRC = People's Republic of China.
Source: ADB estimates based on ILO. ILOSTAT. https://ilostat.ilo.org/data/ (accessed 10 August 2021).

In Cambodia and the Lao People's Democratic Republic (Lao PDR), where male migration is also high, the share of females employed in agriculture remained above 50% in the same period. Such aggregated data may not capture changes in actual work responsibilities and the hours women devote to agricultural activity. In labor surveys, farm households may simply list male members as engaged in agriculture and neglect to report that female family members work their own fields or tend domestic animals.

Women's role and degree of involvement in agriculture vary within and across economies, regions, communities, and cropping systems. They are guided by norms and formal and informal rules that define gender roles and the division of labor, as well as by socioeconomic characteristics such as caste, class, and ethnicity. In South Asia, men take the lead in seedbed and land preparation, crop management, machine operation, and marketing, while women are mainly responsible for postharvest activities, as well as assisting men with seedbed and nursery preparation (Ahmed et al. 2013). In Southeast Asia, men similarly take the lead in seedbed and land preparation, as well as pesticide and fertilizer application. Aside from postharvest activities, women in Southeast Asia are likewise involved in crop establishment, weeding, manual harvesting, and marketing (Akter et al. 2017; Akter et al. 2016). Women in Southeast Asia are more visible than their counterparts in South Asia and exercise more decision-making power and autonomy. Likewise, compared with women in South Asia, those in Southeast Asia face less of a gender gap in access to agricultural extension services and control over farm income and resources (Akter et al. 2017; Akter et al. 2016; Malapit et al. 2020). In Central Asia, the Kyrgyz Republic and Tajikistan rely heavily on remittances from international migrants, who are mostly men. One recent study in Tajikistan found that about half of surveyed rural households had at least one person working abroad, leaving women to take up more responsibility for irrigation management and agriculture production (ADB 2020b). Women in many Asian economies are also responsible for safeguarding seed stores and traditional knowledge of seed varieties, including those that are drought resistant. Women's active participation in community seed banks has been vital in preserving biological diversity, which will be increasingly important under climate change.

Women face discrimination in access to land, capital, inputs, information, and training. Despite their active role in agriculture and their invaluable contribution to global food security, women have limited access to resources, especially land. Evidence of gender inequality in access to land is compelling across all developing regions. Most inheritance systems disadvantage women, who are also vulnerable to loss of land when their household structure changes, especially if the husband dies or leaves (FAO 2011; Doss et al. 2018).

Ensuring women's access to land and other resources is increasingly important in the context of feminization of agriculture in many Asian economies.

The share of older farmworkers has increased over time, especially in economies with low birth rates and rapid rural–urban migration (Figure 2.1.9). In the Republic of Korea, a low birth rate and rapid rural–urban migration has left almost 70% of the agricultural workforce aged 60 or older. In Sri Lanka and Thailand, the share of agricultural workers aged 50 or older rose from only a third in the mid-2000s to almost half in the past few years. The average age of farmworkers was 69.8 years in the Republic of Korea in 2020, 51.0 in Sri Lanka in 2017, and 49.7 in Thailand in 2018. In other economies in Figure 2.1.9, the average age of farmworkers is over 40. It is noteworthy that older farmworkers tend to work fewer hours than do workers in their prime. More than half of agricultural workers in the selected Asian economies aged 60 or older work less than 40 hours per week.

Figure 2.1.9 Age distribution of agricultural workers

...and on older workers.

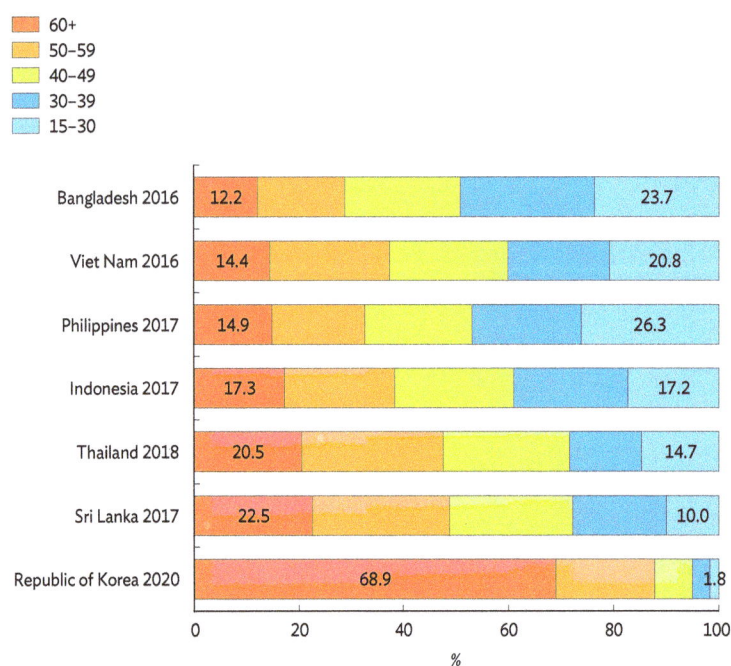

Legend:
- 60+
- 50–59
- 40–49
- 30–39
- 15–30

Economy	60+	...	30–39/15–30
Bangladesh 2016	12.2		23.7
Viet Nam 2016	14.4		20.8
Philippines 2017	14.9		26.3
Indonesia 2017	17.3		17.2
Thailand 2018	20.5		14.7
Sri Lanka 2017	22.5		10.0
Republic of Korea 2020	68.9		1.8

Sources: Labor force surveys of various countries.

As people age, their physical strength and fitness deteriorate, affecting balance, agility, muscle strength, hand precision, and body coordination (Trombetti et al. 2016; Verhaegen and Salthouse 1997). Although older workers tend to be less productive at more physically demanding tasks, such as manual farmwork onsite, they usually have more farm experience and knowledge. An aging workforce requires more intensive agricultural mechanization and adoption of other labor-saving technologies. This may ease labor burdens and improve labor productivity, especially among older farmers and farmworkers.

Some high-income economies have responded to the declining availability of local labor by inviting international migrants to fill seasonal farm jobs. According to the Database on Immigrants in OECD Countries, the number of Asian migrant workers in agricultural jobs in the OECD grew fivefold from 68,000 in 2001 to 328,000 in 2016. About 70% of them were from South or Southeast Asia. In the fiscal year ending in 2016, 2.3% of migrant farmworkers in Australia and New Zealand were from the Pacific and 2.4% from South Asia. Since 2012, Australia's Seasonal Worker Programme has provided more than 40,000 seasonal jobs to workers from the Pacific and Timor-Leste (Clarke and Dercon 2016). While addressing workforce shortages in Australia, the programs provide opportunities for Pacific and Timorese workers to gain experience, earn income, and send remittances home to support their families and communities. Similarly, New Zealand allows overseas workers from the Pacific in horticulture and viticulture, through its Recognized Seasonal Employer (RSE) scheme. From less than 5,000 placements in 2008, the number of visas under the RSE scheme had more than doubled to over 12,000 in 2019, before it declined in 2020 due to the COVID-19 pandemic. Most RSE workers are from Vanuatu, followed by Samoa and Tonga. Most workers in the past years have been men, reflecting a strong gender bias in recruitment (Bedford 2020).

Some middle-income economies in Asia and the Pacific also host Asian migrants, mostly to fill low-skilled farm jobs. Malaysia, for instance, is a large employer of overseas migrant workers. In the 1980s, the Government of Malaysia allowed increasingly large numbers of migrants to work in jobs vacated by locals, especially in agriculture (Kaur 2010). Malaysia and Indonesia signed in 1984 the Medan Agreement, which allowed male workers from Indonesia to work on Malaysian plantations (Abubakar 2002). Malaysia subsequently signed similar agreements with Bangladesh and Thailand. For decades, Indonesian migrants provided labor for planting and harvesting, but the mounting success of Indonesia's own plantations has stemmed this labor flow, with fewer Indonesians choosing to migrate to work on Malaysian plantations.

Figure 2.1.10 Foreign workers on Malaysian plantations

Many migrants, mostly from Indonesia, are employed on Malaysian plantations.

Bangladesh
India
Indonesia
Others

Workers, '000

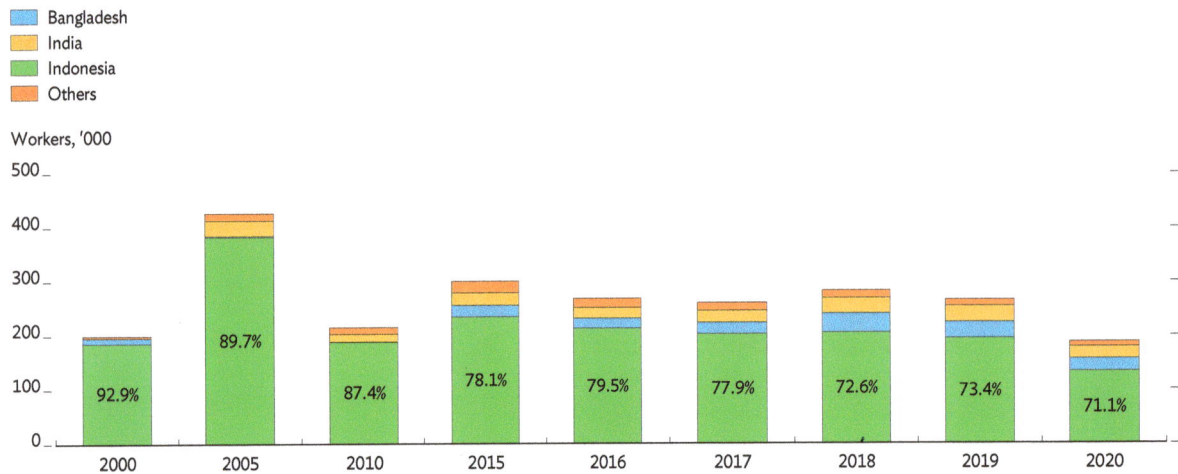

Source: ADB estimates using data from the Ministry of Primary Industries and the Immigration Department cited in P. Wickramasekara. 2020. *Malaysia: Review of Admission and Recruitment Practices of Indonesian Workers in the Plantation and Domestic Work Sectors and Related Recommendations.* International Labour Organization.

Malaysian Palm Oil Board data show that 86% of plantation workers, mostly field and general workers, are foreign migrants (Wickramasekara 2020). According to the Ministry of Primary Industries and the Immigration Department, most plantation migrant workers are Indonesian. However, the Indonesian share declined from almost 93% in 2000 to 71% in 2020 as more workers arrived from other Asian economies, mainly Bangladesh and India (Figure 2.1.10).

The COVID-19 pandemic has highlighted the vital role that migrants play in agricultural supply chains. Many Asian migrant workers have returned to their home countries, notably Cambodia, India, the Lao PDR, and Timor-Leste. As the pandemic evolves, concerns emerge about shortages of migrant workers for planting and harvesting (FAO 2020a). International travel restrictions and the quarantine requirements of subnational states and territories are significantly delaying new recruitment under the Pacific Labour Scheme. From March and October 2020, no Tongan workers entered or left Australia because of complete border closure. In Malaysia, the pandemic is exacerbating labor shortage in its palm oil industry. Thousands of migrant workers have left plantations to head home as borders closed. A foreign labor shortage induced by COVID-19 was expected to disrupt food production, processing, and distribution.

2.1.4 Climate change poses ever greater challenges to agriculture in Asia

Given its reliance on weather and climate, agriculture is especially vulnerable to risks posed by climate change. Changes in temperature and rainfall patterns, and extreme weather events, which are increasing in frequency and intensity due to climate change, cause significant damage and losses to Asian crop and livestock production, as well as fisheries. Aside from the negative agricultural production impacts of these events over the short and medium term, these events have negative long-term impacts as they damage natural resources and the ecosystem services of land and water that sustain agriculture.[6] Figure 2.1.11 illustrates the impact of climate change on agriculture and food security.

Figure 2.1.11 Impact of climate change on agriculture and food security

Agriculture is vulnerable to climate change and extreme weather.

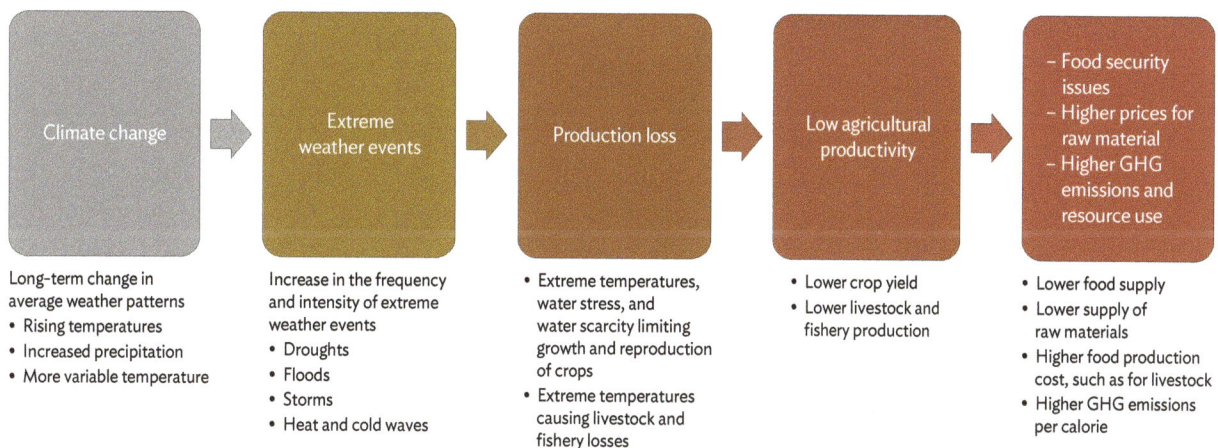

Climate change	Extreme weather events	Production loss	Low agricultural productivity	– Food security issues – Higher prices for raw material – Higher GHG emissions and resource use
Long-term change in average weather patterns • Rising temperatures • Increased precipitation • More variable temperature	Increase in the frequency and intensity of extreme weather events • Droughts • Floods • Storms • Heat and cold waves	• Extreme temperatures, water stress, and water scarcity limiting growth and reproduction of crops • Extreme temperatures causing livestock and fishery losses	• Lower crop yield • Lower livestock and fishery production	• Lower food supply • Lower supply of raw materials • Higher food production cost, such as for livestock • Higher GHG emissions per calorie

GHG = greenhouse gas.
Note: The classification adopted draws on the EM-DAT CRED Guidelines.
Source: ADB illustration.

Crop growth and yields are highly sensitive to significant changes in temperature and precipitation. In the past 6 decades, Asia experienced significant changes in precipitation. Many parts of East, South, and Southeast Asia have experienced declines in precipitation, while precipitation increased in other parts of the region (Figure 2.1.12). As the average temperature continues to rise, the risk of precipitation extremes will further increase over Asia and the rest of the world (Ge et al. 2019; Guo et al. 2016; Li, Zhou, and Chen 2018). Climate change studies predict that, as global warming continues, most of the monsoon area in East and Southeast Asia will experience large increases in precipitation.

---

[6] Climate change may benefit some areas, such as Mongolia, with expected increases in temperature.

Figure 2.1.12 Observed changes in precipitation and temperatures in Asia, 1958–2019

Asia has experienced changes in precipitation and maximum and minimum temperatures.

a. Precipitation change (millimeters)

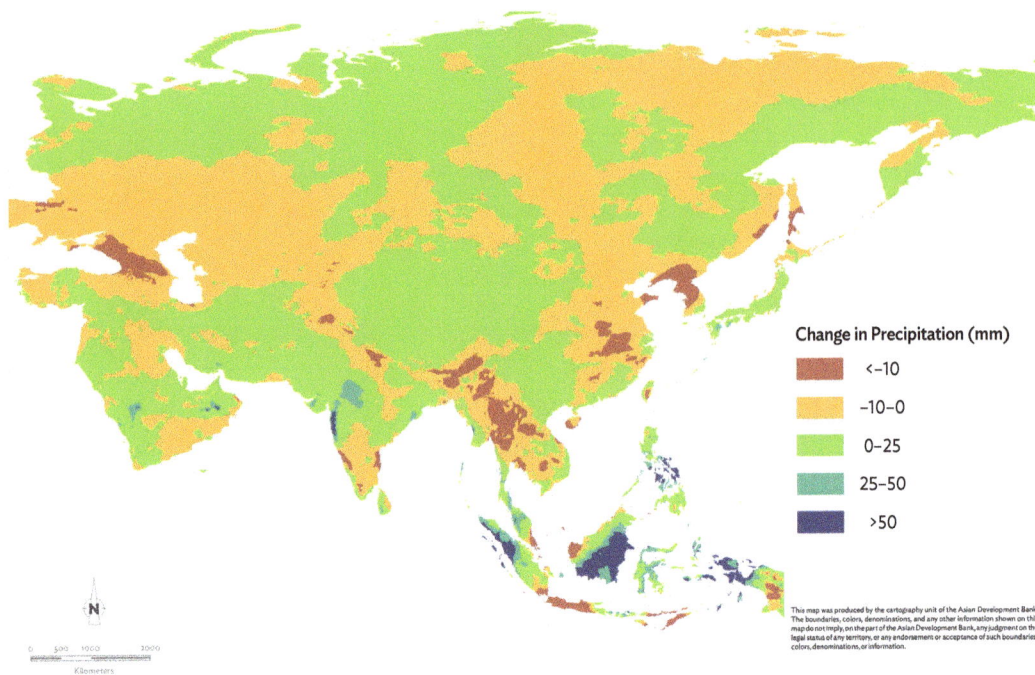

Change in Precipitation (mm)

- <–10
- –10–0
- 0–25
- 25–50
- >50

This map was produced by the cartography unit of the Asian Development Bank. The boundaries, colors, denominations, and any other information shown on this map do not imply, on the part of the Asian Development Bank, any judgment on the legal status of any territory, or any endorsement or acceptance of such boundaries, colors, denominations, or information.

b. Maximum temperature change (°C)

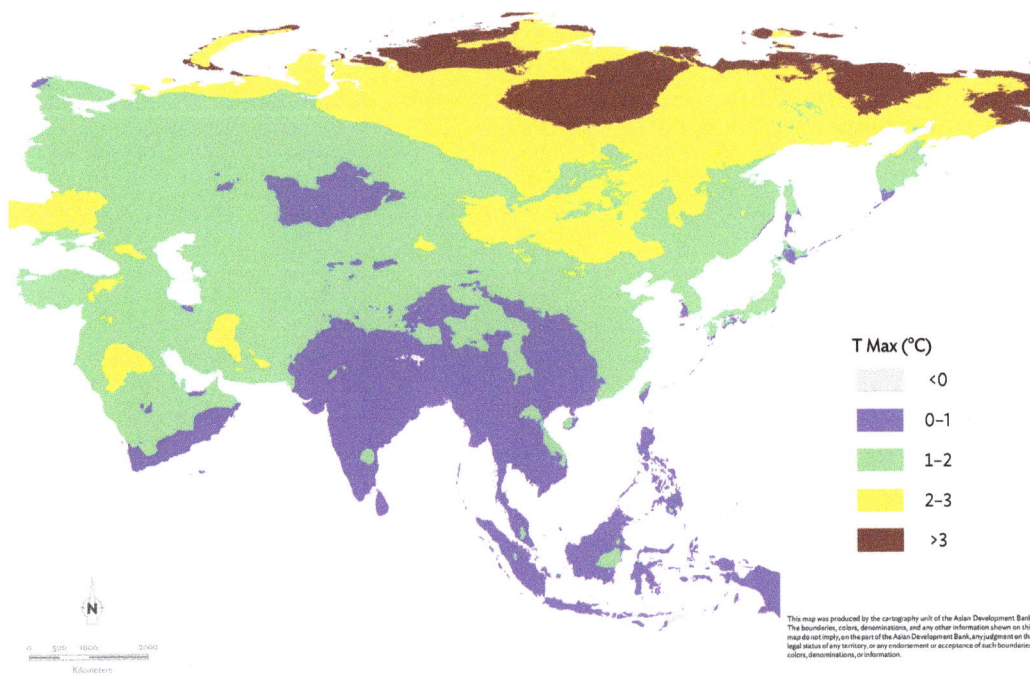

T Max (°C)

- <0
- 0–1
- 1–2
- 2–3
- >3

This map was produced by the cartography unit of the Asian Development Bank. The boundaries, colors, denominations, and any other information shown on this map do not imply, on the part of the Asian Development Bank, any judgment on the legal status of any territory, or any endorsement or acceptance of such boundaries, colors, denominations, or information.

continued on next page

Figure 2.1.12 *Continued*

c. Minimum temperature change (°C)

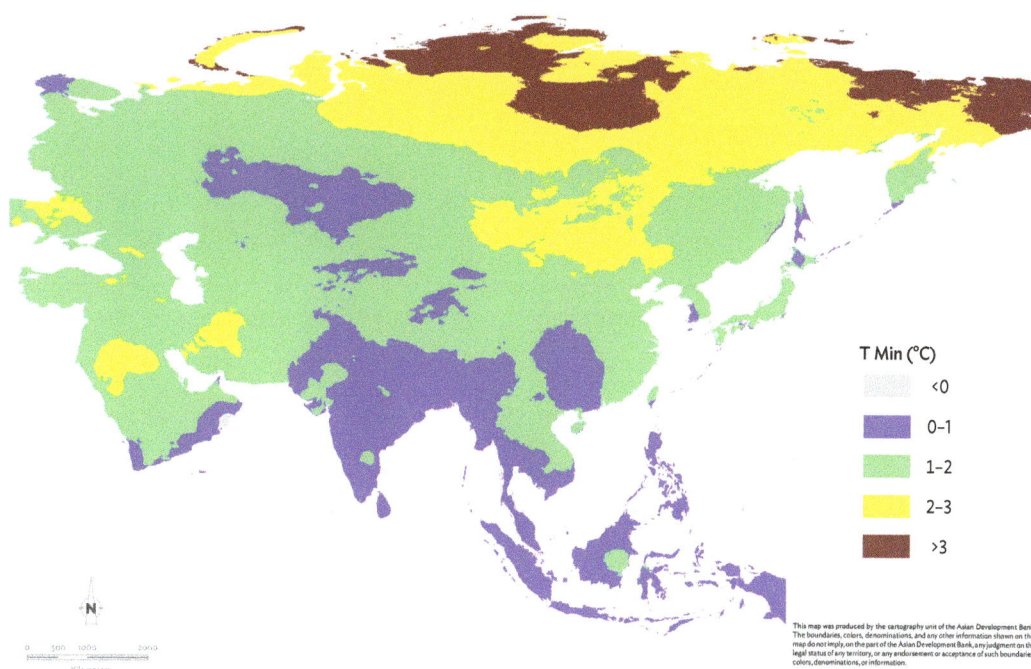

Source: Gumma (2021) based on climate data from J. T. Abatzoglou et al. 2018. Terraclimate, a high-resolution global dataset of monthly climate and climatic water balance from 1958–2015, Scientific Data. Data available at TerraClimate. Climatology Lab. http://www.climatologylab.org/terraclimate.html (accessed 26 March 2021).

Under the worst-case scenario of high GHG emissions—designated representative concentration pathway (RCP) 8.5—by 2050 South Asia will experience an average increase in monsoon precipitation by 6.4% (Mani et al. 2018). Extreme precipitation and floods are also seen increasing in certain areas in Southeast Asia and Central Asia (McKinsey & Company 2020; IPCC 2018; Huang et al. 2014; Jie et al. 2019).

Climate change studies predict higher frequency and intensity of drought as warming accelerates (Sheffield and Wood 2008; Dai 2010). With accelerated warming, studies expect increased water stress and drought in Asia and the Pacific (Kraaijenbrink et al. 2017; Liu et al. 2018; Gao et al. 2018; Wang et al. 2021; Naumann et al. 2018; Cook et al. 2020). Higher drought frequency and intensity are expected in East and Southeast Asia (Amnuaylojaroen and Chanvichit 2019; Zhai et al. 2020). In some areas of West and South Asia, periods of drought are likely to lengthen and occur 5–10 times more frequently (Naumann et al. 2018). For instance, worsening drought severity and frequency are expected across the central, northern, and western parts of India (Gupta and Jain 2018; Shrestha et al. 2020).

Extreme heat stress during the reproductive stage of crop growth can diminish yields in certain crops, notably rice and corn (Wang et al. 2019; Shi et al. 2017; Deryng et al. 2014). Changes in maximum and minimum temperatures accurately describe climate variability over larger areas. They give a frame of reference that allows meaningful comparisons of locations and provide reliable calculations of temperature trends. One study found past drought and extreme heat significantly reducing global grain production by 9%–10% (Lesk, Rowhani, and Ramankutty 2016). While there is less research on the impact on agriculture from heat waves in Asia and the Pacific, evidence hints at their negative impacts on both crop production and human health in the region. Agricultural workers are expected to be the worst affected as their work capacity and productivity are compromised by heat stress, considering that they expend physical effort usually while working outdoors. According to ILO (2019), agriculture is projected to account for 60% of global working hours lost to heat stress in 2030. Pregnant women and people aged over 50 face especially high health risks from heat exposure. Under a scenario of high GHG emissions such as RCP 8.5, at least 600 million and perhaps 1 billion people in Asia will by 2050 be living in areas at risk of lethal heat waves—ones that exceed the human survivability threshold (McKinsey & Company 2020).

More frequent and more intense extreme weather events have caused significant damage and losses to crop and livestock production, as well as fisheries. In developing economies, agriculture absorbs 63% of the damage and loss caused by climate-related disasters across all economic sectors, or 26% of all damage and loss (FAO 2021b). These effects include physical damage from disasters to agricultural infrastructure and assets such as standing crops, farm tools and equipment, postproduction infrastructure, irrigation systems, livestock shelters, and fishing boats, as well as losses from lower crop production, lower income from livestock products, higher input prices, reduced agricultural revenue, higher operational costs, and increased unexpected expenditure to meet immediate needs in the aftermath of a disaster. Damage and loss cascade through the food value chain and other industries such as manufacturing that have backward linkages to agriculture.

Crops absorb 49% of all damage and loss from disasters triggered by natural hazards (FAO 2017). By causing water shortage and heat stress, drought directly affects crop and livestock yields. Recurring or prolonged drought have persistent ecosystem impacts that affect agricultural productivity over the long term. Drought caused by far the most damage and loss in livestock from 2008 to 2018, at 86%. It accounted for 14.6% of damage and loss in crops, albeit far less than 57.7% from floods and 25.4% from storms. Fisheries were damaged mostly by tsunamis, at 68.9%, and storms, at 18.1%.

Extreme weather events have exposed many people and vast agricultural areas in Asia to climate-related disasters (FAO 2015a). Six of the world's 10 climate-related disasters most damaging to agriculture from 2003 to 2013 were in Asia (FAO 2017). They include floods in Pakistan in 2010 and 2011 from extraordinary rainfall that caused $5.3 billion in agricultural damage and loss in one year and $1.9 billion the next. These disasters are followed in ranking by floods in Thailand in 2011 costing $1.9 billion, Typhoon Haiyan in 2013 in the Philippines costing $1.4 billion, a tsunami in 2004 in Indonesia costing $0.9 billion, and Cyclones Ondoy and Pepeng in 2009 in the Philippines costing $0.8 billion (Figure 2.1.13).

Figure 2.1.13 Climate-related disasters that most severely damaged Asian agriculture

Extreme weather has periodically damaged Asian agriculture, causing billions of dollars in losses.

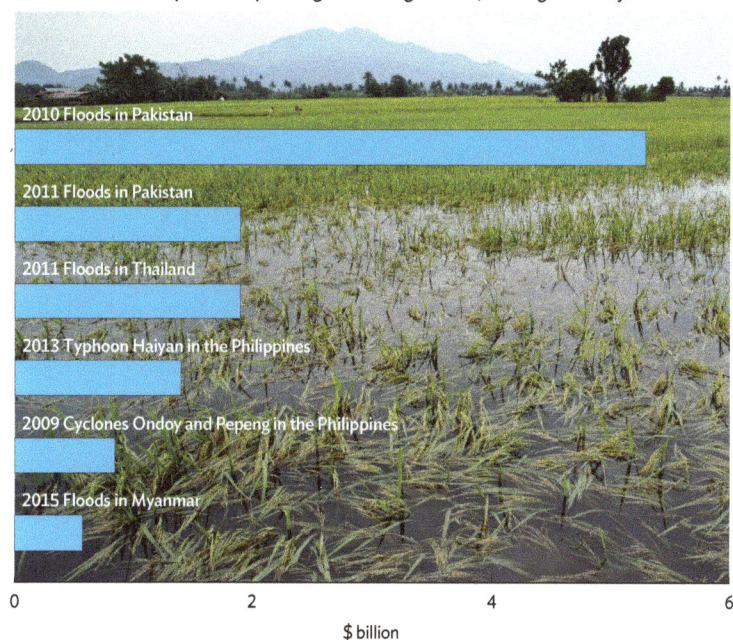

Note: Figures include damage and loss from climate-related disasters, including floods, drought, and tropical storms, based on 2015 and 2017 estimates from the Food and Agriculture Organization (FAO). The classification of disasters adopted by FAO draws on guidelines from the Emergency Events Database (EM-DAT) of the Centre for Research on the Epidemiology of Disasters (CRED) and aligns with United Nations Office for Disaster Risk Reduction definitions and terminology.

Background photo: Drowned harvest. This rice field in the Philippines was flooded by Cyclone Ondoy (photo from the image collection of the International Rice Research Institute. www.irri.org; CC BY-NC-SA 2.0).

From 2008 to 2018, Asia and the Pacific suffered $207 billion in crop and livestock production losses to disasters, or 74% of the global total (FAO 2021b).[7] Of this amount, the PRC accounted for over $153 billion, or 55% of the global agricultural loss,

---

[7]   This equals 283 calories per capita per day, or 11% of the recommended daily allowance.

while developing economies including low and lower-middle income economies in Southeast Asia accounted for $21 billion and in South Asia for $25 billion. The frequency and scale of such events and the damage they cause are rising under climate change and threaten to reverse the economic gains of past decades and worsen poverty, especially in Asia and the Pacific.

2.1.5 Agriculture faces environmental challenges of its own making

The green revolution succeeded in part through heavy use of chemical fertilizers and pesticides, subsidized by governments. To stimulate agricultural production and achieve food self-sufficiency, many Asian governments launched production support programs. These government subsidies lowered the price of fertilizers and encouraged their overuse, which not only burdened national fiscal positions but also caused environmental degradation. Indonesia, for example, began subsidizing fertilizer in 1971, as did the Philippines in 1973, to encourage its use with high-yielding modern rice varieties and reduce rice production cost (Esguerra 1981; Hedley and Tabor 1989). In both Indonesia and the Philippines, average nitrogen fertilizer use per hectare of cropland in 2010–2019 was more than double average use in 1970–1989 (Figure 2.1.14). Nitrogen use likewise intensified in other Southeast Asian economies—most notably Thailand and Viet Nam—and in South Asia, especially Bangladesh, India, and Pakistan.

Figure 2.1.14 Nitrogen fertilizer use in selected Asian economies, 1971–2018

The use of nitrogen fertilizer has intensified in developing countries in Asia.

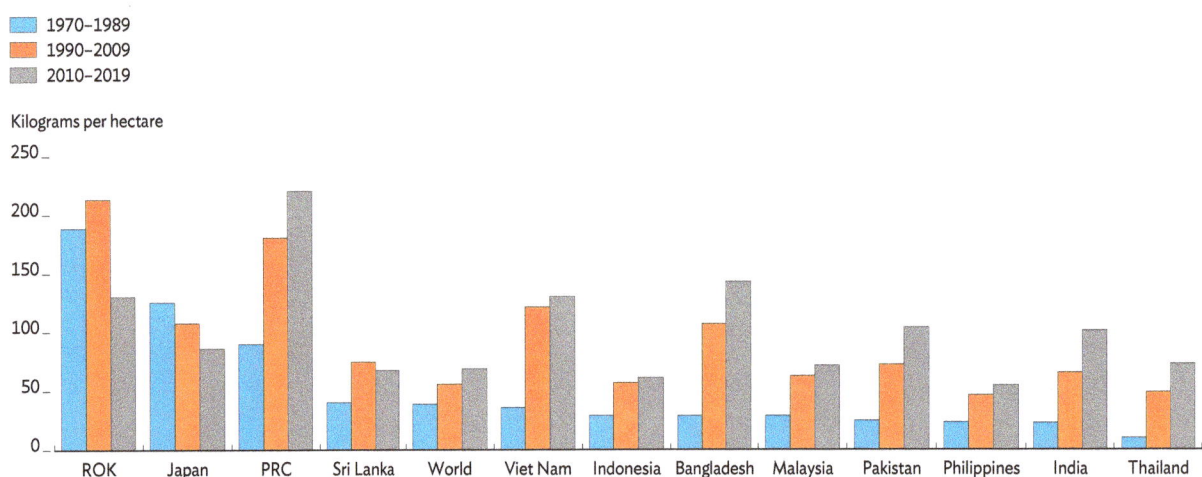

PRC = People's Republic of China, ROK = Republic of Korea.
Source: FAO. FAOSTAT. http://www.fao.org/faostat/en/#data (accessed 21 June 2021).

Fertilizer subsidies have placed a fiscal burden on Asian governments. While intensified fertilizer use contributed to past improvement in agricultural production and food security, their fiscal and environmental costs have outweighed their benefits. Fertilizer subsidies absorbed 1.6% of the national budget in Bangladesh in fiscal 2019, for example, and 1.2% in Indonesia (FPMU 2020; Suryana 2019; Kementerian Keuangan 2019). Further, the primary beneficiaries of fertilizer subsidies have been generally larger, better-off farmers. In Indonesia, for instance, 60% of fertilizer subsidies benefit 40% of the largest farmers (Osorio et al. 2011). Because fertilizer subsidies have consumed a considerable share of government expenditure, phasing out fertilizer subsidy programs offers significant fiscal savings. In the PRC, for instance, the government phased out fertilizer subsidies and invested in nitrogen and waste management (Searchinger et al. 2020).

Fertilizer overuse has caused unwanted phosphorus deficiency, increased water pollution, and led to greater GHG emissions. Fertilizer accounts for 12% of the GHG emissions from agriculture. The manufacture of synthetic nitrogen fertilizer generates significant GHG emissions, while its application is a significant contributor to direct nitrous oxide (N_2O) emissions from agricultural soils. In the PRC, for instance, GHG emissions associated with the manufacture of synthetic nitrogen fertilizers in 2015–2017 were 41.4 metric tCO_2e for wheat and 59.7 metric tCO_2e for maize. In the same period, annual direct N_2O emissions from 12.63 tons/year of synthetic nitrogen application were estimated at 35.82 gigagrams of N_2O for wheat and 69.44 for maize (Chai et al. 2019).

Chemical pesticides are also extensively used in modern agriculture. The success of green revolution encouraged widespread production of only a few varieties of rice, which made production more susceptible to pests and increased the need for pesticides. Farmers started overusing them in the belief that more was better, though studies later found that the use of pesticide during early plant growth was unnecessary, as leaf-feeding insects seldom affected yield (Heong, Escalada, and Mai 1994). Further, pesticides pose threats to farmers' health and food safety (Gomes et al. 2020; Zhang, Zeiss, and Geng 2015; Pingali, Marquez, and Palis 1994).

Water shortages affect a large share of rural population in Asia. FAO (2020a) estimated that 500 million rural people globally are subject to very high water stress in the case of irrigated areas, or very high drought frequency affecting rainfed cropland and pasture. Among them, 453 million people, or 91%, are in Asia, though only 21% of the affected agricultural land is in this region (Figure 2.1.15a). In Asia, 77% of affected areas and 87% of affected rural populations are in only four economies: India, Indonesia, Pakistan, and the PRC. Climate change is expected to further exacerbate water shortages by changing rainfall patterns.

Meanwhile, demand for water is expected to grow because of expanding industrial and residential needs.

Irrigation management, which played an important role in Asia's agriculture, is facing structural challenges. Asia has 70% of the world's irrigated farmland, or 238 million hectares (ha) of the 339 million ha total. About 40% of Asian cropland is irrigated (Figure 2.1.15b). South Asia has 111 million ha of irrigated agricultural land, followed by East Asia with 79 million ha, making about half of cropped area in these two subregions irrigated. However, outmigration of farmers is posing community collective action problem in maintaining the efficiency of irrigation systems. Some farmers have stopped farming altogether, leaving fallow plots in the middle of irrigation systems. While better-off farmers have invested in private irrigation systems using pumps, wells, ponds, sprinklers, and drip irrigation, thereby becoming independent of community irrigation management.

In areas where groundwater use is necessary, private and public irrigation systems need to coexist. Studies have found that the use of private wells in areas with surface irrigation systems can start a vicious cycle (Kajisa et al. 2018). As users of private wells exit surface irrigation systems, their collective management suffers. As surface irrigation systems decline, so does their function of recharging groundwater resources, leaving users of private wells worse off, especially as the increased use of individual wells threatens the water table. Coordination between users of private and public irrigation systems is crucial to finding sustainable modes of irrigation system management (Kajisa 2012). For better coordination, public irrigation systems need to shift conceptually from managing the system to serving users. This transition may require additional user fees and higher water prices. Water pricing has become a fundamental issue. In some cases, farmers pay little or nothing in fees for irrigation water. In many cases, farmers form water-user associations and pay for irrigation water under the principle of the user pays. Yet, when they pay for irrigation water, individual farmers are typically charged according to the size of their landholdings. Because fees may include levies for pump fuel or other operating costs that depend on the volume of irrigation water, association members may collectively have incentive to save water, but the individual user does not. As a result, without effective peer pressure, individual farmers tend to overuse water.

The aquaculture industry faces environmental sustainability concerns. Environmental challenges facing aquaculture include land salinization, which hinders agricultural yields; land subsidence from overuse of groundwater; frequent outbreaks of shrimp disease under

Figure 2.1.15 Agricultural land under water stress and irrigation

Only 21% of agricultural land under water stress is in Asia, but it is home to 91% of affected rural populations.

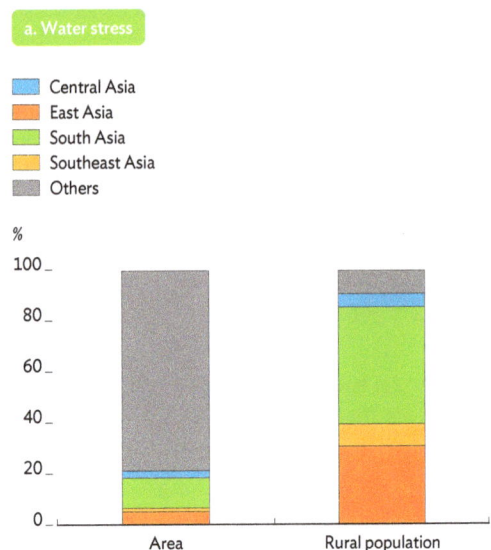

About 70% of irrigated agricultural area is in Asia.

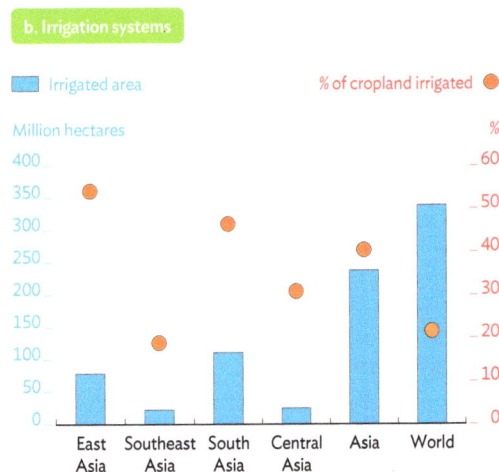

Note: Rainfed areas with very high frequency of drought or irrigated areas with very high levels of water stress.
Source: FAO. FAOSTAT. http://www.fao.org/faostat/en/#data (accessed 21 June 2021).

intensified farming methods; misuse of prohibited antibiotics to prevent and treat shrimp disease, which threatens consumer health; destruction of mangroves, threatening biodiversity in coastal areas; and dependence on wild fish catch for feed, which depletes marine resources.

Some of these environmental problems affect the immediate environment, while others affect coastal land and marine resources, and the health of final consumers. Figure 2.1.16 illustrates a typical market structure for farmed fish and associated environmental problems. Immediate environmental damages occur if excessive groundwater pumping causes ground subsidence or if brackish water directed to ponds affects the salinity of surrounding land. Pond water quality is not easily observable without tests, the equipment for which is not readily available to many fish farmers. Pond effluents can thus spill over and affect neighboring farmers. The conversion of mangrove forests into aquacultural ponds severely affects biodiversity, as natural mangroves function as nurseries and shelters for many aquatic species. As inland aquaculture technologies and practices have been established, there is less need to expand coastal aquaculture. Another important issue is that because feed for farmed shrimp and fish depends heavily on wild-caught fish, the rapid growth of aquaculture worsens the depletion of marine resources. Intensive farming worsens the risk of shrimp disease, and farmers are reported to use antibiotics to prevent or treat them, their residues possibly threatening consumer health.

Figure 2.1.16 Typical market structure and challenges for farmed fish

The market for farmed fish suffers many problems and needs better management for sustainability.

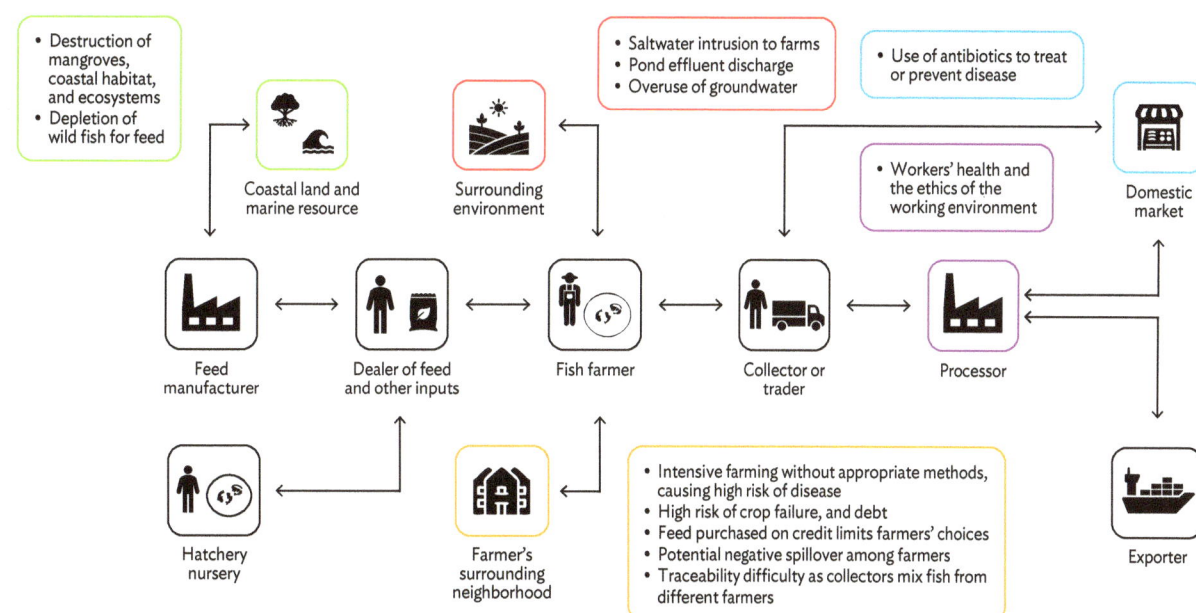

Source: A. Suzuki. 2021. Rising Importance of Aquaculture in Asia: Current Status, Issues, and Recommendations. Background paper for *Asian Development Outlook 2021 Update*. Asian Development Bank.

Finally, fish processing has often been criticized for health and ethical problems affecting workers. Long hours of work while standing in cold factories can undermine workers' health. Child labor and migrants working in environments with subpar labor standards have been reported in media and academic papers, posing ethical issues that if not fully addressed, challenge the sustainability of aquaculture.

The international community has made various efforts to mitigate the negative effects of aquaculture, but problems persist. International standards such as the Code of Conduct for Responsible Fisheries (FAO 1995), International Principles for Responsible Shrimp Farming (FAO et al. 2006), and Better Management Practices have been adopted in many Asian economies. In addition, national standards and certifications and various private standards, such as the Aquaculture Stewardship Certification, have also been established. Yet problems persist because aquaculture is location-specific, with the fish farming community typically comprising numerous smallholders, making it difficult to control good practices. Spillover via canals of others' bad practices discourages farmers from trying to keep their own ponds clean. Other contributing factors include lack of strict monitoring of input markets, constraints on farmer credit, farmers' lack of appropriate knowledge, and difficulty of maintaining clear traceability along the supply chain. The multipolarity of global aquaculture also complicates compliance with numerous standards.

2.2 Innovation to boost productivity and ensure sustainability

Innovative solutions are required to help farmers raise productivity while ensuring long-term environmental sustainability. Faced with increasing labor shortages, innovative arrangements that help Asia's smallholder farmers access agricultural machine services have emerged. Improved technologies and practices such as site-specific nutrient management and volumetric water tariffs can help farmers minimize the negative impact on the environment. The private sector can play an important role in providing these farm extension and advisory services. Finally, the rapidly growing aquaculture sector can provide consumers with animal protein and other essential nutrients, but it needs to be well-regulated to ensure sustainability.

2.2.1 Access to machines for smallholder farmers can be improved

Higher demand for greater agricultural mechanization came in response to rising labor costs under industrialization. Labor scarcity caused by higher demand for industrial labor has encouraged many farmers in Thailand, for example, to increasingly adopt farm machinery such as four-wheeled tractors with harvesters to till their land and harvest their crops (Srisompun, Athipanyakul, and Somporn 2019). Trade liberalization in Asia in the 1990s brought increased supply of agricultural machinery, mainly imported from the PRC, the Republic of Korea, and Japan. In some South and Southeast Asian economies, such as Bangladesh, India, the Philippines, Sri Lanka, and Thailand, local manufacture of adapted small-scale agricultural machinery and parts expanded further as the market for them continued to grow in the 2000s (Diao, Takeshima, and Zhang 2020).

The use of farm machinery saves time and labor. A single hour of combined harvester use, for example, saves some 28 or 29 labor hours of hand harvesting and threshing. The adoption of farm machinery increased over time, albeit at varied rates across economies (Figure 2.2.1). Low-horsepower or small four-wheel tractors were used mainly for land preparation, while small to medium-sized harvesters were also widely used, even by smallholders (Diao, Takeshima, and Zhang 2020).

Figure 2.2.1 Agricultural land productivity, labor productivity, and mechanization, 1961–2014

Agricultural mechanization (shown in circles) has increased labor productivity, but many countries in the region lag behind.

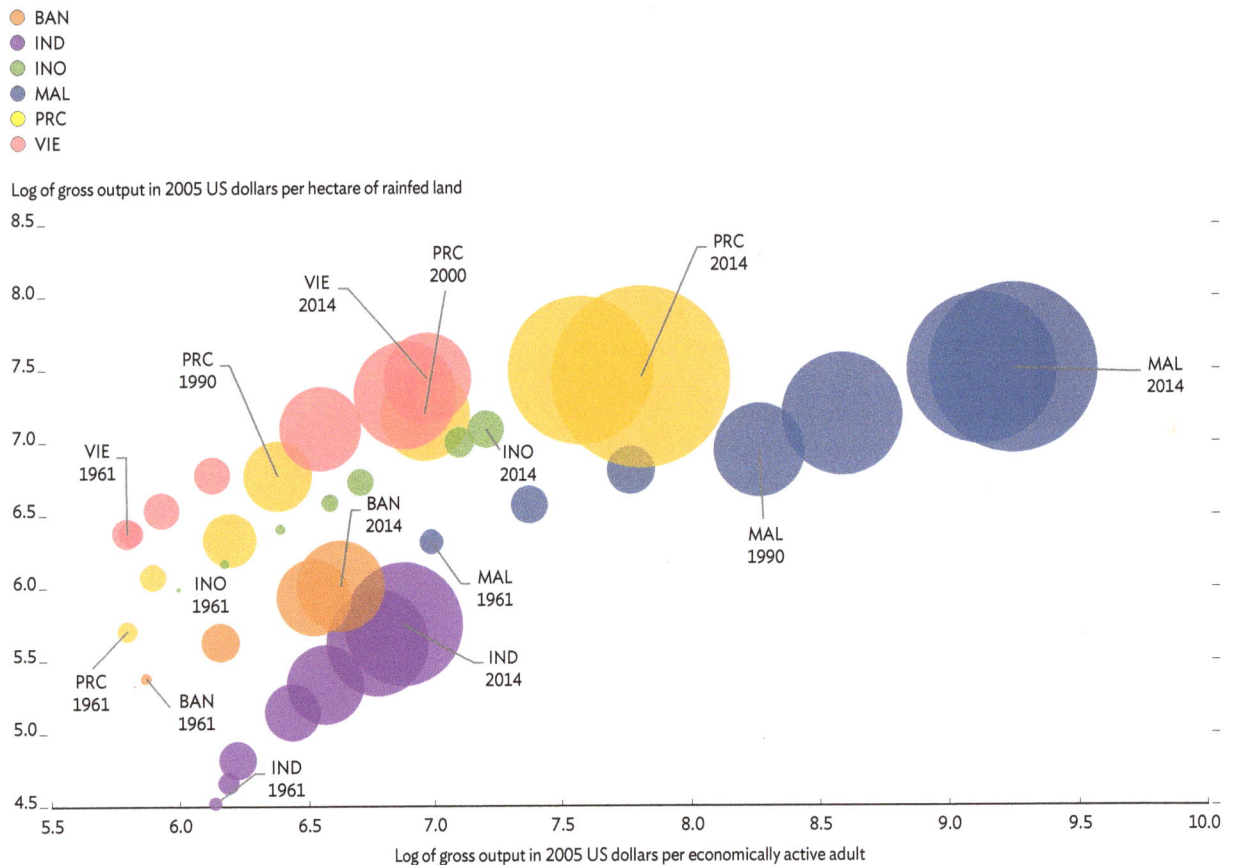

BAN = Bangladesh, IND = India, INO = Indonesia, MAL = Malaysia, PRC = People's Republic of China, VIE = Viet Nam.

Notes: Dots represent data points in 1961, 1970, 1980, 1990, 2000, 2010, and 2014, the last year being when the Food and Agriculture Organization stopped reporting on the use of agricultural machinery. Circle size represents the rate of mechanization as measured by the ratio of machinery in metric horsepower to the number of economically active adults in agriculture. The X axis shows gross agricultural output in 2005 US dollars per economically active adult in agriculture. The Y axis shows gross agricultural output in 2005 US dollars per hectare of rainfed cropland equivalent. On the X and Y axes, equivalent United States dollar values for log 6 is $405, 8 is $3,000, and 9 is $8,150.

Source: US Department of Agriculture. Economic Research Service. https://www.ers.usda.gov/data-products/international-agricultural-productivity/ (accessed 7 October 2019).

Adoption of labor-saving agricultural machinery is critical in the context of the shrinking, aging, and feminizing rural population. Such labor-saving advances enable older workers to prolong their careers and encourage the greater participation of rural women in the workforce. Time-saving agricultural machinery can make it easier for older workers and women to perform heavy, backbreaking agricultural tasks, such as transporting agricultural supplies and produce to and from warehouses. In farming systems in the Philippines and Timor-Leste, with little mechanization, female farmworkers suffer health problems and time poverty because of their workload, especially during peak season.

In contrast, farm mechanization has considerably alleviated women's drudgery in Indonesia and Thailand (Akter et al. 2017; Akter et al. 2016). Time-saving technology—such as a tiller that reduces the need for weeding, a laborious farm task often carried out by women—allow women to pursue work off the farm.

Land productivity has reached a plateau for some advanced Asian economies. In Malaysia, the PRC, and Viet Nam, land productivity has reached a plateau in 2005 at about $3,000 per hectare. This reflects the physical and biological limits of land. These economies have continued to increase agricultural productivity by increasing labor productivity, through mechanization, moving the dots in Figure 2.2.1 to the right. As the dots move from left to right, they become larger to reflect the ratio of machinery in metric horsepower to the number of economically active adults in agriculture.

Compared with advanced Asian economies, labor productivity remains low in other economies where most farmers continue to be smallholders. Asia has 350 million smallholder farmers, or those who manage areas measuring up to 10 ha (FAO 2020b). About 95% of all farms in Asia are smaller than 5 ha (FAO 2020a). In the PRC, 98% of farmers cultivate less than 2 ha (FAO 2015b). In India, 80% of farmers are smallholders. Many of them are poor and food insecure, with little access to capital, markets, or services. Credit is likewise difficult to obtain for lack of collateral and because of the high risks associated with agriculture. These farmers face critical constraints on their adoption of agricultural machinery, as their economic advantage depends critically on scale. Even small agricultural machinery that would be advantageous may be unaffordable without heavy government subsidies. To help smallholder farmers benefit from agricultural machines, innovative arrangements have emerged.

First, farmland consolidation has been promoted through market transactions and institutional arrangements. Historically in many Organisation for Economic Co-operation and Development (OECD) countries, consolidation was achieved largely through market transactions. In the PRC, land transactions were seriously constrained by insecurity affecting farmers' individual land rights. Since the 2000s, however, a variety of institutional innovations consolidated small operations into larger units (Kimura 2021; Yamauchi 2021; Liu et al. 2020). These reforms granted farmers more complete land-use rights and the right to derive nonagricultural income from land, making land transfer much more likely. The PRC Ministry of Agriculture and Rural Affairs reported that "transferred" land soared from 3.9 million ha in 2004 to 31.4 million ha in 2016. With increased land market movements, large-scale agriculture operations have emerged. Caution is needed, however, on land consolidation.

Niroula and Thapa (2005) highlighted that, in the past, land consolidation was not successful partly because of weak land rights, difficulty in evaluating land values, and problems affecting contract enforcement. The study suggested that success in any land consolidation program depends on how well farmers' needs, capabilities, and aspirations are reconciled and integrated.[8]

Second, instead of consolidating land through land rental, there are schemes that consolidate farm activities. In Viet Nam, the Small Farmers, Large Field scheme has received significant attention as a solution to smallholders' problems of mechanization and lack of bargaining power in buying inputs and marketing output. Under the scheme, participating farmers organize themselves into groups and synchronize their operations by adopting a single rice variety to plant, establishing a group nursery, and transplanting and harvesting at about the same time, thus essentially converting their small landholdings into a large field. A similar scheme is now under operation for rice and potatoes in eastern India (Mohanty et al. 2017). In the PRC, the institutional framework to establish farmer professional cooperatives (FPCs) was promulgated in 2007. In addition to jointly owned farm machines, FPCs provide diverse services including technical training and processing, marketing, and purchasing assistance. According to the PRC's State Administration for Market Regulation (2020), the number of legally registered cooperatives reached 2.2 million at the end of 2019. In some cases, FPCs evolved into shareholding cooperatives in which farmers transfer land-use rights in exchange for shares in the cooperative. This arrangement allows members to participate in the allocation of cooperative dividends.

Third, rural entrepreneurs are providing farm machine rental and operation services. By assisting many smallholder farmers, service providers enjoy economies of scale while making labor-saving machines accessible to smallholder farmers. In the PRC, two types of mechanization services exist. One is mechanical services provided by specialized custom plow, planter, and harvester teams that own large machines. The other provides machine rental to farm households that operate the machines themselves. Farmer professional cooperatives and specialized custom plow, planter, and harvester teams have become major driving forces behind agricultural modernization, supported by government machine subsidy program. In addition to offering a wide range of mechanized operation services such as field preparation,

---

[8]   Issues related to land tenure, rights, and regulations are complicated and beyond the scope of this chapter but demand more discussion elsewhere.

planting, harvesting, transportation, and storage, these service providers deliver agricultural machinery technical services and guidance on maintenance and other technical matters, reinforcing smallholder capacity to further mechanize their farms. While these innovations are expected to allow farmers to benefit from agricultural mechanization, careful monitoring and proper regulation are needed to ensure the fair sharing of benefits to participating farmers.

The COVID-19 pandemic continues to hurt rural households (Box 2.2.1). An expansion of innovative services mentioned above may help farmers rebound from the lasting impacts of the pandemic.

2.2.2 Improved practices can help farmers reduce environmental damage

Fertilizer subsidies have encouraged their overuse. Since the beginning of the green revolution, fertilizers have been subsidized in many Asian economies to increase the yields of improved varieties of cereal crops. As fertilizer subsidies are gradually phased out or scaled down in recent decades, farmers have incentive to use fertilizer more efficiently. Even within a single farm plot, the need for fertilizer differs depending on soil condition, topography, and residual from past application. Yet many farmers simply apply fertilizer uniformly, sometimes following outmoded recommendations from local extension services. In response, site-specific nutrient management has been developed. It is a low-tech approach based on plant need for optimally applying fertilizers such as nitrogen, phosphorus, and potassium to crops (Pampolino et al. 2007). Studies found that this approach made nitrogen use more efficient. Mobile phone applications have been developed to help farmers optimize the amount and timing of applications of different types of fertilizers.

Besides chemical fertilizers, excessive use of chemical pesticides is also a problem. The green revolution success encouraged the widespread production of only a few varieties, which made rice production more susceptible to pests and increased the need for agricultural pesticides. Farmers started overusing them in the belief that more was better, though studies later found that the use of pesticide during early plant growth was unnecessary, as leaf-feeding insects seldom affected yield (Heong, Escalada, and Mai 1994). Further, pesticides pose threats to farmers' health and to food safety. To reduce the inappropriate use of pesticide, integrated pest management (IPM) was introduced in the major rice-producing areas of Asia, especially in Southeast Asia.

IPM is an ecosystem-based strategy that aims to control pests and their damage over the long term through a combination of techniques—most notably biological control, habitat manipulation, modification of cultural practices, and the use of resistant crop varieties—to complement, reduce, or replace the application of synthetic pesticides. IPM practices were transferred to farmers not through lectures but by experiential learning in farmer field schools, which attracted the participation of over 2 million rice farmers across Asia.

Although practiced by relatively few farmers in Asia, organic agriculture has gradually expanded in the region. Organic agriculture uses ecologically sound pest controls and biological fertilizers to optimize the productivity and fitness of diverse communities within the agro-ecosystem, including soil organisms, plants, livestock, and people. In 2019, developing Asia had 5.9 million ha of agricultural land under organic agriculture, or 8.2% of the world's total (Figure 2.2.2a). India had the largest share of organic agricultural land in the region, at 38.8%, followed by the PRC, at 37.4%. Southeast Asia had 12.7%, mainly in Indonesia, Thailand, and the Philippines (Figure 2.2.2b). According to *The World of Organic Agriculture, Statistics and Emerging Trends* (Willer et al. 2021), 49.2% of organic agricultural land is used to produce field crops such as cereals, oilseeds, textile crops, and medicinal and aromatic plants, while 13.5% is devoted to permanent crops like coconuts, tea, fruits, and coffee. About 36.2% of organic agricultural land have no specific details on land use, while 1.1% is permanent grassland. There are nearly 1.6 million organic farm producers in Asia, 1.4 million of which are in India and nearly 119,000 are in Thailand. These numbers are believed to be underestimated, as many economies do not report on organic production.

Obtaining organic certification is a complex and expensive process for many farmers in the region. Estimates based on FAOSTAT database suggest that in 2018, only 54% of the organic agricultural land in developing Asia was certified. The low rate of certification may reflect slow adoption of organic regulations in many economies. Table 2.2.1 shows that, as of 2020, only 72 economies globally had fully implemented organic regulations (Willer et al. 2021), and only 10 of them were in Asia. Organic certification requires annual inspections and monitoring that are logistically difficult and costly. Obtaining international certification is even more tedious, expensive, and time consuming, thus not economical for small and marginal farmers. Lack of support in terms of organic product distribution and marketing systems makes it even harder for farmers to meet certification requirements and standards.

Figure 2.2.2 Organic farms in developing Asia

Organic agriculture is expanding in Asia, with most organic agricultural land in the region in India and the People's Republic of China.

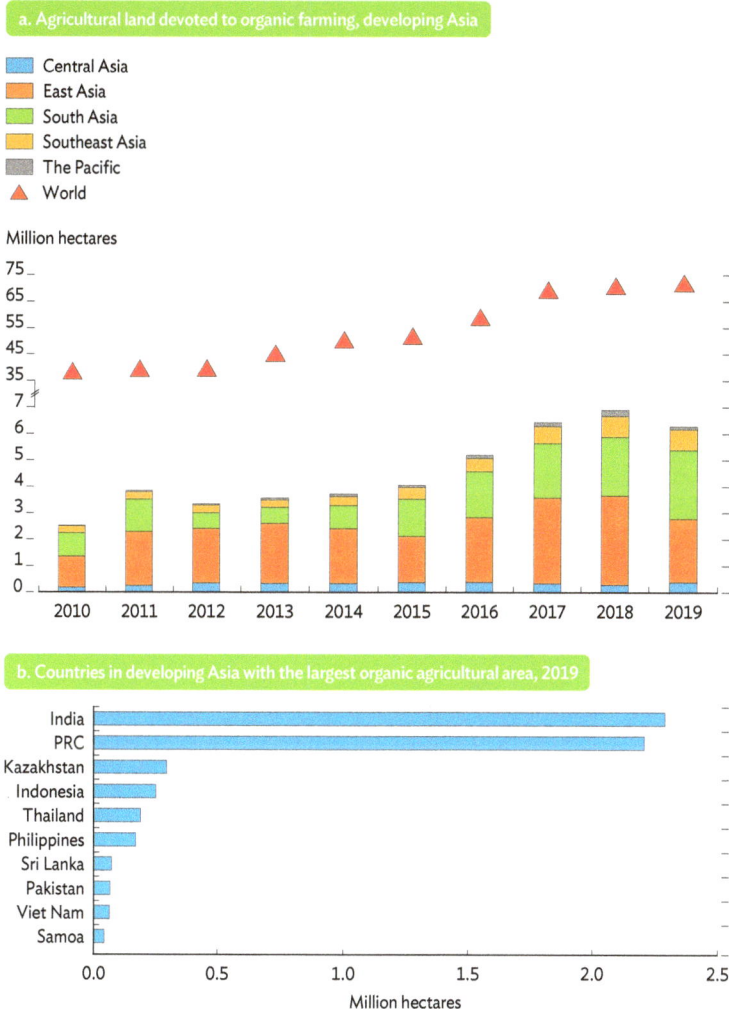

a. Agricultural land devoted to organic farming, developing Asia

Central Asia
East Asia
South Asia
Southeast Asia
The Pacific
▲ World

Million hectares

b. Countries in developing Asia with the largest organic agricultural area, 2019

Million hectares

PRC = People's Republic of China.

Notes: Data are from the Research Institute of Organic Agriculture (FiBL), which is one of the world's leading institutes in organic agriculture. FiBL has long been committed to the international development of organic agriculture, sponsoring the umbrella organization of the organic agriculture movement: IFOAM—Organics International. For research and development projects, FiBL partners with the European Union, the Food and Agriculture Organization, and other national and international institutions.

Source of data: Research Institute of Organic Agriculture FiBL. FiBL Statistics. statistics.fibl.org (accessed 21 June 2021).

An alternative community-based certification system has emerged, as an alternative to costly international certification. The International Federation of Organic Agriculture Movements (IFOAM) has introduced a community-oriented participatory guarantee system (PGS) to build trust, social networks, and local knowledge. PGS employs a peer-to-peer monitoring system and is designed to meet the needs of small farmers producing for local markets. Asia has the largest group of producers and operational PGSs in the world, with 1.1 million certified PGS producers.

Table 2.2.1 Status of organic agriculture regulation

Organic agriculture regulations exist in Asia, but most are not yet fully implemented.

Region	Economies Drafting	Economies Fully Implemented	Economies Partly Implemented	Total
Africa	5	1	4	10
Asia	7	10	11	28
Europe		39	4	43
Latin America and the Caribbean	2	16	3	21
North America		2		2
Oceania		4		4
Total	**14**	**72**	**22**	**108**

Source: IFOAM—Organics International. https://www.ifoam.bio/ (accessed 17 September 2021).

In India, farmers have, for the past 2 years, joined a government initiative called PGS-India, implemented by the National Center of Organic Farming.

As the COVID-19 pandemic shut down markets and other economic activities, the organic food supply chain has been seriously affected by declining demand. The pandemic has also, however, highlighted the importance of healthy food and a healthy lifestyle. Indonesia, the Philippines, and the PRC are among the economies that have recorded significant increases in demand for fresh produce. This generates new opportunities that turn organic production into a hotspot for investment. As economies recover from the pandemic, a strong rebound is expected in demand for high-quality food in restaurants and at home. The post-pandemic period could be a turning point for organic agriculture in Asia.

2.2.3 Irrigation systems need to be upgraded and fit farmers' incentives

Modernizing irrigation infrastructure and management systems is imperative for tackling water stress. Many irrigation systems that were constructed decades ago and have since been poorly maintained are long due for upgrades. Irrigation systems need to be climate resilient, especially able to withstand floods, as climate change is expected to increase the number of floods. More intense flood damage has often been observed in recent years. In addition, investments in irrigation infrastructure need to be designed to be labor saving and supportive of agricultural mechanization and diversified farming. Further, irrigation management systems need to be flexible to allow public and private irrigation systems to coexist and contribute to sustainable water management.

Innovative technologies can promote more sustainable use of water. Implementation of remote water-sensing and control systems, water-saving irrigation technologies such as satellite-based irrigation advisory systems, and such innovative methods as volumetric water charging can lead to a more efficient use of water. However, volumetric water charging systems require effective collective action, highly sophisticated infrastructure that enables accurate volume measurement, and the provision of water supply on demand (Box 2.2.2). Designing appropriate and effective policy for groundwater use must consider the particular agro-ecological and socioeconomic conditions of the area where it applies. To discourage overuse, flat charges should be replaced with metered charges and a so-called Pigouvian tax, levied to compensate for negative externalities associated with both private or communal extraction of groundwater (Kajisa 2012; Kajisa, Palanisami, and Sakurai 2007).

2.2.4 A well-regulated aquaculture sector can support Asian consumers' seafood consumption

The past 3 decades have seen rapid growth in aquaculture in Asia. In 2015, aquaculture provided 53.1% of fishery production, and Asia dominated global aquaculture with an 88% share. Figure 2.2.3 shows that the wild fish catch has been flat at a little above 80 million tons annually since the late 1980s.

Figure 2.2.3 Annual capture fishery and aquaculture production, world and developing Asia

Aquaculture is growing rapidly with developing Asia, which comprises 88% of the global total.

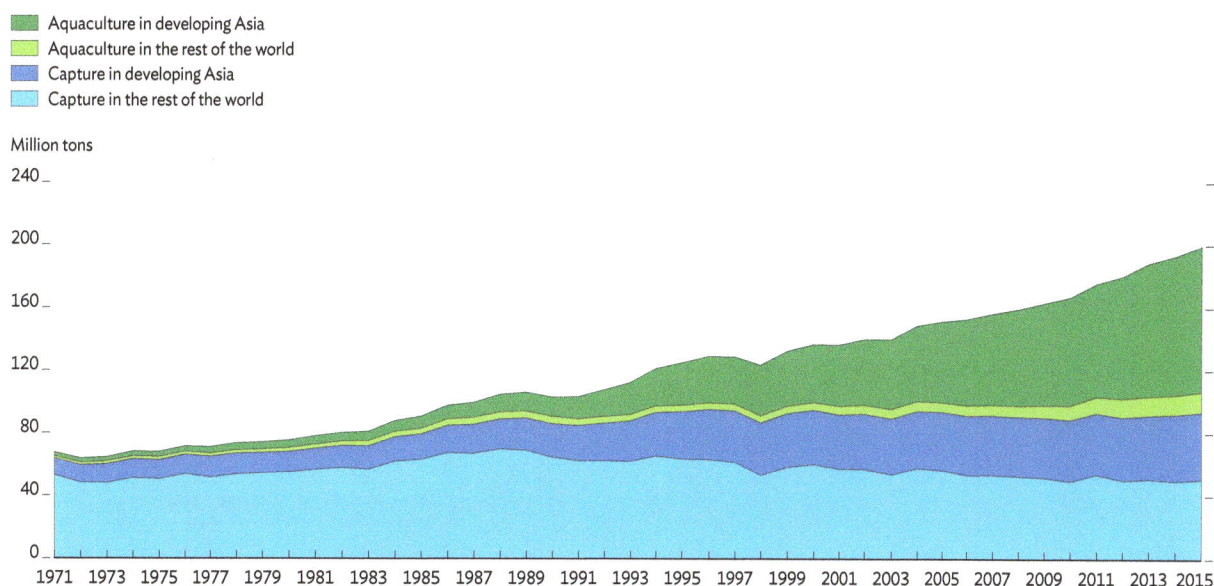

Legend:
- Aquaculture in developing Asia
- Aquaculture in the rest of the world
- Capture in developing Asia
- Capture in the rest of the world

Source: World Bank. World Development Indicators. https://databank.worldbank.org/source/world-development-indicators (accessed 28 July 2021).

Increased human fish consumption has thus been supplied by aquaculture. Growth has come more from inland aquaculture than from marine aquaculture, which has expanded little in the past decade. New technologies and practices have helped the rapid expansion of inland aquaculture. The PRC is by far the world's largest producer of farmed fish, outproducing the rest of the world combined since 1991 (Figure 2.2.4). Aquaculture is growing quickly in East, Southeast, and South Asia. While most of fishery production in the PRC and South Asia is consumed domestically, the share of exports is rising in some Southeast Asian countries, notably Thailand and Viet Nam.

Aquaculture contributes to good nutrition and employment in Asia. While animal protein intake in Asia is generally low, as discussed in section 2.1, the share of dietary protein from fish is larger in Asia than the world average. Employment generated in aquaculture is substantial and rising, providing more work for women than do male-dominated capture fisheries. Further, more than half of workers in fish processing are women (Kruijssen et al. 2018). These income opportunities have empowered women and improved their standing in the household. However, the distribution of benefits from aquaculture is reported to be unequal as men tend to hold jobs in processing with higher pay and benefits (FAO 2021a). Further, aquaculture can serve as a useful social safeguard for people displaced by dam construction, as demonstrated by the Saguling-Cirata dam in Indonesia.

Freshwater fish and shrimp are two major forms of aquaculture in Asia. The success of freshwater aquaculture in Bangladesh, celebrated as a "blue revolution," provides an example of the former. The increase of fish production from inland aquaculture has reduced fish prices in domestic markets, notably benefiting poor consumers. Growth has been spurred by rising domestic demand under stable economic development. Shrimp farming, mainly for export, became widespread after technological innovation intensified shrimp farming in Taipei,China in the 1980s. Private actors, notably conglomerates in Japan and Thailand, played important roles in the growth of shrimp aquaculture in terms of both strengthening the supply side and expanding global demand (Hall 2004). Viet Nam, now one of the world's largest shrimp producers, started allowing the conversion of rice fields to fishponds in 2000, prompting immediate expansion in the fishpond area in coastal areas suitable for fish farming (Box 2.2.4).

Figure 2.2.4 Aquaculture production in Asia

Aquaculture production is rapidly growing in Asia, led by the People's Republic of China.

- Republic of Korea
- Rest of developing Asia
- Bangladesh
- Viet Nam
- India
- Indonesia
- People's Republic of China

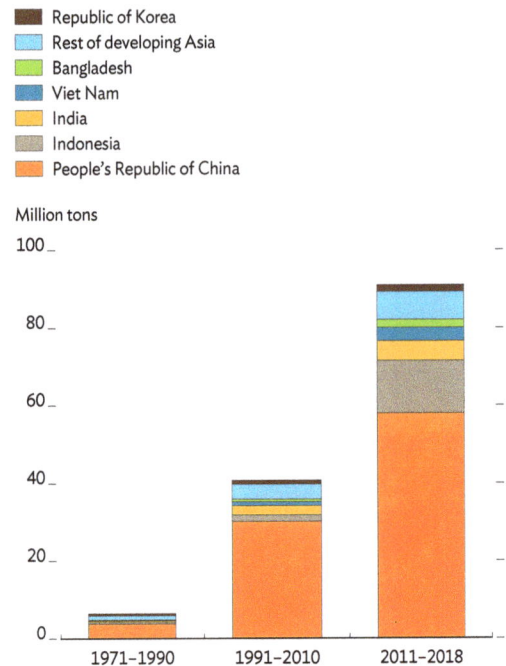

Source: World Bank. World Development Indicators. https://databank.worldbank.org/source/world-development-indicators (accessed 28 July 2021).

Mobile phone technology use can help promote inclusive growth. By providing affordable access to technical information and market access to farmers in remote areas, many phone applications have hastened farmers' adoption of good agricultural practices. Social media can provide platforms for disseminating information and farmers' sharing their experiences (Box 2.2.5). A major concern on the future of aquaculture is its sustainability as discussed in section 2.1. Effective monitoring on environmental effects of aquaculture production, reliable inspections on food safety, and functional regulations are imperative for the sustainable growth of aquaculture in Asia.

Box 2.2.1 Into the second year: farm households under COVID-19 in Pakistan

The COVID-19 pandemic continues to hurt rural households. To empirically investigate the welfare and agricultural marketing of farmers in Pakistan, the Asian Development Bank conducted mobile phone surveys in Punjab and Sindh provinces in June 2020 and 2021. The 2020 survey interviewed 839 farmers, and the 2021 survey re-interviewed 744 of them, or 89% of the original sample. The two surveys found that the COVID-19 pandemic has continued to negatively impact farm households, especially in Sindh province (box figure).

Continuing impact of COVID-19 in Sindh and Punjab, 2020 and 2021

- Family lost wages and off-farm income
- Family members returned from migration destinations
- Reduced food consumption
- Reduced nonfood expenditure

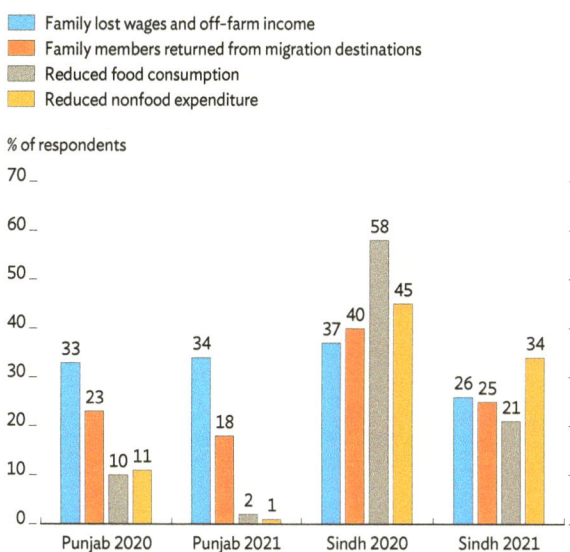

Sources: Yamano, Sato, and Arif (2021a, 2021b).

In Punjab, one-third of farmer households experienced loss of wages and off-farm earnings in 2020, and the reduction has remained unchanged into 2021. Almost one-quarter reported that at least one family member had returned from urban areas in 2020, and the proportion has remained at 18% in 2021. On the other hand, consumption of food and other goods has returned to the pre-pandemic level from about a 10% decline in 2020.

In Sindh Province, negative impacts remain at high levels. In 2020, 37% of rural households in the province experienced reduced wages and off-farm income, and the number remained high at 26% in 2021. One-fourth of rural households continue to report returned family members in June 2021. The percentage of rural households reporting reduced food consumption declined from 58% in 2020 to 21% in 2021, and those reporting lower nonfood expenditure declined from 45% to 34%. These results indicate greater hardship in Sindh than in Punjab. As Pakistan and other economies struggle under the pandemic and prepare for recovery, it is critical to monitor and understand how the pandemic leaves lasting impacts.

Sources:

Yamano, T., N. Sato, and B. W. Arif. 2021a. The Impact of COVID-19 and Locust Invasion on Farm Households in Punjab and Sindh: Analysis from Cross-Sectional Surveys in Pakistan. *ADB Central and West Asia Working Paper Series* No. 10. Asian Development Bank.

——. 2021b. The Impact of the COVID-19 Pandemic into the Second Year: Panel Survey Analysis of Farm Households in Punjab and Sindh Provinces in Pakistan. Mimeo. Asian Development Bank.

Box 2.2.2 Lessons learned from volumetric water pricing in the PRC and the Philippines

Volumetric pricing is an economic approach to saving water. Under such a policy, a fee is based on the volume passing through a canal intake of a water-user group (WUG). Saving water under this scheme requires effective collective action by members of the WUG, who pay a portion of the fee. How effectively such a scheme saves water relies on how well the WUG solves the free-rider problem. While the group has an incentive to save water, individual farmers within a group may overuse water unless they are closely supervised. Facing a rapid increase in water demand for urban and industrial use, the PRC sought to save water in agriculture, especially in rice farming, by replacing area-based pricing with volumetric water pricing.

A case study in the Zhanghe irrigation system in Hubei, PRC, highlighted the importance of setting an appropriate volumetric price and enforcing collective management to prevent free-riding (Kajisa and Dong 2017). The study found that effective collective monitoring and management of water use within a WUG was feasible only when volumetric prices were moderate. If the price was too high, farmers tended to exit the WUG, leaving it with a discontinuous irrigated area, which complicated collective monitoring and management of water use. To keep all members in a WUG, the water price needs to remain at a moderate rate. Another study in northern Luzon, Philippines, similarly highlighted the importance of collective action by WUG members (Kajisa et al. 2018).

First, the study confirmed the tremendous difficulty of measuring water volume in irrigation systems. It also found that the volumetric system has to be sophisticated enough to supply water on demand, or users will not pay fees based on use. These two problems can be solved by upgrading irrigation infrastructure for accurate volume measurement and reliability. A third problem is also complicated. As groundwater flows downhill and recharges wells there, downstream farmers need to buy less water to meet their irrigation needs. Upstream farmers may regard this as unfair. Resolving this problem requires coordination and agreement among water users.

Sources:

Kajisa, K. 2019. Role of Community and Government in Irrigation Management in Emerging States: Lessons from Japan, China, and India. In K. Otsuka and K. Sugihara, eds. *Paths to the Emerging State in Asia and Africa, Emerging-Economy State and International Policy Studies.* Springer. https://doi.org/10.1007/978-981-13-3131-2_12.

Kajisa, K. and B. Dong. 2017. The Effect of Volumetric Pricing Policy on Farmers' Water Management Institutions and Their Water Use: The Case of Water User Organization in an Irrigation System in Hubei, China. *World Bank Economic Review* 31(1).

Kajisa, K. et al. 2018. Lessons from Volumetric Water Pricing Trials at the Three Surface Irrigation Systems in Northern Luzon, Philippines. *DLSU Business & Economic Review* 28(1).

Box 2.2.3 Alternate wetting and drying

Rice production emits 22% of greenhouse gas (GHG) emissions from agriculture in Asia. Under flooded rice fields with little oxygen, microbes decay organic matter in the soil and generate methane gas, which is 28 times more potent a GHG than carbon dioxide. Instead of continuously flooding rice fields, a water-management technique called alternate wetting and drying (AWD) allows rice fields to dry out periodically for one to several days before reflooding (box figure 1). Studies found that AWD reduces methane emissions by 30%–50% and water use by 10%–20% without reducing rice yield (Setyanto et al. 2018).

In 2016 and 2017, over 500 farmers in Chittagong, Bangladesh were trained in AWD water management. With the support of ADB, the Muhuri Irrigation Project demonstrated that AWD requires 22% less water than continuous standing water. In the dry season of 2016, methane emissions were 41%–42% lower from AWD plots than from those with continuous flooding (box figure 2).

Despite AWD's potential benefits, its adoption has been limited for several reasons. First, most irrigation systems charge farmers a fixed irrigation fee for the season, in many cases subsidized by public agents or never collected. Farmers thus have little financial incentive to save water. Second, farmers are not charged for methane and other GHG emissions from their rice fields and are unaware of them. To encourage farmers to adopt AWD, awareness and incentive programs are needed. In light of high GHG emissions from flooded rice fields, it may be reasonable to devise incentive systems that compensate farmers for adopting AWD and reducing their GHG emissions.

Sources:

ADB. 2019. *Climate-Smart Practices for Intensive Rice-Based Systems in Bangladesh, Cambodia, and Nepal.* Asian Development Bank.

Setyanto, P. et al. 2018. Alternate Wetting and Drying Reduces Methane Emission from a Rice Paddy in Central Java, Indonesia without Yield Loss. *Soil Science and Plant Nutrition* 64(1).

1 Alternate wetting and drying

Alternate wetting and drying is a water-management technique that allows rice fields to dry periodically before reflooding...

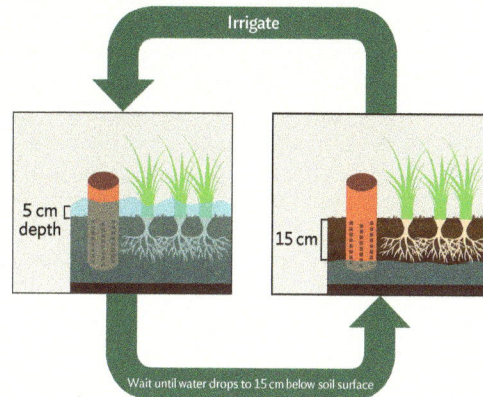

AWD = alternate wetting and drying, cm = centimeter.

Note: Under flooded rice fields (left panel), microbes decay organic matter and generate methane gas, which contributes to global warming. Alternate wetting and drying allows rice fields to dry for one to several days (right panel). Studies found that AWD reduces methane emissions by 30%–50% and water use by 10%–20%.

Source: ADB (2019).

2 Methane emissions under AWD and continuous standing water

...reducing both greenhouse gas emissions and water use.

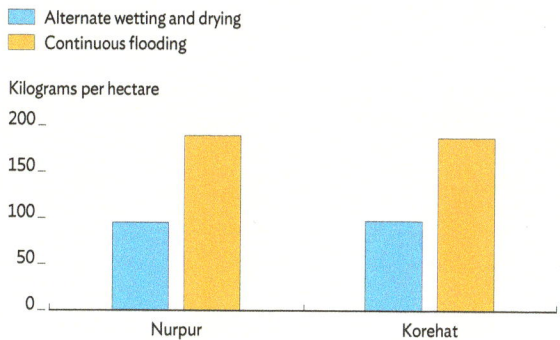

AWD = alternate wetting and drying.
Source: ADB (2019).

Box 2.2.4 Shrimp aquaculture development in Viet Nam

Shrimp farming in Viet Nam grew dramatically as the Government passed a resolution in 2000, allowing the conversion of less-productive rice land in coastal areas to aquaculture ponds. A problem soon developed, however, as many importing economies rejected shrimp from Viet Nam, often citing high antibiotic residue in the product. In some cases, prohibited antibiotics were used, and in others the amount of antibiotic used exceeded maximum limits set by many developed markets (Suzuki and Nam 2018; Lee, Suzuki, and Nam 2019).

Several problems were identified. First, the authorities did not adequately monitor input markets, which allowed the use of uncertified shrimp seed and other prohibited inputs. Second, farmers often purchased shrimp feed on credit from input sellers, which locked them into rigid financial relationships with their input suppliers and deprived them of other options. Third, lab testing was costly and cumbersome for farmers, leaving invisible residues undetected. Fourth, shrimp buyers did not check for residue when making purchases and often mixed shrimp obtained from multiple farmers, scrambling traceability along the supply chain.

Solutions were identified to address these problems. A randomized controlled trial was conducted to investigate how farmers could be induced to adopt better practices (Suzuki, Nam, and Lee 2020). The study conducted three experiments that (i) offered technical training, (ii) quantified antibiotic residue, and (iii) offered price premiums if shrimp passed a quality test. In the second experiment, shrimp were collected from farmers' ponds and lab tested for the presence of four antibiotic markers, and the test results returned to individual farmers in the treatment group. The study found that quantifying antibiotic residue had a positive effect in reducing the antibiotic residue. This finding suggested that providing farmers with the means to detect residue in shrimp was an effective way to change their behavior.

In Thailand, such laboratory testing is freely accessible to shrimp farmers who register with the government. Further, the traceability system in Thailand is well structured, requiring a "movement document" to be updated whenever shrimps are transferred between two parties at every stage, from hatcheries to processing factories (Suzuki and Nam 2019). Through these efforts, antibiotic residues are no longer an issue in Thailand. In recent years, rejection rates for shrimp exports from Viet Nam have declined at Japanese ports. Indeed, Viet Nam has been considered a successful shrimp producer during the COVID-19 pandemic (Fletcher 2020; VASEP 2020). According to the Vietnam Association of Seafood Exporters and Producers, shrimp exports from Viet Nam to the US, its largest market, grew by 33% year on year in January–September 2020. In the same period all shrimp exports from Viet Nam expanded by 11%.

Sources:

Fletcher, R. 2020. *Shrimp Aquaculture: A Tale of Two Pandemics.* Fish Site. 11 August. https://thefishsite.com/articles/shrimp-aquaculture-a-tale-of-two-pandemics.

Lee, G., A. Suzuki, and V. Nam. 2019. Effect of Network-Based Targeting on the Diffusion of Good Aquaculture Practices among Shrimp Producers in Vietnam. *World Development* 124.

Suzuki, A. and V. Nam. 2018. Better Management Practices and Their Outcomes in Shrimp Farming: Evidence from Small-Scale Shrimp Farmers in Southern Vietnam. *Aquaculture International* 26.

Suzuki, A. and V. Nam. 2019. Marketing Risks and Standards Compliance: Challenges in Accessing the Global Market for High-Value Agricultural and Aquacultural Industries. In K. Tsunekawa and Y. Todo, eds. *Emerging States at Crossroads.* Springer.

Suzuki, A., V. Nam, and G. Lee. 2020. Inducing Smallholders' Compliance with International Standards: Evidence from the Shrimp Aquaculture Sector in Vietnam. Mimeo.

VASEP. 2020. Vietnam Association of Seafood Exporters and Producers. http://seafood.vasep.com.vn/.

Box 2.2.5 Digital aquaculture extension

Farmers have formed online groups to share information and crowdsource solutions for their farm problems. For instance, a group of seven shrimp farmers in Asia formed a Facebook group in 2011 to share information and raise issues they encountered on their farms. It grew rapidly to 18,271 by 2017. Administrators of the group closely monitor members' posts and intervene if they see any inappropriate information. While most of the members are shrimp farmers, academic aquaculture experts also joined the group, allowing them to correct misinformation as needed. Lee and Suzuki (2020) examined nearly 11,000 posts in this group from 2011 and 2017 and found that the most common topics were farm skills, inputs, and equipment, followed by disease and prices. This showed that shrimp farmers' major interest in joining this type of virtual group was to obtain information on farming techniques. Other social media and instant messaging platforms, such as Line, WhatsApp, and Telegram, are also widely used by aquaculture producers. YouTube channels that offer technical lessons or interviews with aquaculture producers have been posted in many languages.

Information and communication technology helps measure quality and enables precision aquaculture. Many aspects of aquaculture are not directly observable. If farmers can quantify these aspects, they may be able to improve their performance or mitigate their negative effects on the surrounding environment. Digital meters to test water quality, for example, can measure important water quality parameters such as acidity, dissolved oxygen, oxides of nitrogen, and ammonia. The simple liquid solution test kits often available to farmers offer variable results. A wireless network system has been developed to disseminate results of water quality measures for more consistent monitoring (Tuan 2019). Various phone apps have been developed to help farmers use more appropriate farm practices. One app allows farmers to evaluate shrimp health and growth by taking a smartphone picture and automatically calculating appropriate feed amounts and scheduling (Fish Site 2020).

Sources:

Fish Site. 2020. Vietnamese Shrimp Farmers Flock to New App. 21 October. https://thefishsite.com/articles/vietnamese-shrimp-farmers-flock-to-new-growth-app#:~:text=An%20app%20that%20lets%20shrimp,reviews%20from%20farmers%20in%20Vietnam.

Lee, G. and A. Suzuki. 2020. Motivation for Information Exchange in a Virtual Community of Practice: Evidence from a Facebook Group for Shrimp Farmers. *World Development* 125.

Tuan, K. N. 2019. A Wireless Sensor Network for Aquaculture Using Raspberry Pi, Arduino and Xbee. Paper prepared for the International Conference on System Science and Engineering, Dong Hoi, Viet Nam, 20–21 July.

(Left) A mobile application has been developed to help farmers on shrimp feeding and health management. (Right) Mobile phones used by farmers to check buyers and market prices (photos by Jindra Samson and Mike Cortes).

2.3 Support systems are needed for Asia's farmers

Innovative practices and solutions on the farm need to be supported by complementary systems and technologies. These systems and technologies will help build climate resilience and ensure that farmers benefit from the ongoing agricultural transformation. The future of agriculture depends crucially on the ability of farm communities to cope with climate change. Early warning systems and crop insurance programs that use advanced spatial information systems can mitigate farmers' exposure to climate risks and protect their livelihoods. Agriculture production in Asia is shifting toward high-value crops such as vegetables and fruit supported by new practices and technologies. Contract farming has the potential to benefit both farmers and contractors by allowing product specialization but requires the capacity of local government agencies to monitor and enforce contracts. Similarly, digital technologies can promote inclusive development by helping farmers in remote areas access technical and market information, but this will require better access to mobile technology. To support the ongoing agricultural transformation, agriculture policy should facilitate greater market orientation through research and development.

2.3.1 Early warning systems offer efficient protection from weather risks

Disaster risks can be managed by adopting integrated climate mitigation and adaptation measures. Given intensifying adverse weather events, action to prepare for them is important. At the national level, long-term predictions of extreme weather caused by climate change can guide government agencies and stakeholders to invest in climate-resilient infrastructure and support climate-resilient agricultural production and marketing systems. Investments that offer multiple synergistic dividends in resilience, such as early warning systems for extreme weather, can—combined with other infrastructure such as cyclone shelters in Bangladesh and social capital to facilitate compliance—help government agencies and agricultural producers prepare for such events (ADB 2019c; Shoji and Murata 2021). Various early actions, ideally flexible, can range from cash transfers for fishing communities to safely storing nets ahead of an impending cyclone, livestock vaccination and treatments for herders as drought intensifies, and flood defenses constructed before a severe rainy season to protect crops. In 2019, timely information on floods in northern Bangladesh helped communities and the government prepare and secure necessary supplies, reducing economic losses by two-thirds (FAO 2021b).

Developing and developed economies around the world have implemented drought warning systems at different levels of governance. Studies have demonstrated how effectively such systems empower vulnerable farmers to act early (Pulwarty and Sivakumar 2014). In Mongolia, for instance, pre-season drought predictions motivated government agencies and animal herders to build up stocks of animal feed in preparation for inadequate grazing under drought (FAO 2018b). Because water stress and drought intensity can vary substantially across regions, and crude assessments may miss hotspots in need of appropriate intervention, high-resolution spatial analysis is important. Figure 2.3.1 shows an example of how maps can be used to identify drought areas and assess the magnitude and severity of damage, especially in agricultural areas.

Advanced spatial information systems have several useful applications in agriculture. These advanced systems, which combine high-resolution satellite images, detailed crop models, ground data on agricultural production and management, and machine-learning algorithms, are critically important in developing early warning systems. They are likewise useful for predicting the potential impact on agricultural production from predicted weather events such as cyclones, floods, and drought. Researchers in India, for example, developed a machine-learning algorithm to predict crop types using satellite data in several production areas with mixed crops (Gumma et al. 2020). Area estimates of different crops were more accurate than government statistics derived from ground estimates. This system can likewise inform crop insurance programs as they assess weather-related damage to agricultural production, as discussed below. It can be used to supplement government agricultural statistics, which depend on field observations by government officers and are slow to become available.

Improved site-specific weather monitoring and reliable early warning systems are essential to farmers. These systems enable them to adapt to climate change and mitigate impact on agriculture. Early detection of extreme weather events can help farmers anticipate them and plan accordingly. With advances in crop science toward adaption to climate change, farmers can now select crop varieties that are more resilient under flooding, drought, and high temperatures.

Figure 2.3.1 Spatial distribution of agricultural drought in Myanmar, 2017–2018

Advanced spatial information systems can identify drought areas and reduce damage from extreme weather.

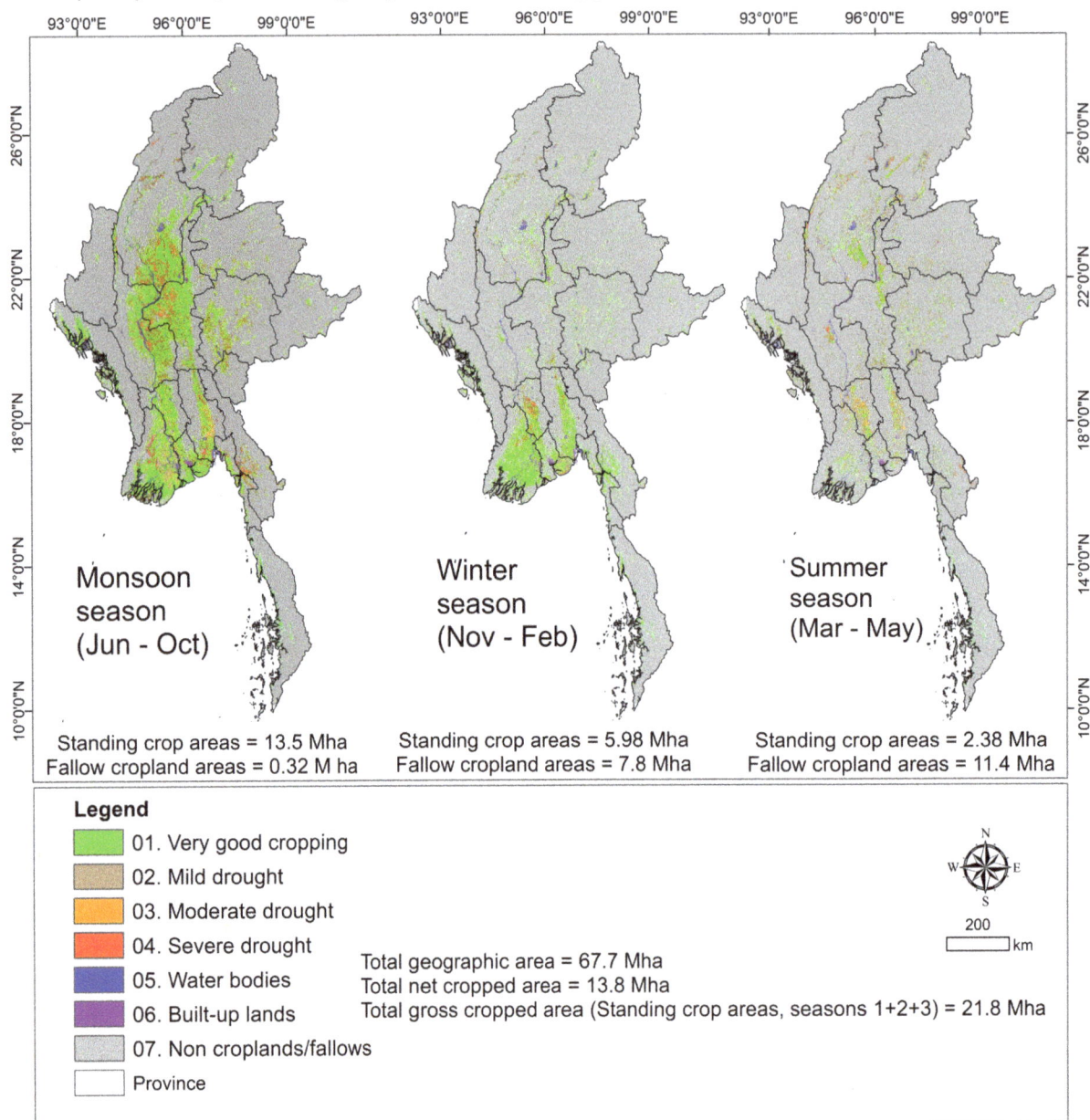

Monsoon season (Jun - Oct)
Standing crop areas = 13.5 Mha
Fallow cropland areas = 0.32 M ha

Winter season (Nov - Feb)
Standing crop areas = 5.98 Mha
Fallow cropland areas = 7.8 Mha

Summer season (Mar - May)
Standing crop areas = 2.38 Mha
Fallow cropland areas = 11.4 Mha

Legend

01. Very good cropping
02. Mild drought
03. Moderate drought
04. Severe drought
05. Water bodies
06. Built-up lands
07. Non croplands/fallows
Province

Total geographic area = 67.7 Mha
Total net cropped area = 13.8 Mha
Total gross cropped area (Standing crop areas, seasons 1+2+3) = 21.8 Mha

200 km

ha = hectare.
Source: M. K. Gumma et al. 2018. Mapping Cropland Fallow Areas in Myanmar to Scale Up Sustainable Intensification of Pulse Crops in the Farming System. *GIScience & Remote Sensing* 55(6): 926–949.

Crop scientists continue to develop varieties that can survive weather stresses or yield well with less water. Such varieties can help make agriculture more climate resilient and render water use more sustainable. However, scaling up the use of climate-resilient crops and production practices requires that farmers have access to timely information and technical support, as discussed in Box 2.3.1.

2.3.2 Innovative crop insurance builds resilience in farm communities in Asia

In the past 2 decades, agricultural insurance systems in the region have evolved and expanded quickly. Disaster risk insurance in Asia has increased from only 35 schemes operating in 2012 to 53 schemes in 2018 (Surminski, Panda, and Lampert 2019). In the past, crop insurance programs have frequently failed for low-income holders mainly because of informational problems, such as adverse selection and moral hazard (Skees et al. 2004; Besley 1995; Binswanger 1986). Index-based agricultural insurance programs have expanded in many Asian economies in recent years. They are attractive because of their potential to overcome asymmetric information problems associated with traditional insurance: adverse selection, when farmers at high risk are more likely to participate in a program than farmers at low risk, and moral hazard, when farmers fully insulated from risk lack incentive to prevent bad outcomes. Also attractive is their potential to attract private sector participation in the management of agricultural risk (Hazell and Hess 2017).[9] Of the 198 million farmers with index-based crop insurance in 2014, 194 million were in Asia—mostly in the PRC, with 160 million, and India, with 33 million (Hazell and Hess 2017).

Public–private insurance arrangements have broadly expanded in recent years. In 2017 and 2018, a third of economies with crop insurance were operating it under public–private partnership, while the public sector operated alone in four economies (Panda 2021). In South Asia, 32% of agricultural insurance was subsidized by governments. Many schemes are voluntary, such as Pradhan Mantri Fasal Bima Yojana and the Restructured Weather Based Crop Insurance Scheme in India.

Although 20 economies in developing Asia have crop insurance, only four governments have fully operational national crop insurance schemes (Table 2.3.1). The four governments include the PRC, India, the Philippines, and Sri Lanka. In Southeast Asia, Cambodia, Malaysia, Myanmar, and Viet Nam are at the cusp of scaling up their agricultural insurance schemes, while Brunei Darussalam, the Lao PDR, and Timor-Leste do not have any form of agricultural insurance. In Azerbaijan, Armenia, and Bangladesh, crop insurance schemes are likewise in pilot stages. Meanwhile, considerable gaps remain in terms of insurance coverage, uptake, and demand among the more established crop insurance schemes.

---

[9]　Crop insurance schemes need to adopt practices that avoid adverse selection and discourage moral hazard in participating farmers. Advanced information technology is expected to help insurance schemes select farmers with good records and provide incentive for them to avoid moral hazard.

Table 2.3.1 Crop insurance programs in Asia

Many economies in developing Asia have crop insurance schemes, but most are in early stages of development.

Type	Economy	Inclusion	Subsidized	Indemnity or Index Based
Private crop insurance				
	Bangladesh	Voluntary	Yes	Both
Public crop insurance				
	Nepal	Voluntary	Yes	Indemnity based
	Philippines	Voluntary	Yes	Both
	Sri Lanka	Mandatory	Yes	Both
	Uzbekistan	Voluntary	No	Indemnity based
Public–private partnership pilots, planning, and preparation at an advanced stage				
	Georgia	Mandatory	Yes	Indemnity based
	India	Voluntary	Yes	Both
	Indonesia	Voluntary	Yes	Both
	Kazakhstan	Mandatory	Yes	Indemnity based
	Kyrgyz Republic	Voluntary	Yes	Indemnity based
	Mongolia	Voluntary	No	Index based
	Myanmar	Voluntary	No	Index based
	Pakistan	Mandatory	Yes	Both
	People's Republic of China	Voluntary	Yes	Both
	Taipei,China	Voluntary	Yes	Indemnity based
	Thailand	Mandatory	Yes	Indemnity based
	Turkmenistan	Voluntary	No	Not applicable
	Viet Nam	Voluntary	Yes	Both

Notes: Premium subsidy can either be in part or full. Indemnity-based crop insurance compensates insured farmers based on verifiable loss at the end of the growing season. Index-based insurance provides claim payments based on the realization of an objectively measured index, such as a weather variable, correlated with production loss.

Source: A. Panda. 2021. Climate Change and Agricultural Insurance in the Asia and the Pacific Region. Background paper for *Asian Development Outlook 2021 Update*. Asian Development Bank.

Farmers covered by insurance are highly concentrated in only a few economies, notably the PRC, India, the Philippines, and Sri Lanka. Coverage and demand for agricultural insurance products remain limited in other economies. While uptake of any formal insurance stands at 16% in a selection of several ADB developing member economies, uptake for crop insurance is less than 2% (Panda, Lambert, and Surminski 2020). Hastening the development of national crop insurance schemes is critical for expanding coverage, especially among vulnerable Asian farmers, and building their climate resilience.

Major obstacles remain for assessing weather-related damage. Lessons can be drawn from the successful implementation of crop insurance systems in some economies. Spatial information systems, for example, are helping insurance programs in the PRC and India rapidly assess crop damage and expedite settlement claims. Imaging technologies such as drones, low Earth orbits, and remote-sensing satellites can capture high resolution images for assessing crop damage. The PRC is using low Earth orbits to capture images of vegetation for monitoring crop growth around the world. In the United States, drones are used to gather data for crop insurance claims. Spatial crop stress maps provide crop insurance programs with timely information, allowing them to expedite claim processing. The map in Figure 2.3.2, for example, was generated for the Indian state of Madhya Pradesh for the period 15–30 October, indicating crop stress at the district level. Similar maps are generated twice a month for Indian states that are covered by crop insurance programs.

Figure 2.3.2 Madhya Pradesh state crop stress map

Spatial information systems can help insurance programs rapidly assess crop damage and expedite settlement claims.

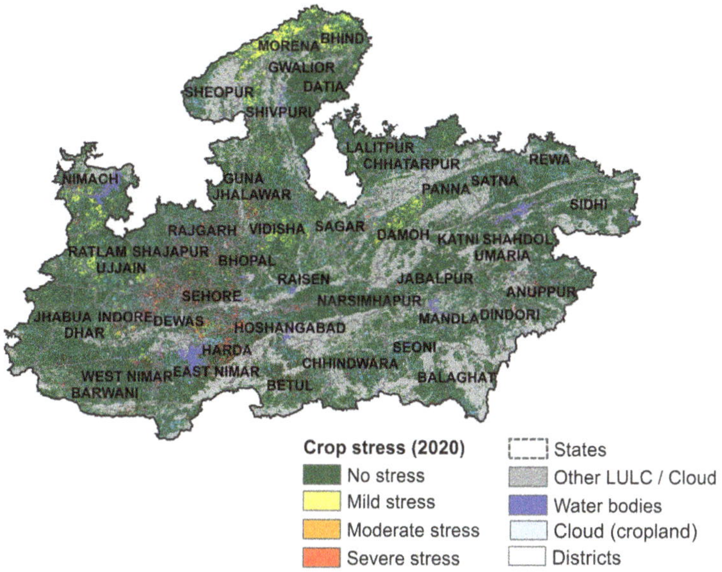

Note: The crop stress map for Madhya Pradesh state on 30 October 2020 shows crop stress by district over the past 15 days. "Other LULC/Cloud" means other land use and land cover or unable to identify land use due to heavy cloud. "Cloud (cropland)" means identified as cropland with unspecified crop stress due to heavy cloud.

Source: M. K. Gumma et al. 2019. Mapping Drought-Induced Changes in Rice Area in India. *International Journal of Remote Sensing* 40(21): 8146–8173.

India's past crop insurance schemes have encountered several problems. The problems include lack of transparency, high premiums, delay in conducting crop-cutting experiments to gauge yield, and absent or delayed payment of claims to farmers. Aware of the limitations of its previous crop insurance schemes, the Government of India launched in 2016 a new crop insurance scheme called Pradhan Mantri Fasal Bima Yojana (PMFBY) (Roy et al. 2018). Its establishment was intended to bring greater transparency and effective implementation, particularly in terms of quick and accurate compensation to farmers for the damage incurred.

PMFBY faced several implementation challenges, especially during its first year of implementation. One was delayed submission of yield data, which were unreliable as they were drawn from thousands of crop-cutting experiments. As a result, state government payment of premium subsidies was delayed. Quick processing and payment of insurance claims require quick and reliable assessment of crop damage. Despite its initial problems, PMFBY has succeeded in increasing insurance coverage from fiscal year 2016 to fiscal year 2017: in terms of area by 5.6%, the number of farmers covered by 20.4%, the sum insured by 74%, and premiums paid by 298%.

2.3.3 Value chains evolve as farmers diversify into high-value crops

The production of high-value crops such as fruit and vegetables have expanded to meet growing demand. Fruit and vegetables currently provide 32% of production value in agriculture, while cereal crops provide only 26%. Today, the PRC, India, and Indonesia are in that order the top three producers of fruit and vegetables in developing Asia, but some other economies are catching up. Commercialization and market integration in food systems have accelerated these shifts in agricultural production shares. Food supply chains have shifted away from being local and fragmented toward broader geographic integration. The transformation of value chains has featured the rapid rise of supermarkets, modern cold storage facilities, and the food-processing industry, as well as the formation of commercialized producers using input-intensive, mechanized agriculture. Information technology has likewise been adopted, as discussed below, to facilitate more efficient processing and distribution of food products and to ensure their quality and safety.

Rising volumes of high-value agricultural products have been produced and marketed through contract farming (Otsuka, Nakano, and Takahashi 2016). Contract farming has become a widely used production and procurement arrangement for various crops in Asia (Table 2.3.2). It can benefit both farmers and contractors. A contract with advance agreement on output prices can provide price stability, and the established business relationship facilitates the provision to farmers of technical assistance, access to credit, new technologies, and ultimately new markets. For farmers, contract farming is a step away from subsistence farming toward market integration. For contractors, contract farming helps ensure greater and more stable supplies of a given commodity with better quality than is available from spot-market procurement. Working with several neighboring farmers helps contractors overcome constraints imposed by small individual plots.

Table 2.3.2 Case studies of contract farming in Asia

Economy	Crops	Number of Studies	Notes
PRC	Fruit and vegetables	3	Reduction in transaction cost, price stability, and access to markets attract farmers; mixed evidence on farm size; product quality attracts processors
	Multiple crops	1	Contract enforcement mechanisms influence growers' decisions
India	Fruit and vegetables	4	Mixed evidence on welfare effects; risk perception, irrigation, extension services, and access to formal credit attract farmers
	Rice	3	Contract enforcement mechanisms influence farmer performance
	Commercial crops	2	Access to inputs on credit attracts farmers
	Poultry and dairy	2	Positive effect on farmer welfare
Indonesia	Palm oil	2	Greater participation among large farmers
	Cereal crops	1	Greater participation among large farmers; mixed evidence regarding return on capital
Nepal	Multiple crops	3	Positive effect on income and productivity
Pakistan	Rice	1	Stabilize farmers' income; large farmers prefer spot markets
	Maize and potato	1	Mixed evidence on income effect
Philippines	Tobacco	1	Greater participation among small farmers; positive effect on income
Viet Nam	Rice	1	Output price and profit attract farmers
	Dairy	2	Third-party quality checks effective

PRC = People's Republic of China.

Source: M. Bellemare. 2017. Contract Farming. Background paper for *Asian Development Outlook 2021 Update*. Asian Development Bank.

Contract farming allows product specialization, which boosts productivity and efficiency, benefiting farmers and contractors alike.

Contract farming can be an effective policy instrument for leveraging agricultural development. A review of studies on contract farming in Asia summarizes the types of farmers who participate, what they produce, and the welfare benefits that accrue to them (Bellemare 2021). While participation in contract farming is popularly associated with large farmers, the actual evidence is mixed (Table 2.3.2). A study on contract farming in Punjab, Pakistan, found that contract farming was more prevalent among medium-sized farmers, as larger farmers who are able to manage considerable risk usually found spot markets more attractive (Dhillon and Singh 2006). Another study found that large palm oil farmers tend to participate in contract farming more than small farmers do (Cahyadi and Waibel 2013). Other studies of multiple crops showed mixed evidence on the relationship between contract farming participation and landholding size. Several studies showed that contract farming can increase and stabilize farmers' income and productivity (Table 2.3.2). It should be noted that contract farming studies reviewed here come from only a handful of economies and may not be representative of actual practice in contract farming across developing Asia.

However, contract disputes often occur due to unclear agreements and lack of contract enforcement mechanisms. Studies highlight contract problems arising from noncompliance on both sides. Noncompliance by farmers includes diverting inputs for contracted products to other uses and selling on the side. Under a contract, a contractor may provide inputs to produce the contracted crop. However, when farmers find higher returns from using the inputs for other crops, they may divert their use to these other crops. Side selling happens when farmers find other buyers who offer a higher price for the contracted crop. On the contractor side, noncompliance may occur when they change their contract terms after signing. Output prices may unexpectedly decline, for instance, or food safety requirements in intended export markets may change. In these situations, contractors may refuse to process transactions, leaving farmers with unsold products or not paying for them. Third party quality assessments can yield better results. On contract enforcement for milk production in Viet Nam, an experimental study showed that having independent quality assessments by third parties encourages farmers to use 12% more inputs and increase their output. This finding highlights the positive influence of independent quality assessments on farmers' performance. This is similar to the use of a mobile phone app to assess the quality of shrimps, as discussed in Box 2.2.5.

The capacity of local agencies to monitor contract farming practices, as well as enforce contracts need to be strengthened. Contract disputes between producers and contracting agents, as discussed above, have possible implications for food safety such as chemical residues in agricultural products, and for environmental damage caused by chemical inputs. To realize the full potential of contract farming, better monitoring of contract farming practices is important. COVID-19 lockdowns and the resulting market disruption affecting the marketing of high-value crops in 2020 provide a vivid illustration. Uncertainty caused by market disruption could have been mitigated by contract farming, under which the costs would have been shared by producers and buyers.

2.3.4 Digital technologies to promote inclusive growth

In recent years, digital technologies have helped farmers in remote areas acquire both technical and market information. They provide tools to collect, store, analyze, and share information more quickly. Big data analytics, the Internet of Things, and sensors can collect real-time data and perform advanced analytics on crops to provide farmers and other actors in value chains with insights and access to data to help them make good decisions. Agricultural extension services and private dealers use mobile technologies to connect with farmers and promote new practices and products.

Many mobile phone applications have been developed to help farmers adopt good agricultural practices. Ranging from simple offline advisory videos for farmers to complex systems for precision agriculture and distributed ledger technologies for value chain traceability, digital technologies can help boost technical efficiency and farm profits, enhance climate resilience, and improve environmental sustainability. However, farmers' use of digital technologies is still limited, leaving large potential gains unexploited. Further, access to mobile phone and internet services remains unequal between men and women in low- and middle-income economies, though the gap is narrowing (GSMA 2021).

Data-driven innovation can reduce transaction costs by improving efficiency and transparency (De Clercq, Vats, and Biel 2018). Conventional food supply chains comprise many transactions between different stakeholders including wholesalers and intermediaries for sales of commodities, equipment, and processed goods. These transactions generate costs as every additional player demands a share of the profit, and every additional transaction increases the risk of fraud. Further, digital technologies can improve productivity on the farm by (i) optimizing the use of machinery and equipment, (ii) facilitating the acquisition of the skills and knowledge needed for agricultural production, and (iii) providing accurate, timely, and location-specific information on prices, weather, and agronomic conditions.

Sensor technologies, big data analytics, and blockchain technology are increasingly being used. These technologies can monitor and analyze climate conditions and initiate mitigation measures. Remote sensing, spectral analysis, and blockchain technology help researchers, policy makers, and businesses monitor, analyze, and initiate investment and other action to conserve and manage landscapes and resources such as forests, oceans, and other water resources. Innovators have developed natural capital accounts at the farm or estate level that use information technology to show how farming depends on ecosystem services and affects ecosystems. These services have been developed to inform farmers on the impacts of their farm management on natural capital and on how changing farm management can mitigate these harmful effects. The testing of these services continues.

The digital transformation of food supply chains can overcome information barriers and emerging mobility challenges. Bridging information gaps and equalizing asymmetries between producers and consumers allows stakeholders with different preferences and incentives to work together more effectively, creating opportunities to improve policy for the agro-food sector and opening new market opportunities, particularly for small stakeholders. Asia is witnessing the emergence of innovative digital start-ups focused on transforming food systems.

Digital transformation can help establish more sustainable and resilient agriculture. In the PRC, e-commerce has emerged as a lifeline during the COVID-19 pandemic. E-commerce helped ensure the delivery of food to urban residents in the midst of strict virus-containment restrictions by pairing input suppliers, agricultural producers, and output marketers, and by facilitating logistical support. Beyond enhancing market connectivity and value chain development, digital technologies can be deployed to shrink environmental and climate footprints in food supply chains and strengthen their risk resilience (Box 2.3.2). The safeguarding of consumer health stands to benefit from improved product traceability and integrity, contract certainty, verification of geographic origin, and compliance with sanitary and phytosanitary requirements. Other direct and indirect benefits to consumers are better information on prices and nutritional value and assurances on production practices and environmental and biodiversity impacts.

Box 2.3.1 Stress-tolerant crop varieties

Submergence has been a persistent problem for rainfed lowland rice farmers in South and Southeast Asia. Rice plants have two ways to survive flooding stress: extend their stalks above rising floodwater, or tolerate submergence. Certain rice varieties can survive submergence for several days. In the 1990s, rice scientists examined several rice varieties and identified a single DNA component, named Sub1, that was responsible for submergence tolerance. Sub1 provides tolerance to complete submergence for up to 14 days. Since this discovery, many submergence-tolerant rice varieties have been developed by crossing popular high-yielding rice varieties with Sub1 varieties. Pilot tests have demonstrated benefits from submergence-tolerant rice varieties on farmers' fields in South Asia.

Despite its potential benefits, adoption of submergence-tolerant varieties has been slow. Slow adoption can be explained by their benefit being hidden most of the time. Under normal conditions, farmers observe no additional benefit from submergence-tolerant rice varieties over other popular varieties, these benefits become apparent only after plants are submerged for longer than most varieties can tolerate. A recent study in Bangladesh by Yamano et al. (2018) found that the adoption of submergence-tolerant rice varieties increased among neighbors of early adopters only after flooding occurred in their area. To encourage farmers to adopt submergence-tolerant or other crops with hidden benefits, including nutrition-enhanced crops, campaigns are needed to disseminate this information to farmers.

Avoiding heat can help crops to be tolerant against drought and heat. Many crops for drought-prone areas are bred for early maturity to avoid heat during their growth periods. However, this trait is generally associated with lower grain yield because plants have less time to grow panicles, prompting crop scientists to search for alternative traits and help them to identify one candidate. Rice plants are sensitive to high temperature as they flower. Exposure to high temperature during flowering can greatly decrease pollen viability, which causes yield loss. If rice plants start flowering early in the morning, when the temperature is low, they can avoid reduced pollen viability. Crop scientists have found rice varieties that open flowers early in the morning and identified the DNA components that are responsible for this characteristic (Hirabayashi et al. 2015). Rice varieties that flower early in the morning and have other desired traits such as high yield and good eating quality have been developed and tested in India and Myanmar.

Sources:

Hirabayashi, H. et al. 2015. qEMF3, a Novel QTL for the Early-Morning Flowering Trait from Wild Rice, Oryza Officinalis, to Mitigate Heat Stress Damage at Flowering in Rice, O. Sativa. *Journal of Experimental Botany* 66(5).

Yamano, T. et al. 2018. Neighbors Follow Early Adopters under Stress: Panel Data Analysis of Submergence-Tolerant Rice in Northern Bangladesh. *Agricultural Economics* 49(3).

Box 2.3.2 Agricultural e-commerce in the PRC

The recent development of agricultural e-commerce in the People's Republic of China (PRC) follows three models. The first uses nationwide e-commerce platforms for online sales of fresh agricultural products to consumers, serving as major channels with wide market scope and large transaction volume. These platforms offer a full range of agricultural products suitable for shipping long distances. As the entry barrier for merchants is low and competition is fierce, price remains the main basis of competition. The second model has local governments organizing agriculture e-commerce using third-party platforms. In this model, merchants must obtain government permission to enter the platform, which guarantees to some extent the quality of the agricultural products on offer. The third model uses unofficial social network channels that are active in agricultural e-commerce. Transaction volume is relatively small, but this model has potential for growth because of interpersonal trust and the convenience that social networks offer.

Traditional vegetable supply chains have many weaknesses, both upstream and down. Each intermediary link—connecting producers, farmers' brokers, wholesale markets in production areas, wholesale markets in sales areas, and vendors in the vegetable market—incurs costs that increase final food prices. Because of information asymmetry in traditional vegetable supply chains, farmers often grow produce without good information on market demand. Farmers' brokers must cope with unstable vegetable supply as farmers produce blindly and with fluctuating selling prices to wholesalers. Wholesalers and vegetable vendors bear such logistics expenses as trucking costs, loading and unloading charges, and the labor costs involved. Moreover, wholesalers and vendors pay booth or entry fees for the right to trade in a market.

E-commerce can help vegetable supply chains address their weaknesses. For instance, Songxiaocai, a business-to-business trading platform for vegetables, innovatively tackled supply chain problems. Songxiaocai designed a demand-driven supply chain informed and underpinned by advanced information technology and has positioned itself as a one-stop intermediary connecting producers to final consumers and eliminating some of the middlemen in traditional vegetable supply chains. Small vendors and wholesalers place orders through one of the mobile applications maintained by Songxiaocai. Specific orders from vendors and wholesalers allow producers to prepare accurate deliverables to meet specified demand. Standardized products are packaged and transported directly to end users, thus improving product quality and reducing the lead time required for unpacking shipments and sorting them at various stages along a traditional supply chain. Through Songxiaocai, vendors in the same area may choose to order products from the same supplier and pool their orders. Vendors thus strengthen their bargaining power in price negotiations and stabilize the quality of the produce they buy.

Sources:

Guo, H. et al. 2020. The Role of E-commerce in the Urban Food System under COVID-19: Lessons from China. *China Agricultural Economic Review* 13(2). https://doi.org/10.1108/CAER-06-2020-0146.

Yao, Y. et al. 2019. How to Become a System Integrator Streamlining Vegetable Supply Chains: The Case of Songxiaocai Company. *International Food and Agribusiness Management Review* 22(4). DOI: 10.22434/IFAMR2018.0115.

2.4 Policies need to shift toward transforming agriculture in Asia

Government policies toward agriculture need to evolve to meet new challenges. This chapter has discussed many of the challenges facing agriculture in Asia in its ability to provide nutritious and diverse food, while ensuring environmental sustainability and climate resilience. At the same time, several opportunities have emerged, sometimes with private sector involvement, and with the application of new technologies and practices. Agriculture policy in the region needs to be reoriented to meet these challenges by fully exploiting these new opportunities.

First, subsidies and other producer support programs often distort market incentives and can spur overproduction. Such policies often fail to provide consistent incentives to preserve natural capital or support sustainable production. Subsidies for chemical inputs can lead to pollution of soil and the surrounding environment that can cause health problems for farmers and consumers. Direct support for producers can also distort incentives and encourage misallocation of resources away from more productive use.

Second, resource-intensive agricultural production requires monitoring and better regulation to protect the environment and consumers. Production of livestock and high-value crops requires intensive use of natural resources and chemical inputs. In addition, rice production on irrigated land and livestock production emit high levels of greenhouse gases. The rapid expansion of aquaculture can cause deforestation of mangroves and raises concerns over land and water pollution and food safety. To monitor and reduce adverse environmental effects from resource-intensive agricultural and aquaculture production, policy makers must account for these impacts when crafting agricultural policies. Well-designed regulations, effective monitoring programs on chemical contaminations in soil, water, and agricultural products, and enforcement programs to reduce contamination need to be put in place to safeguard the environment and ensure food safety for consumers.

Third, governments need to modernize agricultural laws and regulations to provide an enabling environment for farmers and business agents. Agricultural processers and traders offer contracts to farmers with advance pricing, technical assistance, and access to markets, which have the potential to benefit both farmers and traders.

However, unclear agreements and contract enforcement mechanisms often lead to contract disputes and prevent farmers and traders from fully benefiting from such services. Agricultural laws and regulations need to be modernized so that agricultural business agents can engage in innovative arrangements that stimulate agricultural development.

Fourth, investments are needed for climate-resilient agricultural infrastructure and support systems to mitigate impacts from weather shocks. Climate-resilient agriculture infrastructure and practices, early warning systems, and crop insurance can all help to mitigate negative impacts of weather shocks at various stages. For example, investments in early warning systems and other complementary programs, such as building cyclone shelters or providing cash assistance to stock emergency goods, can mitigate damage to rural communities. These investments need to increase as more frequent and devastating weather shocks are expected due to climate change. Because they have a public good element—the benefits accrue to a wide range of participants—the public sector has an important role to play in assuring or encouraging adequate provision. But such investments in support systems could be pursued in collaboration with private agents, who may already be providing similar services and who are often more familiar with the latest technological advances. Many private firms are already involved in crop insurance and weather forecasting, for example, and tapping their expertise could be helpful. More generally, agricultural policies need to shift toward support for innovation, market development, and fostering effective business ecosystems with updated regulations.

Finally, instead of direct producer support, economies in developing Asia need to focus more on supporting market-oriented development by encouraging innovation and investing in research and development (R&D). Economies in developing Asia depend on technology transfer from developed economies through public research networks and private companies. However, public research funds from international organizations and other development partners have declined in recent years. Private research funds are oriented toward commercial agricultural products for which demand is high from consumers in developed economies. As discussed above, Asian agriculture faces serious challenges and needs improved technologies. In the last decades, scientists have made many discoveries, such as identifying DNA components associated with drought tolerance. However, it will take further R&D to adapt these scientific discoveries into agricultural technologies that farmers can use. Policy makers in the region need to invest in agricultural R&D to help farmers benefit from such scientific discoveries.

Background papers

Akter, S. 2021. Gender Inequality and Food Insecurity in the Asian Food System During the COVID-19 Pandemic. Background paper for *Asian Development Outlook 2021 Update*. Asian Development Bank.

Bellemare, M. 2021. Contract Farming in Asia. Background paper for *Asian Development Outlook Update 2021*. Asian Development Bank.

Gumma, M. 2021. Spatio-temporal Distribution of Croplands Using Earth Observation Data for Decision Making. Background paper for *Asian Development Outlook 2021 Update*. Asian Development Bank.

Kajisa, K. 2021. Contemporary irrigation issues in Asia. Background paper for *Asian Development Outlook 2021 Update*. Asian Development Bank.

Panda, A. 2021. Climate Change and Agricultural Insurance in the Asia and the Pacific Region. Background paper for *Asian Development Outlook 2021 Update*. Asian Development Bank.

Suzuki, A. 2021. Rising Importance of Aquaculture in Asia: Current Status, Issues, and Recommendations. Background paper for *Asian Development Outlook 2021 Update*. Asian Development Bank.

Yamauchi, F. 2021. Changing Farm Size and Agricultural Productivity in Asia. Background paper for *Asian Development Outlook 2021 Update*. Asian Development Bank.

References

Abubakar, S. 2002. *Migrant Labor in Malaysia: Impact and Implications of the Asian Financial Crisis*. East Asian Development Network Regional Project on the Social Impact of the Asian Financial Crisis.

Ahmed, A. et al. 2013. *The Status of Food Security in the Feed the Future Zone and Other Regions of Bangladesh: Results from the 2011–2012 Bangladesh Integrated Household Survey*. International Food Policy Research Institute.

Akter, S. et al. 2016. Gender in Crop Production in Timor-Leste. *Australian Centre for International Agricultural Research Proceedings Series* No. 146.

——. 2017. Women's Empowerment and Gender Equity in Agriculture: A Different Perspective from Southeast Asia. *Food Policy* 69.

Aldaco, R. et al. 2020. Food Waste Management during the Covid-19 Outbreak: A Holistic Climate, Economic and Nutritional Approach. *The Science of the Total Environment* 742.

Amnuaylojaroen, T. and P. Chanvichit. 2019. Projection of Near-Future Climate Change and Agricultural Drought in Mainland Southeast Asia under RCP8.5. *Climate* 155.

Asian Development Bank (ADB). 2019a. *Ending Hunger in Asia and the Pacific by 2030: An Assessment of Investment Requirements in Agriculture*. Manila.

——. 2019b. *Climate-Smart Practices for Intensive Rice-Based Systems in Bangladesh, Cambodia, and Nepal*. Manila.

——. 2019c. *Asian Development Outlook 2019: Strengthening Disaster Resilience*. Manila.

——. 2020a. *Asia's Journey to Prosperity: Policy, Markets, and Technology over 50 Years*. Manila.

——. 2020b. *A Study of Women's Role in Irrigated Agriculture in the Lower Vaksh River Basin, Tajikistan*. Manila.

Bedford, R. 2020. *Patterns of Seasonal Employment of RSE Workers in New Zealand, 1 July 2013–30 June 2017*. Bedford Consulting.

Besley, T. 1995. Nonmarket Institutions for Credit and Risk Sharing in Low-Income Countries. *The Journal of Economic Perspectives* 9(3).

Binswanger, H. 1986. Risk Aversion, Collateral Requirements, and the Markets for Credit and Insurance in Rural Areas. In Hazell, P., C. Pomerada, and A. Valdes, eds. *Crop Insurance for Agricultural Development*. Johns Hopkins University.

Cahyadi, E. and H. Waibel. 2013. Is Contract Farming in the Indonesian Oil Palm Industry Pro-Poor? *Journal of Southeast Asian Economies* 30(1).

Chai, R. et al. 2019. Greenhouse Gas Emissions from Synthetic Nitrogen Manufacture and Fertilization for Main Upland Crops in China. *Carbon Balance and Management* 14(1).

Clarke, D. and S. Dercon. 2016. *Dull Disasters? How Planning Ahead Will Make a Difference*. Washington, DC: World Bank.

Cook, B. et al. 2020. Twenty-First Century Drought Projections in the CMIP6 Forcing Scenarios. *Earth's Future* 8. https://doi.org/10.1029/2019EF001461.

Dai, A. 2010. Drought Under Global Warming: A Review. *Wiley Interdisciplinary Reviews Climate* 2.

De Clercq, M., A. Vats, and A. Biel. 2018. *Agriculture 4.0: The Future of Farming Technology*. Proceedings of the World Government Summit. Dubai, UAE. 11–13 February.

Deryng, D. et al. 2014: Global Crop Yield Response to Extreme Heat Stress under Multiple Climate Change Futures. *Environmental Research Letters* 9.

Dhillon, S. and N. Singh. 2006. Contract Farming in Punjab: An Analysis of Problems, Challenges and Opportunities. *Pakistan Economic and Social Review* 44(1).

Diao, X., H. Takeshima, and X. Zhang. 2020. *An Evolving Paradigm of Agricultural Mechanization Development: How Much Can Africa Learn from Asia?* International Food Policy Research Institute.

Doss, C. et al. 2018. Women in Agriculture: Four Myths. *Global Food Security* 16.

Esguerra, E. F. 1981. An Assessment of the Masagana 99 Credit Subsidy as an Equity Measure. *Philippine Review of Economics* 18 (3–4).

Food and Agriculture Organization of the United Nations (FAO). 1995. *FAO Code of Conduct for Responsible Fisheries*. Rome.

——. 2011. *The State of Food and Agriculture 2010–11: Women in Agriculture, Closing the Gender Gap for Development*. Rome.

——. 2015a. *The Impact of Disasters and Crises on Agriculture and Food Security: 2015*. Rome.

——. 2015b. *The Economic Lives of Smallholder Farmers*. Rome.

——. 2017. *The Impact of Disasters and Crises on Agriculture and Food Security: 2017*. Rome.

——. 2018a. *The Future of Food and Agriculture—Alternative Pathways to 2050*. Rome.

——. 2018b. *Mongolia, Impact of Early Warning Early Action*. Rome.

——. 2019. *The State of Food and Agriculture 2019: Moving Forward on Food Loss and Waste Reduction*. Rome.

——. 2020a. *State of Food and Agriculture in Asia and the Pacific Region, including Future Prospects and Emerging Issues*. Thirty-fifth Session of the FAO Regional Conference for Asia and the Pacific. Rome.

——. 2020b. *Migrant Workers and the COVID-19 Pandemic*. Rome. https://doi.org/10.4060/ca8559en.

——. 2021a. *Hunger and Food Insecurity*. Rome. http://www.fao.org/hunger/en.

——. 2021b. *The Impact of Disasters and Crises on Agriculture and Food Security: 2021*. Rome.

FAO et al. 2006. *International Principles for Responsible Shrimp Farming*. FAO and Network of Aquaculture Centres in Asia-Pacific.

Food Planning and Monitoring Unit (FPMU). 2020. *Bangladesh Second Country Investment Plan Nutrition-Sensitive Food Systems (CIP2 2016–2020) Monitoring Report 2020, July*. Ministry of Food, Government of Bangladesh.

Gao, X. et al. 2018. The Impact of Climate Change Policy on the Risk of Water Stress in Southern and Eastern Asia. *Environmental Research Letters* 13(6).

Ge, F. et al. 2019. Risks of Precipitation Extremes over Southeast Asia: Does 1.5°C or 2°C Global Warming Make a Difference? *Environmental Research Letters* 14(4).

Global System for Mobile Communications Association (GSMA). 2021. *State of the Industry Report on Mobile Money 2021*. GSMA.

Gomes, H. et al. 2020. A Socio-Environmental Perspective on Pesticide Use and Food Production. *Ecotoxicology and Environmental Safety* 197. https://doi.org/10.1016/j.ecoenv.2020.110627.

Grantham-McGregor, S. et al. 2007. Developmental Potential in the First 5 Years for Children in Developing Countries. *Lancet* 369(9555).

Gumma, M. et al. 2020. Agricultural Cropland Extent and Areas of South Asia Derived Using Landsat Satellite 30-M Time-Series Big-Data Using Random Forest Machine Learning Algorithms on the Google Earth Engine Cloud. *GIScience & Remote Sensing* 57(3).

Gumma, M. K., A. Nelson, and T. Yamano. 2019. Mapping Drought-Induced Changes in Rice Area in India. *International Journal of Remote Sensing* 40(21).

Gumma, M. K. et al. 2018. Mapping Cropland Fallow Areas in Myanmar to Scale Up Sustainable Intensification of Pulse Crops in the Farming System. *GIScience & Remote Sensing* 55(6).

Guo, X. et al. 2016. Projection of Precipitation Extremes for Eight Global Warming Targets by 17 CMIP5 Models. *Natural Hazards* 84.

Gupta, V. and M. Jain. 2018. Jain Investigation of Multi-Model Spatiotemporal Mesoscale Drought Projections over India under Climate Change Scenario. *Journal of Hydrology* 567.

Hall, D. 2004. Explaining the Diversity of Southeast Asian Shrimp Aquaculture. *Journal of Agrarian Change* 4(3).

Hazell, P. and U. Hess. 2017. Beyond Hype: Another Look at Index-Based Agricultural Insurance. In P. Pangali and G. Feder, eds. *Agriculture and Rural Development in a Globalizing World*. Routledge.

Hedley, D. and S. Tabor. 1989. Fertilizer in Indonesian Agriculture: The Subsidy Issue. *Agricultural Economics* 3(1).

Heong, K., M. Escalada, and V. Mai. 1994. An Analysis of Insecticide Use in Rice: Case Studies in the Philippines and Vietnam. *International Journal of Pest Management* 40(2).

Hickson, M. and A. Julian. 2018. Consequences of Undernutrition. In M. Hickson, S. Smith, and K. Whelan, eds. *Advanced Nutrition and Dietetics in Nutrition Support*. John Wiley & Sons.

Huang, A. et al. 2014. Changes of the Annual Precipitation over Central Asia in the Twenty-First Century Projected by Multimodels of CMIP5. *Journal of Climate* 27.

Intergovernmental Panel on Climate Change (IPCC). 2018. *Global Warming of 1.5°C: An IPCC Special Report on the Impacts of Global Warming of 1.5°C Above Pre-Industrial Levels and Related Global Greenhouse Gas Emission Pathways, in the Context of Strengthening the Global Response to the Threat of Climate Change, Sustainable Development, and Efforts to Eradicate Poverty*. IPCC.

International Diabetes Federation (IDF). 2019. *IDF Diabetes Atlas, 9th Edition*.

International Labour Organization (ILO). 2019. *Working on a Warmer Planet: The Impact of Heat Stress on Labour Productivity and Decent Work*. Geneva.

Jie, J. et al. 2019. Future Changes in Precipitation Over Central Asia Based on CMIP6 Projections. *Environmental Research Letters* 15(5).

Kajisa, K. 2012. The Double Tragedy of Irrigation Systems in Tamil Nadu, India: Assessment of the Replacement of Traditional Systems by Private Wells. *Water Policy* 14.

Kajisa, K. et al. 2018. Lessons from Volumetric Water Pricing Trials at the Three Surface Irrigation Systems in Northern Luzon, Philippines. *DLSU Business & Economic Review* 28(1).

Kajisa, K. and B. Dong. 2017. The Effect of Volumetric Pricing Policy on Farmers' Water Management Institutions and Their Water Use: The Case of Water User Organization in an Irrigation System in Hubei, China. *World Bank Economic Review* 31(1).

Kajisa, K., K. Palanisami, and T. Sakurai. 2007. Effects on Poverty and Equity of the Decline in the Collective Tank Irrigation Management in Tamil Nadu, India. *Agricultural Economics* 36(3).

Kaur, A. 2010. Labour Migration Trends and Policy Challenges in Southeast Asia. *Policy and Society* 29(4).

Kementerian Keuangan. 2019. *APBN 2019 (2019 Budget)*. Ministry of Finance, Republic of Indonesia. https://www.kemenkeu.go.id/apbn2019.

Kimura, S. 2021. China Agricultural Institutional Reform. Background paper for *Asian Development Outlook 2021 Update*. Asian Development Bank.

Kraaijenbrink P. et al. 2017. Impact of a Global Temperature Rise of 1.5 Degrees Celsius on Asia's Glaciers. *Nature* 549.

Kruijssen, F. et al. 2018. Gender and Aquaculture Value Chains: A Review of Key Issues and Implications for Research. *Aquaculture* 493.

Lesk, C., P. Rowhani, and N. Ramankutty. 2016. Influence of Extreme Weather Disasters on Global Crop Production. *Nature* 529.

Li, P., T. Zhou, and X. Chen. 2018. Water Vapor Transport for Spring Persistent Rains over Southeastern China Based on Five Reanalysis Datasets. *Climate Dynamics* 51.

Liu, D. et al. 2018. Long-term Experimental Drought Combined with Natural Extremes Accelerate Vegetation Shift in a Mediterranean Holm Oak Forest. *Environmental and Experimental* 151.

Liu, Y. et al. 2020. The Intertemporal Evolution of Agriculture and Labor over a Rapid Structural Transformation: Lessons from Vietnam. *Food Policy* 94. https://doi.org/10.1016/j.foodpol.2020.101913.

McKinsey & Company. 2020. *Climate Risk and Response Physical Hazards and Socioeconomic Impacts*.

Madjdian, D. et al. 2018. Socio-Cultural and Economic Determinants and Consequences of Adolescent Undernutrition and Micronutrient Deficiencies in LLMICs: A Systematic Narrative Review. *Annals of the New York Academy of Sciences* 1416(1).

Malapit, H. et al. 2020. Empowerment in Agricultural Value Chains: Mixed Methods Evidence from the Philippines. *Journal of Rural Studies* 76.

Mani, M. et al. 2018. *South Asia's Hotspots: The Impact of Temperature and Precipitation Changes on Living Standards*. Washington, DC: World Bank.

Mohanty, S. et al. 2017. Piloting the Vietnamese Small Farmers, Large Field Scheme in Eastern India. *Rice Today* 16(1).

Naumann, G. et al. 2018. Global Changes in Drought Conditions under Different Levels of Warming. *Geophysical Research Letters* 45(7).

Niroula, T. and G. Thapa. 2005. Impacts and Causes of Land Fragmentation, and Lessons Learned from Land Consolidation in South Asia. *Land Use Policy* 22.

Osorio, C. et al. 2011. Who Is Benefiting from Fertilizer Subsidies in Indonesia? *World Bank Policy Research Working Paper* No. 5758. Washington, DC: World Bank.

Otsuka, K., Y. Nakano, and K. Takahashi. 2016. Contract Farming in Advanced and Developing Countries. *Annual Review of Resource Economics* 8.

Pampolino, M. et al. 2007. Environmental Impact and Economic Benefits of Site-Specific Nutrient Management (SSNM) in Irrigated Rice Systems. *Agricultural Systems* 93.

Panda, A., P. Lambert, and S. Surminski. 2020. Insurance and Financial Services across Developing Countries: An Empirical Study of Coverage and Demand. *Centre for Climate Change Economics and Policy Working Paper/Grantham Research Institute on Climate Change and the Environment Working Paper* No. 367/336. London School of Economics and Political Science.

Pingali, P., C. Marquez, and F. Palis. 1994. Pesticides and Philippine Rice Farmer Health: A Medical and Economic Analysis. *American Journal of Agricultural Economics* 76(3).

Popkin, B. 2001. The Nutrition Transition and Obesity in the Developing World. *Journal of Nutrition* 131(3).

Pulwarty, R. S. and M. V. K. Sivakumar. 2014. Information systems in a changing climate: Early warnings and drought risk management. *Weather and Climate Extremes* 3.

Roy, B. C. et al. 2018. *Performance Evaluation of Pradhan Mantri Fasal Bima Yojana (PMFBY) in West Bengal*. West Bengal Agro-Economic Research Centre.

Searchinger, T. et al. 2019. *Creating a Sustainable Food Future (Final Report)*. World Resources Institute.

Searchinger, T. et al. 2020. *Revising Public Agricultural Support to Mitigate Climate Change*. Washington, DC: World Bank.

Setyanto, P. et al. 2018. Alternate Wetting and Drying Reduces Methane Emission from a Rice Paddy in Central Java, Indonesia without Yield Loss. *Soil Science and Plant Nutrition* 64(1).

Sheffield, J. and E. F. Wood. 2008. Projected Changes in Drought Occurrence under Future Global Warming from Multi-model, Multi-scenario, IPCC AR4 Simulations. *Climate Dynamics* 31(1).

Shi, C. et al. 2017. A Quantitative Analysis of High Temperature Effects during Meiosis Stage on Rice Grain Number per Panicle. *Chinese Journal of Rice Science* 31(6).

Shoji, M. and A. Murata. 2021. Social Capital Encourages Disaster Evacuation: Evidence from a Cyclone in Bangladesh. *Journal of Development Studies* 57.

Shrestha, A. et al. 2020. Climatological Drought Forecasting Using Bias Corrected CMIP6 Climate Data: A Case Study for India. *Forecasting* 2(2).

Skees, J. et al. 2004. Can Financial Markets Be Tapped to Help Poor People Cope with Weather Risks? In Darcon, S., ed. *Insurance Against Poverty*. Oxford University Press.

Srisompun, O., T. Athipanyakul, and I. Somporn. 2019. The Adoption of Mechanization, Labour Productivity and Household Income: Evidence from Rice Production in Thailand. *TVSEP Working Paper* No. 16. Leibniz Universität Hannover, Thailand Vietnam Socio Economic Panel.

State Administration for Market Regulation. 2020. In Y. Xue, K. Mao, N. Weeks, and J. Xiao. 2021. Rural Reform in Contemporary China: Development, Efficiency, and Fairness. *Journal of Contemporary China* 30(128).

Surminski, S., A. Panda, and P. Lampert. 2019. Disaster Insurance in Developing Asia: An Analysis of Market-Based Schemes. *Economics Working Paper Series* No. 590. Manila: ADB.

Suryana, A. 2019. *Fertilizer Subsidy and Retail Price Policies to Support Food and Nutrition Security in Indonesia*. Food and Fertilizer Technology Center for the Asian and Pacific Region.

Suzuki, A. 2021. A Short Note on the Asian Aquaculture. Background paper for *Asian Development Outlook 2021 Update*. Asian Development Bank.

Taylor, M., A. McGregor, and B. Dawson, eds. 2016. *Vulnerability of Pacific Island Agriculture to Climate Change*. Pacific Community.

Trombetti, A. et al. 2016. Age-Associated Declines in Muscle Mass, Strength, Power, and Physical Performance: Impact on Fear of Falling and Quality of Life. *Osteoporosis International* 27.

United Nations Department of Economic and Social Affairs (UN DESA). 2019. *World Population Prospects 2019 Online Edition (Revision 1)*. New York. https://population.un.org/wpp/Download/Standard/Population/.

United Nations Environment Programme (UNEP). 2021. *Food Waste Index Report*. https://www.unep.org/resources/report/unep-food-waste-index-report-2021.

Verhaegen, P. and T. Salthouse. 1997. Meta-Analyses of Age-Cognition Relations in Adulthood: Estimates of Linear and Nonlinear Age Effects and Structural Models. *Psychological Bulletin* 122(3).

Wang, T. et al. 2021. Atmospheric Dynamic Constraints on Tibetan Plateau Freshwater under Paris Climate Targets. *Nature Climate Change* 11.

Wang, Y. et al. 2019. Research Progress on Heat Stress of Rice at Flowering Stage. *Rice Science* 26.

Wickramasekara, P. 2020. *Malaysia: Review of Admission and Recruitment Practices of Indonesian Workers in the Plantation and Domestic Work Sectors and Related Recommendations*. International Labour Organization.

Willer, H. et al. eds. 2021. *The World of Organic Agriculture, Statistics and Emerging Trends 2021*. Research Institute of Organic Agriculture and International Federation of Organic Agriculture Movements (Organics International).

World Bank. 2016. Health and Communicable Diseases. *Pacific Possible Background Paper* No. 5. Washington, DC: World Bank.

World Health Organization (WHO). 2014. *Global Nutrition Targets 2025: Childhood Overweight Policy Brief*. Geneva.

——. 2021. WHO Global Anaemia estimates, 2021 Edition. https://www.who.int/data/gho/data/themes/topics/anaemia_in_women_and_children.

World Resources Institute. 2019. *Reducing Food Loss and Waste: Setting a Global Action Agenda*. https://doi.org/10.46830/wrirpt.18.00130

Yamano, T. et al. 2018. Neighbors Follow Early Adopters under Stress: Panel Data Analysis of Submergence-Tolerant Rice in Northern Bangladesh. *Agricultural Economics* 49(3).

Zhai, J. et al. 2020. Future Drought Characteristics through a Multi-Model Ensemble from CMIP6 over South Asia. *Atmospheric Research* 246.

Zhang, M., M. Zeiss, and S. Geng. 2015. Agricultural Pesticide Use and Food Safety: California's Model. *Journal of Integrative Agriculture* 14(11).

3

ECONOMIC TRENDS
AND PROSPECTS
IN DEVELOPING ASIA

Central Asia

Most economies in Central Asia are recovering more swiftly than expected from downturns in 2020 caused by the COVID-19 pandemic. Accordingly, combined subregional growth projections for 2020 and 2021 are raised from forecasts published in April in *Asian Development Outlook 2021*. With strong recovery in domestic demand, subregional inflation projections are also raised for both years, and the current account deficit for 2022 is now projected to be wider than forecast in April.

Subregional assessment and prospects

With continued economic recovery from the pandemic, projected growth in Central Asia this year is revised up from 3.4% in *Asian Development Outlook 2021* (*ADO 2021*) to 4.1% in this *Update* (Figure 3.1.1). The forecast for 2022 is raised from 4.0% to 4.2%. The revised outlook reflects buoyant performance in the first half of 2021 in most countries in the subregion. The growth outlook in 2021 improves for five of eight countries: Armenia, Azerbaijan, Georgia, Kazakhstan, and Uzbekistan. For 2022, growth projections have been adjusted upward for four: Armenia, Georgia, Kazakhstan, and Uzbekistan. However, many countries in Central Asia have been hit by a strong new wave of the virus, and some have reimposed movement restrictions. These developments pose risks to growth prospects, as does slow progress in vaccination.

Among hydrocarbon exporters, Azerbaijan grew by 2.1% in the first 6 months of 2021 on gains outside of the hydrocarbon industry and higher net exports. The 2021 growth forecast for Azerbaijan is therefore raised from 1.9% in *ADO 2021* to 2.2% in this *Update*. In Kazakhstan, the economy expanded by 2.3% in the first half of 2021. In view of supportive fiscal policy and rising commodity prices, its growth projections are raised from 3.2% to 3.4% for 2021 and from 3.5% to 3.7% for 2022. Uzbekistan recorded particularly strong growth at 6.2% in the first half of 2021, with gains of 8.5% in industry and 8.0% in services. Its growth projections are thus revised up from 4.0% to 5.0% for 2021 and from 5.0% to 5.5% for 2022.

Figure 3.1.1 GDP growth in Central Asia

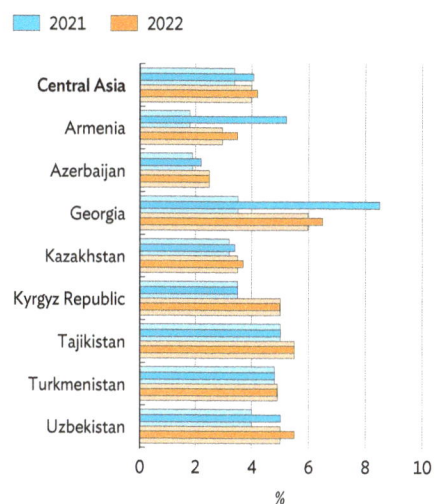

GDP = gross domestic product.
Note: Lighter colored bars are *Asian Development Outlook 2021* forecasts.
Source: *Asian Development Outlook* database.

The subregional assessment and prospects were written by Kenji Takamiya. Kazakhstan was written by Genadiy Rau, and the other economies by Muhammadi Boboev, Begzod Djalilov, Grigor Gyurjyan, Jennet Hojanazarova, George Luarsabishvili, Gulkayr Tentieva, and Nail Valiyev. All authors are in the Central and West Asia Department of ADB.

Several hydrocarbon importers also enjoyed robust growth. Notably, Georgia's economy grew by 12.7% in the first half of 2021 with recovery in all sectors, prompting upward revisions to its growth forecasts from 3.5% to 8.5% for 2021 and from 6.0% to 6.5% for 2022. Armenia's economy expanded by 4.9% in the first half of 2021, with gains in all sectors and in both consumption and investment. Its growth projections are thus revised up from 1.8% to 5.2% for 2021 and from 3.0% to 3.5% for 2022. Despite growth in Tajikistan accelerating to 8.7% in the first half of 2021, this *Update* retains April growth forecasts in light of uncertain prospects for containing the pandemic, weak remittances, and a slowdown affecting a major public investment project. The economy of the Kyrgyz Republic contracted by 1.7% in the first 6 months of 2021; this *Update* retains earlier projections for growth this year and next.

Inflation in the first 6 months of 2021 was higher than in the same period of 2022 in most Central Asian countries. The factors pushing up inflation vary but generally include strong recovery in aggregate demand, currency depreciation, and higher prices for food and other commodities. Inflation projections for the subregion as a whole are raised from 6.8% to 7.7% for 2021 and from 6.3% to 6.7% for 2022 (Figure 3.1.2). Seven countries with higher projections for inflation in 2021 are Armenia, Azerbaijan, Georgia, Kazakhstan, the Kyrgyz Republic, Tajikistan, and Turkmenistan. This list for 2022 does not include Azerbaijan or the Kyrgyz Republic.

With domestic demand recovering in most subregional economies, this *Update* maintains April projections for the aggregate current account deficit in 2021 at the equivalent of 1.2% of GDP but raises it to 1.6% in 2022 (Figure 3.1.3). Larger deficits are forecast for Uzbekistan in 2021 and 2022 and, with deficits in services and primary income expected to persist, also for Kazakhstan in 2022. For Turkmenistan a narrower surplus is projected in 2021 and now a deficit in 2022. Azerbaijan, on the other hand, saw its current account surplus reach 5.6% of GDP in the first quarter of 2021, and this upward trend is expected to continue with relatively high oil prices. The prospect of sharply rising oil export earnings motivates upward revisions to Azerbaijan's projected current account surpluses from 3.9% of GDP to 7.0% in 2021 and from 5.5% to 8.1% in 2022. In both Georgia and Tajikistan, higher exports call for narrower current account deficit forecasts than in *ADO 2021*.

Figure 3.1.2 Inflation in Central Asia

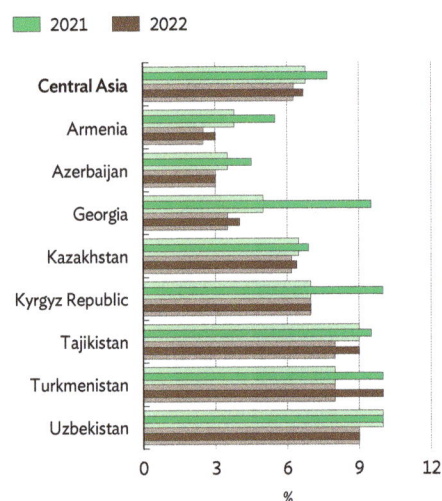

Note: Lighter colored bars are *Asian Development Outlook 2021* forecasts.
Source: *Asian Development Outlook* database.

Figure 3.1.3 Current account balances in Central Asia

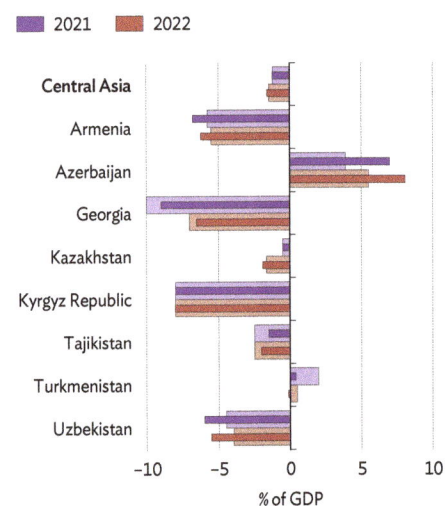

GDP = gross domestic product.
Note: Lighter colored bars are *Asian Development Outlook 2021* forecasts.
Source: *Asian Development Outlook* database.

Kazakhstan

GDP saw gains in services and industry in the first half of 2021, but they were limited by the slow pace of easing quarantine measures. This *Update* marginally raises projected growth in 2021 and 2022, assuming a pickup in vaccinations but with new COVID-19 variants posing downside risks to the outlook. Higher inflation projections for both years reflect higher commodity prices and rising real incomes resulting from expansionary fiscal policy. The forecast for the current account deficit is unchanged for 2021 but marginally widened for 2022 as faster growth boosts imports.

Updated assessment

In contrast to contraction by 1.8% recorded in the first half of 2020, the economy expanded at an annual rate of 2.3% in the first half of this year. Services rebounded from 5.6% decline with 1.7% growth as pent-up demand boosted consumption, raising wholesale and retail trade by 8.5% (Figure 3.1.4). However, COVID-19 travel restrictions and quarantine measures continued to restrain growth in transportation, hospitality, and catering. Industry rose by 1.3% as fiscal support and import-substitution programs helped manufacturing expand by 5.6%. Mining declined by 3.0% as oil and gas production fell by 5.3% to meet production cuts agreed with the Organization of the Petroleum Exporting Countries and other major oil producers (OPEC+). Growth in construction remained strong at 11.9%, benefiting from state housing and infrastructure programs and legislative changes that permit some pension funds to finance housing. Agriculture expanded by 3.2% as livestock production grew by 3.4% and crops by 0.2%.

Demand-side data, available for only the first quarter of 2021, show consumption expanding by 4.6% as private consumption grew by 3.7% and public by 8.3%. Strong housing and infrastructure spending boosted investment by 3.4%. Net exports declined as exports fell more than imports. Prolonged quarantine restrictions raised the unemployment rate marginally to 4.9%, driving labor force participation from 66.4% in the first quarter of 2020 down to 65.8% (Figure 3.1.5). Real wages rose by 7.4%, with health care and social workers' salaries surging by 21.0%, and teachers' salaries by 15.9%.

In the first half of 2021, state budget expenditure was 10.1% higher than a year earlier as government spending rose by 18.1% for education, 11.9% for health care, and 8.6% for social assistance. In the first 6 months of 2021, tax revenue increased by 29.2%, with receipts of corporate income tax rising by 32.6%, value-added tax by 24.4%, and personal income tax by 14.1%. Higher receipts reflected a doubling of oil export duty collection, expanding economic activity, and a phasing out of tax holidays and waivers. Moreover, unprecedented demand for

Figure 3.1.4 Supply-side contributions to growth

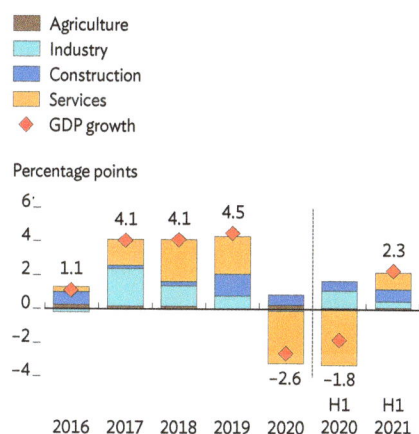

GDP = gross domestic product, H1 = first half.
Source: Republic of Kazakhstan. Agency for Strategic Planning and Reforms. Bureau of National Statistics.

Figure 3.1.5 Unemployment rate

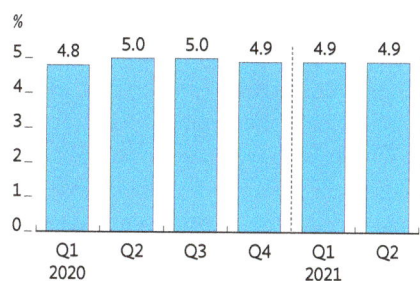

Q = quarter.
Source: Republic of Kazakhstan. Agency for Strategic Planning and Reforms. Bureau of National Statistics.

government support to the economy motivated the authorities in May 2021 to draw from the National Fund of the Republic of Kazakhstan, the sovereign wealth fund, an additional amount equal to 1.2% of GDP. This raised the share of state budget revenue from the fund to 30.0%. The state budget deficit equaled 1.6% of GDP in the first half of 2021 (Figure 3.1.6).

Average inflation in the first 7 months of 2021 accelerated from 6.5% in the same period a year earlier to 7.5%, reflecting price increases of 10.6% for food, 6.2% for other goods, and 4.6% for services (Figure 3.1.7). Rising global commodity prices and fiscal stimulus boosted demand, causing shortages of raw materials and low inventories. In July 2021, a survey on inflationary expectations commissioned by the National Bank of Kazakhstan, the central bank, reported responders anticipating further price increases by two to one, an all-time high, and that 89% of responders voiced concern over food prices. The central bank expects inflation to exceed its target of 4%–6% in 2021 before gradually subsiding into the target range in 2022.

In the first half of 2021, monetary policy remained accommodative, the policy rate unchanged at 9.0% since July 2020 despite inflation exceeding the target range. Broad money growth followed a 16.9% surge in the whole of 2020 with 13.0% growth in the first half of 2021 (Figure 3.1.8). In that half, credit expanded by 6.2% and deposits by 13.7%. Lending to firms grew modestly by 4.4%, while consumer credit grew by 13.3% and mortgages by 10.9%. Foreign currency deposits, constituting 38.4% of all deposits, rose by 13.0%, while deposits in Kazakhstan tenge rose by 14.2%. Official figures from the government agency that regulates the financial market show the share of nonperforming loans declining further from 6.9% at the end of 2020 to 4.8% in June 2021.

In the first half of 2021, the tenge remained stable, occasionally appreciating to reflect higher oil prices (Figure 3.1.9). However, its average value against the US dollar was 4.8% lower than in the same period of 2020. The central bank reported no net intervention in the foreign exchange market, but the sovereign wealth fund converted foreign exchange worth $4.3 billion into tenge before transferring the funds to the state budget.

Preliminary central bank estimates for the first half of 2021 indicate a current account deficit of $1.7 billion, equal to 1.0% of GDP, as the trade surplus in goods shrank by 5.9% and foreign investor profit repatriation increased by 42.4%. Merchandise exports increased by 3.4% to $26.9 billion despite a 10.8% drop in oil and gas exports. Merchandise imports expanded by 9.2% to reach $17.5 billion, driven by increases of 27.3% for consumer goods and 36.0% for nonfood products. Foreign direct investment fell by two-thirds to $1.4 billion owing to a global decline in international investment flows.

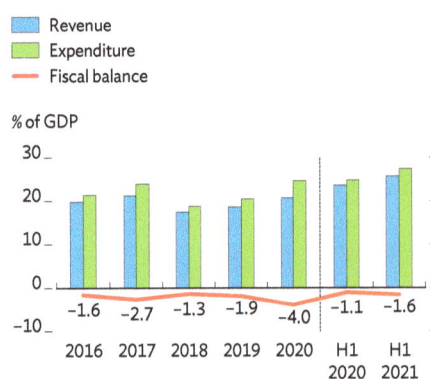

Figure 3.1.6 Fiscal indicators

- Revenue
- Expenditure
- Fiscal balance

% of GDP

GDP = gross domestic product, H1 = first half.
Sources: Ministry of Finance; Ministry of National Economy.

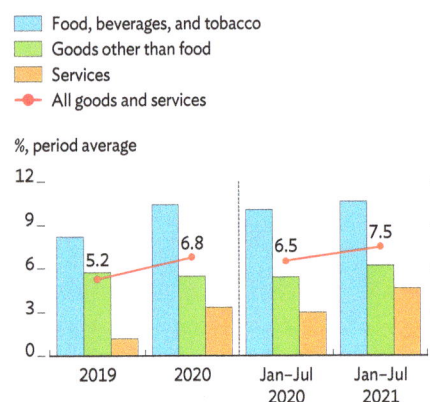

Figure 3.1.7 Average inflation

- Food, beverages, and tobacco
- Goods other than food
- Services
- All goods and services

%, period average

Source: Republic of Kazakhstan. Ministry of National Economy. Statistics Committee.

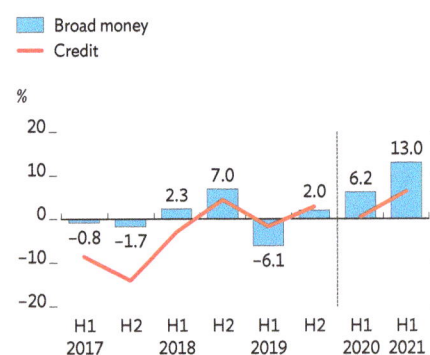

Figure 3.1.8 Broad money and credit growth

- Broad money
- Credit

%

H = half.
Note: Broad money growth refers to change from December of the previous year.
Source: National Bank of the Republic of Kazakhstan.

Gross foreign exchange reserves reached $35.1 billion in June 2021, of which 62.2% was monetary gold. Reserves provided cover for 9.5 months of imports of goods and services. Sovereign wealth fund assets declined slightly to an estimated $57.5 billion despite transfers to the budget being smaller in the year to June than a year earlier (Figure 3.1.10). In the first half of 2021, net receipts into the sovereign wealth fund were one-third of those in the same period of 2020 as lower investment income and declining tax revenue from oil companies outweighed a substantial increase in privatization earnings. External debt at the end of March 2021 reached $164.1 billion, equal to 96.6% of GDP (Figure 3.1.11). Intercompany debt, primarily for oil and gas projects, increased to $100.7 billion, or 59.3% of GDP, with $6.3 billion coming due in 2021. Public sector external debt increased to $36.6 billion, or 21.5% of GDP, with $3.7 billion due in 2021.

Prospects

Kazakhstan gradually removed social distancing and quarantine restrictions until mid-June 2021, when the more contagious Delta coronavirus variant arrived and spurred infection rates. In response, the government reintroduced many quarantine measures while accelerating vaccination efforts. By the end of August 2021, more than 6.6 million people, or 34.9% of the population, had received a first dose of vaccine, and 5.4 million, or 28.2%, were fully vaccinated. The government is on track to administer vaccines to at least two-thirds of the population by the end of 2021.

On the supply side, growth prospects for mining are improving as global demand for commodities recovers and oil production rises in accord with a relaxed cap under the OPEC+ agreement of July 2021. Government infrastructure and manufacturing-support programs are expected to boost the economy. Severe drought weakened the outlook for agriculture in 2021, but additional state support mitigated its impact and should boost activity in 2022. Similarly, growth in services in the second half of 2021 will be limited because of quarantine measures to contain the Delta variant, then accelerate in 2022.

On the demand side, consumption is projected to grow by 2.9% in 2021, benefiting from higher private and public spending. In 2022, consumption growth is forecast to reach 3.2% as real household income growth accelerates further. Total investment will rebound, reflecting substantial government support for housing and infrastructure. Recovering exports are projected to turn net exports of goods and services positive. With growth in consumption accelerating, this *Update* marginally raises projections for growth in both 2021 and 2022 (Table 3.1.1).

Figure 3.1.9 Exchange rate

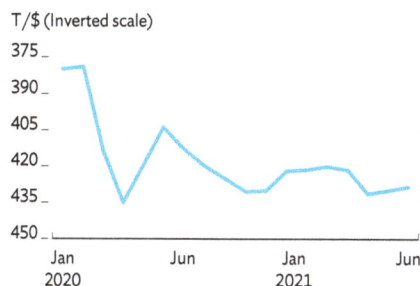

T/$ (Inverted scale)

Source: National Bank of the Republic of Kazakhstan.

Figure 3.1.10 Reserves and assets

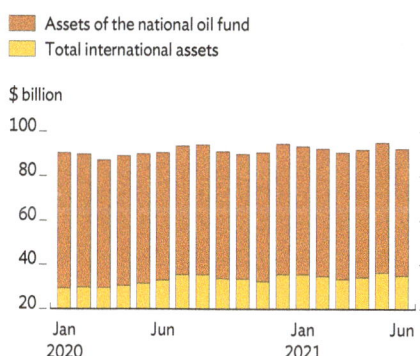

■ Assets of the national oil fund
■ Total international assets

$ billion

Source: National Bank of the Republic of Kazakhstan.

Figure 3.1.11 External and public sector external debt

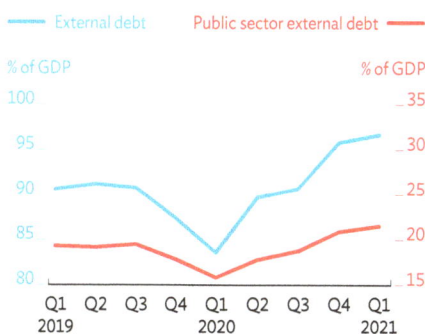

—— External debt   Public sector external debt ——

% of GDP   % of GDP

GDP = gross domestic product, Q = quarter.
Source: National Bank of the Republic of Kazakhstan.

Domestic and external factors alike have raised inflationary pressures. Expansionary fiscal policy has helped raise incomes, while global food price increases have undermined state price controls on staple foods, as the country is a net food importer. Rising oil prices and consumption have put pressure on gasoline prices, which increased by 6.1% in the first half of 2021. Following years of constraint, utility prices rose by 4.5% in the same period. These increases have reverberated through the economy, raising production and transportation costs. To moderate inflationary pressure, the central bank raised the key policy rate by 25 basis points to 9.25% on 26 July 2021 and warned of possible further policy rate increases and measures to absorb excess liquidity and bring inflation within its target range. Nevertheless, this *Update* raises inflation projections for both years, though tighter monetary policy should slow inflation in 2022.

With a May 2021 amendment to the state budget, revenue is now projected to equal 19.4% of GDP, below 19.8% as forecast in *ADO 2021*, reflecting less tax revenue but higher transfers from the sovereign wealth fund. Expenditure is now estimated at 23.5% of GDP, marginally above the *ADO 2021* projection because of higher allocations for social and growth-supporting programs. Thus, the projected 2021 budget deficit is revised from 3.5% of GDP to 4.0%, with the non-oil deficit deepening from 10.3% of GDP to 10.8% to bolster ongoing economic support measures. Public debt is now forecast to exceed the equivalent of 30.3% of GDP at the end of 2021 and moderate to 29.0% at the end of 2022.

Higher commodity prices and export volumes are projected to restore the merchandise trade surplus in 2021 to the pre-crisis high of $25.0 billion, equal to 13.5% of GDP, before it subsides in 2022 with forecast lower oil prices. The forecast for imports is also increased, reflecting higher consumption supported by rising incomes and accelerating economic activity. With deficits in services and primary income expected to persist, this *Update* maintains the current account deficit forecast for 2021 and marginally expands it for 2022. Higher transfers to the budget are now projected to trim sovereign wealth fund assets to $56.5 billion at the end of 2021 before assets rise to $59.0 billion at the end of 2022. Projections for international reserves are raised to $32.0 billion at the end of 2021, or cover for 8.5 months of imports of goods and services, subsiding to $30.5 billion at the end of 2022. External debt including intercompany debt is now forecast at the equivalent of 93.0% of GDP at the end of 2021, revised up from 90.0%, and at 91.0% at the end of 2022, revised up from 85.0%, as Kazakhstan attracts more investment for mining projects and increases overseas borrowing to finance the budget deficit.

Table 3.1.1 Selected economic indicators in Kazakhstan, %

	2020	2021 ADO 2021	2021 Update	2022 ADO 2021	2022 Update
GDP growth	-2.6	3.2	3.4	3.5	3.7
Inflation	6.8	6.5	6.9	6.2	6.4
CAB/GDP	-3.7	-0.5	-0.5	-1.7	-1.9

ADO = *Asian Development Outlook*, CAB = current account balance, GDP = gross domestic product.

Source: Asian Development Bank estimates.

Other economies

Armenia

The economy reversed 5.5% contraction in the first half of 2020 to grow by 4.9% a year later. This marked recovery from a low base but also from multiple economic shocks in the second half of 2020.

On the supply side, all sectors contributed to growth. Agriculture expanded by a strong 7.1% on higher crop production. Services grew by 5.3%, with increases in trade, transportation, food, and administrative and real estate services that outstripped declines in recreation, accommodation, and education services. Construction grew by 5.5%, supported by public infrastructure and private construction. Industry grew by 1.3% as gains in mining and quarrying, electricity generation, and water and waste management more than outweighed a 4.4% decline in manufacturing.

On the demand side, private consumption expanded by 5.4% on higher remittances, and public consumption grew by 3.2% with higher spending on social services. Investment, measured by gross fixed capital formation, surged by 9.5% on higher government and private capital spending. With the economy recovering faster than anticipated, this *Update* raises growth projections for 2021 and 2022 (Table 3.1.2).

Inflation accelerated in the first 7 months of 2021, reflecting recovery in domestic demand, currency depreciation from November 2020 to March 2021, and rebounding global commodity prices. Average annual inflation in the period jumped from 0.7% a year earlier to 6.1%, propelled by increases of 8.5% for food and 8.2% for other goods, with services up 1.9%. Inflation hit 8.2% year on year in July, well above the Central Bank of Armenia target of 2.5%–5.5%. To contain inflation, the central bank gradually raised its benchmark rate by 175 basis points to 7.00% in four steps from December 2020 to August 2021. With inflation in the first half exceeding expectations, this *Update* raises the inflation forecast substantially for 2021 and less so for 2022.

The current account recorded surpluses in services, current transfers, and remittances, as well as a smaller deficit in goods, slashing the overall deficit from the equivalent of 8.9% of GDP in the first quarter of 2020 to 3.4% a year later. The merchandise trade deficit narrowed from 12.4% of GDP to 8.6% as a 13.3% drop in imports outpaced a 1.5% decline in exports. With imports expected to rise more than exports because of increased demand for capital goods to supply investments, the merchandise trade deficit is projected to widen during the rest of 2021. This development should be partly offset by rising remittances from the Russian Federation, higher current transfers, and increased gains from tourism, transportation, and financial services. With increases in both external and domestic demand, this *Update* raises projections for current account deficits in both 2021 and 2022.

Table 3.1.2 Selected economic indicators in Armenia, %

	2020	2021		2022	
		ADO 2021	*Update*	ADO 2021	*Update*
GDP growth	−7.4	1.8	5.2	3.0	3.5
Inflation	1.2	3.8	5.5	2.5	3.0
CAB/GDP	−3.8	−5.8	−6.8	−5.5	−6.2

ADO = *Asian Development Outlook*, CAB = current account balance, GDP = gross domestic product.

Source: Asian Development Bank estimates.

Azerbaijan

The economy reversed 2.7% contraction in the first half of 2020 to grow by 2.1% in the same period of this year. This reflected gains outside of hydrocarbon extraction, where the economy expanded by 5.1% as wage growth and retail sales improved and manufacturing surged by 16.4%, led by food processing and petrochemicals. Services grew by 4.3% on rebounds in transportation as well as retail trade. Growth in agriculture accelerated to 5.6% as crop production expanded by 8.9% and livestock by 2.4%.

As agreed with the Organization of the Petroleum Exporting Countries and other major oil producers, Azerbaijan cut oil production by 3.7%. A further decline occurred because Azerbaijan's main oil platform was closed for maintenance. Hydrocarbons thus shrank by 4.7% despite gas production rising by 8.8% and high oil prices that boosted export earnings. Industry contracted by 1.2% with lower oil production and a 1.1% decline in construction.

On the demand side, higher credit and household income helped lift private consumption by 1.7% in the first half of 2021. Public consumption declined by 1.0% despite continued government support for social services and economic recovery. Subdued investment in major oil and gas projects dragged down total investment, but net exports rose by 12.2% as import volume fell. By mid-August 2021, 23.0% of the population had received a second vaccine dose, facilitating firm reopening and economic revival. With higher oil and gas earnings, rising household income, and stronger domestic demand, this *Update* raises the growth forecast for 2021 while maintaining it for 2022 (Table 3.1.3).

Inflation accelerated from 3.0% year on year in the first half of 2020 to 4.3% in the same period of this year. Prices rose by 4.9% for food, 3.9% for other goods, and 3.5% for services. The main inflation drivers were transport costs driven higher by a rise in fuel tariffs and elevated global prices for food, while the exchange rate held steady. Despite higher inflation, the central bank policy interest rate has remained at 6.25% since December 2020. With inflation higher in the first half, this *Update* raises projected inflation for 2021 but not for 2022, as controlled prices are unlikely to change.

The current account achieved a surplus equal to 5.6% of GDP in the first quarter of 2021. With higher oil prices, the merchandise trade surplus doubled from $1.5 billion in the first half of 2020 to $3.1 billion a year later as exports jumped by 33%. Imports grew by only 5.5%, with machinery, equipment, and metals lower. In the full year, unexpectedly rapid oil price rises should more than offset lower export volume. On balance, this *Update* projects higher current account surpluses in 2021 and 2022.

Table 3.1.3 Selected economic indicators in Azerbaijan, %

	2020	2021		2022	
		ADO 2021	Update	ADO 2021	Update
GDP growth	−4.3	1.9	2.2	2.5	2.5
Inflation	2.8	3.5	4.5	3.0	3.0
CAB/GDP	−0.5	3.9	7.0	5.5	8.1

ADO = *Asian Development Outlook*, CAB = current account balance, GDP = gross domestic product.

Source: Asian Development Bank estimates.

Georgia

Reversing 6.2% contraction a year earlier, economic growth rebounded strongly and broadly to 12.7% year on year in the first half of 2021, with expansion in agriculture, industry including construction, and services including trade, transportation, and finance. Underpinning recovery were significant government support to firms and households and sizable assistance from development partners.

On the demand side, positive contributions to GDP growth came from growth in private consumption, estimated at 5.5%; a 15.0% rise in net exports of food, beverages, and industrial supplies; and public investment spending equal to 8.0% of GDP. Following land border reopening in June 2021, foreign exchange inflow is expected to accelerate, despite less than 14% of the population fully vaccinated and only modest gains in tourism and travel by the end of August. Meanwhile, the unemployment rate rose to 21.9% in the first quarter of 2021, and absolute poverty, using the national poverty line, to 21.3%, each up by about 3 percentage points from 2020 despite the pickup in growth. With encouraging growth figures and optimistic business expectations, this *Update* raises growth projections for 2021 and 2022, despite downside risks from delayed vaccination and new COVID-19 variants (Table 3.1.4).

Inflation averaging 5.2% in 2020 started accelerating in 2021 to reach 11.9% year on year in July 2021. This reflected rapid price increases beginning in March for food, health care, transport, and utilities because of higher import prices, particularly for energy, and the removal of subsidies for certain items, notably utilities. Core inflation, which excludes food, energy, and tobacco, was 6.3% year on year in July, and the producer price index was 15.1% higher, reflecting elevated input costs. After inflation exceeded 7% in March 2021, more than twice the National Bank of Georgia inflation target, the central bank had by August raised the policy rate to 10.0% in three steps. Having depreciated by 5.3% against the US dollar from January to early May, the Georgian lari has since appreciated by about 10% but without taming imported inflation. With inflation accelerating, this *Update* raises inflation forecasts for 2021 and 2022.

The current account deficit narrowed slightly from the equivalent of 11.2% of GDP in the first quarter of 2020 to 10.7% a year later, mainly from higher exports of copper ore and concentrate to the People's Republic of China and of wine and spirits to the Commonwealth of Independent States—and despite higher imports to meet recovering domestic demand. Merchandise exports increased by 25.2%, and merchandise imports by 19.7%. Net income inflow increased, as did current transfers by 40.8%. Accordingly, this *Update* projects faster narrowing of the current account deficit in both 2021 and 2022.

Table 3.1.4 Selected economic indicators in Georgia, %

	2020	2021		2022	
		ADO 2021	*Update*	*ADO 2021*	*Update*
GDP growth	−6.2	3.5	8.5	6.0	6.5
Inflation	5.2	5.0	9.5	3.5	4.0
CAB/GDP	−12.5	−10.0	−9.0	−7.0	−6.5

ADO = *Asian Development Outlook*, CAB = current account balance, GDP = gross domestic product.

Sources: National Statistics Office of Georgia; National Bank of Georgia; Asian Development Bank estimates.

Kyrgyz Republic

The economy shrank by 1.7% in the first half of 2021 as contraction since the second half of 2020 persisted in industry, and despite other sectors slowly starting to recover. Industry retreated from scant 0.1% growth year on year in the first 6 months of 2020 to decline by 10.6% as the production of pharmaceuticals and chemical products and the processing of gold and other metals plunged by 16.2%, though the mining subsector grew by 2.1% on gains in output other than gold. Construction fell by 14.2% as combined public and private investment dropped by 11.8%. Agriculture grew by 1.3% as livestock production rose by 1.5%. Services expanded by 4.8% as trade recovered by 10.0% and transportation by 19.4%, while hospitality contracted by 5.0%.

Growth is expected to recover in the second half of 2021 as mining, trade, and other services bounce back from last year's low base, given a favorable outlook in trade partners. However, the adverse effects of COVID-19 are expected to continue, as borders have not completely reopened, flights and road traffic have not fully resumed, and business confidence remains low. Any recurring pandemic waves or slow vaccine rollout could derail growth. On balance, this *Update* keeps growth projections unchanged for 2021 and 2022 (Table 3.1.5).

In the first half of 2021, average inflation nearly doubled from 5.8% a year earlier to 10.8%. Food price inflation remained high at 11.0% as supply chains were slow to recover and pass-through continued from 20% depreciation of the currency against the US dollar in 2020. To curb inflationary pressure from currency depreciation and manage a floating exchange rate, the National Bank of the Kyrgyz Republic, the central bank, raised its policy rate by 1.0 percentage point to 6.5% in April 2021 and kept it unchanged in its June meeting. This *Update*, expecting inflation in the second half of 2021 to remain high with persistent and rapid food price increases, substantially raises the inflation forecast for 2021. However, it keeps the 2022 inflation forecast unchanged, assuming further restoration of economic stability in 2022.

In the first quarter of 2021, the current account deficit equaled 4.6% of GDP. Data for the first 6 months of 2021 showed the merchandise trade deficit widening by 21.9% from a year earlier. Exports contracted by 9.5%, mainly from lower exports of gold and other metals. Higher imports of machinery and equipment, apparel, and sugar boosted total imports by 40.2%, enabled by remittances that were 41.0% above the same period in 2020. As these developments align with earlier forecasts, this *Update* leaves unchanged projections for current account deficits in 2021 and 2022.

Table 3.1.5 Selected economic indicators in the Kyrgyz Republic, %

	2020	2021		2022	
		ADO 2021	*Update*	*ADO 2021*	*Update*
GDP growth	−8.6	3.5	3.5	5.0	5.0
Inflation	6.3	7.0	10.0	7.0	7.0
CAB/GDP	5.2	−8.0	−8.0	−8.0	−8.0

ADO = *Asian Development Outlook*, CAB = current account balance, GDP = gross domestic product.

Sources: National Statistics Committee; National Bank of the Kyrgyz Republic; Ministry of Economy; International Monetary Fund staff report for the Article IV Consultation, May 2021; Asian Development Bank estimates.

Tajikistan

After slowing sharply in 2020 because of COVID-19, economic growth bounced back in the first half of 2021, more than doubling from 3.5% a year earlier to 8.7%. This reflected higher production and exports and, despite weak remittances, revived consumption as private lending skyrocketed. In the same period, expansion in industry jumped from 9.2% to 23.4%, reflecting accelerated efforts at industrialization. Less favorable weather slowed growth in agriculture marginally from 8.2% to 8.1%.

Although remittances from the Russian Federation fell by 9.2% in the first 3 months of 2021 from the same period last year, services recovered from a 4.8% decline in the first half of 2020 to a 16.5% gain a year later as retail trade reversed 1.1% contraction with 17.1% growth. Also in the first half, gross fixed investment grew by 23.7% as construction growth soared by 33.5%, propelled by investment linked to celebrations of the 30th anniversary of Tajikistan's independence. The deficit in net exports narrowed by 27.2%.

Despite high GDP growth in the first half of 2021, this *Update* does not upgrade growth projections for 2021 and 2022 (Table 3.1.6). One reason is uncertainty tied to a second wave of the pandemic, with only 13.5% of the adult population fully vaccinated against COVID-19 as of the end of August 2021, and 35.3% having received their first shot. Other factors are the expectation that weak remittances will moderate private consumption later this year and the Rogun hydropower project proceeding more slowly than expected because of financing issues.

Inflation averaged 9.0% in the first half of 2021, unchanged from the first half of 2020 but above the target range of the National Bank of Tajikistan, the central bank. Reflecting seasonal factors and external supply shocks from COVID-19, prices rose by 10.9% for food and 8.4% for other goods but only 5.1% for services. To mitigate inflation, the central bank raised the policy interest rate from 10.75% to 12.00% on 28 April 2021, and further to 13.00% on 2 August 2021. With electricity tariffs projected to rise by 15% in September, credit surging by 64.2% in the first half of this year, possible currency depreciation under greater exchange rate flexibility, and an expanded fiscal deficit from revenue shortfalls and increased health-care expenditure, this *Update* raises inflation forecasts for both 2021 and 2022.

The merchandise trade deficit narrowed from $851.1 million in the first half of 2020 to $619.2 million in the same period of this year as borders reopened and merchandise exports nearly doubled to $1,231.6 million, while merchandise imports rose by 23% to $1,850.8 million. Thus, despite weak remittances, this *Update* narrows projections for current account deficits in both 2021 and 2022.

Table 3.1.6 Selected economic indicators in Tajikistan, %

	2020	2021		2022	
		ADO 2021	*Update*	ADO 2021	*Update*
GDP growth	4.5	5.0	5.0	5.5	5.5
Inflation	9.4	9.0	9.5	8.0	9.0
CAB/GDP	4.3	−2.5	−1.5	−2.5	−2.0

ADO = *Asian Development Outlook*, CAB = current account balance, GDP = gross domestic product.

Source: Asian Development Bank estimates.

Turkmenistan

The government reported growth accelerating from 5.9% in the first half of 2020 to 6.1% in the first half of 2021. On the supply side, it estimated 15.2% growth in industry including construction and 5.2% growth in agriculture, offsetting sluggish growth in services. Industry was thus the main growth driver as a 23.4% rise in gas production led expansion in hydrocarbon output and processing. Growth also benefited from steady expansion in chemicals, electricity, textiles, food, and other industries enjoying government support under import substitution programs.

Record wheat harvests boosted growth in agriculture, and cotton will likely meet government production goals in the second half of the year. Growth in services has lagged, however, as a pandemic response plan imposed stringent and persistent travel restrictions and quarantine requirements that have hampered trade, transport, and tourism and hospitality.

On the demand side, rising public investment and net exports aided growth, while the adverse effects of inflation on real household income limited private consumption. Even as pandemic containment measures affected trade volume, gas exports to the People's Republic of China began to recover. This *Update* retains *ADO 2021* growth projections for 2021 and 2022 (Table 3.1.7).

Monetary policy remained focused on controlling inflation by limiting cash in circulation and maintaining the official exchange rate at TMT3.5 per US dollar, supplemented by price controls and the distribution of selected foodstuffs at subsidized prices. While the gap between official and parallel market exchange rates narrowed somewhat during the first half of 2021, import restrictions and resulting shortages have continued to boost inflation for food and other goods, including medicines. This *Update* therefore revises upward inflation forecasts for 2021 and 2022.

Citing a slight rise in revenue from gas exports, the International Monetary Fund projects fiscal surpluses equal to 0.4% of GDP in 2021 and 0.1% in 2022, based on revenue at 12.3% of GDP in 2021 and 11.9% in 2022, and expenditure close to 11.8% of GDP in both years.

The government reported a 37.2% increase in the value of natural gas exports in the first half of 2021, mainly from higher global energy prices. Exports should rise this year and next with continued recovery in gas shipments to the People's Republic of China—and as full vaccination of the population, expected in the second half of 2021, allows gradual easing of trade and transport restrictions. This *Update* nevertheless reverses the *ADO 2021* projection of a wider current account surplus in 2021 and forecasts a small deficit in 2022, in anticipation of some relaxation of import controls, particularly in 2022.

Table 3.1.7 Selected economic indicators in Turkmenistan, %

	2020	2021 ADO 2021	2021 Update	2022 ADO 2021	2022 Update
GDP growth	1.6	4.8	4.8	4.9	4.9
Inflation	10.0	8.0	10.0	8.0	10.0
CAB/GDP	0.5	2.0	0.4	0.5	−0.1

ADO = *Asian Development Outlook*, CAB = current account balance, GDP = gross domestic product.
Source: Asian Development Bank estimates.

Uzbekistan

The government reported growth recovering from only 0.5% year on year in the first half of 2020 to 6.2% in the same period of 2021. Industry reversed 1.2% decline a year earlier to expand by 8.5% with increases in manufacturing, mining, and quarrying. Growth in services accelerated from 0.3% to 8.0% on gains in trade, transport, and storage. Growth in construction slowed from 7.1% to 0.1% with contraction in building starts but expansion in infrastructure and specialized construction including repairs. Agriculture growth slowed from 2.8% to 1.8% as water shortage constricted crop production but livestock expanded.

On the demand side, gross capital formation reversed a 12.8% decline in the first half of 2020 to rise by 5.9% year on year with higher infrastructure development and upgrades to machinery and equipment in industry. Consumption reversed 1.2% decline with growth estimated at 4.5% as recovering household income boosted demand. Trade deficits widened by 35.1% for goods and 12.6% for services.

Uzbekistan began vaccinations in April 2021 and targeted to cover 20.0% of its population in 2021. As of the end of July, 3.2% of the population was fully vaccinated. Assuming a smooth vaccine rollout and continued rapid recovery in industry, services, investment, and private consumption, this *Update* raises growth projections for 2021 and 2022 (Table 3.1.8).

Despite wage increases, inflation slowed in the first half of 2021 from 13.9% a year earlier to 10.9%. Improved food production helped slow the rise in food prices from 17.5% to 14.5%, though food inflation has recently reaccelerated. Inflation for other goods slipped from 9.6% to 8.6% and, with tariffs for electricity and gas unchanged, fell for services from 13.8% to 8.4%. To bring inflation below 10% in 2021, the central bank has kept its policy rate at 14.0% since September 2020. With continuing tight monetary policy and energy tariffs unlikely to change, this *Update* retains earlier projections for inflation in 2021 and 2022.

The current account deficit widened in the first half of 2021 from the equivalent of 7.4% of GDP a year earlier to 9.6% on rising imports of capital and intermediate goods and transport services. Exports of goods expanded by 13.7%, reflecting large gains in textiles, copper, and petrochemicals, though gold exports fell by 34.7% with a 9.0% drop in world market prices. Imports rose by 23.5% on higher imports of machinery and equipment, ferrous metals, and petrochemicals. Service exports remained unchanged as the pandemic limited demand for transport and travel services, but imports rose by 5.6% on higher demand for cargo services. Recovery in remittances increased primary and secondary income by 14.3%. With imports rising notably, this *Update* widens projections for current account deficits in 2021 and 2022.

Table 3.1.8 Selected economic indicators in Uzbekistan, %

	2020	2021		2022	
		ADO 2021	*Update*	*ADO 2021*	*Update*
GDP growth	1.6	4.0	5.0	5.0	5.5
Inflation	12.9	10.0	10.0	9.0	9.0
CAB/GDP	−5.4	−4.5	−6.0	−4.0	−5.5

ADO = Asian Development Outlook, CAB = current account balance, GDP = gross domestic product.

Source: Asian Development Bank estimates.

East Asia

Subregional GDP expanded in the first half of 2021, lifted by global recovery and expanding vaccination campaigns. The aggregate GDP forecast for the whole year is upgraded from the April projection in *Asian Development Outlook 2021*, but the forecast for 2022 is unchanged. Inflation has been mostly low and stable and is unlikely to stray far from earlier forecasts. Similarly, this *Update* foresees subregional current account surpluses in both years that are slightly lower than projected earlier.

Subregional assessment and prospects

The economies of East Asia expanded in aggregate in the first half (H1) of 2021, recovering sharply from a year earlier. In the People's Republic of China (PRC), the economy reversed 1.6% contraction in H1 2020 to grow by 12.7% a year later, driven by improved domestic and robust external demand. Unexpectedly strong exports and rebounding private consumption and investment fueled 3.9% growth year on year in the Republic of Korea (ROK). Growth in Taipei,China accelerated from 1.4% a year earlier to 8.3%. Hong Kong, China grew by 7.8% on vigorous domestic and external demand. In Mongolia, mining staged a strong recovery.

Subregional inflation remained generally subdued in H1 2021. In the first 7 months of 2021, inflation in the PRC averaged 0.6%, 3.1 percentage points lower than in the same period in 2020 driven by declining food prices. Inflation surged in the second quarter in the ROK to average 1.9% in the first 7 months of 2021, led by higher global prices for fuel and other commodities and by strong domestic demand. Similar factors had similar results in Taipei,China. Larger electricity subsidies helped keep inflation low in Hong Kong, China.

Figure 3.2.1 GDP growth in East Asia

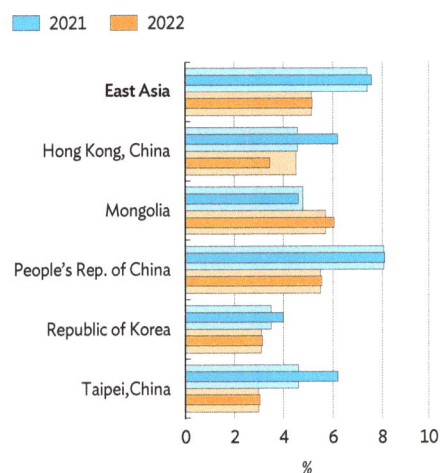

GDP = gross domestic product.
Note: Lighter colored bars are *Asian Development Outlook 2021* forecasts.
Source: *Asian Development Outlook* database.

The section on the PRC was written by Dominik Peschel and Wen Qi, and the part on other economies by Cindy Castillejos-Petalcorin, Matteo Lanzafame, Declan Magee, Donghyun Park, Irfan Qureshi, Bold Sandagdorj, Priscille Villanueva, and Michael Timbang, consultant. All authors are in the East Asia and Economic Research and Regional Cooperation departments of ADB. Subregional assessment and prospects were written by Eric Clifton, consultant, Economic Research and Regional Cooperation Department.

Available information suggests that the East Asia subregional current account surplus widened in H1 2021, boosted by strong exports. In the PRC, the current account surplus increased from the equivalent of 0.9% of GDP in H1 2020 to 1.5% a year later on a higher merchandise trade surplus. In Hong Kong, China, goods exports soared in H1 with a rebound in global demand. Elsewhere, Taipei,China and the ROK enjoyed widening current account surpluses thanks mostly to high global demand for semiconductors.

Subregional GDP growth is forecast to rise from 1.8% in 2020 to 7.6% in 2021—slightly higher than expected in *Asian Development Outlook 2021 (ADO 2021)*—before easing back to 5.1% in 2022 (Figure 3.2.1). Growth in the PRC is likely to decelerate from the rapid pace set in H1 as tailwinds from base effects subside. Consequently, PRC growth forecasts are maintained at 8.1% in 2021 and 5.5% in 2022. For Taipei,China, the 2021 GDP growth forecast is revised up from 4.6% to 6.2% following a remarkable performance in the second quarter, but the 2022 forecast is maintained at 3.0%. Forecasts for the ROK and Hong Kong, China are also revised up for 2021. However, the 2022 forecast for Hong Kong, China is revised down mainly to accommodate a base effect. As Mongolia's recovery lags, the growth forecast is revised down to 4.6% for 2021 and up to 6.0% for 2022.

Inflation in East Asia as a whole is forecast at 1.4% in 2021 and 2.2% in 2022, close to *ADO 2021* projections (Figure 3.2.2). Inflation in the PRC in 2021 is forecast to stay well below its 2020 high as pork price deflation keeps food price inflation in check. In Mongolia, inflation is accelerating and much higher than the subregional norm, forecast to reach 6.9% in 2021 and 8.5% in 2022. Elsewhere in the subregion, inflation is expected to be low, notwithstanding strengthening demand.

The subregional current account surplus is forecast to equal 2.5% of GDP in 2021 and 1.9% in 2022, narrowing slightly more than projected in April (Figure 3.2.3). The PRC current account surplus is expected to be 1.7% of GDP in 2021 and 1.1% in 2022, both forecasts similarly less than projections in *ADO 2021*. Current account surpluses in the ROK and Hong Kong, China are now expected to be somewhat wider than forecast earlier but still a least a bit narrower than in 2020. Taipei,China is expected to run large surpluses in 2021 and 2022. Mongolia will have the only current account deficit in the subregion in both years, deepening to 8.7% of GDP in 2021 and 10.2% in 2022 as the domestic economy recovers.

Downside risks to the growth outlook substantially outweigh upside risks. The most significant risk is from new waves of coronavirus variants, both within the subregion or elsewhere, that threaten to hinder economic activity further and disrupt international trade.

Figure 3.2.2 Inflation in East Asia

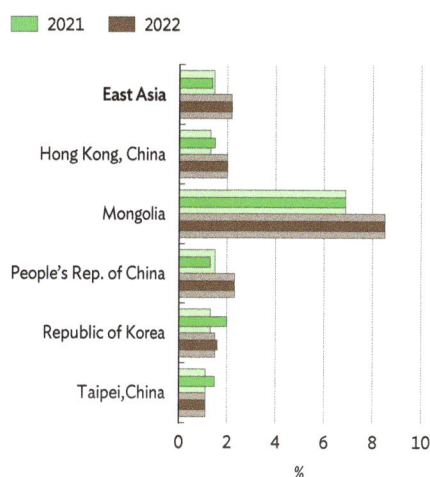

Note: Lighter colored bars are *Asian Development Outlook 2021* forecasts.
Source: *Asian Development Outlook* database.

Figure 3.2.3 Current account balances in East Asia

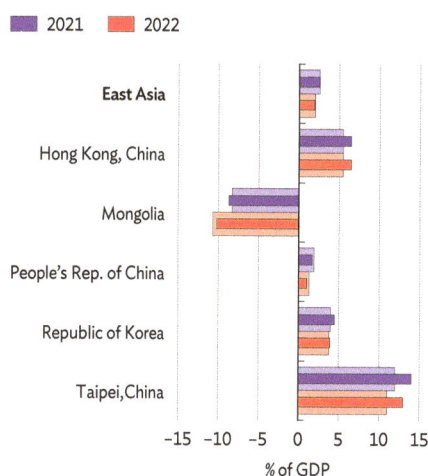

GDP = gross domestic product.
Note: Lighter colored bars are *Asian Development Outlook 2021* forecasts.
Source: *Asian Development Outlook* database.

People's Republic of China

The economy recovered further in the first half (H1) of 2021, driven by strong exports and improving consumption. The April GDP growth forecast in *ADO 2021* remains unchanged as a recovery in household consumption that was slightly weaker than expected will be offset by an increase in fiscal support in H2 2021 and continued export growth. With a more protracted recovery in consumer demand, inflation is now forecast to come in slightly lower in 2021. Current account forecasts are lowered for both years, reflecting higher commodity prices.

Updated assessment

The economy continued to recover in H1 2021. Driven by improved domestic demand and robust exports, it reversed 1.6% contraction year on year in H1 2020 to grow by 12.7% a year later. Benefiting from a low base, GDP increased by 18.3% in the first quarter (Q1) of 2021 and 7.9% in Q2 (Figure 3.2.4).

On the demand side, the first 6 months of 2021 saw consumption stage a comeback. With solid recovery in household consumption and retail sales, consumption regained its position as the main contributor to growth, adding 7.8 percentage points in H1 2021, in sharp contrast with 2.9 points subtracted a year earlier (Figure 3.2.5). Thanks to a 12.0% increase in real household income in H1 2021, real growth in household consumption reversed 9.3% contraction in H1 2020 to expand strongly by 17.4% (Figure 3.2.6). In the first 7 months of 2021, retail sales recovered from 12.0% contraction in real terms a year earlier to increase by an estimated 19.4%.

Investment contributed 2.4 percentage points to growth in H1 2021, or 0.9 points more than a year earlier. In the first 7 months, driven by investment in manufacturing and real estate, fixed asset investment came back from 1.6% contraction in nominal terms a year earlier to increase by 10.3% (Figure 3.2.7). Manufacturing investment grew by 17.3% on strong export performance and improved domestic demand, while real estate investment increased by 12.7%. By contrast, infrastructure investment expanded by only 4.6% as new issues of local government special bonds were low in Q4 2020 and Q1 2021.

As external trade picked up substantially in H2 2020 and merchandise exports stayed healthy throughout H1 2021, net exports reversed 0.2 percentage point subtraction from growth in H1 2020 to contribute 2.4 percentage points in H1 2021.

On the supply side, recovery in services gained speed as segments hit hard by the pandemic benefited from a gradual loosening of mobility restrictions and the rollout of COVID-19 vaccinations. Services came back from 1.6% contraction in H1 2020 to expand by 11.8% a year later, contributing 6.7 percentage points to growth (Figure 3.2.8).

Table 3.2.1 Selected economic indicators in the People's Republic of China, %

	2020	2021		2022	
		ADO 2021	*Update*	*ADO 2021*	*Update*
GDP growth	2.3	8.1	8.1	5.5	5.5
Inflation	2.5	1.5	1.3	2.3	2.3
CAB/GDP	1.9	1.9	1.7	1.3	1.1

ADO = *Asian Development Outlook*, CAB = current account balance, GDP = gross domestic product.
Source: Asian Development Bank estimates.

Figure 3.2.4 Economic growth

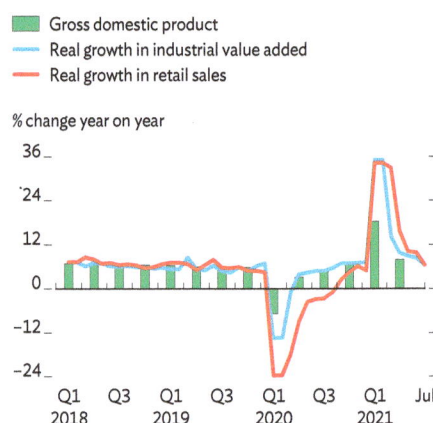

- Gross domestic product
- Real growth in industrial value added
- Real growth in retail sales

% change year on year

Q = quarter.
Sources: CEIC Data Company (accessed 16 August 2021); Asian Development Bank estimates.

Figure 3.2.5 Demand-side contributions to growth

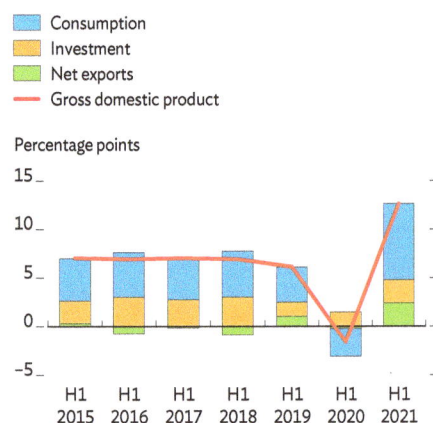

- Consumption
- Investment
- Net exports
- Gross domestic product

Percentage points

H1 = first half.
Source: CEIC Data Company (accessed 2 August 2021).

The recovery in services was broad, with accommodation and catering growing by 29.1%, transportation and logistics by 21.0%, and information technology by 20.3%. The secondary sector—manufacturing, mining, construction, and utilities—continued its strong performance and expanded by 14.8% to contribute 5.5 percentage points to growth. Within the sector, manufacturing grew rapidly by 17.0%, while construction expanded by 8.6%. Growth in agriculture recovered from 0.9% to 7.8%, driven by increased investment, contributing 0.4 percentage points to GDP growth in H1 2021. Widespread flooding in July 2021 had only temporary and limited effects on food supply.

A depressed and distorted base in H1 2020 renders economic recovery in H1 2021 difficult to gauge accurately. Looking at 2-year average growth rates to compensate, GDP grew by 5.3% in H1 2021. In the same period, industry grew by 6.1% on average, faster than services at 4.9%. On the demand side, real household income expanded by 5.2% on average, only slightly slower than GDP growth, but growth in real household consumption lagged at 3.2%. Fixed asset investment expanded by 4.4% on average with mixed performances by its components as investment in manufacturing grew by 2.0% and in infrastructure by 2.4% but in real estate by 8.2%.

Though labor market statistics do not measure underemployment (as discussed in *ADO 2020 Update*), available data indicate that the labor market has improved in line with economic recovery. By the end of June 2021, rural labor migrants in urban areas had nearly returned to their 2019 numbers. The surveyed urban unemployment rate was 5.1% at the end of July 2021, or 0.2 points lower than at the same point in 2019.

Food prices moderated inflation. In the first 7 months of 2021, inflation averaged 0.6%, dragged 3.1 percentage points lower than in the same period in 2020 by a 0.7% decline in food prices (Figure 3.2.9). Pork prices, which had been declining for 10 months following a surge caused by African swine fever, plunged by 23.2% on average in the first 7 months of 2021 as the pork supply improved. Nonfood price inflation stood at 0.9% on average, 0.3 percentage points higher than a year earlier.

Rebounding from a low base at 2.0% deflation, and driven by higher prices for commodities and raw materials, producer prices increased by 5.7% on average. Despite government measures that tightened financing for property developers and mortgage loans, prices for newly constructed homes in the top 70 cities were still on average 4.2% higher in the first 7 months of 2021 than a year earlier, with price increases more pronounced in first-tier cities (Figure 3.2.10).

The government budget deficit shrank significantly from the equivalent of 4.5% of GDP in H1 2020 to 0.9% in H1 2021 as revenue improved alongside the recovering economy (Figure 3.2.11). Fiscal revenue increased by 21.8% in H1 2021 as

Figure 3.2.6 Growth in income and consumption expenditure per capita

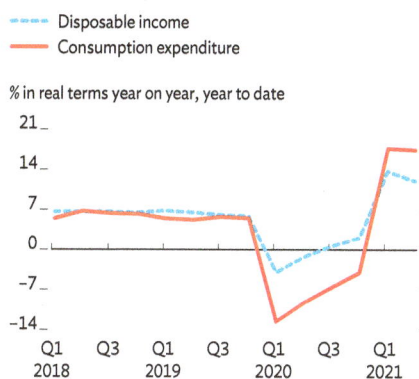

Q = quarter.
Source: CEIC Data Company (accessed 2 August 2021).

Figure 3.2.7 Growth in fixed asset investment

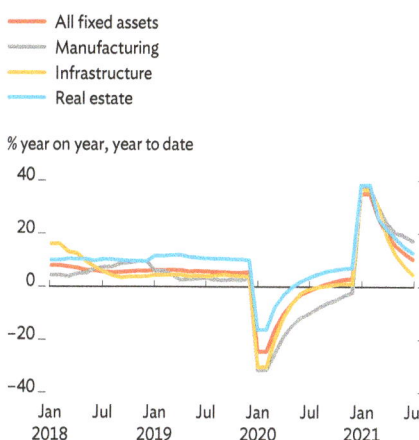

Source: CEIC Data Company (accessed 16 August 2021).

Figure 3.2.8 Supply-side contributions to growth

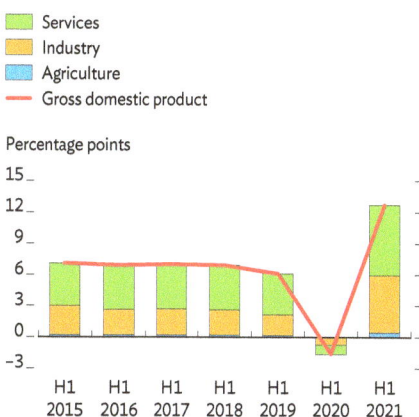

H1 = first half.
Source: CEIC Data Company (accessed 2 August 2021).

tax revenue grew by 22.5%. In line with retail sales expanding, value-added tax—the most significant tax source—grew by 22.5% in the first 6 months of 2021. Corporate tax expanded by 17.7% as industrial enterprise profit jumped by 66.9%, though from a very low base reflecting a pandemic-induced profit slump a year earlier. Fiscal expenditure increased only moderately by 4.5%. In addition, issues of new local government special bonds—not included in the general budget— amounted to CNY1.70 trillion by the end of July 2021, filling 46.6% of the annual quota (Figure 3.2.12).

Turning to monetary policy, the People's Bank of China, the central bank, kept the medium-term lending facility unchanged at 2.95% and the loan prime rate at 3.85% (Figure 3.2.13). On 9 July, the central bank announced a cut in the reserve requirement ratio by 0.5 percentage points for all banks to help them roll over maturing medium-term lending facilities and prepare for higher upcoming government bond issues, and to support credit expansion. Interest rates in the secured interbank market were broadly stable apart from a brief episode in late January and early February 2021.

Total social financing—a broad credit aggregate that includes bank loans, shadow bank lending, government and corporate bonds, and equity financing—was up by 10.7% at the end of July 2021 from a year earlier (Figure 3.2.14). While bank loans outstanding increased by 12.2%, shadow bank finance outstanding declined by 10.6% as the government aimed to control financial risks and rein in off-budget financing. Broad money (M2) stood 8.3% higher at the end of July 2021 than a year earlier.

The merchandise trade surplus drove the current account surplus from the equivalent of 0.9% of GDP in H1 2020 to 1.5% a year later (Figure 3.2.15). The service deficit held steady as outbound tourism remained highly restricted. At the same time, trade in goods expanded significantly in H1 2021 as merchandise imports grew by 36.6% on higher commodity prices and improved domestic demand. Merchandise exports, growing by 36.4%, profited from high global demand for mechanical and electrical products and consumer goods such as clothing and footwear. Growth in exports of personal protective equipment slowed from a high base in H1 2020. Geographically, exports to the three biggest PRC trade partners—the US, the European Union, and collectively Southeast Asia—grew strongly across the board in H1 2021.

Foreign direct investment was robust, expanding from the equivalent of 0.3% of GDP in H1 2020 to 1.5% a year later on much higher inflow, reflecting improved foreign investor confidence (Figure 3.2.16). In Q1 2021, net portfolio investment was balanced, while notably increased outflow in the form of loans to foreign entities and deposits abroad eased appreciation pressure on the renminbi.

Figure 3.2.9 Monthly inflation

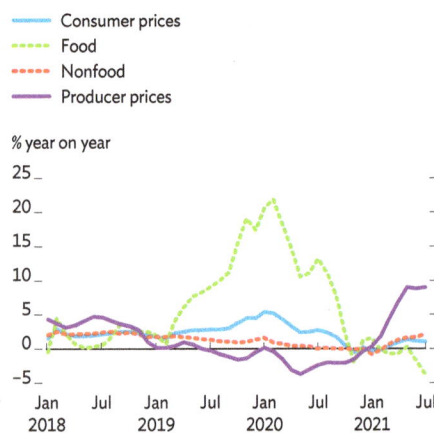

- Consumer prices
- Food
- Nonfood
- Producer prices

% year on year

Source: CEIC Data Company (accessed 16 August 2021).

Figure 3.2.10 Price increase for newly constructed homes

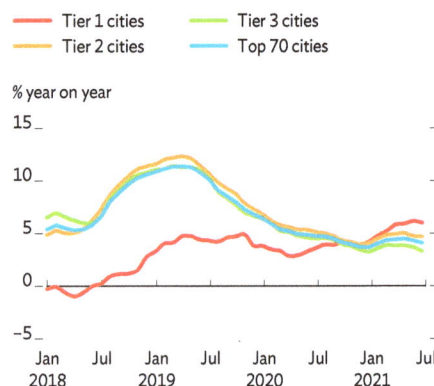

- Tier 1 cities
- Tier 2 cities
- Tier 3 cities
- Top 70 cities

% year on year

Note: Tier 1 cities are Beijing, Guangzhou, Shanghai, and Shenzhen; tier 2 has 31 provincial capitals and larger municipalities; and tier 3 has 35 other cities.
Source: Asian Development Bank calculations using data from CEIC Data Company (accessed 16 August 2021).

Figure 3.2.11 General government fiscal revenue and expenditure

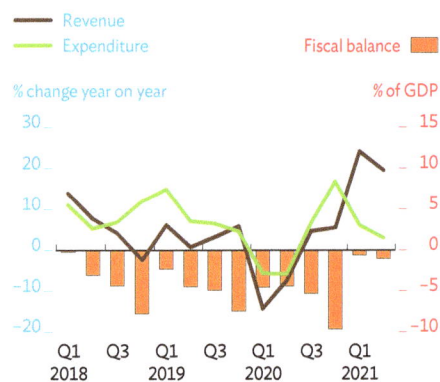

- Revenue
- Expenditure
- Fiscal balance

% change year on year   % of GDP

GDP = gross domestic product, Q = quarter.
Note: Central and local government public finance budget only.
Source: Asian Development Bank calculations using data from CEIC Data Company (accessed 2 August 2021).

Reserve assets decreased marginally in the first 7 months of 2021 to $3.37 trillion. By the end of July 2021, the renminbi had appreciated by 3.4% from the end of 2020 in nominal effective terms, against a trade-weighted basket of currencies, and by 1.0% in real effective terms. In nominal terms, it appreciated by 0.9% against the US dollar in the first 8 months of 2021 (Figure 3.2.17).

Prospects

Economic growth is expected to decelerate further from 7.9% in Q2 2021 as recovery dynamics weaken and base effects turn from tailwinds to headwinds in Q4 2021. COVID-19 weighed on recovery in household consumption and services when new case numbers bumped up from late July into August 2021 (Figure 3.2.18). Though slowing, export growth is expected to continue to support growth in industry and manufacturing investment. Monetary policy is likely to ease marginally in H2 2021, supporting higher fiscal expenditure to avoid economic growth decelerating too quickly in H2 2021. On balance, the GDP growth forecast remains unchanged from *ADO 2021* at 8.1% in 2021 and 5.5% in 2022 (Table 3.2.1).

On the demand side, consumption is expected to improve only gradually in the remainder of 2021. COVID-19 persistence has prompted strict virus-control measures, which weigh on consumer confidence and thus dampen growth in household demand and slow recovery in the job market. Investment performance will likely remain mixed in the remainder of 2021. Though the housing market will continue to be a driver of growth, measures to tame real estate developers and home buyers will likely stay in place, moderating growth in real estate investment into 2022. However, new issues of local government special bonds will pick up and support infrastructure investment in H2 2021 (Figure 3.2.12), and manufacturing investment should expand solidly in line with robust exports.

Overall in 2021 and 2022, consumption will be the main growth driver, followed by investment and net exports. Given solid export performance, net exports are now projected to contribute slightly more to growth in 2021 than earlier expected despite a projected decline in the trade surplus reflecting higher commodity prices. The net export contribution to growth should retreat in 2022 as the current account surplus moderates.

On the supply side, services should catch up with further recovery in household consumption. Retail sales should sustain their gradual revival in the remainder of 2021. Industry will continue to perform well thanks to manufacturing. While slower expansion in real estate investment will likely dampen growth in construction and related industries, growth in manufacturing is expected to stay strong in H2 2021. In addition to robust external demand, the domestic machinery

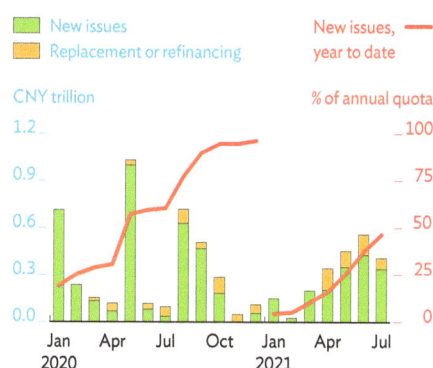

Figure 3.2.12 Local government special bond issues

Source: Asian Development Bank calculations using data from CEIC Data Company (accessed 24 August 2021).

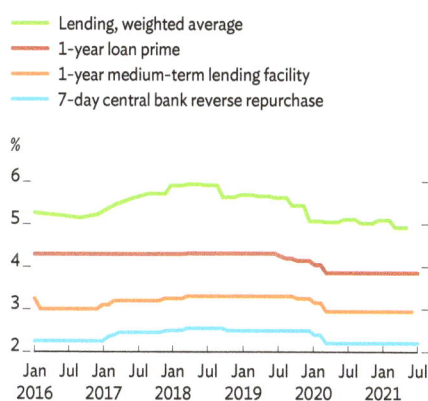

Figure 3.2.13 Banking lending and policy rates

Source: CEIC Data Company (accessed 24 August 2021).

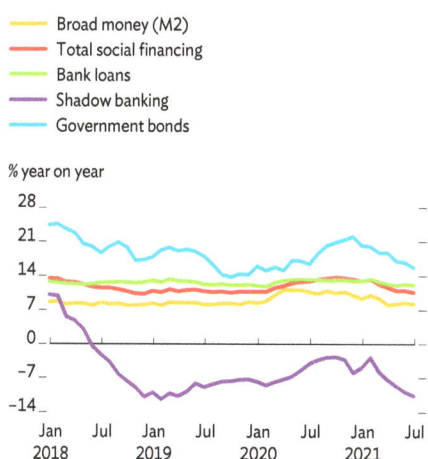

Figure 3.2.14 Growth in broad money, credit outstanding, and government bonds outstanding

Note: Shadow banking comprises entrust loans, trust loans, and banks' acceptance bills.

Source: Asian Development Bank calculations using data from CEIC Data Company (accessed 16 August 2021).

and equipment industry looks set to profit from continued solid manufacturing investment, while high-tech manufacturing and innovative industries continue to profit from government support. Finally, agriculture is expected to expand steadily.

Consumer price inflation in 2021 is forecast to stay well below its 2020 rate as pork price deflation keeps food price inflation in check. Nonfood inflation is expected to remain moderate in H2 2021. As household demand will recover only gradually, companies will find it difficult to increase prices for services.

Producer price inflation may have peaked in Q2 2021 but is expected to stay elevated for most of 2021 given increased commodity prices. However, only moderate transmission from higher producer prices to consumer prices is expected because the bulk of price increases for commodities will not be passed on to downstream producers. One reason is that commodity price increases are buffered along the value chain by market participants upstream and midstream, many of them state-owned enterprises. Prices for many inputs such as energy and utilities can be influenced by the government, either by regulatory measures or by setting administered prices. In addition, competition downstream in the value chain tends to be stiff, and participants are wary about household demand still recovering. As a result, little of the commodity price shock should reach final consumers (Figure 3.2.19).

For these reasons, the inflation forecast for 2021 is lowered to 1.3%, but the forecast for 2022 remains unchanged at 2.3% to accommodate revived food price inflation.

Fiscal policy is expected to become more supportive in H2 2021 on the spending side as economic growth declines with base effects increasingly coming to bear. Recovering fiscal revenue will provide some room to increase fiscal spending in the remainder of 2021 while keeping the budget deficit under control. In addition, new issues of local government special bonds picked up in Q2 2021 and will likely remain high in the remainder of 2021, providing additional funds for infrastructure investment. Despite high nominal GDP growth, general government debt is expected to increase further in 2021, after climbing by 9.7 percentage points in 2020 to equal 67.1% of GDP (Figure 3.2.20).

Monetary policy is expected to ease marginally in H2 2021. At the same time, credit to real estate will remain tightly regulated, as will shadow bank financing. The central bank will likely keep policy interest rates unchanged, opting instead to adjust liquidity in the interbank market as needed. Having moderated in H1 2021, credit growth is unlikely

Figure 3.2.15 Current account balance and merchandise trade

GDP = gross domestic product, Q = quarter.
Note: January and February data are combined to exclude the Lunar New Year effect.
Source: Asian Development Bank calculations using data from CEIC Data Company (accessed 16 August 2021).

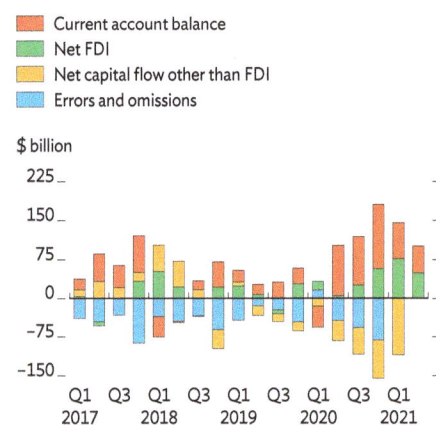

Figure 3.2.16 Balance of payments

FDI = foreign direct investment, Q = quarter.
Note: Only net FDI and current account balance available for Q2 2021.
Source: Asian Development Bank calculations using data from CEIC Data Company (accessed 16 August 2021).

Figure 3.2.17 Renminbi exchange rates

Source: Asian Development Bank calculations using data from CEIC Data Company (accessed 1 September 2021).

to slow much further, to avoid an adverse impact on economic recovery. To manage liquidity in the interbank market and support banks, the central bank may deploy another cut in the reserve requirement ratio later this year. This would align with central bank efforts to lower banks' funding costs to create room for them to lower their lending rates marginally without the central bank having to lower policy rates.

Nonperforming loans stood at 1.8% of commercial loans at the end of June 2021. The ratio is expected to rise in 2022 as deferred loan repayments come due (as discussed in *ADO 2021*).

External trade should continue to perform well in H2 2021 despite a moderating rate of export growth caused by base effects. Strong economic recovery forecast for the advanced economies should support PRC merchandise exports in the remainder of 2021, and import growth will reflect recovering domestic demand as well as higher commodity prices. Merchandise trade growth is expected to moderate to single digits in 2022. Ongoing foreign travel restrictions should prevent the service trade deficit from widening in 2021, but likely not in 2022 as international travel is seen picking up by then. On balance, the current account surplus is now forecast to narrow to the equivalent of 1.7% of GDP in 2021 and 1.1% in 2022, both 0.2 percentage points lower than earlier forecast.

Inflow of foreign direct investment in 2021 is expected to exceed last year's inflow as domestic demand in the PRC has been picking up. The PRC bond market should continue to benefit from a spread in yields over US Treasury notes, attracting capital. In August 2021, a 10-year PRC government bond yielded 2.88% per annum, more than double the rate of a US Treasury note with the same maturity.

Domestic risks to the outlook include the unpredictability of COVID-19 outbreaks and virus mutations, which could endanger recovery in domestic consumer demand. One external risk is the global tendency to tighten access to key technologies, which has potential to disrupt supply chains. Another is further hikes in commodity prices and high shipping costs, which could necessitate increases in PRC export prices and thus weigh on export performance. Finally, new pandemic outbreaks in key trade partners could weaken demand for PRC exports.

Figure 3.2.18 New confirmed COVID-19 cases weekly

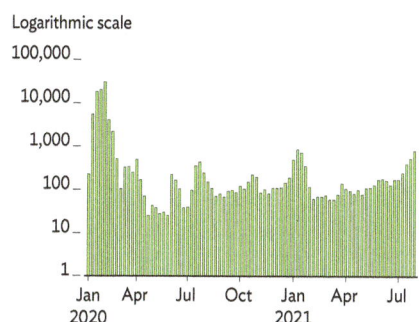

Source: Asian Development Bank calculations using data from CEIC Data Company (accessed 16 August 2021).

Figure 3.2.19 Commodity prices and inflation

Notes: Base metals include aluminum, copper, lead, nickel, steel, tin, and zinc. Crude oil is the average spot price of Brent, Dubai, and West Texas Intermediate.
Sources: CEIC Data Company (accessed 16 August 2021); Asian Development Bank calculations using World Bank Commodity Price Data. https://www.worldbank.org/en/research/commodity-markets (accessed 16 August 2021).

Figure 3.2.20 Debt structure

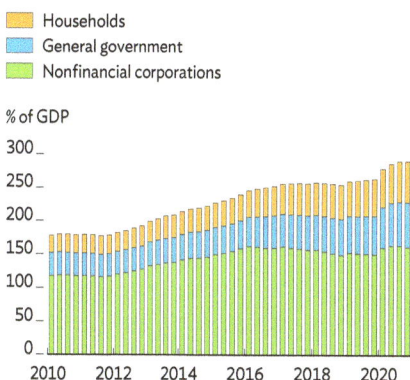

GDP = gross domestic product.
Source: Bank for International Settlements. https://www.bis.org/statistics/totcredit.htm (accessed 2 August 2021).

Other economies

Hong Kong, China

Recovery in both domestic and external demand led GDP to grow by 7.8% year-on-year in the first half of 2021. With the vaccination program progressing rapidly, private consumption expenditure rose as consumer activity picked up in the second quarter (Q2) despite an earlier drop in consumer confidence in Q1 with the arrival of a fourth wave of the COVID-19 pandemic. Gross fixed capital formation performed even better than private consumption in the first half amid significant improvement in business sentiment in Q2, while government spending still increased in the first half and net exports were positive as exports outgrew imports.

The recovery in global trade in Q1 2021 provided a boost to the services sector, which grew by 6.7% year-on-year in real terms. The manufacturing sector recovered in the quarter, reversing a decline in Q4 2020. Agriculture, fishing, mining and quarrying also grew, but the decline in construction deepened.

Economic growth is likely to moderate in the coming quarters as external demand stabilizes, and as the pandemic's continuing drag on business sentiment, domestic consumption, and tourism dents economic recovery despite the rapid pace of inoculation. More than 60% of the eligible population had received at least one dose of vaccine by late August and over 50% were fully vaccinated. Unexpectedly strong growth in the first half nevertheless pushes the growth forecast for 2021 higher than the *ADO 2021* projection. The forecast for 2022 is revised down, reflecting base effects.

Headline consumer price inflation slowed to 0.7% in June 2021 year-on-year from 1.0% in May, mainly reflecting larger electricity subsidies. Price pressures will continue to be moderate overall as significant slack remains in the economy and global inflation is likely to stay largely contained. However, inflation is expected to revive slightly alongside economic recovery. This *Update* thus raises the inflation forecast for 2021 and maintains the forecast in *ADO 2021* for somewhat higher inflation in 2022.

The current account turned to a surplus in Q1 2021 compared to a deficit in Q1 2020, as exports of goods surged more than imports on a sharp increase in demand from the People's Republic of China and other major export markets. The surplus in services widened, and the net inflow of primary income increased. In light of these developments and an anticipated strong global upturn, projections for current account surpluses in both 2021 and 2022 are now wider than in *ADO 2021*, essentially sustaining the 2020 surplus.

The economic outlook is subject to downside risk arising from uncertainty about the pandemic, particularly the emergence and evolution of new virus strains and how effectively vaccines control their spread.

Table 3.2.2 Selected economic indicators in Hong Kong, China, %

	2020	2021		2022	
		ADO 2021	*Update*	*ADO 2021*	*Update*
GDP growth	−6.1	4.6	6.2	4.5	3.4
Inflation	0.3	1.3	1.5	2.0	2.0
CAB/GDP	6.5	5.5	6.5	5.5	6.5

ADO = *Asian Development Outlook*, CAB = current account balance, GDP = gross domestic product.

Source: Asian Development Bank estimates.

Mongolia

In the first half (H1) of 2021, GDP expanded by 7.1%, driven by strong recovery in mining and services. Contraction in construction continued, and a rapid increase in COVID-19 infections and consequent lockdowns caused unexpected 3.5% contraction in agriculture. Extended lockdowns turned consumption negative, subtracting 9.9 percentage points from growth. Despite over 63% of the population becoming fully vaccinated, increased COVID-19 cases and the arrival of new coronavirus variants in both Mongolia and the People's Republic of China disrupted coal exports in the second quarter as quotas restricted truck movements across the border. Net exports nevertheless added 2.7 points to growth. Investment contributed 14.3 points, supported by credit availability and government programs for smaller enterprises.

In light of these developments, this *Update* forecasts GDP growth in 2021 slightly lower than projected in *ADO 2021* but still sustained by accommodative fiscal and monetary policies (Table 3.2.3). Social protection and household support introduced in response to COVID-19 have been extended through H2 2021, which should support growth in private consumption, assuming no further lockdowns. Credit expansion recovered to 12.2% year on year and will be maintained in H2, supported by the Bank of Mongolia, the central bank, through its repo financing scheme and by the government's stimulus measures for smaller businesses. The contribution to GDP growth from investment is forecast to remain positive through 2022 on growing private and public outlays and foreign direct investment. The contribution in 2021 from agriculture and industry together is revised down by 0.4 percentage points to 2.5%, but the contribution from services including wholesale and retail trade is revised up by 0.2 points to 2.1%.

Growth will accelerate in 2022 more than forecast in *ADO 2021* as COVID-19 concerns ease, benefits from the vaccination program materialize, transportation and logistics issues affecting exports are resolved, and domestic demand rises.

Annual inflation in the year to July 2021 reached 7.4%, mainly on double-digit increases for food and for transportation and dining services. Inflation forecasts remain unchanged as April inflation forecasts reflected these rising costs and likely supply shocks. The current account deficit narrowed in H1 2021 but it is now forecast to widen more in 2021 than projected in *ADO 2021* and less in 2022, as the export growth projection is revised down for 2021 and up for 2022. Import growth forecasts are unchanged.

Risks to the outlook are on the downside as public health concerns and economic uncertainty remain high. Persistent border restrictions in particular could continue to disrupt coal exports, undermine industrial output, and keep inflation high by disrupting supplies of food and construction materials and raising transportation costs.

Table 3.2.3 Selected economic indicators in Mongolia, %

	2020	2021		2022	
		ADO 2021	Update	ADO 2021	Update
GDP growth	−5.3	4.8	4.6	5.7	6.0
Inflation	3.7	6.9	6.9	8.5	8.5
CAB/GDP	−5.1	−8.3	−8.7	−10.7	−10.2

ADO = Asian Development Outlook, CAB = current account balance, GDP = gross domestic product.

Source: Asian Development Bank estimates.

Republic of Korea

Fueled by unforeseen strength in net exports, solid private investment, and rebounding private consumption, GDP expanded by 3.9% year on year in the first half of 2021. Growth benefited from competent pandemic management that saw 32.6% of the eligible population fully vaccinated by end August 2021 and allowed mobility restrictions to be eased. Economic expansion in the second quarter reached 5.9% year on year, the highest quarterly expansion rate in more than 10 years.

On the supply side, industry surged by 6.7% on rebounds in manufacturing and in mining and quarrying, and as services recovered after two semesters of contraction. Agriculture contracted by 0.7% because of bad weather.

Consumer price inflation averaged 1.9% in the first 7 months of 2021 after a surge in the second quarter caused by higher global fuel and commodity prices and stronger domestic demand. During its August 2021 meeting, the central bank raised the policy interest rate by 25 basis points to 0.75%, to help temper rising debt and prices.

Merchandise exports rebounded by 14.4% in the first 6 months of 2021 on continuing high global demand for semiconductors, for which the Republic of Korea is a key supplier. Merchandise imports also expanded, by 12.5%, on growing demand for raw materials and intermediate goods. The current account surplus in the first 6 months of 2021 equaled 4.0% of GDP, shored up by a widening trade surplus, an increase in net income, and a lower service deficit.

The GDP growth projection for 2021 is revised up in light of the strong performance in the first half and an economic outlook brightened by continuing improvement in exports, a higher manufacturing purchasing managers' index in July, recovering consumption, expected private sector outlays in the semiconductor industry, and a $30.2 billion supplementary budget approved in July. The 2022 GDP forecast is retained.

Inflation is now projected to trend higher than forecast in *ADO 2021* on the combined impact of rising global prices for oil and other commodities, persistent supply chain bottlenecks, and increase in interest rates in the second half on concerns about financial stability. With exceptional growth in both exports and imports so far this year, and with demand rising for electronic products and vehicle parts, forecasts for the current account surplus are adjusted up from *ADO 2021* for both 2021 and 2022.

Uncertainty over COVID-19 remains the biggest risk to the forecasts. Stringent social distancing rules introduced in July following a resurgence in COVID-19 cases may dampen private consumption. Upside risks include stronger global economic recovery, continuing strong growth in exports of electronic products, and an accelerated vaccine rollout.

Table 3.2.4 Selected economic indicators in the Republic of Korea, %

	2020	2021		2022	
		ADO 2021	Update	ADO 2021	Update
GDP growth	-0.9	3.5	4.0	3.1	3.1
Inflation	0.5	1.3	2.0	1.5	1.6
CAB/GDP	4.6	4.0	4.5	3.8	4.0

ADO = *Asian Development Outlook*, CAB = current account balance, GDP = gross domestic product.
Source: Asian Development Bank estimates.

Taipei,China

With 2 quarters of decade-high expansion in 2021 fueled by improved global trade, particularly in 5G mobile applications and high-performance computing devices, GDP growth accelerated year on year in the first half (H1) of 2021 from 1.4% to 8.3%. Imports rebounded by 16.8% while exports soared by 22.4%, such that net exports contributed 5.6 percentage points to GDP growth. Gross capital formation expanded by 8.9%, contributing 2.2 points to growth with massive investment in machinery, transportation equipment, infrastructure for green energy, 5G network development, urban renewal, and social housing projects. Government consumption grew by 3.4%, but a COVID-19 spike in mid-May constrained expansion in private consumption, which nevertheless reversed 3.5% decline in H1 2020 with 1.0% growth.

On the supply side, high-tech and export-oriented companies propelled growth in industry, which contributed 5.7 percentage points to growth in H1 2021. Growth in services was supported by robust activity in finance and insurance and in wholesale and retail trade. Agriculture shrank by 2.3% but with negligible impact on GDP.

Growth will likely continue for the rest of this year. With more than 40% of the population inoculated as of mid-August, the pandemic seems to be largely contained without damaging lockdowns. Continued expansion in industry is signaled by a higher manufacturing purchasing managers' index in July and double-digit growth in industrial production in recent months. Improved consumer sentiment in July bodes well for recovery in private consumption, and 22.4% growth in June in export orders indicates a robust external sector. Fiscal and monetary policies are expected to remain accommodative. This *Update* thus revises up the forecast for high growth in 2021, assuming continued strong global demand for high-tech products, but maintains the forecast for a return to trend in 2022 (Table 3.2.5).

Inflation averaged 1.5% in the first 7 months of 2021 in line with higher global prices for oil and other raw materials, strong recovery in domestic demand, and price increases in services. The forecast for inflation is thus revised up for 2021 from the *ADO 2021* projection, given rising consumer demand and strengthening global commodity markets, but kept unchanged for 2022.

The current account surplus widened to equal 14.6% of GDP in H1 2021 as strong export growth outpaced rising imports. With this export trend expected to continue, the current account surplus is now forecast higher than projected in *ADO 2021* for both 2021 and 2022.

The main downside risks to the outlook would be new outbreaks of coronavirus variants and vaccine rollout delayed by supply constraints. On the upside, greater expansion may occur if growth in exports of electronic products exceeds expectations or if global recovery accelerates further with effective vaccination.

Table 3.2.5 Selected economic indicators in Taipei,China, %

	2020	2021		2022	
		ADO 2021	Update	ADO 2021	Update
GDP growth	3.1	4.6	6.2	3.0	3.0
Inflation	−0.2	1.1	1.5	1.1	1.1
CAB/GDP	14.2	12.0	14.0	11.0	13.0

ADO = *Asian Development Outlook*, CAB = current account balance, GDP = gross domestic product.

Sources: CEIC Data Company; Asian Development Bank estimates.

South Asia

The subregional economy is forecast to expand, but less in 2021 than projected last April in *Asian Development Outlook 2021* and, as the pandemic fades, more in 2022 than foreseen. Inflation is now expected to run higher this year than forecast in April, but the projection for 2022 is unchanged, largely following the pattern in India. South Asia's current account deficit is forecast slightly wider than projected in April in both years as domestic demand recovers.

Subregional assessment and prospects

Aggregate GDP is forecast to expand by 8.8% in 2021, less than projected in *ADO 2021* following the spread of COVID-19 in the subregion and consequent containment measures and their economic consequences (Figure 3.3.1). If the pandemic dissipates before the end of 2021, the subregional economy is projected to grow by 7.0% in 2022, more than forecast in April. The growth outlook reflects expected sharp expansion in the Indian economy, which is 80% of the subregional economy. This outlook excludes forecasts for Afghanistan, as the uncertain situation precludes meaningful projections.

The Indian economy surged year on year in the first quarter of fiscal year 2021 (FY2021, ending 31 March 2022) as substantial fiscal stimulus was introduced and monetary policy remained accommodative in response to a second wave of COVID-19 in April–May 2021. The central bank kept its policy rate at 4.0%, set in May 2020, and injected liquidity through other instruments despite headline inflation persisting above the medium-term target range of 2%–6%. Growth is now forecast at 10.0% in FY2021, below the *ADO 2021* projection, and at 7.5% in FY2022, higher than projected in April with a significant proportion of the population expected to be vaccinated and economic activity to further normalize.

Figure 3.3.1 GDP growth in South Asia

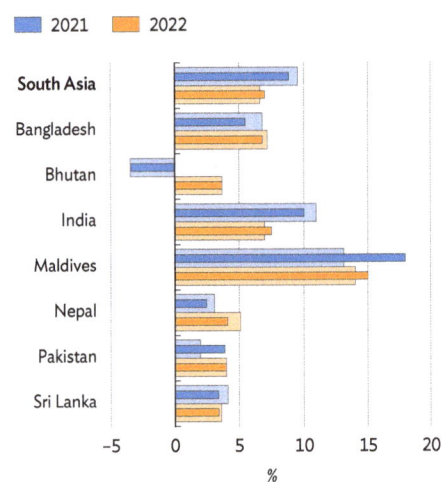

GDP = gross domestic product.
Note: Lighter colored bars are *Asian Development Outlook 2021* forecasts.
Source: *Asian Development Outlook* database.

The section on Bangladesh was written by Jyotsana Varma, Soon Chan Hong, Barun K. Dey, and Mahbub Rabbani; India by Rana Hasan and Shalini Mittal; Pakistan by Kiyoshi Taniguchi, Ali Khadija, and Maleeha Rizwan; and other economies by Nirukthi Kariyawasam, Manbar Singh Khadka, Utsav Kumar, Masato Nakane, and Madhavi Pundit, as well as consultants Abdulla Ali, Macrina Mallari, Nyingtob Norbu, and Thilina Panduwawala. Authors are in the Central and West Asia and South Asia departments of ADB. The subregional assessment and prospects was written by Reza Vaez-Zadeh, consultant, Economic Research and Regional Cooperation Department.

Growth forecasts for Maldives and Pakistan are upgraded. Tourist arrivals in Maldives exceeded expectations in the first half of 2021 as the country benefited from large increases in visitors from India and the Russian Federation. In Pakistan, GDP recovered more strongly in fiscal year 2021 (FY2021, ended 30 June 2021) than forecast in *ADO 2021* and growth in FY2022 is expected to be the same as projected in April, supported by a vaccination rollout, economic stimulus measures, and structural reforms. The economies of Bangladesh and Nepal underperformed relative to projections in FY2021 (ended 30 June 2021 in Bangladesh and 15 July 2021 in Nepal), held back by restrictions imposed to contain the pandemic. Growth in both countries is now projected to be lower in FY2022 than forecast in April because infection rates remain high and, in Nepal, heavy rains damaged infrastructure.

Bhutan saw GDP contract in FY2021 (ended 30 June 2021), owing mainly to closed borders and a freeze on international tourism, but the FY2022 outlook remains unchanged as government capital spending is scaled up. In Sri Lanka, growth in the first half of 2021 was positive, but COVID-19 containment measures, weakness in the external sector, and heavy foreign debt repayments will suppress growth in both 2021 and 2022 below April forecasts.

The subregional forecast for inflation in 2021 is revised up from 5.5% in *ADO 2021* to 5.8%, largely reflecting supply chain disruption and a delayed monsoon sustaining FY2021 inflation in India at 5.5% (Figure 3.3.2). Higher food prices in FY2021 propelled inflation in Bhutan beyond the forecast in April and kept it so in Pakistan. Increased imports of food into Bangladesh and a good harvest in Nepal lowered inflation in FY2021 beyond expectations. Subregional inflation is forecast at 5.1% in 2022, as projected in *ADO 2021*, as Indian inflation moderates to the rate forecast in April. Inflation forecasts are revised up for Sri Lanka and Bhutan, owing to rising oil and food prices. Inflation will return to Maldives this year but, with increases in price subsidies, at downgraded rates this year and next.

The combined South Asian current account deficit is now seen to equal 1.2% of subregional GDP in 2021 and 1.1% in 2022, slightly wider in both years than April projections as domestic demand picks up and oil prices rise (Figure 3.3.3). India's deficit will equal 1.1% of GDP this fiscal year and 1.0% next, as forecast in April, but still mark deterioration from a small surplus in FY2020. Pakistan's current account deficit narrowed in FY2021 more than forecast in April and is now projected to widen less in FY2022 than earlier expected. The deficit in Maldives is projected to be lower this year and the next than forecast in April as tourism receipts expand. Higher imports spell bigger deficits than earlier foreseen in Nepal and Sri Lanka in both years, and deficits instead of surpluses in Bangladesh.

Figure 3.3.2 Inflation in South Asia

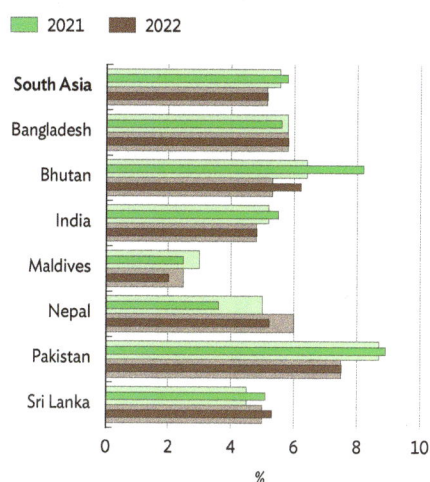

Note: Lighter colored bars are *Asian Development Outlook 2021* forecasts.
Source: *Asian Development Outlook* database.

Figure 3.3.3 Current account balances in South Asia

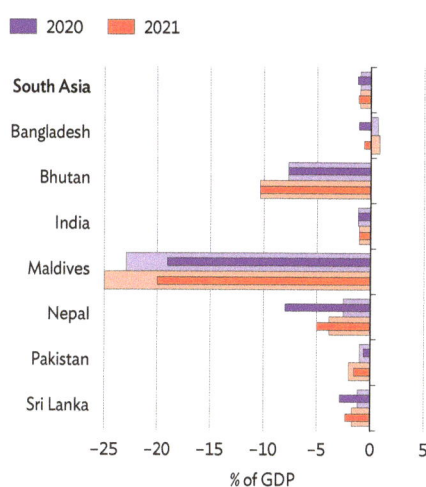

GDP = gross domestic product.
Note: Lighter colored bars are *Asian Development Outlook 2021* forecasts.
Source: *Asian Development Outlook* database.

Bangladesh

GDP growth began to revive in fiscal year 2021 (FY2021, ended 30 June 2021) from the COVID-19 pandemic induced slump of the previous year. This reflected timely implementation of fiscal and monetary stimulus measures, a recovery in global trade flows and the start of a vaccinations program. With a modest rise in domestic demand, inflation moderated, and the current account deficit narrowed. Given the expected continued expansion in the global economy and maintained government recovery policies, FY2022 growth is expected to strengthen but remain below pre-pandemic levels. Inflation will edge up and the current account deficit will narrow.

Updated assessment

GDP growth strengthened to 5.5% in FY2021 from 3.5% in FY2020, according to official preliminary estimates. This was lower than 6.8% forecast in *ADO 2021* due to restrictions imposed from early April 2021 to contain a second wave of infections from the Delta coronavirus variant that slowed activities. Exports nevertheless rebounded from a marked fall in FY2020 as global trade recovered, such that net exports again contributed to growth. A large increase in remittances supported growth in private consumption. Growth in public investment, however, was less than planned because no additional financing of development expenditure was allocated in the fourth quarter. Though net foreign direct investment increased by 39%, total private investment stagnated, reflecting investor confidence undermined by the prolonged pandemic.

On the supply side, agriculture growth slowed to 3.5% due to a cyclone and prolonged flooding. Growth in industry increased to 6.1% underpinned by improvement in medium and large-scale manufacturing, reflecting increased exports bolstered by large increases in garment orders from key export destinations and a surge in other exports. However, growth in small-scale industries slowed. Services increased by 5.6%, on recovery in wholesale and retail trade, hotels and restaurants, and transport services (Figure 3.3.4).

Inflation eased to average 5.6% in FY2021 from 5.7% in FY2020, as nonfood inflation continued to drift lower in the first half of the year on weak domestic demand, though it rose in the second half on strengthening global demand boosting domestic income (Figure 3.3.5). Food inflation followed an opposite pattern, markedly increasing in the first half on the repeated floods but moderating in the later part of the year on a good winter crop harvest and increased rice imports.

Broad money growth accelerated to 13.6% in FY2021, from 12.6% in FY2020, against a monetary program target of 15.0% (Figure 3.3.6). Private sector credit growth was slow at 8.3% against the target of 14.8%, as both investors and banks continued to be cautious in making new investments

Figure 3.3.4 Supply-side contributions to growth

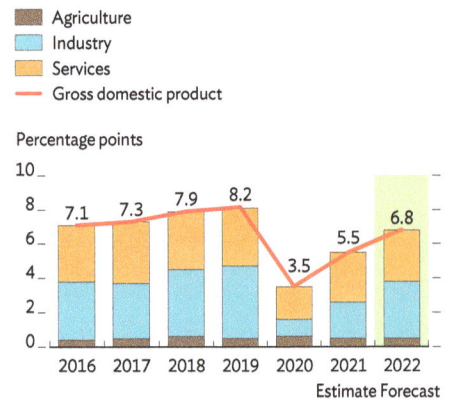

- Agriculture
- Industry
- Services
- Gross domestic product

Percentage points

Note: Years are fiscal years ending on 30 June of that year.
Sources: Bangladesh Bureau of Statistics. http://www.bbs.gov.bd; Asian Development Bank estimates.

Figure 3.3.5 Monthly inflation

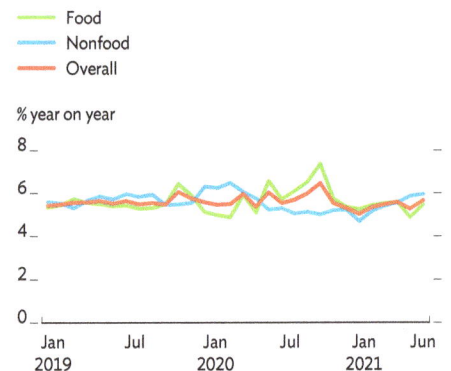

- Food
- Nonfood
- Overall

% year on year

Source: Bangladesh Bank. 2021. *Monthly Economic Trends.* July. https://www.bb.org.bd.

Figure 3.3.6 Growth of monetary indicators

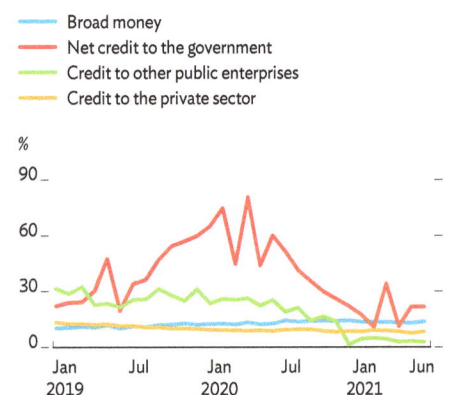

- Broad money
- Net credit to the government
- Credit to other public enterprises
- Credit to the private sector

%

Source: Bangladesh Bank. 2021. *Major Economic Indicators, Monthly Update.* July. https://www.bb.org.bd.

amid continuing uncertainty. Growth in net credit to the public sector decelerated to 19.0%, against the program target of 31.7%, reflecting strong demand for national savings certificates driven by attractive interest rates that buoyed borrowing from nonbank sources. Market interest rates declined substantially on a build-up of reserves at commercial banks, and as part of its accommodative monetary policy, Bangladesh Bank, the central bank, cut policy rates to a 4.0% to 4.75% band in July 2020 (Figure 3.3.7).

Revenue collection by the National Board of Revenue increased by 20.1% in FY2021, although below the revised budget target of 32.2%. Lower-than-budgeted capital spending in April–June 2021 period is estimated to offset the revenue shortfall, as government gave priority to implementing stimulus and relief program packages. With adjustments to shortfalls in revenue and spending, the budget deficit is estimated at 6.1% of GDP, crossing the intended policy ceiling of 5.0% for the third consecutive year. Yet, Bangladesh continues at a low risk of debt distress due to its moderate debt–GDP ratio.

Exports growth rebounded to 15.4% in FY2021, reflecting economic recovery and greater demand from major export destinations (Figure 3.3.8). Garment exports, accounting for more than 80% of total exports, grew by 12.5% bolstered by reinstatement of previously cancelled or delayed orders. Exports of jute goods, agricultural products, leather and leather products, and engineering products increased sharply to lift growth of all other exports by a striking 27.5%.

Imports increased by 19.7% to $65.6 billion in FY2021, with about a third of the rise accounted for by the increased cost of petroleum and petroleum products, mainly due to sharply higher prices. Excluding petroleum, imports increased by 14.5%. Reflecting the solid economic advance, intermediates for the garment industry rose by 8.0%, while there were double-digit increases in imports of other intermediates, consumer products, and capital goods. Rice imports also increased sharply to replenish government stocks and contain pressure on prices.

The FY2021 trade deficit widened to $22.8 billion or 6.4% of GDP, as the $10.0 billion increase in imports surpassed the $5.1 billion rise in exports. Remittance grew by a stunning 36.1% to $24.8 billion, driven by the 2% cash incentive given for transfers through official channels and relaxed documentation requirements (Figure 3.3.9). Remittances held the current account deficit to $3.8 billion or 1.1% of GDP (Figure 3.3.10).

The combined capital and financial account surplus, adjusted for errors and omissions, increased to $13.1 billion in FY2021, mainly reflecting greater use of trade credit and other short-term loans. With net financial inflows significantly exceeding the current account deficit, gross foreign exchange reserves increased to $46.4 billion, covering 7.8 months of imports of goods and services (Figure 3.3.11).

Figure 3.3.7 Interest rates

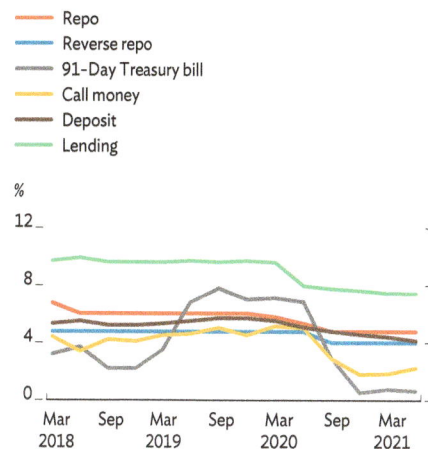

Source: Bangladesh Bank. 2021. *Major Economic Indicators, Monthly Update*. July. https://www.bb.org.bd.

Figure 3.3.8 Export and export growth

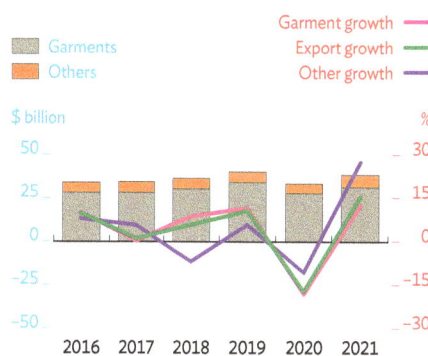

Note: Years are fiscal years ending on 30 June of that year.
Sources: Export Promotion Bureau; Asian Development Bank estimates.

Figure 3.3.9 Remittances

Note: Years are fiscal years ending on 30 June of that year.
Source: Bangladesh Bank. 2021. *Major Economic Indicators, Monthly Update*. July. https://www.bb.org.bd.

The Bangladesh taka remained stable against the US dollar in FY2021, as Bangladesh Bank continued its managed float policy, aided by the country's large foreign exchange reserves (Figure 3.3.12). It bought $7.9 billion from the inter-bank foreign exchange market and sold $235 million to commercial banks to curb excessive volatility. Accounting for inflation differentials, the real effective exchange rate index depreciated by 2.1% over FY2021, suggesting improved export competitiveness.

Prospects

GDP growth is projected at 6.8% in FY2022, revised down from the 7.2% forecast in *ADO 2021* because containment measures were needed to bring down high infection rates that lingered on in the first months of the year (Table 3.3.1). With continued robust growth expected in major country destinations, export earnings should reach pre-pandemic levels. Remittances are also expected to remain strong, firming up private consumption. Improving consumer confidence and government stimulus measures will help boost private and public investment. The main downside risk to the forecast would be sustained escalation of infection rates in major advanced economies, clipping external demand.

On the supply side, agriculture growth is projected to edge up to 3.7% in FY2022, driven by budget priority given to agriculture for subsidies on seeds, fertilizer, irrigation, and farm mechanization (Figure 3.3.13). With improved external demand and stronger public and private investment, industry is expected to grow by 9.5%. Services will expand by 5.8% on strengthening in agriculture and industry.

Inflation is projected to increase to 5.8% in FY2022, as forecast in *ADO 2021*. A favorable agricultural outlook, underutilized capacity, and continued vigilance of Bangladesh Bank should keep in check inflationary pressures from higher global oil and commodity prices. Domestic administered prices for fuel may cushion the impact of increased crude oil prices.

Monetary policy will continue to be accommodative in FY2022, while containing inflation and maintaining financial stability. To support recovery, Bangladesh Bank will emphasize full implementation of the government's stimulus programs and strengthen its refinancing windows. In addition, it will continue to support priority sectors for productivity and employment with strengthened monitoring of loan quality.

With primacy placed on people's lives and livelihoods during the second wave of COVID-19 infections, the FY2022 budget focuses on speeding the pace of economic recovery by strengthening the health-care system, increasing agriculture production, and expanding social protection, human capital development, and employment generation, while implementing ongoing priority mega projects.

Figure 3.3.10 Current account components

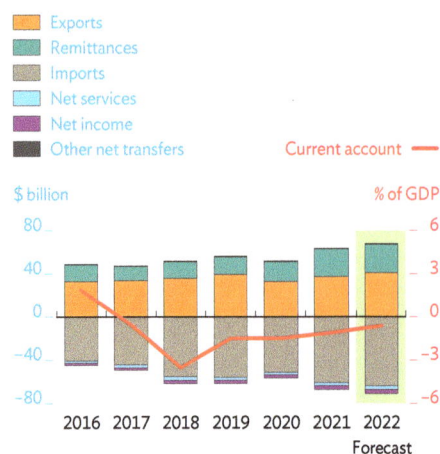

GDP = gross domestic product.
Note: Years are fiscal years ending on 30 June of that year.
Sources: Bangladesh Bank. *Annual Report 2019–2020* and *Economic Data*. http://www.bb.org.bd; Asian Development Bank estimates.

Figure 3.3.11 Foreign exchange reserves

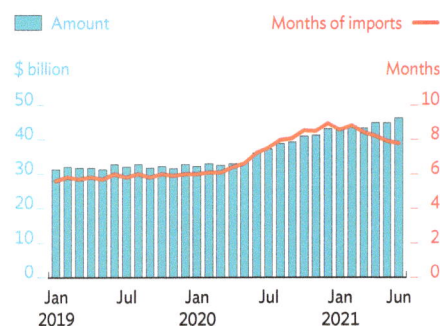

Source: Bangladesh Bank. 2021. *Major Economic Indicators, Monthly Update*. July. https://www.bb.org.bd.

Table 3.3.1 Selected economic indicators in Bangladesh, %

	2020	2021		2022	
		ADO 2021	*Update*	*ADO 2021*	*Update*
GDP growth	3.5	6.8	5.5	7.2	6.8
Inflation	5.7	5.8	5.6	5.8	5.8
CAB/GDP	–1.5	0.7	–1.1	0.8	–0.6

ADO = Asian Development Outlook, CAB = current account balance, GDP = gross domestic product.
Note: Years are fiscal years ending on 30 June of that year.
Sources: Bangladesh Bureau of Statistics. http://www.bbs.gov.bd; Bangladesh Bank. http://www.bb.org.bd; Asian Development Bank estimates.

The budget targets revenue at 11.3% of GDP and government expenditures of 17.5% of GDP (Figure 3.3.14). Current spending is targeted to grow by 8.7% over the FY2021 revised budget, mostly for higher interest payments, pay and allowances, and current transfers, while growth in development spending is targeted at 14.0%. The budget deficit is set at 6.2% of GDP. Domestic financing will cover 52.8% of it, of which 67.4% will be from banks and 32.6% from nonbank sources, mostly national saving certificates.

Though the revenue target is lower than those planned in earlier budgets, achieving it will be challenging because of revenue losses incurred by tax concessions and exemptions, and the economic impact of containment measures. Government spending will rise as the government continues to implement economic stimulus through the budget, increasing the size of financial assistance and accelerating implementation of priority mega projects. Achieving the spending target will also be a challenge, though, because of limited implementation capacity and revenue constraints. Considering shortfalls on both sides of the ledger, the planned budget deficit of 6.2% of GDP is expected to be met.

Exports are expected to expand by 8.0% in FY2022 on continued robust growth expected in major export destinations. Export industries will be aided by flexibility in implementing containment measures, improving incentives for export-oriented activities, and measures taken to improve the business climate. Moreover, the potential trade diversion from other countries facing increasing labor costs or political instability could benefit Bangladesh positively.

Imports are expected to grow by 5.0% from a high base. As the readymade garment industry continues robust growth, its substantial input requirements will expand. An increase in the volume of imports of petroleum and petroleum products is expected, but with a more moderate price adjustment than in FY2021. Accelerated implementation of large infrastructure projects and robust real estate development are expected to boost imports of inputs for construction, capital equipment and other materials. Meanwhile, the need for food grain imports will fall.

Growth in remittances is likely to moderate to 7.0% in FY2022, reflecting a high base. Providing vaccinations for workers is key to job placement in destination countries and to maintaining robust remittance growth. The trade deficit is expected to be stable in dollar terms as both exports and imports increase. With moderate growth expected in remittances, the current account deficit is expected to narrow to 0.6% of GDP in FY2022 from 1.1% of GDP in FY2021.

Figure 3.3.12 Exchange rates

GDP = gross domestic product.
Source: Bangladesh Bank. 2021. *Monthly Economic Trends*. July. https://www.bb.org.bd.

Figure 3.3.13 GDP growth

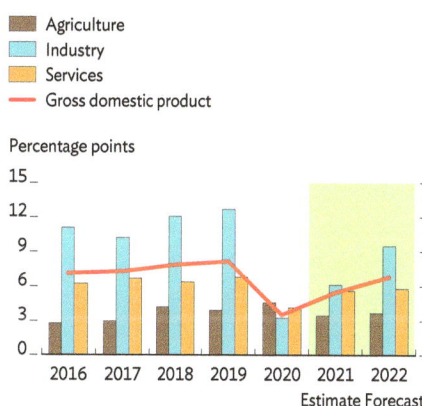

GDP = gross domestic product.
Note: Years are fiscal years ending on 30 June of that year.
Sources: Bangladesh Bureau of Statistics. http://www.bbs.gov.bd; Asian Development Bank estimates.

Figure 3.3.14 Fiscal indicators

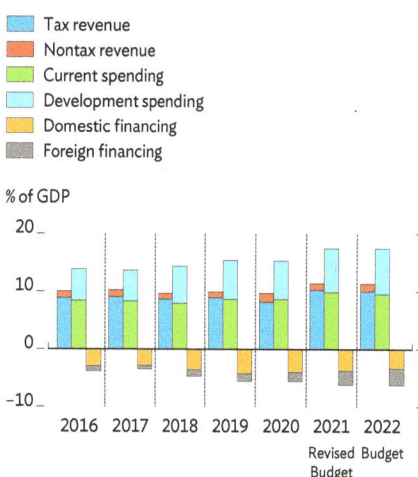

GDP = gross domestic product.
Note: Years are fiscal years ending on 30 June of that year.
Source: Ministry of Finance. https://www.mof.gov.bd.

India

Compared to last year, the economy rebounded strongly in the first quarter (Q1) of fiscal year 2021 (FY2021, ending 31 March 2022). It is expected to grow this year almost as quickly as forecast in *ADO 2021*, notwithstanding a dramatic second wave of COVID-19 infections that struck in April and May. Inflation is now projected to stay higher in FY2021 than forecast in *ADO 2021* because of rising input prices, but the forecast for lower inflation in FY2022 is sustained. Forecasts for current account deficits in both years are unchanged from *ADO 2021*.

Updated assessment

GDP grew in Q1 FY2021 by 20.1% year on year, rising by double digits because of a large base effect. Despite the high pace of year on year growth, it has yet to recover to its value in Q4 FY2019, just before the pandemic hit. At the same time, reflecting the adverse impact of a second wave of COVID-19, the economy contracted in Q1 FY2021 by 12.4% quarter on quarter in seasonally adjusted terms (Figure 3.3.15).

On the supply side, agriculture remained resilient, growing by 4.5% year on year. Industry grew by 46.1% on robust expansion in manufacturing and construction. Growth in services reached double digits, supported by strong expansion in trade, hotels, transport, and communication. Quarter on quarter, though, industry contracted in Q1 2021 even as mining grew by 6.2% on support from higher global commodity prices. Construction was severely hit in the quarter by local lockdowns in several states and shrank by 27.6%. Services similarly declined by 17.6%.

On the demand side, private consumption contracted by 16.1% quarter on quarter as households battled the second COVID-19 wave. Government consumption expenditure shrank by 22.2%, reflecting the government's constrained resources (Figure 3.3.16). Gross capital formation fell by 26.5% quarter on quarter but showed a strong rebound year on year. Exports of goods and services benefited from rising global demand to grow by 15.3% quarter on quarter, while imports of goods and services contracted by 6.7% as domestic demand was affected by the second wave.

Rising global oil prices, higher excise duties on gasoline and diesel fuel, and double-digit consumer price inflation for pulses and vegetable oil—both important staples in India—caused inflation to breach again in May and June 2021 the 2%–6% inflation target set by the Reserve Bank of India, the central bank (Figure 3.3.17). Inflation then fell back in July to 5.6%, its average rate in the first 4 months of FY2021. With headline inflation persistently high since last year, core inflation, which excludes energy and food, inched up as well, averaging 6.0% in the same 4 months. This development and a deficient monsoon may mean there is further inflationary pressure to come.

Figure 3.3.15 Supply-side contributions to growth

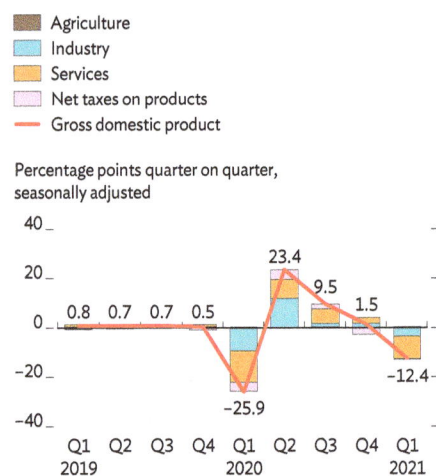

■ Agriculture
□ Industry
□ Services
□ Net taxes on products
— Gross domestic product

Percentage points quarter on quarter, seasonally adjusted

Q = quarter.
Notes: Q1 refers to first quarter of fiscal year (April–June). Net taxes on products are tax receipts minus subsidies.
Sources: Ministry of Statistics and Programme Implementation. http://www.mospi.nic.in; Haver Analytics (accessed 3 September 2021).

Figure 3.3.16 Demand-side contributions to growth

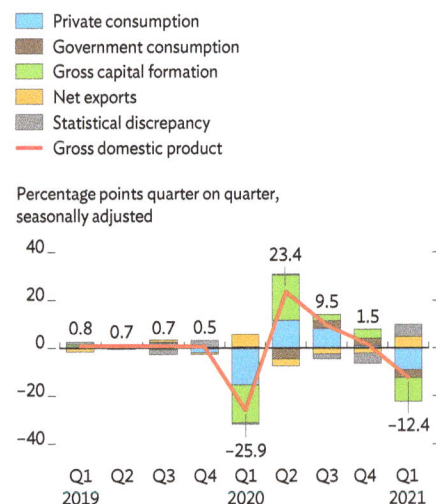

□ Private consumption
■ Government consumption
□ Gross capital formation
□ Net exports
□ Statistical discrepancy
— Gross domestic product

Percentage points quarter on quarter, seasonally adjusted

Q = quarter.
Note: Q1 refers to first quarter of fiscal year (April–June).
Sources: Ministry of Statistics and Programme Implementation. http://www.mospi.nic.in; Haver Analytics (accessed 3 September 2021).

With the second wave of COVID-19 disrupting economic activity, the government announced a new fiscal stimulus package equal to 2.7% of GDP, of which an amount equal to 2.4% of GDP is to be spent in FY2021. The package includes a 5-year scheme to reform electric power distribution, support for health-care infrastructure especially in rural areas, extension of a food guarantee scheme, and support to farmers through fertilizer subsidies. In addition, the government increased minimum agricultural support prices in June and September 2021.

Government revenue rose in the first 4 months of FY2021 thanks to substantially improved revenue collection through higher excise duties and measures to ensure tax compliance, notably the Vivaad se Vishwas (no dispute but trust) scheme (Figure 3.3.18). Goods and services tax receipts, on the other hand, slumped below ₹1 trillion in June 2021 for the first time since September 2020 before bouncing back in July–August 2021 as the economy reopened after the second wave. Expenditure remained as planned, with the central government budgeting a fiscal deficit equal to 6.8% of GDP for FY2021.

With health care, social services, and other critical aspects of containment, such as testing and monitoring, falling under the jurisdiction of Indian states even as their revenue declined, states have grappled with constrained fiscal space. States that reported budgets after the onset of the pandemic recorded deficits averaging 4.6% of state GDP in FY2020, breaching the 3% maximum set for them. Recognizing the need for states to fight the pandemic and continue with structural reform, both the central government and the devolution-enabling Fifteenth Finance Commission introduced reform-linked loans and grants equal to 1% of state GDP. Several state governments have consequently initiated reforms that, notably, implement "portable" rations that remains accessible to migrants far from home, improve the ease of doing business and thus the investment climate, and establish floor rates for property taxes and water charges in urban areas. Reform to electric power generation and distribution is an area where progress remains slow, with only some states implementing only partial reform.

Given elevated inflation, the central bank last lowered its policy rate in May 2020 (Figure 3.3.19). It is, however, undertaking measures to enhance liquidity: acquiring government securities on the secondary market, extending its On Tap Targeted Long-term Repurchase Operations, and providing liquidity support to its list of All India Financial Institutions and to emergency health-care services and contact-intensive industries. Despite these liquidity measures, the yield spread between 10-year government bonds and 91-day Treasury bills was 295 basis points at the end of August 2021, only marginally lower than 300 points at the end of March 2021.

Figure 3.3.17 Inflation

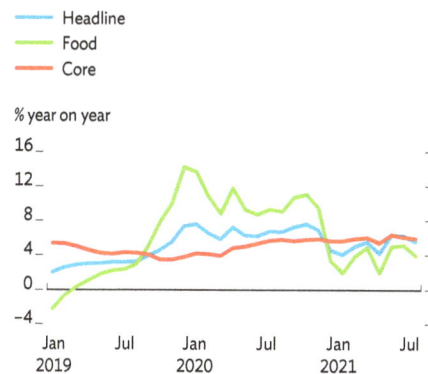

Source: CEIC Data Company (accessed 3 September 2021).

Figure 3.3.18 Fiscal revenue and expenditure

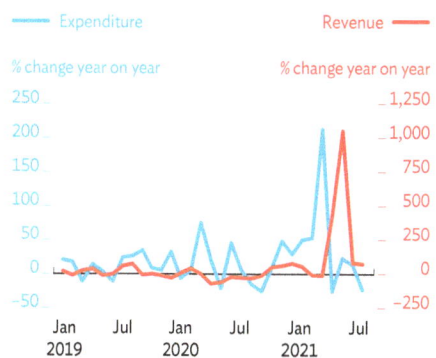

Source: CEIC Data Company (accessed 3 September 2021).

Figure 3.3.19 Interest rates

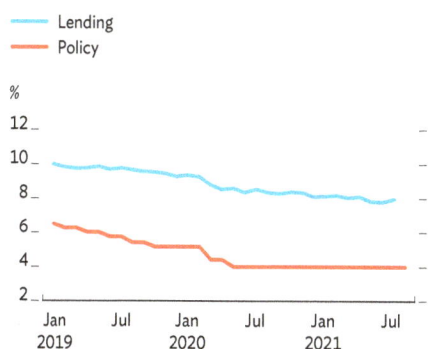

Source: CEIC Data Company (accessed 3 September 2021).

Despite central bank measures and liquidity support, nonfood credit, which excludes public sector loans for procuring crops from farmers, contracted by 1.2% from the end of March to mid-June 2021 (Figure 3.3.20). Contraction crossed all sectors, sparing only aviation, medium-sized industrial firms, and banking and finance services other than nonbank financial companies. Despite reduced household savings, personal loans contracted by 0.9%, weakening domestic consumption as households struggled with increased out-of-pocket health-care expenses incurred during the second COVID-19 wave, except for housing and loans against gold jewelry. Priority sector lending also weakened in the period, but not for housing, renewable energy, or social infrastructure.

The ratio of nonperforming loans (NPLs) to all loans increased from 6.8% at the end of December 2020 to 7.5% in March 2021 (Figure 3.3.21). This increase was smaller than expected, held down by pandemic-related measures announced by the government such as a loan repayment moratorium and credit restructuring without a downgrade in asset classification. As reported in the July 2021 edition of its *Financial Stability Report*, the central bank expects NPLs to worsen to 9.8% by March 2022 under its baseline scenario.

Imports shrank more than exports in FY2020, generating a current account surplus equal to 0.9% of GDP, or 0.1 percentage points lower than estimated in *ADO 2021*. Merchandise exports bounced back in the first 4 months of FY2021 with growth at 71.1% year on year, surpassing the prepandemic value, while imports grew by 88.7%. The trade deficit in goods widened from the equivalent of 1.9% of GDP in Q1 FY2020 to 4.4% in Q1 FY2021. The trade surplus in services grew by 8.1% year on year in Q1 FY2021, down from double-digit growth a year earlier.

Foreign direct investment inflow contracted by 1.9% in FY2020 despite a strong investment climate supported by reform designed to attract investment. It rose in Q1 FY2021 from $2.1 billion a year earlier to $16.6 billion. After record growth in FY2020, net foreign portfolio investment turned negative in the first 4 months of FY2021 before turning positive again in August 2021, even though global incomes improved and international stock market indexes rose by 16.2% (Figure 3.3.22). Disincentives to inbound investment were an unsettled international tax dispute, hurdles to the implementation of new data privacy laws, and antitrust cases against large e-commerce companies.

The Indian rupee depreciated by 0.9% in the first 5 months of FY2021 but appreciated by 0.3% over the FY2020 average (Figure 3.3.23). Large inflows of foreign direct investment contributed to an increase in foreign exchange reserves to $616.9 billion at the end of August 2021, providing cover for 16.1 months of imports (Figure 3.3.24).

Figure 3.3.20 Bank credit

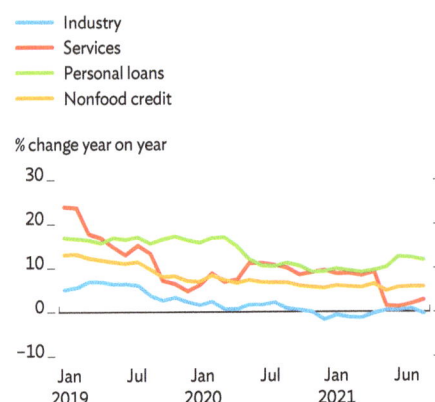

Note: Nonfood credit excludes public sector loans for procuring crops from farmers.
Source: Reserve Bank of India. https://rbi.org.in (accessed 3 September 2021).

Figure 3.3.21 Nonperforming loans

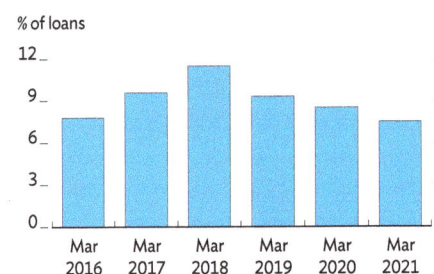

Source: Reserve Bank of India. https://rbi.org.in/ (accessed 3 September 2021).

Figure 3.3.22 Stock prices

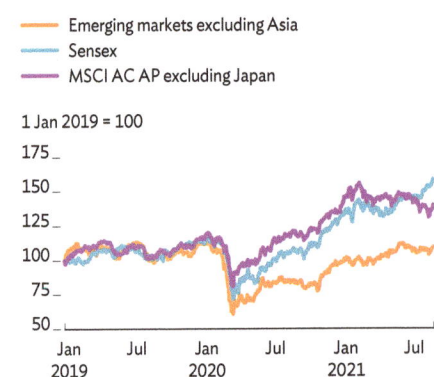

Source: Bloomberg (accessed 3 September 2021).

Prospects

The second COVID-19 wave dissipated more quickly than anticipated, with daily cases averaging about 40,000 by the end of August 2021. Several states have eased lockdown measures, and Google Mobility data show travel patterns starting to return to normal. This *Update* assumes that the economic impact of a third wave, if it occurs, will be limited thanks to the vaccination drive progressing on schedule, better preparedness in firms and households, and two-thirds of the population found by nationwide serological surveys to possess some antibodies against the SARS-CoV-2 virus.

Deep GDP contraction in FY2020 is seen providing a springboard for growth in the remaining 3 quarters of FY2021. High-frequency indicators show dissipating impact from the second wave and a return to normal economic activity. The purchasing managers' index for services increased sharply in August after remaining in contractionary territory below 50 in the previous months (Figure 3.3.25). It remained above 50 for manufacturing in July–August, indicating expansion in the sector. Electronic way bills grew by 30.3% in July–August over a year earlier, providing evidence of more movement of goods. Freight traffic grew by double digits in July 2021, and electricity generation and finished steel production expanded, though only by single digits (Figure 3.3.26).

Growth may be driven less by private consumption and more by government expenditure and exports as global demand picks up. COVID-19 severely hit household incomes and spending capacity as household debt rose sharply to equal 37.9% of GDP by the end of December 2020. Household debt will likely rise further after households borrowed against gold jewelry to pay out-of-pocket health-care expenses incurred in the second wave in April–May 2021. Consumer confidence fell in May 2021 to its lowest reading ever recorded and remained low in July 2021 (Figure 3.3.27).

Overall, investment remains weak as new project announcements amounted in Q1 FY2021 to only 44.3% of their prepandemic level and, in the same quarter, only 0.3% of outstanding projects were completed (Figure 3.3.28). In Q1 FY2021, of the 1,779 central sector projects worth more than ₹10 billion and less than ₹10.0 billion but more than ₹1.5 billion, 480 suffered cost overruns of ₹4.5 trillion in aggregate, and 559 suffered delays ranging from 1 to 324 months, caused mainly by delays in acquiring land and environmental clearances, and by a lack of infrastructure support and linkage. At the same time, rising NPLs and low uptake of bank credit are likely to deter private investment.

With private consumption and investment weak nevertheless, public investment should support recovery. The government's national monetization plan for brownfield infrastructure assets is expected to free resources worth

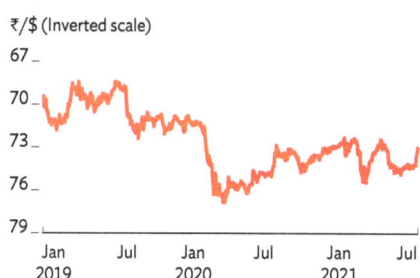

Figure 3.3.23 Exchange rates

₹/$ (Inverted scale)

Source: Bloomberg (accessed 3 September 2021).

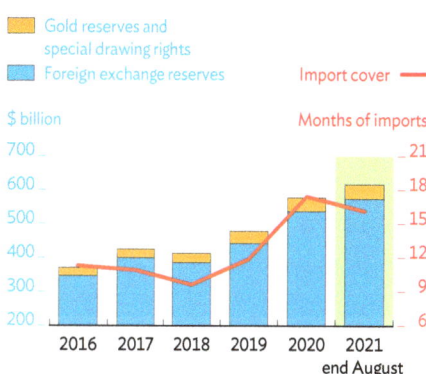

Figure 3.3.24 Gross international reserves

Gold reserves and special drawing rights
Foreign exchange reserves
Import cover

$ billion   Months of imports

Note: Years are fiscal years ending on 31 March of the next year.
Source: CEIC Data Company (accessed 3 September 2021).

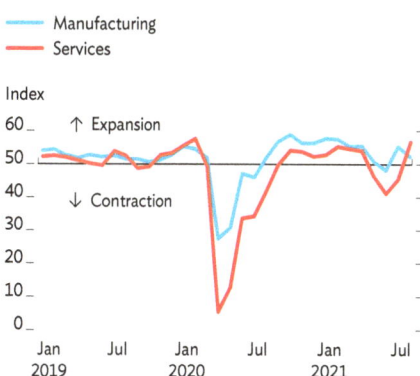

Figure 3.3.25 Purchasing managers' indexes

Manufacturing
Services

Index

↑ Expansion

↓ Contraction

Note: Purchasing managers' indexes are based on Nikkei, Markit.
Source: Bloomberg (accessed 3 September 2021).

₹6 trillion over the next 3 years with which to finance infrastructure development. Effective implementation of the plan will be, however, crucial. Further, government loans and grants have provided additional fiscal space to state governments as an inventive to increase capital expenditure, and it provides interest-free loans to enable state initiatives to monetize their public assets.

Growth in agriculture, affected by COVID-19 spreading into rural areas and a slightly delayed monsoon, may be marginally lower than projected in *ADO 2021*. The area sown for winter crops is smaller than last year. Rising international commodity prices caused a hike in fertilizer prices by 58% on 1 April 2021, prompting increased subsidies from the government in May. While this promises to ease some pressure on farmers' input costs, it burdens the government budget with an additional cost equal to 0.1% of GDP. Delays in implementing agricultural reform may undermine agricultural productivity in the medium term.

The service sector, a major contributor to growth in India, has been severely curtailed, especially subsectors requiring a physical interface with the public. The government estimates that the tourism industry lost 21.5 million jobs from April to December 2020. When the second wave hit the economy in Q1 FY2021, there likely were further job losses, especially affecting workers in the urban informal sector, which offers little access to social safety nets. After India opened to foreign tourists in March 2021, arrivals stopped again in May 2021 with the imposition of a ban on international travel, battering tourist revenue.

On balance, the economy is expected to grow by 10.0% in FY2021 as more people get vaccinated and economic activity rebounds (Table 3.3.2). The forecast is 1.0 percentage point below that in *ADO 2021* to take into account the impact of the second wave. Growth is forecast to moderate to 7.5% in FY2022, above the *ADO 2021* projection, assuming that a significant proportion of the population will be vaccinated by then and that domestic demand returns to normal. The government has ramped up its vaccination campaign, administering more than 10 million doses in 2 days in August. It approved vaccination for children as young at 12 years, which will help protect the younger population and facilitate normalization.

Inflation is expected to moderate in the rest of FY2021 as containment measures are eased and supply chain bottlenecks are resolved. Upward pressure on food prices will come from demand left unmet because of the delayed monsoon and consequent delay in crop sowing, coupled with higher procurement prices announced by the government. Rising global prices for oil and other commodities will further increase input and transportation costs for producers, which they will pass on to consumers. These push factors and the second-round effects of persistently high headline inflation

Figure 3.3.26 Selected high-frequency indicators

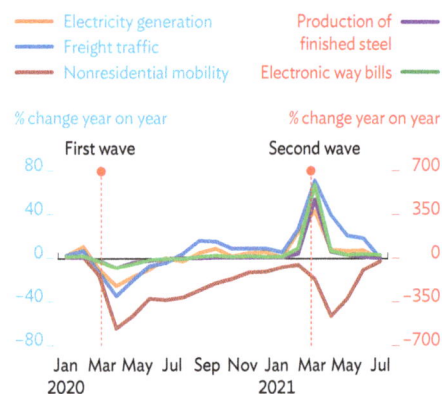

Note: Nonresidential mobility is percentage change from the baseline.
Sources: CEIC Data Company; Centre for Monitoring Indian Economy Pvt. Ltd.; Google COVID-19 Community Mobility Reports (all accessed 3 September 2021).

Figure 3.3.27 Consumer confidence

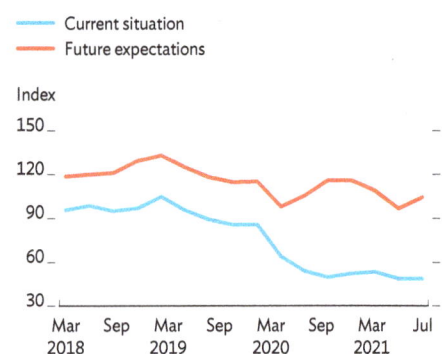

Source: Reserve Bank of India. https://www.rbi.org.in (accessed 3 September 2021).

Figure 3.3.28 Investment projects

Source: Centre for Monitoring Indian Economy Pvt. Ltd. https://www.cmie.com (accessed 3 September 2021).

from last year will keep core inflation elevated. Inflation in FY2021 is thus forecast to slow only to 5.5%, but the forecast for further slowing to 4.8% in FY2022 is retained.

The central government now aims for slower fiscal consolidation than envisaged under the Fiscal Responsibility and Budget Management Act, 2003, with the fiscal deficit scheduled to fall below 4.5% by FY2026. Domestic resource mobilization remains an issue. Key measures needed to augment tax revenue and generate fiscal space are streamlining income tax brackets to build the tax base, digitizing land and property records, strengthening goods and services tax administration and compliance, and mobilizing municipal resources.

The central bank is likely to continue its accommodative stance and support the economy through liquidity measures and reform in the financial industry. However, improving credit flow to support domestic investment requires making the resolution process for stressed assets more efficient. The central bank introduced a restructuring scheme for the stressed assets of individuals and smaller enterprises to lift some of the stress off them and improve credit flow in the system. Consequent haircuts and a slow resolution process have lowered net returns to lenders. Further, the resolution process remains skewed under the Insolvency and Bankruptcy Code, 2016. Setting aside two large recoveries, only 31% of defaulted assets have been recovered.

Increased global demand and a large base effect will fuel a strong rebound in exports of goods and services in FY2021. Imports of goods and services are expected to grow more quickly, however, as domestic demand resumes and the oil import bill increases, widening the trade deficit. This may be offset by improved remittances as global income recovers. On balance, the current account deficit in FY2021 is expected to equal 1.1% of GDP, as forecast in *ADO 2021* (Figure 3.3.29). In FY2022, exports and imports of goods and services will grow moderately as global demand continues to normalize. As economic growth moderates in FY2022, the current account deficit will narrow marginally to 1.0%, as forecast in April.

Higher US interest rates and a further increase in bond buying may trigger capital outflows as foreign investors search for higher returns (Figure 3.3.30). Ample foreign exchange reserves exist to cope with a higher import bill caused by any consequent depreciation of the rupee. Rolling back retrospective taxes on asset transfers should improve the climate for foreign investment.

Risks to the outlook tilt to the downside and depend mainly on the evolution of the pandemic. While the government has taken several measures to improve health-related interventions, especially in rural areas, vaccination remains key to reducing disease severity, easing the burden on hospitals, and speeding a return to normal.

Table 3.3.2 Selected economic indicators in India, %

	2020	2021		2022	
		ADO 2021	Update	ADO 2021	Update
GDP growth	−7.3	11.0	10.0	7.0	7.5
Inflation	6.2	5.2	5.5	4.8	4.8
CAB/GDP	1.0	−1.1	−1.1	−1.0	−1.0

ADO = Asian Development Outlook, CAB = current account balance, GDP = gross domestic product.

Note: Years are fiscal years ending on 31 March of the next year.

Sources: Ministry of Statistics and Programme Implementation (accessed 3 September 2021); Asian Development Bank estimates.

Figure 3.3.29 Current account

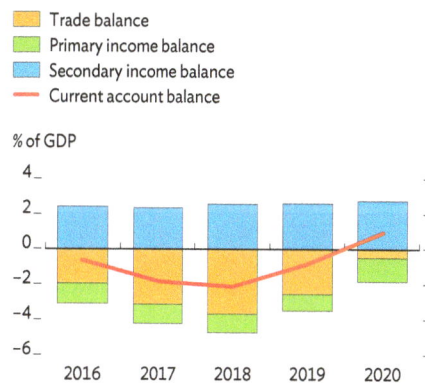

GDP = gross domestic product.

Note: Years are fiscal years ending on 31 March of the next year.

Sources: CEIC Data Company (accessed 3 September 2021); Asian Development Bank estimates.

Figure 3.3.30 Portfolio capital flows

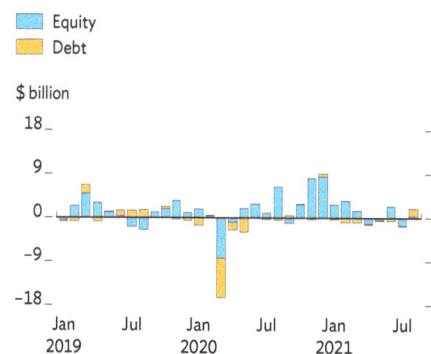

Source: National Securities Depository Limited. https://www.fpi.nsdl.co.in/web/Reports/Archive.aspx (accessed 3 September 2021).

Pakistan

The government's budget paper reported that the economy staged a strong recovery in fiscal year 2021 (FY2021, ended 30 June 2021). Improved COVID-19 containment strategies, including some mobility restrictions, helped to hold down reported cases. Through second and third waves of infections, the government maintained accommodative fiscal and monetary policies that accelerated recovery across all sectors. Pakistan's prospects in the near term depend on the course of the pandemic and on how well policy manages to sustain economic recovery while achieving fiscal consolidation as required.

Updated assessment

Real GDP rebounded from pandemic-induced 0.5% contraction in FY2020 to grow by 3.9% in FY2021 (Figure 3.3.31). The government implemented strong fiscal and monetary policy responses to the pandemic that included temporary fiscal stimulus, significant expansion of the social safety net, lower interest rates, subsidized credit, and relief on servicing bank loans. These measures lifted consumer and business confidence, as did a steady vaccine rollout, a gradual narrowing of mobility restrictions to small specific areas, and speedy resumption of most economic activity. As of 13 September 2021, 21.6 million people, or 10.0% of the population, had been fully vaccinated, and 50.8 million people, or 23.6%, had received one shot. The government aims to vaccinate 70 million people by the end of the current calendar year.

On the supply side, growth in agriculture slowed from 3.3% in FY2020 to 2.8% in FY2021, trimming the contribution of agriculture to GDP growth from 0.6 percentage points to 0.5 points. The slowdown reflected a cotton harvest significantly reduced by excessive rain, pest attacks, and a continued fall in cultivated area. Production of other major crops—notably wheat, rice, sugarcane, and maize—increased robustly thanks to a relief package for agriculture offering subsidies on seed, pesticides, fertilizer, and locally manufactured tractors, as well as bank credit and higher minimum procurement prices for wheat and sugarcane. Credit to agriculture increased by 14.1% year on year in the first 11 months in FY2021, and sales of farm tractors rose by 62.2% in the first 10 months. Growth in livestock, which contributes about 60% of agricultural output, accelerated from 2.1% in FY2020 to 3.1% in FY2021.

Industry reversed 3.8% contraction in FY2020 to expand by 3.6% in FY2021. Robust manufacturing and construction flipped the sector's contribution to GDP growth from −0.7 percentage points in FY2020 to 0.7 points in FY2021. Despite new outbreaks of COVID-19 and the reimposition of some mobility restrictions, business sentiment improved with the revival of economic activity, bolstered by fiscal incentives

Figure 3.3.31 Supply-side contributions to growth

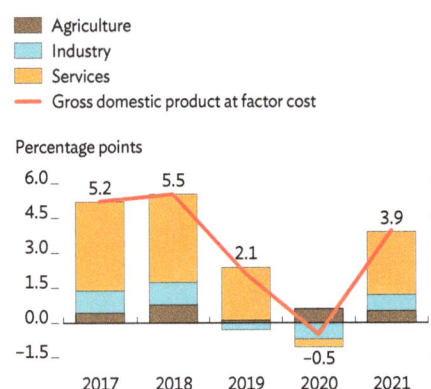

Note: Years are fiscal years ending on 30 June of that year.
Source: Ministry of Finance. *Pakistan Economic Survey 2020–21.* http://www.finance.gov.pk.

Figure 3.3.32 Demand-side contributions to growth

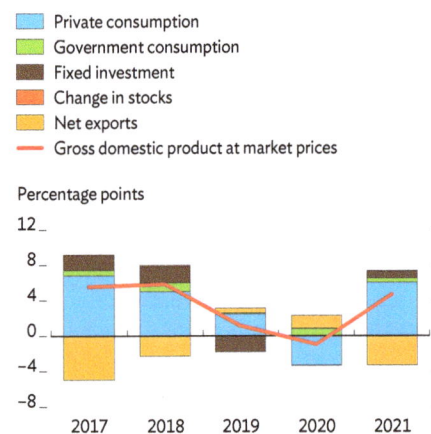

Note: Years are fiscal years ending on 30 June of that year.
Source: Ministry of Finance. *Pakistan Economic Survey 2020–21.* http://www.finance.gov.pk.

to key construction and export industries and subsidized credit to protect employment. The countrywide launch of a vaccination program in the second half of FY2021 further strengthened recovery in industry. Large-scale manufacturing, which accounts for about half of sector output, grew by 12.8% in the first 10 months in FY2021, reversing 8.7% contraction in the same period a year earlier. This trend saw double-digit increases in textiles, food, automobiles, pharmaceuticals, chemicals, iron and steel products, and nonmetallic mineral products. Growth in services also resumed with the normalization of most business activity following the removal of most restrictions on movement to contain COVID-19 and from buoyant growth in agriculture and industry. Reversing 0.6% decline in FY2020, services expanded by 4.4% in FY2021, boosting the sector's contribution to GDP growth from −0.3 percentage points to 2.7 points.

On the demand side, private consumption, which constitutes 81.6% of GDP, rebounded strongly in FY2021 to contribute 6.0 percentage points to GDP growth (Figure 3.3.32). The rebound reflected improved consumer confidence, a record increase in workers' remittances, and cash transfers to the impoverished through the Ehsaas Emergency Cash Program. However, growth in public consumption slowed as the government sought to consolidate its fiscal position by curtailing subsidies and gradually scaling back measures to mitigate the economic impact of COVID-19. Fixed investment contributed 0.7 percentage points to GDP growth as public investment increased, but private investment subtracted marginally from growth, subdued by uncertainty about the course of the pandemic nationally and globally. Net exports reduced growth by 3.3 percentage points as imports grew considerably faster than exports in FY2021 on account of recovery in domestic economic activity and higher imports of essential foodstuffs to stabilize domestic prices.

Average consumer inflation slowed from 10.7% in FY2020 to 8.9%, but rising food and energy prices kept it above the 6.5% target for the year set by the State Bank of Pakistan, the central bank (Figure 3.3.33). Food price inflation remained elevated at 12.5% in urban areas and 13.2% in rural areas, primarily reflecting higher prices for nonperishable food items caused by supply chain disruption, increased farmer-support prices for wheat and sugarcane, and an extended wet monsoon. Rising international oil prices and a January 2021 increase in electricity tariffs boosted energy price inflation. However, inflation for other goods eased thanks to Pakistan rupee appreciation and the postponement in the wake of the pandemic of other planned hikes for electricity tariffs and domestic fuel prices. Core inflation, excluding food and energy, fell from an average of 8.1% in FY2020 to 6.8% in FY2021.

The central bank has kept the policy rate unchanged at 7.00% after reducing it by a cumulative 625 basis points in the early days of the pandemic in March 2020 (Figure 3.3.34).

Figure 3.3.33 Monthly inflation

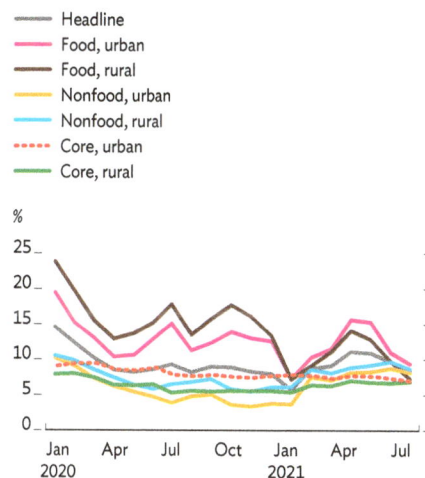

- Headline
- Food, urban
- Food, rural
- Nonfood, urban
- Nonfood, rural
- Core, urban
- Core, rural

Notes: Core inflation excludes food and energy. Fiscal year 2016, ended on 30 June 2016, equals 100.
Source: State Bank of Pakistan. *Economic Data.* http://www.sbp.org.pk (accessed 12 August 2021).

Figure 3.3.34 Interest rates and inflation

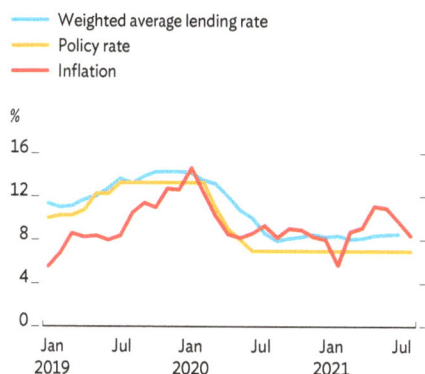

- Weighted average lending rate
- Policy rate
- Inflation

Source: State Bank of Pakistan. *Economic Data.* http://www.sbp.org.pk (accessed 21 August 2021).

It aims to support economic recovery while keeping inflationary expectations under control. Further, the central bank has introduced a host of time-bound, targeted measures to help firms and households cope with pandemic-induced challenges by keeping businesses solvent, supporting export-oriented industries, encouraging investment, and sustaining financial services. Responding to the improving outlook, the central bank has gradually trimmed several of these measures, ending in FY2021 a subsidized lending scheme to finance employee wages and salaries and thus prevent layoffs and, for bank borrowers, regulatory relief that facilitated loan deferment and restructuring.

Private sector credit expanded by 6.1% in the first 11 months in FY2021 as demand recovered under accommodative monetary conditions. Growth in private sector credit has featured increases in lending by 3.1% to manufacturers, 28.6% for consumer finance, 6.0% for construction, and 6.9% for electricity generation. Nevertheless, as a share of GDP, outstanding credit to the private sector declined from 15.1% at the end of May 2020 to 13.9% a year later.

In FY2021, lower expenditure reined in the consolidated federal and provincial fiscal deficit to the equivalent of 7.1% of GDP, down from 8.1% of GDP a year earlier (Figure 3.3.35). The primary balance was a deficit of 1.4% of GDP. Revenue collection fell from 15.1% of GDP to 14.5%, primarily because of a large decline in nontax receipts from an exceptionally high peak in the preceding year. Tax revenue decreased marginally from 11.4% of GDP in FY2020 to 11.1% in FY2021 despite a higher petroleum levy and more effective federal and provincial tax collection. Expenditure decreased from 23.2% of GDP to 21.6% as spending on defense and development was significantly curtailed as fiscal space shrank and outlays for health care and social spending rose. As a share of GDP, interest payments declined marginally because of reduced foreign interest payments after Pakistan joined the Group of Twenty (G-20) Debt Service Suspension Initiative. The fiscal deficit was financed largely through domestic borrowing, which provided 66.0% of financing, 48.3% from banks and 17.7% from nonbank sources. External borrowing financed the rest of the deficit.

The current account deficit narrowed significantly from the equivalent of 1.7% of GDP in FY2020 to 0.6% in FY2021, the improvement driven by exceptional growth in remittances, a turnaround in exports, and a more robust primary income balance with deferred interest repayments under the G-20 initiative (Figure 3.3.36). Supported by the government's Roshan Digital Accounts initiative to help the Pakistani diaspora make online bank payments, transfers, and investments, remittances rose by 27% in FY2021, reaching an average of $2.4 billion per month (Figure 3.3.37). By the end of FY2021, international

Figure 3.3.35 Government budget indicators

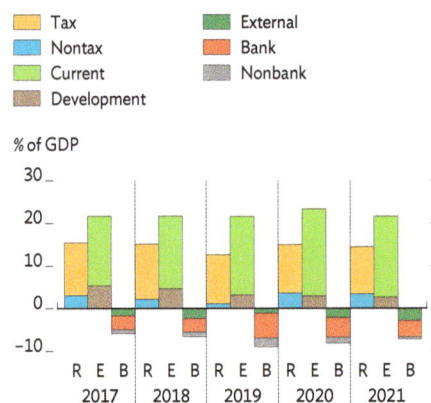

B = budget financing, E = expenditure, GDP = gross domestic product, R = revenue.
Note: Years are fiscal years ending on 30 June of that year.
Source: Ministry of Finance, Pakistan Summary of Consolidated Federal and Provincial Budgetry Operations, July–December 2021.

Figure 3.3.36 Current account components

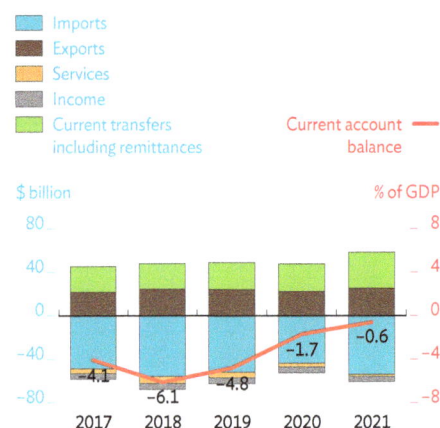

GDP = gross domestic product.
Note: Years are fiscal years ending on 30 June of that year.
Source: State Bank of Pakistan. http://www.sbp.org.pk (accessed 12 August 2021).

Figure 3.3.37 Remittances

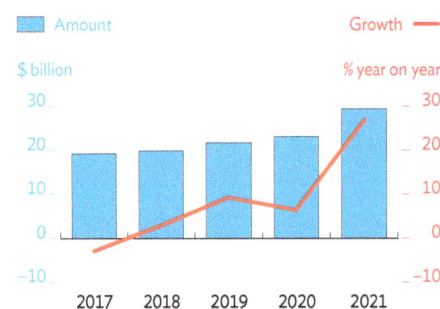

Note: Years are fiscal years ending on 30 June of that year.
Source: State Bank of Pakistan. http://www.sbp.org.pk (accessed 12 August 2021).

reserves had reached $17.3 billion, improving import coverage to 3.4 months (Figure 3.3.38). In addition, the merchandise trade deficit widened from the equivalent of 8.0% of GDP a year earlier to 9.4% as imports surged to meet rising demand for intermediate goods with the revival of economic activity and to counter supply shocks affecting key agricultural products, notably wheat, sugar, and cotton. This occurred despite exports reversing contraction by 7.1% with 13.7% expansion, mainly from supportive government policy and strong economic recovery in key export markets.

Prospects

The economy is expected to continue recovering in FY2022, with real GDP projected to rise by 4.0% (Table 3.3.3 and Figure 3.3.39). This growth forecast assumes recovery in private investment as consumer confidence and business activity improve amid the ongoing vaccination rollout and various economic stimulus measures announced in the budget for FY2022. It also assumes the resumption of structural reform later in the year in an ongoing program under the International Monetary Fund (IMF) Extended Fund Facility. The economic outlook is clouded, however, by high uncertainty because it is closely tied to the course of the pandemic in Pakistan and globally.

On the supply side, the outlook for agriculture is encouraging in view of the government's ambitious Agriculture Transformation Plan. The plan aims to achieve food security for a growing population by expanding land under cultivation, revamping extension services, boosting water-use efficiency, developing postharvest storage and food processing plants, augmenting bank credit, and introducing the Kissan Card as a digital wallet for the direct and swift transfer of subsidies for seed, pesticides, and fertilizer. Growth in industry is forecast to improve in FY2022, driven by fiscal incentives announced in the FY2022 budget, a substantial rise in budgeted development spending, and strong private consumption underpinned by adequate agricultural harvests, strong remittance inflow, and a pickup in earnings as social restrictions are reduced and most economic activity resumes. Also expected to buttress industry are the steady normalization of global merchandise trade, improved market sentiment, and stronger business and consumer confidence expected from the continuing rollout of COVID-19 vaccines and an accommodative monetary policy. Enhanced growth in agriculture and industry and an expected improvement in domestic demand are projected to boost growth in services, strengthening their contribution to growth in FY2022. On this outlook, this *Update* maintains the *ADO 2021* projection for GDP growth at 4.0% in 2022.

Inflation is projected to slow to 7.5% in FY2022, unchanged from the forecast in *ADO 2021*, as food prices moderate with supply chain improvement and production increases

Figure 3.3.38 Gross official reserves and import coverage

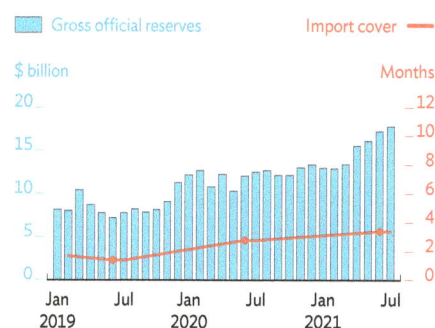

Source: State Bank of Pakistan. http://www.sbp.org.pk (accessed 12 August 2021).

Table 3.3.3 Selected economic indicators in Pakistan, %

	2020	2021		2022	
		ADO 2021	Update	ADO 2021	Update
GDP growth	−0.5	2.0	3.9	4.0	4.0
Inflation	10.7	8.7	8.9	7.5	7.5
CAB/GDP	−1.7	−1.0	−0.6	−2.0	−1.5

ADO = *Asian Development Outlook*, CAB = current account balance, GDP = gross domestic product.
Note: Years are fiscal years ending on 30 June of that year.
Sources: Ministry of Finance. *Pakistan Economic Survey 2020–21*; Asian Development Bank estimates.

Figure 3.3.39 GDP growth

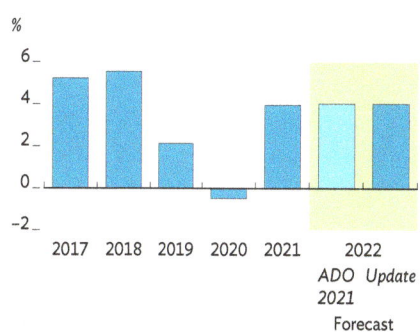

ADO = *Asian Development Outlook*, GDP = gross domestic product.
Note: Years are fiscal years ending on 30 June of that year.
Sources: Ministry of Finance. *Pakistan Economic Survey 2020–21*. http://www.finance.gov.pk; Asian Development Bank estimates.

facilitated by the government's Agriculture Transformation Plan (Figure 3.3.40). Price rises for other goods are expected to moderate as well thanks to tax relief in the FY2022 budget. Inflationary pressures will likely come from ongoing economic recovery and rising global oil prices but should be tempered by expenditure reform and the government's commitment not to borrow directly from the central bank. Risk of inflation higher than forecast derives from any unusual increase in oil prices or from potential currency depreciation in the wake of any early winding down of the ongoing IMF program.

The fiscal deficit is forecast to narrow to the equivalent of 6.9% of GDP in FY2022, which is still higher than the target set earlier under a medium-term fiscal consolidation program supported by the IMF. Growth in revenue is projected to accelerate with the rapid pickup in domestic economic activity and higher imports. Further bolstering revenue growth are the introduction of new tax measures under the Finance Act, 2021; a renewed focus on streamlining tax exemptions; and additional policy and administrative measures to broaden the tax base. Expenditure is also projected to rise in FY2022, as the government has budgeted substantial increases in subsidies and in social and development spending to protect the vulnerable and fortify growth and economic recovery.

Pakistan's public debt outlook is sustainable in the medium term. With primary and fiscal deficits, high borrowing costs, and currency depreciation, public external debt reached $95.2 billion in FY2021 (Figure 3.3.41). However, the government has been implementing a medium-term debt strategy for FY2020–FY2023. The maturity structure of public debt has improved by reprofiling public debt into longer-term instruments. With strong economic growth prospects for FY2022 and beyond, public debt remains on a downward path over the medium term.

As domestic demand picks up and international oil prices rise, the current account deficit is seen widening to the equivalent of 1.5% of GDP in FY2022, which is a smaller deficit than forecast in *ADO 2021* in line with the FY2021 deficit being smaller than projected (Figure 3.3.42). Export growth is expected to accelerate in FY2022, supported by a projected upturn in economic activity in Pakistan's major trade partners. Exports will further benefit from continued initiatives to reduce the cost of doing business and especially from the government's newly introduced export facilitation scheme, which allows the duty- and tax-free acquisition of inputs: intermediate goods, plant, and machinery. Imports are expected to rise in FY2022 in response to domestic economic recovery, higher international oil prices, and rationalization of custom and regulatory duties in the FY2022 budget. Remittances are likely to remain elevated, supported by the Roshan Digital Accounts initiative, and will continue to narrow the current account deficit.

Figure 3.3.40 Inflation

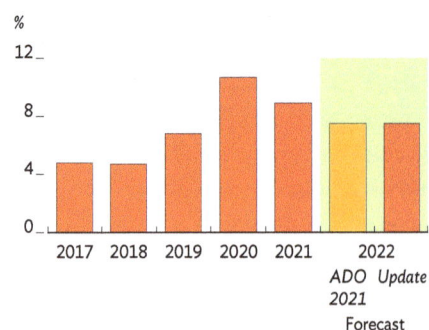

ADO = Asian Development Outlook.
Note: Years are fiscal years ending on 30 June of that year.
Sources: Ministry of Finance. *Pakistan Economic Survey 2020–21.* http://www.finance.gov.pk; Asian Development Bank estimates.

Figure 3.3.41 Government domestic and external debt

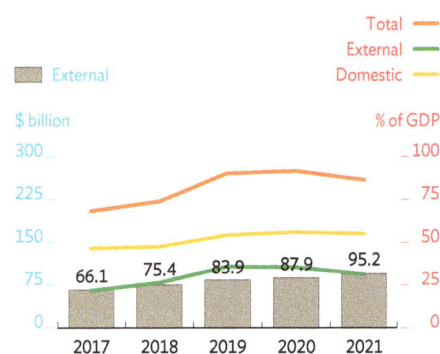

GDP = gross domestic product.
Notes: Years are fiscal years ending on 30 June of that year. External debt includes government and other external liabilities and public corporations.
Source: State Bank of Pakistan. *Economic Data.* http://www.sbp.org.pk (accessed 30 August 2021).

Figure 3.3.42 Current account balance

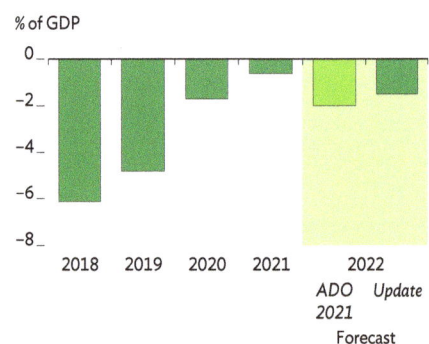

ADO = Asian Development Outlook, GDP = gross domestic product.
Note: Years are fiscal years ending on 30 June of that year.
Sources: Ministry of Finance. *Pakistan Economic Survey 2020–21.* http://www.finance.gov.pk; Asian Development Bank estimates.

Other economies

Afghanistan

Before the Taliban took over on 15 August 2021, the Afghan economy faced fallout from the COVID-19 pandemic, deepening insecurity, and drought. With the consequent withdrawal of international assistance, Afghanistan confronts an even greater crisis.

In April, ADB estimated in *ADO 2021* that GDP growth would recover to 3% in 2021 and improve further to 4% in 2022. These forecasts have been overtaken by events. Afghanistan has long depended heavily on grant inflows, which equaled 43% of GDP in 2020 and funded 56% of the budget but are now suspended by most development partners. With the freezing of over $9 billion in Afghan assets abroad, foreign reserves that recently covered 15 months of imports now cover only days. The afghani has depreciated significantly, spurring inflation such that the price of flour has risen by an estimated 11% since mid-August and the price of rice by 9%. Falling government revenue has disrupted the delivery of government services.

The country's economic prospects will depend on the policy choices of the new administration and how the international community responds. Looking ahead, ADB distinguishes three scenarios for the Afghan economy, simulating the economic impact using a computable general equilibrium model, the results subject to wide margins of error given data limitations and general uncertainty.

In the first scenario, the economy would severely contract under prolonged suspension of development and humanitarian assistance, frozen foreign reserves, and economic sanctions. Against a base scenario of business as usual with no takeover, real GDP could contract by up to 30% and unemployment increase by about 43%, dramatically increasing the poverty rate to as high as 97%, based on a United Nations estimate. Potentially significant refugee outflow could impose difficulties on neighboring countries.

In the second scenario, the provision of humanitarian aid and limited bilateral assistance could have mitigating economic impact. While adversity would still be significant—with real GDP contracting by up to 20% against the base scenario, household consumption by about 27%, and government expenditure by 30%—humanitarian support and some resumption of economic activity would avert a crushing humanitarian crisis. Afghanistan's economic ties would likely be strengthened with countries formally recognizing the new government, and some foreign investment would arrive, particularly into utilities and mining.

In the third scenario, sanctions are lifted, multilateral assistance resumes, and access to external reserves and international markets is unlocked. Afghanistan could then resume development and perhaps even improve its trajectory.

A peace dividend with better security could enhance the investment environment, catalyzing foreign direct investment and economic activity. With help from development partners, the government would be able to deliver basic services and build on development gains achieved during the past 20 years. Economic growth could accelerate in line with an annual growth rate of 4%, as projected by ADB prior to the takeover.

Bhutan

Bhutan has fully vaccinated 90% of its eligible population, which bodes well for a return to normal economic activity. However, borders may stay largely closed due to conditions in neighboring countries and a return to normalcy will be protracted. Accordingly, growth and current account forecasts made in *ADO 2021* have been retained.

GDP is estimated to have contracted by 3.4% in fiscal year 2021 (FY2021, ending 30 June 2021) (Table 3.3.4). While containment measures including two nationwide lockdowns controlled COVID-19 to only 2,585 cases and 3 deaths since the beginning of the pandemic in March 2020, economic activities came to a virtual standstill.

On the supply side, services experienced the steepest contraction of 4.7%, as the freeze on international tourism for a full year knocked down allied sectors. Industry contracted by 3.2%, despite a boost in hydropower, as manufacturing and construction contracted markedly on shortages of imported materials and the departure of much of the large expatriate labor force. Agriculture grew by 2.8%, given policy focus on food supply.

On the demand side, private investment contracted as disruptions obstructed activities. Falling incomes and lockdown measures also resulted in sharp contractions in private consumption. Increased public consumption and investment moderately cushioned the contraction in domestic demand.

Fiscal policy was expansionary as total expenditure was set to increase by 21.2% in FY2021. While current expenditure was lowered to fulfill constitutional requirements, capital spending was increased to support recovery. Fiscal stimulus will continue in FY2022 as a "No Capital Budget Ceiling" principle has been adopted by including a large share of planned capital outlays in the Twelfth Five-Year Plan into the budget for the year. Similarly, monetary policy will continue to support businesses with a continuation of interest waiver schemes, restructuring options for loans and concessional financing for small and medium industries.

Growth is forecast to rebound to 3.7% in FY2022 as the nationwide vaccination drive restores mobility and economic activity; the government markedly boosts investment spending; and global economic recovery revives tourism and trade with India.

Table 3.3.4 Selected economic indicators in Bhutan, %

	2020	2021		2022	
		ADO 2021	Update	ADO 2021	Update
GDP growth	0.9	-3.4	-3.4	3.7	3.7
Inflation	3.0	6.4	8.2	5.3	6.2
CAB/GDP	-12.1	-7.7	-7.7	-10.4	-10.4

ADO = *Asian Development Outlook*, CAB = current account balance, GDP = gross domestic product.
Note: Years are fiscal years ending on 30 June of that year.
Source: Asian Development Bank estimates.

Average inflation in FY2021 increased to 8.2%, well above the 6.4% forecast in *ADO 2021*. This was mainly driven by higher food prices, both domestic and imported, which rose to average 14.7%. Nonfood prices averaged 3.0%. Inflation in FY2022 is now expected to moderate to 6.2%, higher than the *ADO 2021* 5.3% forecast. Lower inflation in India, the major supplier of imports; a steep decline in import tariffs from third countries to a uniform rate of 10%; and the progressive restoration of supply lines underpin more moderate inflation than in FY2021.

Maldives

Tourist arrivals rebounded strongly in the first half (H1) of 2021, although the number of arrivals in the second quarter weakened. Nevertheless, arrivals increased by 33.4% year on year to 510,549, boosted by very large increases in visitors from the Russian Federation and India that brought their combined market share to 42.0% from only 16.7% in H1 of 2020. Increased visitors from Europe (excluding the Russian Federation), however was slightly up at about 1.0%, but still amounted to 41.5% of arrivals, somewhat below their 44.1% share of the 1.7 million peak arrivals in 2019 before the pandemic. Arrivals from the People's Republic of China, which held a major 16.7% market share in 2019, only accounted for 0.1% of total tourists in H1 2021, reflecting the country's outbound (and inbound) travel policies to mitigate the spread of COVID-19.

In contrast to tourism, construction and investment remain in decline as evidenced by a 33.5% year on year fall in imports of construction materials in H1 2021, as well as stagnation in private sector credit for construction and real estate.

More favorable tourism prospects are expected during the latter part of the year, reflecting higher vaccination rates in major markets drumming up arrivals, peak seasonal tourism in the fourth quarter and the appeal of the country's "one island, one resort" model in controlling risk of infection. With arrivals at 510,549 in H1 2021, the *ADO 2021* projection of roughly 850,000 visitors in 2021 is likely to be exceeded to reach a little over one million. Accordingly, the GDP forecasts are upgraded to 18.0% in 2021 and to 15.0% in 2022, nevertheless GDP would be 21.6% lower in 2021 and 9.9% lower in 2022 than in 2019 (Table 3.3.5). The main downside risk to these forecasts is the emergence of more virulent and contagious variants prompting travel restrictions disrupting economic recovery, further deteriorating fiscal and debt sustainability in the face of the country's very high public debt ratio and limited usable foreign exchange reserves.

Inflation averaged only 0.8% in H1 2021 given large price cut in information and communication services and the impact of COVID-19 relief for housing rent. Government has historically

Table 3.3.5 Selected economic indicators in Maldives, %

	2020	2021 ADO 2021	2021 Update	2022 ADO 2021	2022 Update
GDP growth	–32.0	13.1	18.0	14.0	15.0
Inflation	–1.4	3.0	2.5	2.5	2.0
CAB/GDP	–29.8	–23.0	–19.0	–25.0	–20.0

ADO = *Asian Development Outlook*, CAB = current account balance, GDP = gross domestic product.

Source: Asian Development Bank estimates.

used administrative pricing policies to underpin meeting its citizens basic needs. Given the incomplete economic recovery, the inflation forecast for 2021 is lowered to 2.5% despite global price pressure as utility and other price subsidies are put in place. The 2022 forecast is also lowered to 2.0% on expected receding global pressures, although introduction of a minimum wage may risk some cost-push inflation.

The trade deficit rose by 16.1% year on year in H1 2021 as imports climbed by 14.6%. Given better tourism performance in this period travel receipts rose by 104.5% year on year boosting the services balance. Owing to the stronger-than-expected tourism recovery, current account deficits are revised lower.

Nepal

The economy is reviving from the COVID-19 pandemic induced contraction of 2.1%, despite a surge in infections that led to strict containment measures in May and June 2021 in most districts, including the Kathmandu valley.

GDP growth in fiscal year 2021 (FY2021, ended 15 July 2021) is estimated at 2.3%, below the 3.1% *ADO 2021* forecast (Table 3.3.6). Agriculture expanded by 2.4%, up from 2.2% a year earlier, owing to a good monsoon and increased acreage under cultivation. Industry grew by 1.7%, after contracting by 3.7%, on stronger domestic demand and a large increase in exports. Services, which had contracted by 4.0%—mainly on account of tourism, which directly and indirectly accounts for about 8.0% of GDP, and saw an 80.8% collapse in arrivals—grew modestly by 2.5%. On the demand side, private consumption dominated spending on strong growth in remittances. Fixed investment expanded modestly by 4.0%, following a large 12.4% contraction, as public and private activity increased.

Growth in FY2022 is revised to 4.1% from 5.1% in *ADO 2021* because high infection rates, though reduced, continue and will limit growth in tourism and services. Heightened public precautions and government's plan to vaccinate 72% of the population are expected over time to quell infection rates. Fiscal policy for FY2022 remains expansionary, focused on strengthening health care, employment generation, expansion of social protection for the poor and vulnerable, and promoting agricultural productivity. Monetary policy for FY2022 will continue to be accommodative through a dedicated large refinancing facility, concessional lending for priority projects, and facilities for affected businesses.

Average inflation fell to 3.6% in FY2021 from 6.2% a year earlier. Food inflation eased to 5.0%, while nonfood inflation fell markedly to 2.5% on a rebound in imports and very slight price increases for most goods and services. With growth in FY2022 accelerating less than forecast, projected inflation is revised to 5.2%, somewhat below the *ADO 2021* forecast.

Table 3.3.6 Selected economic indicators in Nepal, %

	2020	2021		2022	
		ADO 2021	*Update*	*ADO 2021*	*Update*
GDP growth	-2.1	3.1	2.3	5.1	4.1
Inflation	6.2	5.0	3.6	6.0	5.2
CAB/GDP	-0.9	-2.5	-8.0	-3.8	-5.0

ADO = Asian Development Outlook, CAB = current account balance, GDP = gross domestic product.
Note: Years are fiscal years ending 15 July of that year.
Source: Asian Development Bank estimates.

Imports surged by 25.7% in FY2021 after contracting by 19.3% a year earlier as the economy began to normalize. Despite a 30.0% increase in exports and 8.2% increase in remittances, the current account deficit rose sharply to 8.0% of GDP, substantially above the 2.5% deficit forecast in *ADO 2021*. Financing, nevertheless, was adequate to meet the large deficit and gross foreign exchange reserves grew marginally to $11.7 billion, cover for 10.2 months of imports of goods and services. Import growth will remain high in FY2022 as investment activity intensifies based on a sustained revival in economic activity. Even with continued strong growth in exports and favorable remittances, the current account deficit will stay high, estimated at 5.0% of GDP, exceeding the *ADO 2021* forecast.

Sri Lanka

GDP grew by 4.3% year on year in the first quarter of 2021, as COVID-19 infection rates eased. Despite an upturn in cases from April, timely indicators pointed to a recovery in manufacturing and services amid localized containment measures. However, detection of Delta coronavirus variant outbreaks led to a nationwide lockdown in late August and early September that will slow growth momentum. Further, Sri Lanka's debt and fiscal situation continues to be challenging, with central government debt to GDP growing to 101.0% in 2020. Moreover, the budget deficit is likely to be higher than expected as revenue suffers and expenditure increases amid new outbreaks. External sector pressures and low reserves stemming from softening in remittances, lackluster recovery in tourism, and large debt repayments will constrain growth.

Accordingly, *ADO 2021* GDP growth forecasts are revised down to 3.4% in 2021 and 2022 as macroeconomic headwinds will hold back a strong rebound (Table 3.3.7). By 9 September, 60.5% of the population received one dose of vaccine and 46.6% were fully vaccinated, and indeed rapid vaccination is key to economic recovery. Risks to the outlook are from fresh pandemic outbreak, low foreign reserves, and currency related stress.

Inflation increased from 3.0% in January to 6.0% in August, averaging 4.5% in the first 8 months of 2021. Volatile food prices, rising global oil and commodity prices, and exchange rate depreciation will keep prices elevated in the second half of 2021. Consequently, inflation forecasts are raised to 5.1% for 2021 and 5.3% for 2022.

The central bank raised policy rates by 50 basis points in August 2021 to a 5.0%–6.0% corridor, stating concerns on inflation and external imbalances. By early September, the exchange rate depreciated by 7.3% against the US dollar from end-2020 as the official exchange rate was maintained

Table 3.3.7 Selected economic indicators in Sri Lanka, %

	2020	2021		2022	
		ADO 2021	*Update*	*ADO 2021*	*Update*
GDP growth	–3.6	4.1	3.4	3.6	3.4
Inflation	4.6	4.5	5.1	5.0	5.3
CAB/GDP	–1.3	–1.1	–2.8	–1.7	–2.3

ADO = *Asian Development Outlook*, CAB = current account balance, GDP = gross domestic product.
Source: Asian Development Bank estimates.

at just below SLRs200/$ since May 2021, barring a few days when the official indicative rate moved up to SLRs210/$. Foreign exchange reserves declined to $2.8 billion by end-July from $5.7 billion at end-2020 but improved to $3.55 billion by end-August supported by special drawing rights allocation and other efforts to buffer reserves. Further restrictions on outward transfers were imposed to manage the pressure on reserves.

During the first half of 2021, the merchandise trade deficit increased by 32.3% year on year as imports outpaced exports amid higher commodity prices and relaxation of some import restrictions. With remittances starting to soften in June and July, and tourist arrivals a trickle, the current account deficit is expected to widen to 2.8% of GDP in 2021 and to 2.3% in 2022.

Southeast Asia

The resurgence of the more contagious Delta COVID-19 variant in late April this year has slowed Southeast Asia's growth momentum. GDP growth for the subregion's 11 economies is now forecast at 3.1% for 2021, down from 4.4% forecast in *Asian Development Outlook 2021*. Subregional growth in 2022 is forecast at 5.0% after an earlier projection of 5.1%. Despite rising oil prices, inflation will ease this year as aggregate demand softens. The subregion's current account surplus will shrink due to supply chain disruptions.

Subregional assessment and prospects

In late April, authorities in Southeast Asian economies started to impose mobility restrictions as COVID-19 cases soared. The 7-day moving average of cases per 1 million people rose almost six times from 28.9 at the end of April 2021 to 167.5 at the end of August. Malaysia, Brunei Darussalam, Thailand, and Timor-Leste at the end of August had the subregion's highest average daily cases per million. Lockdowns imposed to contain the virus have disrupted the movement of goods, services, and people across Southeast Asia.

Increasing the availability of COVID-19 vaccines offers Southeast Asia a way out of the crisis, but so far only Malaysia (55.3%), Cambodia (59.2%), and Singapore (78.5%) have vaccinated more than half of their populations.

This *Update*'s lower growth forecast for 2021 and 2022 applies to most economies in Southeast Asia with the exception of Singapore and the Philippines in both years, and Brunei Darussalam, Cambodia, and Malaysia in 2022 (Figure 3.4.1).

Consumer spending improved in the first half of 2021—but at a modest pace—as lockdowns weakened retail and discretionary spending. Mobility restrictions reversed employment gains, reducing household income. The International Labour Organization forecasts 9.3 million fewer jobs in Southeast Asia in 2021 compared with a no-pandemic scenario.

Figure 3.4.1 GDP growth in Southeast Asia

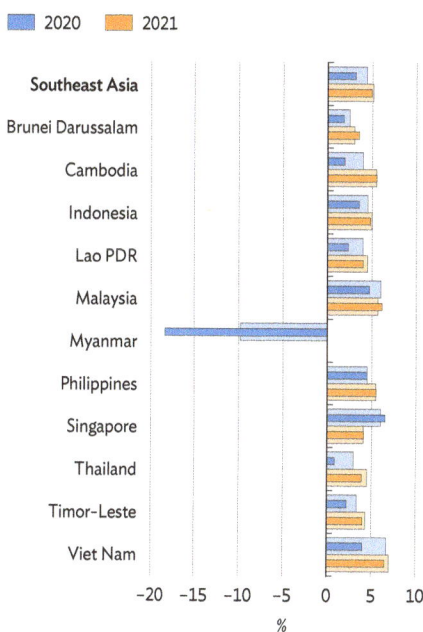

GDP = gross domestic product, Lao PDR = Lao People's Democratic Republic.

Note: Lighter colored bars are *Asian Development Outlook 2021* forecasts.

Source: *Asian Development Outlook* database.

The subregional assessment and prospects were written by James Villafuerte and Dulce Zara. The section on Indonesia was written by Henry Ma and Priasto Aji; Malaysia by James Villafuerte and Maria Theresa Bugayong; the Philippines by Cristina Lozano and Teresa Mendoza; Thailand by Chitchanok Annonjarn; Viet Nam by Cuong Minh Nguyen, Nguyen Luu Thuc Phuong, and Chu Hong Minh, and the other economies, by Emma Allen, Shiela Camingue-Romance, Poullang Doung, David M. Freedman, Kavita Iyengar, Yothin Jinjarak, Soulinthone Leuangkhamsing, Eve Cherry Lynn, Joel Mangahas, Pilipinas Quising, and Shiu Tian. Authors are in the Southeast Asia and Economic Research and Regional Cooperation departments of ADB.

Fiscal policy continued to support domestic demand amid rising COVID-19 cases. Based on International Monetary Fund data, COVID-19 policy responses taken across Southeast Asia in the first 7 months of this year totaled an estimated $48.2 billion, equivalent to 3.1% of subregional GDP. COVID-19 policy responses totaled an estimated $218.6 billion last year. Fixed investment also aided growth on a rebound in private sector capital spending, increased manufacturing output and exports, and a recovery in construction on pent-up demand.

The global recovery shored up external demand for merchandise exports from Malaysia, Singapore, Thailand, and Viet Nam. Automotive and parts, chemical and petroleum products, electronic and electrical appliances, and some agriculture products saw strong first-half export growth from these economies. But purchasing managers' index readings in August point to sharp contractions in manufacturing in Indonesia, Malaysia, the Philippines, Thailand, and Viet Nam, and weakness in Singapore. The rapid growth in industrial output has also eased somewhat in June and July as the momentum of global recovery slows and persistent COVID-19 outbreaks force firms to suspend operations anew. Services exports, especially tourism, remained weak in the first half.

Amid slower growth, this *Update* forecasts lower subregional inflation at 2.2% in 2021, down from the earlier projection of 2.4% in *Asian Development Outlook 2021* (*ADO 2021*). Inflation will decelerate in Cambodia, Indonesia, the Lao People's Democratic Republic, and Viet Nam, but higher global oil and commodity prices will fuel inflationary pressures in Brunei Darussalam, Malaysia, Singapore, and Timor-Leste. The subregional inflation forecast for 2022 is maintained at 2.4% (Figure 3.4.2).

For the current account balance forecasts, no change from *ADO 2021* is made for Cambodia. Deteriorations are forecast for Brunei Darussalam, the Philippines, Thailand, Timor-Leste, and Viet Nam, and smaller deficits or larger surpluses are projected for Indonesia, the Lao People's Democratic Republic, Malaysia, Myanmar, and Singapore. In 2021, the estimated subregional current account surplus is expected to fall to the equivalent of 2.2% of GDP from the earlier projection of 3.0% and to 2.4% from 3.4% in 2022 (Figure 3.4.3).

Central banks in Southeast Asia kept policy rates unchanged in the first half of 2021, except in Indonesia. With low inflation and interest rates on reserves, some central banks in the region also continue to help finance the COVID-19 recovery program by purchasing government bonds. From January to August, currencies in the subregion weakened against the US dollar. The baht fell the most (10.3%), followed by the ringgit (5.2%).

Figure 3.4.2 Inflation in Southeast Asia

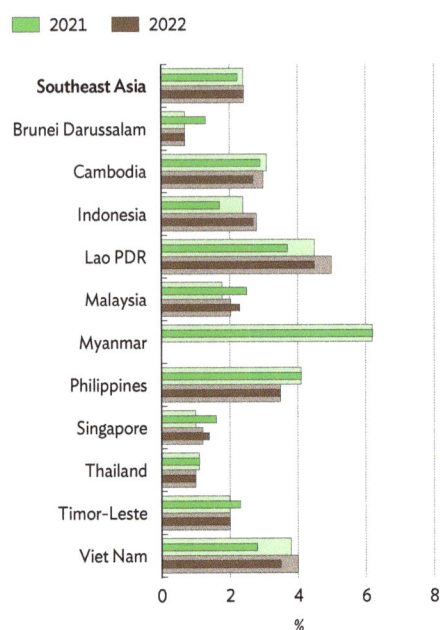

Lao PDR = Lao People's Democratic Republic.
Note: Lighter colored bars are *Asian Development Outlook 2021* forecasts.
Source: *Asian Development Outlook* database.

Figure 3.4.3 Current account balances in Southeast Asia

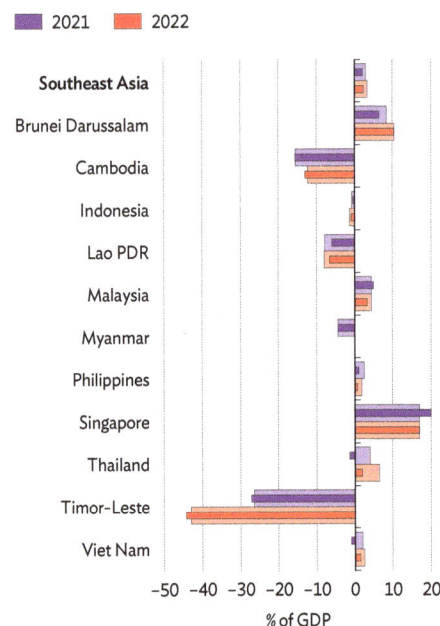

GDP = gross domestic product, Lao PDR = Lao People's Democratic Republic.
Note: Lighter colored bars are *Asian Development Outlook 2021* forecasts.
Source: *Asian Development Outlook* database.

The slow vaccination rollout in most Southeast Asian economies and the possibility of further COVID-19 variants remain the key risks to the outlook. Prolonged measures to contain COVID-19's resurgence in Southeast Asia could undermine fiscal and debt sustainability as government spending to tackle the pandemic rises and tax revenue shrinks further.

Indonesia

Growth is expected to be lower than the forecast in *ADO 2021*. An earlier surge of COVID-19 infections and the ensuing mobility restrictions will constrain the economy's recovery. Growth will increase in 2022 as conditions normalize, the global economy recovers, and domestic reforms spur investment. Inflation and the current account deficit will remain low this year and rise slightly next year.

Updated assessment

Real GDP grew by 3.1% in the first half of 2021, enabled by the pickup in mobility and demand (Figure 3.4.4). GDP contracted by 0.7% year on year in the first quarter (Q1) and grew by 7.1% in Q2, the first positive growth rate on a yearly basis since the onset of the COVID-19 pandemic. The economic recovery started in Q3 2020 when seasonally adjusted GDP grew from the previous quarter.

Private consumption, which is about 55% of GDP, grew by 1.7% in the first half of 2021. The effects of job and income losses in 2020, continuing uncertainty over the economy and how COVID-19 unfolds, and an only partial return of mobility dampened consumer demand, although income support through the national economic recovery plan and subsidies to low-wage earners helped prop up consumer demand.

Government consumption and fixed investment were the main first-half growth drivers (Figure 3.4.5). Government consumption grew by 5.5%, reflecting outlays from the national economic recovery plan, whose budgeted amount and pace of disbursement have increased since 2020. Fixed investment rose by 3.5% after declining by 6.3% in the second half of 2020, due to businesses gearing up to meet recovering domestic demand and strong demand for Indonesian exports.

Net exports contributed 0.7 percentage points to GDP growth in the first half of 2021, continuing their positive contribution since the start of the COVID-19 pandemic. In 2020, the positive net contribution resulted from imports shrinking faster than exports due to the domestic and global recessions. In the first half of 2021, however, imports recovered in step with domestic demand, but exports grew even faster, especially to the People's Republic of China, a major trading partner.

Figure 3.4.4 Quarterly GDP growth

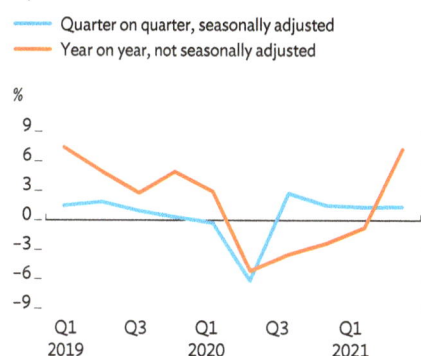

GDP = gross domestic product, Q = quarter.
Sources: CEIC Data Company (accessed 20 August 2021); Asian Development Bank estimates.

Figure 3.4.5 Demand-side contributions to growth

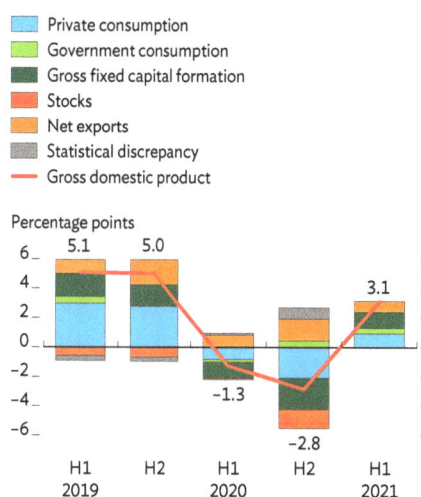

H = half.
Source: CEIC Data Company (accessed 20 August 2021).

Growth picked up across the three main productive sectors (Figure 3.4.6). Services contributed just over half of total growth, with a solid performance in wholesale and retail trade, and information and communication. Industry grew by 2.5%, with transport equipment, basic metals, and chemicals and pharmaceuticals doing well. The plantation sector mainly drove the 1.8% growth in agricultural output.

Inflation remained low despite the pickup in activity (Figure 3.4.7). Headline inflation averaged 1.5% and core inflation 1.4% in the first 8 months. Both measures were well below the central bank's target range of 2%–4%. Inflation for price-volatile goods was quite high, at 2.7%. But overall inflation was held down by assistance programs to contain food-price inflation.

Merchandise trade was buoyant and the trade surplus continued, albeit lower than in the second half of 2020 (Figure 3.4.8). Exports in US dollar terms grew by 35.8% year on year in the first half, with exports of crude petroleum, oil and gas, and minerals being particularly robust. Between July 2020 and July 2021, the prices of Indonesia's main commodity exports more than doubled (Figure 3.4.9). Imports of goods grew by 29.6% year on year in the first half, in line with the recovery of economic activity, with double-digit growth across all three categories of consumer goods, raw materials and intermediate inputs, and capital goods. The trade surplus totaled $15.7 billion, down from $19.8 billion in the second half of 2020.

The reduction in the trade surplus, along with persistent deficits in services and primary income, turned the current account from a surplus of $1.9 billion in the second half of 2020 to a deficit of $3.3 billion in the first half of 2021 (Figure 3.4.10). The current account deficit, however, was more than offset by substantial positive net inflows of portfolio capital and foreign direct investment in the financial account (Figure 3.4.11). The rise in yields in financial markets in the United States partly contributed to net portfolio outflows in April, but portfolio debt inflows quickly recovered and net portfolio inflows were positive in the first half. Consequently, gross international reserves rose from $135.9 billion at the end of December 2020 to $137.1 billion at the end of June 2021 and to $144.8 billion at the end of August (including Indonesia's share of the International Monetary Fund special drawing rights allocation), cover for 8.7 months of imports and government debt payments. The rupiah, after depreciating against the US dollar by an average of 3.0% in 2020, depreciated by a further 1.9% over January–August.

Fiscal policy continued to support the recovery. The budget deficit was 1.7% of GDP in the first half, slightly above the deficit in the same period last year. Public investment surged by 90% in the first half, and spending on materials rose by 80%. Social spending, however, fell by 24% as the government reallocated funds to support health; micro, small, and medium-

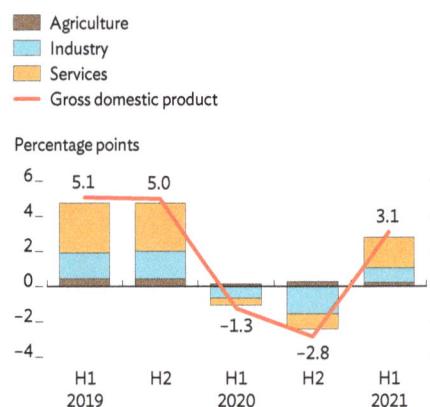

Figure 3.4.6 Supply-side contributions to growth

H = half.
Source: CEIC Data Company (accessed 20 August 2021).

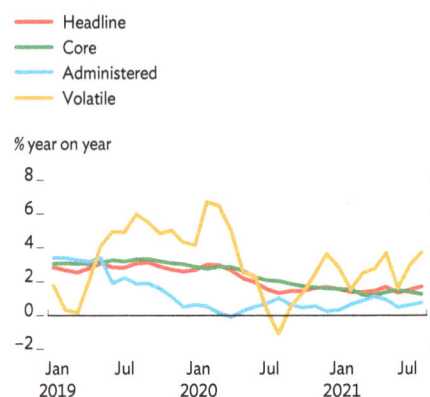

Figure 3.4.7 Monthly inflation

Source: CEIC Data Company (accessed 20 August 2021).

Figure 3.4.8 Merchandise trade

Source: CEIC Data Company (accessed 31 August 2021).

sized enterprises (MSMEs); and priority programs under the national economic recovery plan. Government revenue improved, reflecting better economic conditions. Tax collection rose by 8.8% and nontax collection by 11.4%.

Monetary policy also continued to be accommodative. Bank Indonesia, the central bank, cut the policy rate (the 7-day reverse repo rate) six times and by a total of 125 basis points since February 2020 to 3.5% by February 2021, its lowest since 2016. Bank Indonesia has kept the policy rate at that level, citing low inflation, a stable exchange rate, and a tentative economic recovery. It also extended the policy of reducing fines for late credit card payments to stimulate borrowing and consumption.

To support fiscal policy, the central bank will buy Rp439 trillion in government bonds during 2021–2022. Rp341 trillion will go to social assistance and MSME relief; the interest rate will be equal to the 7-day reverse repo rate. Rp98 trillion will pay for vaccinations and bear zero interest. This transaction will be the third "burden-sharing," following similar operations in April and July 2020.

The nonperforming loan ratios of banks have been unchanged since mid-2020, capital adequacy has remained comfortably above the regulatory minimum, and provisions for nonperforming loans have increased. But private credit growth remains weak, despite higher deposits (Figure 3.4.12). Credit contracted every month since September 2020, although it eked out 0.4% growth in June. The collapse in credit has been broad except for housing loans, which have benefited from higher demand stimulated by cuts in the VAT rate for new home purchases.

The pandemic continued to set back economic and social progress. The World Bank reclassified Indonesia as a lower-middle-income country in July 2021, due to a lower per capita income, after being classified upper-middle-income in 2020. The poverty rate rose from 9.2% in 2019 to 10.2% in September 2020 and was 10.1% in July 2021. The number of people living below the poverty line increased to 26.4 million in March 2020, the first reversal of its downward trend since 2015, and stood at 27.5 million in March 2021. The unemployment rate rose from 5.2% in 2019 to 7.1% in August 2020 and eased to 6.3% in February 2021.

Prospects

The economy's rebound in 2021 had been predicated on a recovery of pent-up demand, aided by accommodative macroeconomic policies; a steady resumption of activity as COVID-19 vaccinations progress; and a supportive external environment. All these conditions held until the end of June. Since then, only the support of accommodative fiscal and monetary policies seems likely to hold up to the end of the year, with the other drivers weakening somewhat.

Figure 3.4.9 Commodity prices

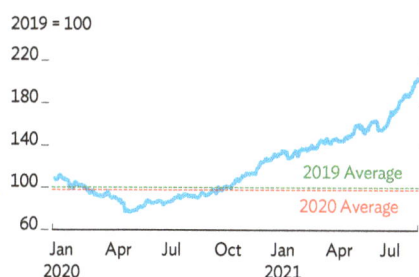

2019 = 100

Note: Prospera commodity price index comprising palm oil, coal, nickel, rubber, and copper weighted by export shares of those commodities in 2019.
Source: Prospera. https://prospera.or.id (accessed 30 August 2021).

Figure 3.4.10 Current account balance

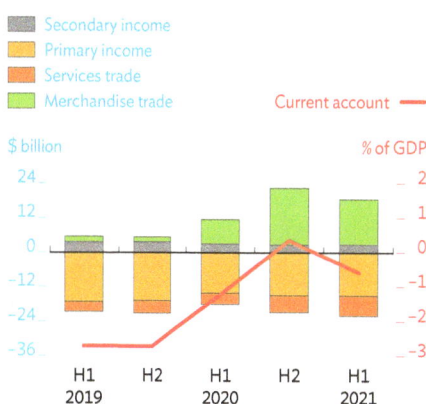

GDP = gross domestic product, H = half.
Source: CEIC Data Company (accessed 20 August 2021).

Figure 3.4.11 Balance of payments

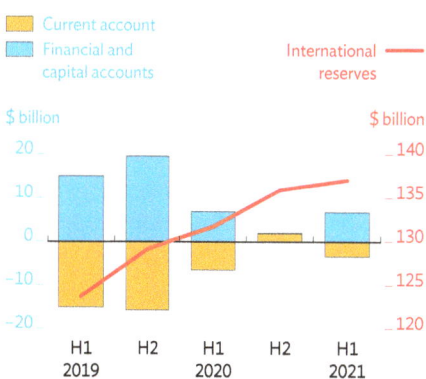

H = half.
Note: Financial and capital accounts include errors and omissions.
Source: CEIC Data Company (accessed 20 August 2021).

Until June, the pandemic seemed contained and the recovery proceeded smoothly. The daily number of new cases fell from about 12,000 in January 2021 to about 6,000 by mid-June, when second vaccinations had been administered to 13.5 million people, 7.4% of the targeted population (Figure 3.4.13). Several leading indicators showed healthy growth during Q2, such as retail and motor vehicle sales, consumer confidence, and the purchasing managers' index (Figures 3.4.14 and 3.4.15). And demand for Indonesian exports was strong.

Despite these encouraging developments, downside risks from a possible resurgence of COVID-19 infections, a slow rollout of vaccinations, and a resultant lockdown had always been present. Infections jumped in late June after being relatively low and stable since February 2021. The upsurge triggered mobility restrictions in Bali and Jakarta during 2–20 July, but the restrictions were later extended to 43 regions and 20 provinces until 20 September. Daily infections peaked at 56,157 on 15 July but abated after that. Daily infections were about 10,500 and the cumulative number of deaths reached about 133,000 as of end-August.

The pace of recovery in 2021 and 2022 will be slower than earlier expected. The resurgence of COVID-19 and mobility restrictions will crimp domestic demand and growth. Consequently, activity will pick up only modestly in Q4. Similar upswings of COVID-19 infections in Indonesia's major trading partners, as well as continuing supply blockages in semiconductors and shipping, could dampen export prospects in the second half.

There are early indications of the scale of the lockdown's negative impact on the economy. The manufacturing purchasing managers' index peaked at 55.3 in May and was at 53.5 in June, marking 8 consecutive months of the index exceeding 50, which points toward expansion. After the lockdown was declared, the index plunged to 40.1 in July and 43.7 in August. The consumer confidence index in April 2021 exceeded the 100 threshold, which indicates consumer optimism, for the first time in 12 months and peaked at 107.4 in June. In July, it plunged to 80.2.

Because of these developments, this *Update* revises down the growth projection for 2021 to 3.5% from the forecast of 4.5% in *ADO 2021*. The prolonged slow pace of growth in 2021 will carry over to 2022, leading to growth next year of about 4.8%, lower than the 5.0% projected earlier (Table 3.4.1).

Even before the lockdown the slow pace of COVID-19 vaccinations was hindering a fast return to normal economic activity. A weak recovery in private consumption is expected in 2021, growing by about 2.5%, half its prepandemic pace. In 2022, however, private consumption should resume its prepandemic trend growth of 5.0%.

Investment will also recover in 2021, albeit less strongly than previously projected. Investment is expected to remain

Figure 3.4.12 Loans and deposits

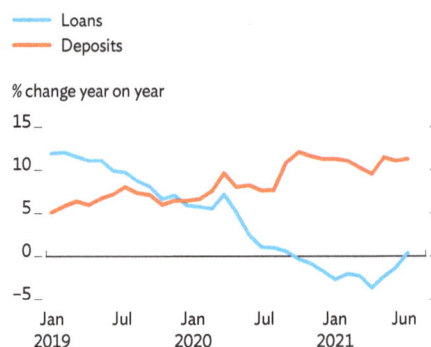

Source: Haver Analytics (accessed 30 August 2021).

Figure 3.4.13 COVID-19 indicators

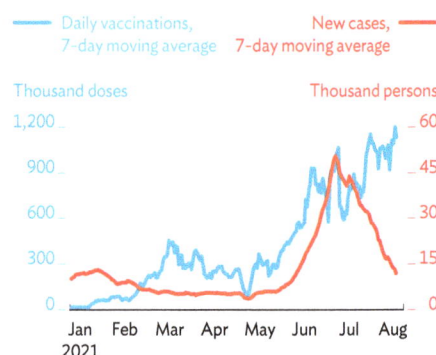

COVID-19 = Coronavirus Disease 2019.
Source: Our World in Data. https://ourworldindata.org (accessed 3 September 2021).

Figure 3.4.14 Consumer activity

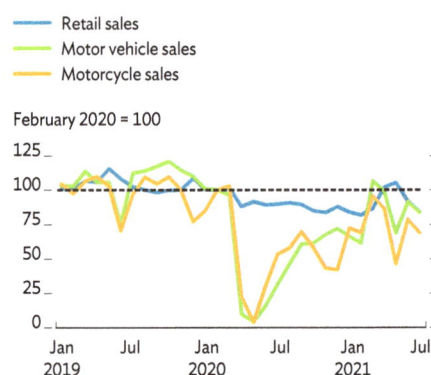

Source: CEIC Data Company (accessed 24 August 2021).

weak through September due to lower demand and increased uncertainty. In 2022, investment growth should pick up due to the normalization of conditions and recent reforms to improve the business and investment climate. Business licensing, for instance, has started moving toward an online, risk-based approach that will reduce processing times and costs.

Fiscal policy will continue supporting growth. The budget deficit target for 2021 is 5.7% of GDP, slightly lower than 6.2% in 2020. The actual deficit will likely be closer to 6.0% of GDP, as the slowdown in Q3 holds back revenue growth and spurs increased emergency spending. As in 2020, outlays from the national economic recovery plan are allotted to health, social assistance, support for MSMEs, and priority programs. To mitigate the economic costs of the July–August lockdown, the government continued the subsidy for low-earning workers and increased emergency social assistance by reallocating funds from other budgetary outlays.

Monetary policy will remain accommodative. With inflation low and the rupiah broadly stable, the central bank is expected to keep the policy rate at 3.5% through the end of 2021. Credit growth, however, is unlikely to be robust in the second half.

The slower recovery will push down inflation. With the recovery moderating and few signs of inflationary pressures over the rest of the year, the forecast for inflation in 2021 is cut to 1.7% from 2.4% in *ADO 2021*. The pickup in growth in 2022 will be accompanied by inflation returning to close to its prepandemic rate of 3.0%.

The current account deficit is projected at 0.5% of GDP in 2021, down from the earlier forecast of 0.8%. The merchandise trade surplus will continue in 2021 and is forecast at about $30 billion. Merchandise exports will remain healthy in the second half and grow by about 21% for the full year. Merchandise imports are expected to increase by about 23%, somewhat less than projected earlier due to weaker growth in the second half. The surplus in merchandise trade will offset the continuing deficit in services trade as international tourism remains on hold and imports of services pick up. In 2022, import demand will grow in step with the economy, and the current account deficit is expected to rise to 0.9% of GDP.

Net inflows in the financial account will approximately offset the current account deficit in the second half of 2021, leaving international reserves by the end of December at about the same level as at the end of August. This level of reserves will be comfortable and consistent with external sustainability.

The risks to the outlook remain on the downside due to the potential for further COVID-19 outbreaks, perhaps of new variants; future lockdowns; and disruptions to economic activity in Indonesia and abroad. Measures should therefore continue to try to contain the pandemic, promote economic recovery, and further pending domestic reforms.

Figure 3.4.15 Consumer confidence and purchasing managers' indexes

Source: CEIC Data Company (accessed 1 September 2021).

Table 3.4.1 Selected economic indicators in Indonesia, %

	2020	2021		2022	
		ADO 2021	Update	ADO 2021	Update
GDP growth	–2.1	4.5	3.5	5.0	4.8
Inflation	2.0	2.4	1.7	2.8	2.7
CAB/GDP	–0.4	–0.8	–0.5	–1.3	–0.9

ADO = *Asian Development Outlook*, CAB = current account balance, GDP = gross domestic product.

Sources: CEIC Data Company; Asian Development Bank estimates.

Malaysia

The resurgence of COVID-19 in April this year and mobility restrictions weakened consumer confidence and business conditions. Politically, it forced Prime Minister Muhyiddin Yassin to resign, causing the ringgit to fall to a 1-year low. Because of these developments, this *Update* revises down the 2021 growth forecast in *ADO 2021*. Increasing oil and commodity prices are driving inflation higher. The current account surplus will continue to expand, as export growth outpaces import growth. The main near-term downside risks are a weaker global recovery, protracted political instability, and rising public debt.

Updated assessment

Although GDP growth bounced back by 7.1% in the first half of 2021 from an 8.4% contraction in the same period last year, quarter-on-quarter growth slowed in the second quarter on a strict COVID-19 lockdown imposed in June.

Total consumption—which comprises about 70% of GDP—rebounded, increasing by 4.8% in the first half of this year (Figure 3.4.16). Private consumption was particularly strong, growing by 4.3% and reversing the contraction since the second quarter of 2020. Mobility controls and travel restrictions in January weighed on consumer spending, but the effect was softer compared with the impacts of these curbs in 2020. The value of retail trade rose by 9.7% in the first half, underpinned mainly by online purchases and higher car sales. Consumer spending was also supported by fiscal stimulus and wage subsidies. These lifted the consumer sentiment index to an average 81.6 in the first half from 70.6 in the same period last year (Figure 3.4.17). Public consumption increased by 7.5%.

Investments picked up strongly, despite rising input costs, declining profit margins, and business uncertainties. Fixed investment grew by 5.5% in the first half of 2021 after contracting by 17.3% in the same period last year. The improvement in private fixed investment was underpinned by continued capital spending on telecommunications and manufacturing industries exporting electrical and electronic products. The business condition index rose to 99.7 in the first half from 72.0 in the same period last year. Government fixed investment rose by 12% in the second quarter after falling for 3 consecutive years.

Exports of goods and services continued their 2021 rebound, growing by 23.5% in the first half on stronger global growth, particularly in the country's largest markets: the United States, the People's Republic of China, and Singapore. Exports of electrical and electronic products continued to grow on rising demand for semiconductors (Figure 3.4.18). Imports of goods and services rose 24.3% in the first half after contracting 11.3% in the same period a year ago.

Figure 3.4.16 Demand-side contributions to growth

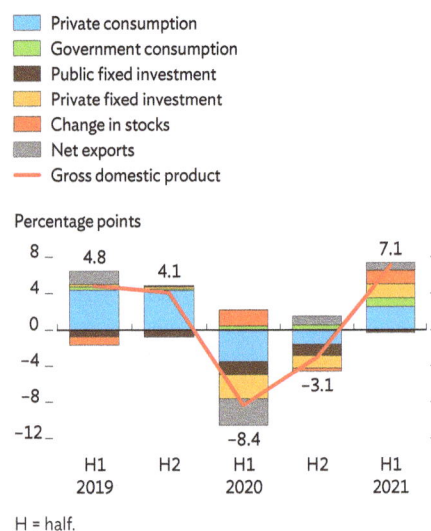

Legend:
- Private consumption
- Government consumption
- Public fixed investment
- Private fixed investment
- Change in stocks
- Net exports
- Gross domestic product

Percentage points

H = half.
Source: CEIC Data Company (accessed 3 September 2021).

Figure 3.4.17 Consumer and business confidence indexes

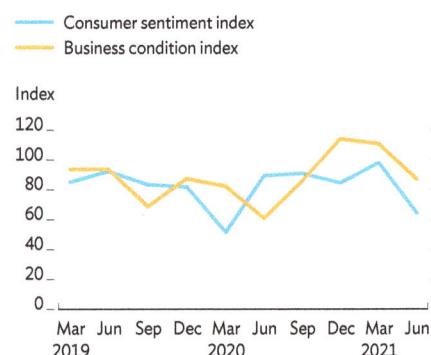

Legend:
- Consumer sentiment index
- Business condition index

Index

Note: Above 100 indicates improving business conditions and rising consumer confidence.
Source: Haver Analytics (accessed 31 August 2021).

Agriculture production contracted by 0.7% in the first half of 2021 (Figure 3.4.19). Industry output strengthened as economic conditions in the second quarter were considerably better than during the same period last year, when most factories were closed due to COVID-19 lockdown. Manufacturing rose a robust 15.8% after contracting by 8.7% in the first half of 2020. By subsector, growth was strongest in transport equipment (23.3%), electrical and electronics (17.7%), and petroleum (16.9%).

Mining output rose on higher commodity prices in the first half of 2021, although its contribution to the economy remains below 10% of GDP. Construction grew by 8.3%, supported by higher fixed investment, after contracting 26% in the same period a year earlier. Site shutdowns due to the COVID-19 lockdown affected large construction projects.

The growth in services in the first half of 2021 was still far below prepandemic levels. Even so, financial, insurance, information, and communication services did well, and wholesale and retail trade improved significantly despite capacity restrictions. Tourism remained subdued, with COVID-19 severely affecting accommodation and air travel services.

Consumer prices started rising in February 2021 after deflation in 2020. Inflation accelerated to 4.7% in April, the biggest monthly increase since 2017, but decelerated to 2.2% in July (Figure 3.4.20). Inflation averaged 2.3% in the first 7 months of 2021. Higher oil prices were the main source of inflation.

The unemployment rate has fallen since the start of 2021, although it remains high, averaging 4.7% in the first half. Private sector wages improved, led by a 2.7% rise in manufacturing wages.

COVID-19's resurgence kept the budget stance expansionary. Revenue collection in the first half of 2021 was about $26.0 billion and expenditure $28.7 billion. On 31 May, the government announced a further stimulus package, totaling $10.0 billion, to cushion the economic impact of the resurgence in COVID-19 cases. The package is expected to further increase the budget deficit, equivalent to 7.7% of GDP in the first half compared with 7.9% for the same period in 2020.

Export earnings in US dollar terms have risen consistently since the start of 2021, growing by an average of 38.2% in the first 6 months. Imports were up 36.5%. With exports outpacing imports, the trade balance improved over the first half, when the services and primary income deficits both widened. The current account of the balance of payments turned a surplus equivalent to 3.6% of GDP in the first half, up from 2.5% in the same period of last year.

Figure 3.4.18 Selected exports

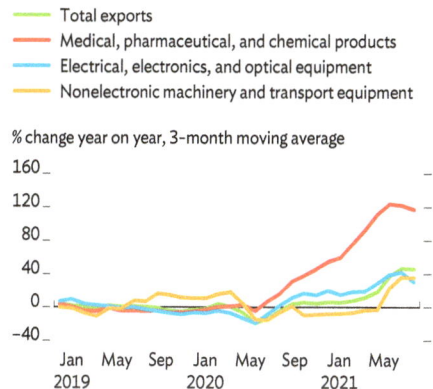

— Total exports
— Medical, pharmaceutical, and chemical products
— Electrical, electronics, and optical equipment
— Nonelectronic machinery and transport equipment

% change year on year, 3-month moving average

Notes: Medical, pharmaceutical, and chemical products generally refer to Standard International Trade Classification (SITC) Revision 3 Division codes 51, 52, 54, 848, and 872; electrical, electronics, and optical equipment covers SITC Revision 3 codes 75, 76, 77, and 87; nonelectronic machinery and transportation covers codes 71 to 74 and 78 to 79.

Source: Asian Development Bank estimates using data from CEIC Data Company and Haver Analytics (both accessed 1 September 2021).

Figure 3.4.19 Supply-side contributions to growth

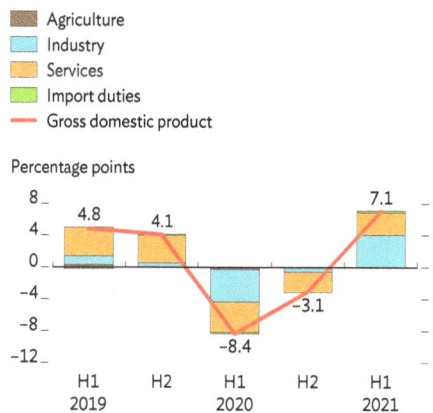

■ Agriculture
■ Industry
■ Services
■ Import duties
— Gross domestic product

Percentage points

H = half.
Source: CEIC Data Company (accessed 3 September 2021).

Figure 3.4.20 Monthly inflation

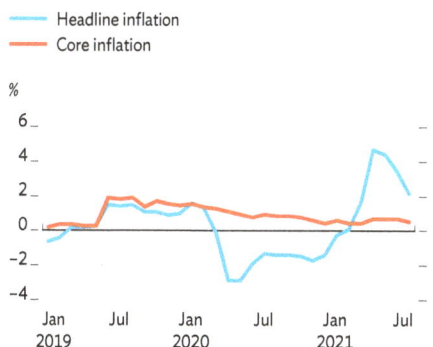

— Headline inflation
— Core inflation

%

Sources: Haver Analytics; Bank Negara Malaysia. 2021. *Monthly Highlights and Statistics*. March. http://www.bnm .gov.my (accessed 2 September 2021).

International reserves at Bank Negara Malaysia, the central bank, totaled $116.3 billion as of 30 August, cover for 8.3 months of imports and higher than the short-term external debt. Monetary policy has remained largely accommodative, with the overnight policy interest rate at 1.75% since July 2020. Trade tensions, political instability, uncertainty over COVID-19, and rising debts pressured the ringgit, which depreciated by 3.1% from January to the end of August, when it was at RM4.2 = $1.0.

Prospects

This *Update* revises down Malaysia's GDP growth prospects to 4.7% from the forecast of 6.0% in *ADO 2021* (Table 3.4.2). The main factors for the revision are COVID-19's resurgence, causing the reimposition of nationwide containment measures and a lockdown, and continued political instability. The lower growth outlook is consistent with weaker growth prospects for the US and Japan, key markets for Malaysian exports. In June and July, the manufacturing purchasing managers' index, electricity generation, and wholesale and retail trade, among other indicators, eased somewhat, pointing to weaker domestic economic activity. Indeed, the growth of the leading index of economic activities fell from 17.2% in March to 0.5% in June, indicating that growth could ease in the second half (Figure 3.4.21). GDP growth is expected to accelerate to 6.1% in 2022 (Figure 3.4.22). This higher projection than the one made in *ADO 2021* is contingent on the progress of the national COVID-19 vaccination campaign. But even if there is a robust recovery next year, growth will still be about 10% lower than its prepandemic trajectory.

Growth in private consumption will remain buoyant and support near-term growth, despite the impact of the COVID-19 lockdown. Although the consumer confidence index fell from 98.9 in the first quarter of 2021 to 64.3 in the second, the growth of wholesale and retail trade sales improved from a 2.7% contraction in January to growth of 9.3% in March and 28.3% in May. This trend is expected to continue on purchases of essential and discretionary items in the second half. Even so, the spending momentum will be significantly slowed by the continuing rise in COVID-19 cases and still weak consumer confidence. The improving labor market should support household spending, and higher government spending on supplies and services will also support growth.

Business sentiment remains fragile because of disruptions caused by the pandemic, political uncertainty, and a sluggish business climate. In the second quarter of 2021, the business conditions index fell to 87.5 from 111.8 in the first. The manufacturing purchasing managers' index declined to 39.9 in June on a slower global recovery. Investment growth will remain moderate in the second half, before picking up

Table 3.4.2 Selected economic indicators in Malaysia, %

	2020	2021		2022	
		ADO 2021	Update	ADO 2021	Update
GDP growth	–5.6	6.0	4.7	5.7	6.1
Inflation	–1.1	1.8	2.5	2.0	2.3
CAB/GDP	4.2	4.4	5.0	4.4	3.4

ADO = Asian Development Outlook, CAB = current account balance, GDP = gross domestic product.
Source: Asian Development Bank estimates.

Figure 3.4.21 Manufacturing purchasing managers' index and leading index

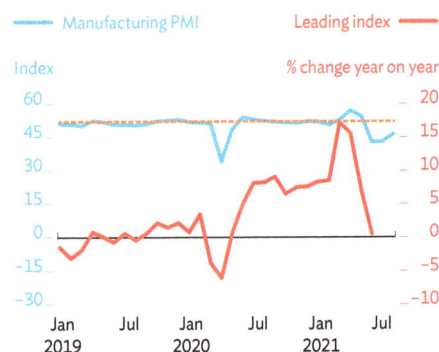

PMI = purchasing managers' index.
Notes: The manufacturing PMI series for Malaysia is adjusted by adding 3 points, as historical experience suggests that a value above 47 is consistent with expansion. A manufacturing PMI above 50 indicates expansion, below 50 indicates contraction.
Source: CEIC Data Company (accessed 14 September 2021).

Figure 3.4.22 GDP growth

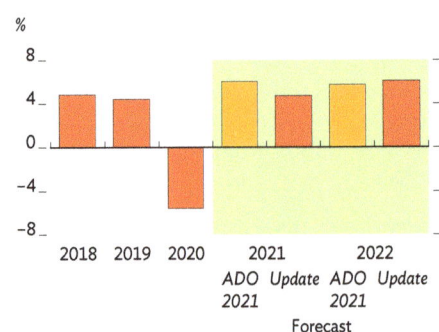

ADO = Asian Development Outlook, GDP = gross domestic product.
Source: ADO database.

strongly next year as COVID-19 vaccinations allow the economy, particularly services, to reopen more permanently. This will contribute to a wider and more diversified growth in 2022.

Public investment will remain subdued this year, but contribute to growth next year via investments in transport, industrial parks, rural areas, digital connectivity, and education infrastructure. Notable public investments coming up are RM15 billion on transport infrastructure projects, including the Pan Borneo Highway and the rapid transit system link connecting Singapore and Malaysia; RM2.7 billion on rural infrastructure to help narrow the rural–urban divide; and RM825 million to upgrade school buildings and improve internet connectivity in the education system, among other education interventions. For this year, political wrangling and a low revenue base will dampen public investment.

Manufacturing will lead Malaysia's economic recovery, which will be underpinned by higher commodity prices and demand, as well as robust growth in electrical and electronics exports. Construction will be spurred by higher gross national savings, an expected easing in mobility restrictions over the rest of the year, and better financial conditions that will support growth in loans and housing loan approvals. In the first half of 2021, total loans grew by 0.8% on average on a quarterly basis, similar to their growth during the same period last year. Liquefied natural gas operations will benefit from stronger commodity prices.

Services should see a steady expansion in the second half as increased COVID-19 vaccinations allow the economy to reopen, and on rising domestic consumption and growth in business services. That said, the rebound in all sectors of the economy will not be as strong as that forecast in *ADO 2021* as rising COVID-19 cases disrupted domestic production.

Monetary policy will remain accommodative, with Bank Negara Malaysia likely to hold the policy rate at 1.75% until the end of 2021 because of upward pressure on prices. This stance is expected to cushion the impact of the pandemic and promote stable prices and a sustainable economic recovery.

With inflation pressures stronger than previously anticipated, *ADO 2021*'s inflation forecast is raised to 2.5% from the earlier projection of 1.8%. For next year, stable oil prices, despite improving demand, and a stronger ringgit will likely temper inflation, with the rate forecast at 2.3% (Figure 3.4.23).

The favorable external environment should increase the current account surplus in 2021 to the equivalent of 5.0% of GDP and keep net trade in surplus. The current account surplus next year is expected to moderate to 3.4% (Figure 3.4.24). The balance of payments will also turn a surplus, although portfolio inflows and foreign direct investment could wane if political instability persists.

Figure 3.4.23 Annual inflation

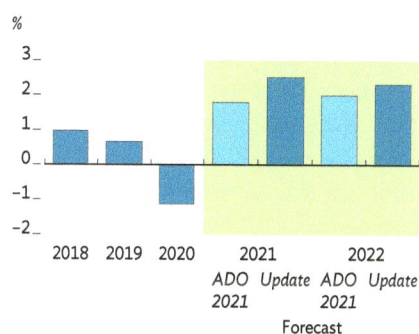

ADO = Asian Development Outlook.
Source: ADO database.

Figure 3.4.24 Current account balance

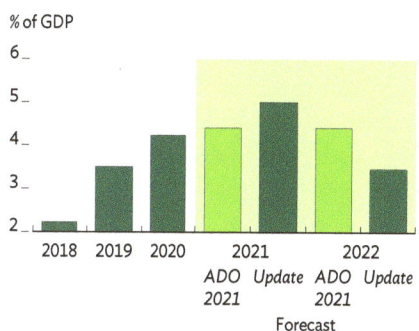

ADO = Asian Development Outlook, GDP = gross domestic product.
Source: ADO database.

Malaysia's COVID-19 vaccine rollout is raising hopes that while the resurgence of cases will peak in the third quarter, the number of people requiring critical care in the fourth quarter will significantly decline. As of 28 August, 33.7 million doses had been administered at a rate of some 395,723 jabs per day. During the same period, 58.8% of the population received at least one dose and about 44.3% had been fully vaccinated.

Fiscal policy will continue to support growth in 2021, as it did last year when the government injected fiscal stimulus equivalent to 24% of GDP to support economic recovery from the COVID-19 pandemic. For this year, the budget allocated 5.3% of expenditure—about $4 billion—to the COVID-19 fund. As of July, about $62.5 billion is estimated have been allocated to COVID-19 response, some 16.6% of GDP. Measures to tackle the pandemic have focused primarily on equity and liquidity support, direct long-term lending, and health and income support. These are countercyclical interventions to mitigate the impact of the pandemic and steer the economy through the storm.

Several downside risks could undermine Malaysia's near-term prospects. Externally, a weaker global economic recovery, coupled with tapering in the US, could cause greater financial market volatility and trigger capital outflows. Domestically, COVID-19 mutations and weak political support for the new government could cause further uncertainty, undermine business confidence, and delay the passage of the Twelfth Malaysia Plan and reforms that are crucial for the economy to recover from the pandemic.

Malaysia's credit ratings have remained broadly stable, but with some concerns for a negative outlook. In early June 2021, Moody's Investors Service affirmed its A3 stable credit rating for the Government of Malaysia, citing the country's competitive and diversified economy, large pool of domestic savings, and favorable debt structure. Later in that month, S&P Global Ratings affirmed Malaysia's A– and A–2 sovereign credit ratings with a negative outlook, noting that net indebtedness could rise from the domestic political uncertainty and the resurgence of COVID-19. In July, Fitch Ratings affirmed Malaysia BBB+ stable outlook, noting that the country's highly diversified export base, persistent current account surpluses, and broad-based medium-term growth have offset concerns over political uncertainty, increasing debt, and a low revenue base.

Philippines

This *Update* leaves unchanged the growth forecasts for this year and next as recovering domestic demand and global trade align with the projections made in *ADO 2021* in April. An expansionary fiscal policy will continue to support growth, especially infrastructure investment. Progress on COVID-19 vaccination in Metro Manila will help support further easing of mobility restrictions in the coming months. The outlook is still for modest inflation and a small current account surplus.

Updated assessment

GDP rose by 3.7% year on year in the first half of 2021, rebounding from a 9.3% contraction in the same period of 2020. GDP contracted by 3.9% in the first quarter (Q1), but grew by 11.8% in Q2, reversing a deep contraction in Q2 2020. Movement and business restrictions have been partially lifted in phases and lockdowns are now more localized than widespread. Investment was the most significant contributor to Q2 2021 growth, followed by household consumption (Figure 3.4.25).

Total investment including inventories rose by 20.2% in the first half of 2021, with a sharp rebound in Q2 on a doubling of private investment. Fixed investment rose by 37.4% in the same quarter, reversing contractions in the preceding 5 quarters; outlays for machinery and transport equipment, and private construction, bounced back (Figure 3.4.26).

Although household consumption, about three-fourths of GDP, rose by only 0.9% in the first half, it picked up in Q2 with 7.2% growth. Continued uncertainty over the course of the COVID-19 pandemic and the slow recovery in the labor market weighed on household spending. The unemployment rate fell from a peak of 17.6% in April 2020 to 7.7% in June 2021, but it is still high compared with its prepandemic level of 5.3% in January 2020. Remittances from overseas workers, which rose by 6.7% in the first half, supported consumption.

Government consumption rose by 3.5% in the first half on continued spending on social services and economic recovery programs, but less than the 15.5% growth in same period last year when a large-scale social amelioration program was rolled out for the poor, and low-income households and workers, among other stimulus measures.

Merchandise trade recovered in the first half, with exports growing by 17.1% and imports 19.6% in real terms. Services exports posted a smaller contraction of 5.0% compared with last year's slump. The decline in travel and transport offset the increase in exports of business services, telecommunications, and computer and information services, including business process outsourcing (BPO). Overall, net exports of goods and services dampened growth as imports outpaced exports.

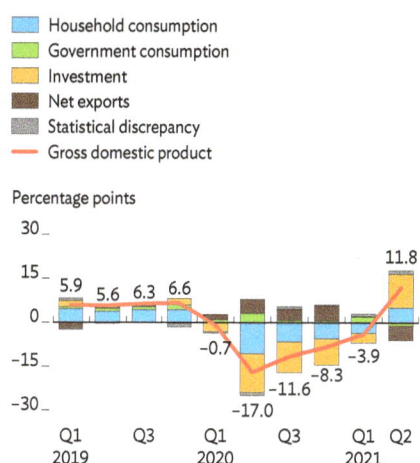

Figure 3.4.25 Demand-side contributions to growth

Q = quarter.
Sources: *Asian Development Outlook* database; CEIC Data Company (downloaded 3 September 2021).

Figure 3.4.26 Contributions to fixed investment growth

Q = quarter.
Sources: *Asian Development Outlook* database; CEIC Data Company (downloaded 3 September 2021).

All sectors of the economy contributed to GDP growth in the first half of 2021 except agriculture, which contracted by 0.7% mainly on lower pork production (Figure 3.4.27). Industry grew by 7.4%, contributing nearly 60% of GDP growth in the first half. Manufacturing, comprising two-thirds of industry, expanded by 10.4% on gains in food and beverage, pharmaceutical products, transport and electrical equipment, computer and electronic products, and construction material. Although construction grew by only 0.8% in the first half, it rose by 25.7% in Q2 as private construction rebounded on relaxed restrictions on construction activity. Public construction posted solid growth of 42.2% in the first half as government accelerated infrastructure projects, including roads and railways.

Services, accounting for 60% of GDP, reversed 2020's slump by expanding 9.6% in Q2, bringing first-half services growth to 2.6%. Growth drivers included information and communication, retail trade, finance, education, and health and business services. Transport, accommodation, and food services continued to contract in the first half, although by a lower rate than in the same period last year.

Inflation averaged 4.4% in the first 8 months of 2021. In May, the government took temporary measures to augment food supplies, including reducing tariffs on rice and meat imports and allowing more pork imports under low-tariff minimum access volume terms. These measures helped temper food inflation.

The monetary authorities, at their August meeting, maintained the policy interest rate at a record low of 2% for the overnight reverse repurchase rate (Figure 3.4.28). Liquidity (M3) growth expanded by 5.9% year on year in July 2021 mainly on credit to the government. Private sector credit remained weak with 0.4% growth year on year in July, following a steady contraction since December 2020.

The fiscal deficit widened to the equivalent of 7.9% of GDP in the first half of 2021 compared with 6.5% in the same period in 2020. Revenue rose by 2.5% year on year; expenditure was 9.6% higher. While tax revenue increased by 10.3%, dividend remittances from corporations owned or controlled by the government narrowed compared with last year's sharp increase to support fiscal stimulus measures. Government debt rose to 60.4% of GDP in June 2021 from 54.6% at the end of 2020 to fund COVID-19 pandemic response and economic recovery programs.

The current account turned a deficit equal to 0.7% of GDP in the first half of 2021 on a wider merchandise trade deficit after a 2.8% surplus in the same period in 2020. Merchandise exports rose by 21.3% and imports by 31.6% in US dollar terms, widening the trade deficit to 11.9% of GDP from 9.1% a year earlier. Services exports contracted by 1.3% on lower tourism

Figure 3.4.27 Supply-side contribution to growth

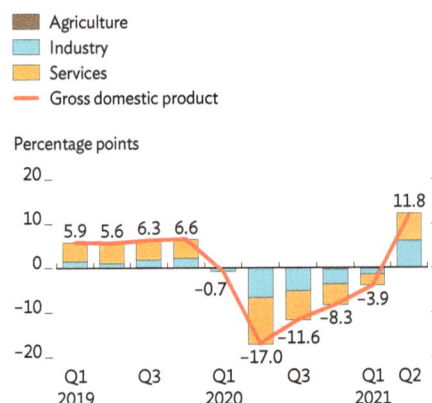

Q = quarter.
Sources: *Asian Development Outlook* database; CEIC Data Company (downloaded 3 September 2021).

Figure 3.4.28 Policy interest rate

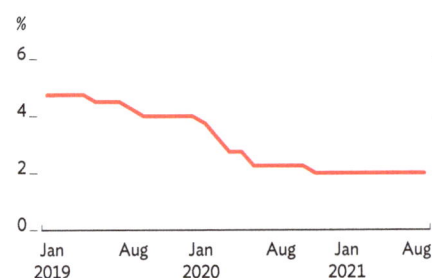

Note: Refers to the overnight reverse repurchase rate.
Source: Bangko Sentral ng Pilipinas. https://www.bsp.gov .ph (accessed 3 September 2021).

receipts, although this was partly offset by higher revenue from computer, information, and other business services. Remittances also continued to grow. Net outflows of portfolio investments rose, but this was partly tempered by higher direct investment. In sum, the balance of payments reversed to a deficit equivalent to 1.0% of GDP from 2.4% surplus in the first half of 2020.

Official reserves were at $108.1 billion as of August 2021, cover for 12.3 months of imports and service and income payments. The ratio of external debt to GDP was 26.5% in June, down from 27.2% at the end of 2020. The peso depreciated 4% against the US dollar in the year to August.

Prospects

The economy is recovering, but remains fragile because of periodically tighter COVID-19 mobility restrictions, particularly in Metro Manila.

Growth forecasts are maintained at 4.5% in 2021 and 5.5% in 2022 as recovering domestic demand and improving global trade align with the forecasts from April (Table 3.4.3). A resurgence of COVID-19 cases from July led to the reimposition of tighter lockdowns in Metro Manila and some provinces from 6 to 20 August in a preemptive response to curb the spread of highly transmissible variants. Lockdowns are being eased in phases and implemented in targeted locations depending on transmission levels rather than broadly.

The roll out of the national vaccine program has accelerated in recent months and is therefore making good progress towards meeting the government's year-end targets. The government has focused on vaccinating the population in the major urban areas like Metro Manila because they have the highest incidence of COVID-19 cases. As of 15 September 2021, 84% of Metro Manila's target population ages 18 and older—8.2 million people—have received at least one dose and 63% of the target population in Metro Manila have been fully vaccinated. The government forecasts that around 80% of the target population in Metro Manila will be fully vaccinated by the end of October, which helps improve the conditions for further easing of mobility restrictions that will help restore consumer and business confidence. With substantial deliveries of vaccines expected over the rest of this year, the vaccination rollout outside Metro Manila is expected to accelerate. Overall, 22 million people nationwide had received a first jab as of mid-September and 17.7 million have completed their vaccination or about 16% of the population (Figure 3.4.29).

Improved consumer confidence based on the central bank's survey conducted in Q2 and rising remittances from workers overseas supported a continued recovery in household consumption. Remittances further expanded in July largely from land-based workers with work contracts of 1 year or longer (Figure 3.4.30).

Table 3.4.3 Selected economic indicators in the Philippines, %

	2020	2021		2022	
		ADO 2021	Update	ADO 2021	Update
GDP growth	–9.6	4.5	4.5	5.5	5.5
Inflation	2.6	4.1	4.1	3.5	3.5
CAB/GDP	3.6	2.5	1.0	1.8	0.8

ADO = Asian Development Outlook, CAB = current account balance, GDP = gross domestic product.
Source: Asian Development Bank estimates.

Figure 3.4.29 COVID-19 indicators

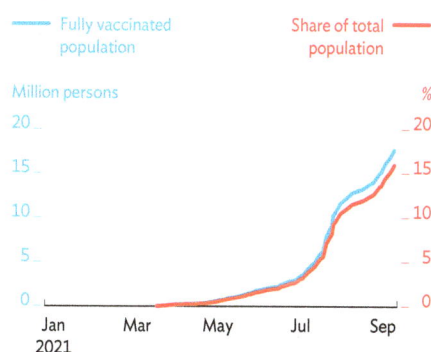

COVID-19 = Coronavirus Disease 2019.
Source: Our World in Data. https://ourworldindata.org (accessed 17 September 2021).

Figure 3.4.30 Remittances

Note: Refers to cumulative growth rate of personal remittances.
Sources: Bangko Sentral ng Pilipinas. https://www.bsp.gov.ph; CEIC Data Company (both accessed 3 September 2021).

Employment is expected to recover gradually as intermittent lockdowns hamper the operation of businesses, including in Metro Manila. The unemployment rate further decreased to 6.9% in July (Figure 3.4.31). However, the labor force participation rate fell from 65.0% in June to 58.9% in July, and the absolute number of jobs fell by 3.4 million in July. Job losses were recorded in services and agriculture. Among the employed, there was a shift from wage and salary employment to self-employment. Widespread vaccination will allow lockdowns to be eased further and for more businesses to operate.

Public investment will remain a key driver of domestic investment. Growth in infrastructure disbursements continued to rise in July by 39.1% year on year. Roads, bridges, expressways, ports, and railways are among the major investment projects underway. The government aims to raise infrastructure spending from the equivalent of 4.8% of GDP in 2020 to at least 5.0% in 2021 and 2022.

Private investment indicators point to recovery, albeit a fragile one. Imports of capital goods rose by 24.1% in the first 7 months of 2021 and raw materials by 29.5%. Industrial production has picked up, with the purchasing managers' index slightly above the 50-threshold indicating expansion from December 2020 to July 2021. It slipped, however, to 48.6 in August on tighter quarantines in Metro Manila after a new spike in COVID-19 cases (Figure 3.4.32).

Loans for production expanded modestly by 0.8% year on year in July, the first increase since December 2020. Credit rose for information and communication, transport, construction, and real estate. But loans to wholesale and retail trade, manufacturing, accommodation, and food services continued to decline, although at a slower rate. Some leading indicators appear favorable. Retail vehicle sales and private construction permits for residential and nonresidential projects showed strong Q2 growth. Merchandise exports continued to rebound in July, growing by 12.7%, particularly electronic products, which comprise over half of total exports. Rising merchandise exports are expected to continue to spur growth in industry and lift investment in manufacturing. Among services exports, BPO receipts will continue to rebound in line with the improved prospects of major advanced economies, but tourism will take longer to recover. International tourist arrivals were 95.9% in the first half of 2021 compared with the same period in 2020.

Fiscal policy will continue to support growth. A fiscal deficit is planned at the equivalent of 7.5% of GDP for 2022, with budget expenditure 11.5% higher than in 2021 with larger outlays for infrastructure and social programs. Social spending includes programs to implement universal health care and conditional cash transfers for poor families, and for livelihood assistance and education programs.

Figure 3.4.31 Unemployment rate

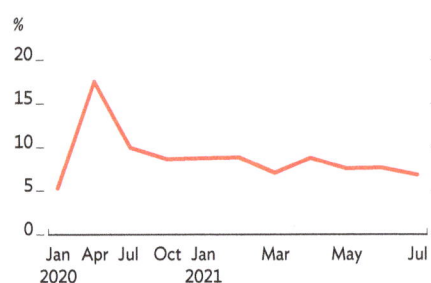

Sources: CEIC Data Company; Philippine Statistics Authority. https://psa.gov.ph (both accessed 3 September 2021).

Figure 3.4.32 Manufacturing purchasing managers' index

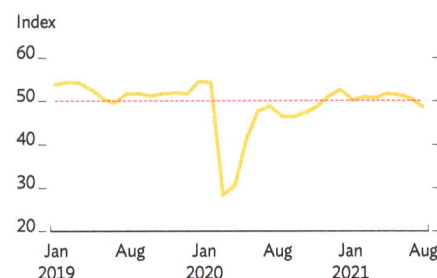

Note: Above 50 indicates expansion, below 50 indicates contraction.

Source: Bangko Sentral ng Pilipinas. https://www.bsp.gov.ph (accessed 3 September 2021).

Reforms are ongoing to support the economic recovery. A National Employment Recovery Strategy was institutionalized in June 2021 to create a policy environment that fosters quality employment. The strategy harmonizes the programs of various government agencies for a whole-of-government approach, including social protection, training, upskilling, and support to businesses. The Philippine Identification System for a national ID has been accelerated to improve targeting and the delivery of public services. Having a national ID will help enable poor Filipinos to open bank accounts and draw more people into the formal financial system. This year's notable reforms include the Corporate Recovery and Tax Incentives for Enterprises Act, which reduces the corporate income tax rate for micro, small, or medium-sized enterprises from 30% to 20%, and to 25% for all other businesses, and enhances fiscal incentives to investors to make them time-bound and performance-based. The Financial Institutions Strategic Transfer Act helps banks to offload bad debts and nonperforming assets onto asset management companies to free up liquidity for lending. Other priority reforms include easing restrictions on foreign participation in some investment areas by amending the Public Services Act, the Retail Trade Liberalization Act, and the Foreign Investments Act.

This *Update* maintains *ADO 2021*'s inflation forecast of 4.1% this year and 3.5% next year. The forecasts take into consideration the continued impact of the government's supply-side measures to contain food prices. With inflation expected to fall within the central bank's 2%–4% target range for the rest of the year, and domestic demand recovering only gradually, the monetary stance will likely remain accommodative.

The current account is projected to remain in surplus, albeit at the equivalent of 1.0% of GDP in 2021, compared with *ADO 2021*'s projection of 2.5%, and at 0.8% in 2022 (1.8%). Weighing on the current account will be the stronger-than-expected rebound in imports, including for capital goods and raw materials; a rebound in merchandise exports, and BPO receipts, and higher remittances will help lift the current account.

The main risk to the outlook is the spread of more contagious COVID-19 variants, leading to the reimposition of strict quarantines and stalling economic recovery. Daily new COVID-19 cases have spiked since July 2021, driven in part by highly transmissible new variants. From less than 6,000 daily infections in May and June, cases had risen to over 18,000 a day by early September, with total cases reaching 2.2 million (Figure 3.4.33). The government is adopting a granular lockdown approach targeting specific areas to be piloted in Metro Manila in September. The scheme uses 5 alert levels depending on the number of COVID-19 cases and hospital utilization rates. It specifies the businesses and establishments that will be allowed to operate at certain capacity rates and gives mobility guidelines, including activities open for vaccinated individuals.

Figure 3.4.33 COVID-19 cases

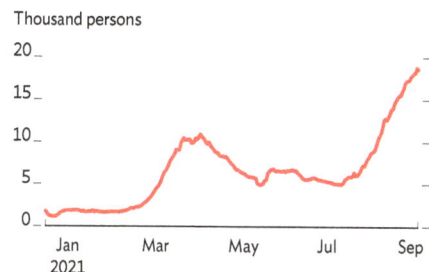

COVID-19 = Coronavirus Disease 2019.
Note: Refers to 7-day moving average of daily new cases.
Source: Our World in Data. https://ourworldindata.org (accessed 16 September 2021).

Thailand

Thailand's latest wave of COVID-19 outbreak threatens to undermine the country's economic recovery this year and next. But strong growth in merchandise exports and an enabling policy environment could partly offset the large negative impact of COVID-19 on growth. Even so, the risks to the economic outlook are tilted downward on the current third wave of the outbreak adding to concerns over the efficacy of vaccines and delays in the country's vaccination program.

Updated assessment

COVID-19 continued to hit the economy hard in the first half of 2021. The latest wave of infections began in April 2021 and most cases have been from the highly transmissible Alpha and Delta variants. The vaccination program has progressed slowly because of inadequate supplies. As of August 2021, only 10% of the population was fully vaccinated. The pandemic worsened in July and August when new infections rose above 10,000 cases per day, more than double the daily cases during the previous wave in December 2020.

In response, the government suspended most domestic flights and expanded areas under curfew during July and August. Most businesses in shopping malls were closed with a few exemptions for food outlets and other essential businesses. Restaurants and food stalls may only offer takeaway services. Employees have been encouraged to work from home as much as possible. These measures dragged growth down. GDP in the first half of 2021 grew by 2.0% after a 6.9% contraction in the first half of 2020 (Figure 3.4.34).

The accelerating global recovery shored up external demand for Thailand's exports. The dollar value of merchandise exports grew by 15.7% in the first half of 2021 after a 7.1% contraction in the same period last year. Exports of automobiles and auto parts, chemical and petroleum products, electronics and electrical appliances, fruit, rubber, and tapioca saw strong growth—as did exports to major markets, including Australia, Europe, India, the People's Republic of China, the Republic of Korea, Southeast Asia, and the United States. But the dollar value of services exports, especially tourism and tourism-related sectors, remained weak in the first half of this year. International tourist arrivals fell by 99.4% after a 66.2% drop in the first half of 2020 (Figure 3.4.35).

Private consumption rose by 2.1% in the first half of 2021. Household income and consumer confidence, however, deteriorated in the second quarter due to the latest wave of COVID-19 and stricter containment measures. This was despite government relief measures to support household spending. The unemployment rate rose from 1.5% at the end 2020 to 1.9% in the second quarter of 2021. The labor market is still highly vulnerable to the pandemic, especially the services sector

Figure 3.4.34 Demand-side contributions to growth

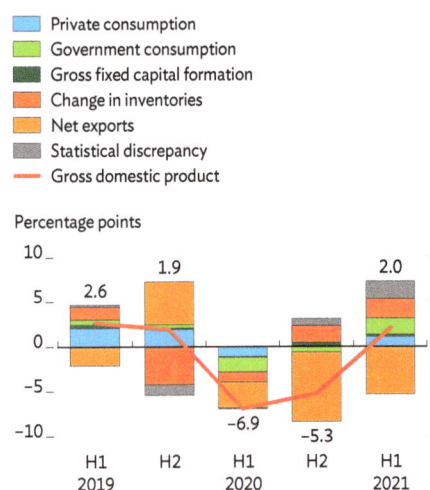

- Private consumption
- Government consumption
- Gross fixed capital formation
- Change in inventories
- Net exports
- Statistical discrepancy
- — Gross domestic product

H = half.
Source: Office of the National Economic and Social Development Council. http://www.nesdc.go.th (accessed 30 August 2021).

Figure 3.4.35 International tourist arrivals

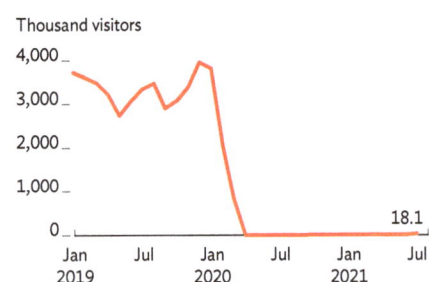

Source: CEIC Data Company (accessed 31 August 2021).

and the self-employed. The ratio of household debt to GDP rose in the first quarter to 90.5% from 89.4% in the previous quarter. From May to July, the government extended cash transfers to welfare card holders and vulnerable groups, and co-payment programs for purchases at small shops. It also introduced new schemes, including the *Ying Chai Ying Dai* (the more you spend, the more you get) scheme, aimed at encouraging middle- and high-income consumers to buy goods and services at participating shops using mobile applications. Under the *Ying Chai Ying Dai* scheme, registrants can spend up to B10,000 a day and receive cashback e-vouchers for 10%–15% of their spending into their e-wallet accounts up to B7,000 per person. The government is providing 2-month cash aid for workers covered by the Social Security Act and discounts on electricity and water bills for all households in July to August. The Ministry of Finance and the Bank of Thailand allowed financial institutions to give a 2-month debt-payment moratorium for individuals and micro, small, or medium-sized enterprises hit by COVID-19 containment measures.

Private investment rose by 5.9% year on year in the first half of 2021 on the recovery in merchandise exports. The resurgence of COVID-19, however, continuously weakened business sentiment for domestic sectors from April to July. The Business Sentiment Index fell, with declines in almost all subindices. The weaker sentiment was mainly for services, including hospitality and retail trade, which were directly affected by stricter containment measures. Imports rose by 14.8% in the first half, in line with growth in private investment and rising merchandise exports.

Public spending on consumption grew by 1.6% year on year in the first half and investment by 12.1%, with both helping to support the economy. Some infrastructure projects were delayed due to the closure of construction sites in high pandemic-risk areas to contain the outbreak. In May, the government's additional B500 billion (around $16 billion) borrowing plan to mitigate COVID-19 impacts was endorsed. Of this, 60% will be used to help people and businesses affected by the pandemic, 34% for public projects to help businesses retain employees and to stimulate investment, and 6% for health benefits. Most of the spending will be government transfers, which could help stimulate private consumption and investment.

Agriculture increased by 1.7% year on year in the first half of 2021 on rising global demand for agricultural products and favorable weather, among other factors. Manufacturing continued to strengthen in line with the recovery in merchandise exports. Services remained weak. The accommodation and food services segments contracted by 17.2% on the impact of COVID-19 containment measures and travel restrictions for foreign tourists (Figure 3.4.36).

Figure 3.4.36 Supply-side contributions to growth

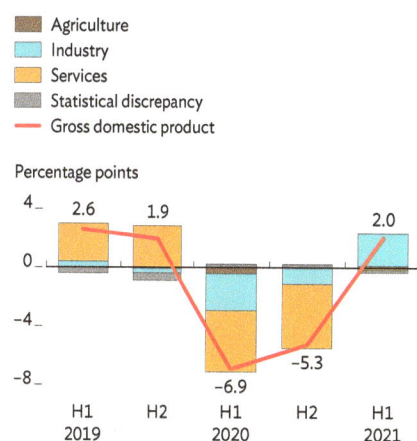

- Agriculture
- Industry
- Services
- Statistical discrepancy
- Gross domestic product

Percentage points

H = half.

Source: Office of the National Economic and Social Development Council. http://www.nesdc.go.th (accessed 30 August 2021).

With subdued aggregate demand, inflation remained low, despite higher energy prices. Headline inflation in the first half of 2021 was at 0.89% and core inflation at 0.27%. The inflation rates for electricity and water, rice products, fresh food, textiles, and entertainment, among other categories, remained low (Figure 3.4.37).

The current account, as a percentage of GDP, turned a deficit of about 3.4% in the first half of 2021 due mainly to the collapse of tourism. The trade balance turned a surplus in tandem with the recovery in merchandise exports. The net outflow in the capital and financial accounts was due to increasing Thai investments abroad. The overall balance of payments turned a deficit of $8.5 billion (Figure 3.4.38). External payments remained sustainable, with international reserves at $246.5 billion, cover for 14 months of imports.

The central bank held the policy rate at 0.5% on the view that the policy rate has already levelled off. Thailand's banking system remained resilient with high levels of capital funding, sustainable provisions for loan losses, and enough liquidity to accommodate increasing economic uncertainty. The nonperforming loan ratio was 3.1% in the second quarter of 2021, unchanged from the end of 2020.

Prospects

The economic situation has deteriorated since *ADO 2021*. This *Update* forecasts GDP growth this year at 0.8% from the earlier projection of 3.0%. And it lowers the growth forecast for 2022 to 3.9% from 4.5% (Table 3.4.4). These revisions are largely in line with government forecasts, which have GDP growth this year ranging 0.7%–1.2%. Low inflation will persist this year and next, as aggregate demand remains sluggish (Figure 3.4.39).

External demand is expected to improve on mainly rising merchandise exports, but services exports are likely to remain below *ADO 2021*'s forecast. Foreign tourist arrivals in 2021 are projected at just 140,000 compared with 4 million forecast earlier. Foreign tourist arrivals are forecast at 20 million in 2022, up from the earlier projection of 7 million. The European Union, in July, removing Thailand from the COVID-19 safe list could upset the country's plan to fully reopen more pilot provinces to foreign tourists by October.

Receipts from international tourism may get a boost from the government's tourism recovery pilot program, Phuket Sandbox and Samui Plus, that allowed foreign tourists who are fully vaccinated to enter Thailand without quarantine from July 2021. According to the Tourism Authority of Thailand, advance hotel bookings in Phuket from July to September were 244,703 room nights—an average occupancy rate of just 10.1%. Under current requirements, tourists must first stay in Phuket or Samui for 14 nights before they can travel to other parts of the country.

Figure 3.4.37 Inflation and policy interest rate

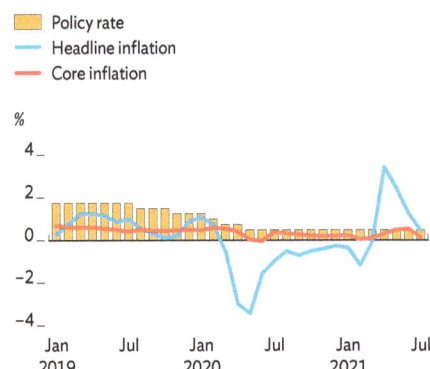

Source: CEIC Data Company (accessed 30 August 2021).

Figure 3.4.38 Balance of payments

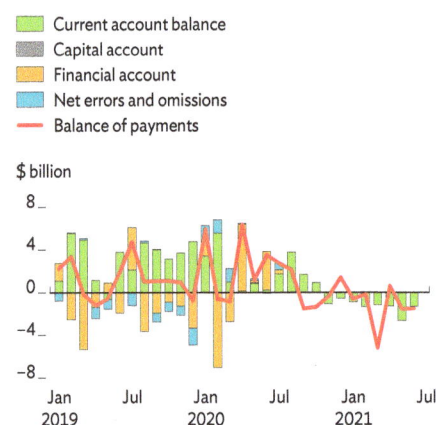

Source: CEIC Data Company (accessed 30 August 2021).

Table 3.4.4 Selected economic indicators in Thailand, %

	2020	2021		2022	
		ADO 2021	*Update*	*ADO 2021*	*Update*
GDP growth	−6.1	3.0	0.8	4.5	3.9
Inflation	−0.8	1.1	1.1	1.0	1.0
CAB/GDP	3.5	4.0	−1.4	6.5	2.0

ADO = Asian Development Outlook, CAB = current account balance, GDP = gross domestic product.
Source: Asian Development Bank estimates.

Private consumption is expected to remain subdued as jobs and income are lost, particularly in tourism, retail trade, and clothing manufacturing. Support from the government is unlikely to fully compensate for these losses. Hence, growth in private consumption this year is revised down from the 2.1% forecast in *ADO 2021* to 1.0%, rebounding to 3.9% in 2022.

Weak domestic demand could hold back private investment, which is expected to decline in the second half of 2021. For the year, private investment is projected to grow by 3.0%, down from the earlier forecast of 3.5%. The forecast for private investment growth next year, at 5.0%, remains unchanged. Public investment is likely to hold up well, supported by the government's efforts to reduce COVID-19 infections. Still, several construction projects are expected to be delayed, causing a mild downward revision of public investment this year.

This *Update* projects public consumption growing by 4.3% in 2021, down from *ADO 2021*'s 5.2% estimate. For next year, public consumption growth is expected to turn negative, partly because the budget for fiscal year 2022 (ending 30 September 2022) is cut by 5.7% to avoid breaching the government's target of a ratio of 60% public debt to GDP. Public consumption for 2022 is expected to contract by 0.9% after an earlier projection of 2.0% growth. Most public spending this year and next year will be transfers to relieve the impact of COVID-19 and support economic recovery. The bulk of the spending will be off-budget under two borrowing decrees, endorsed in April 2020 and May 2021.

Imports are expected to recover in tandem with rising merchandise exports, despite weakening domestic demand and delays in private and public investment. Imports are forecast to grow a robust 16.1% in 2021, up from 4.7% forecast in *ADO 2021*. Import growth next year is projected to expand by 3.9%, revised down from 8.4%.

The outlook for agriculture remains unchanged at 2.6% growth this year and 3.4% next year. Industrial output is being hit by the latest wave of COVID-19. Some factories have already been temporarily closed because of infections among workers. Slowing domestic demand will also undermine industrial output. Industry growth this year is revised down to 2.0% from the earlier projection of 2.3%. Industry growth in 2022, forecast at 5.1%, is below the earlier 5.7% projection. Services in the first half of 2021 performed below *ADO 2021*'s expectations. Forecasts for the sector are revised down for this year and next, with services expected to contract by 0.1% after an earlier forecast of 1.7% growth.

The current account of the balance of payments is expected to record a deficit equivalent to 1.4% of GDP in 2021 and a surplus of 2.0% in 2022 as services exports decline significantly this year but gradually recover next year (Figure 3.4.40).

Figure 3.4.39 GDP growth

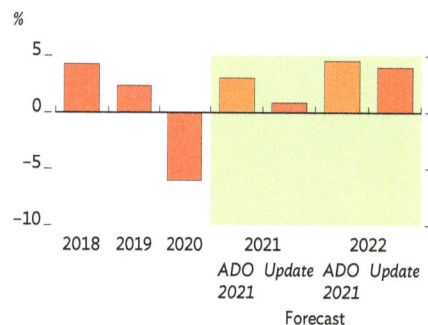

ADO = Asian Development Outlook, GDP = gross domestic product.
Source: ADO database.

Figure 3.4.40 Current account balance

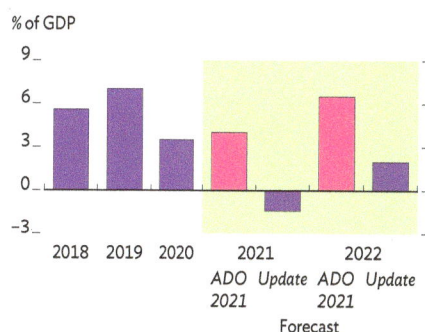

ADO = Asian Development Outlook, GDP = gross domestic product.
Source: ADO database.

A net outflow in the capital and financial accounts is likely on investor concerns over the latest COVID-19 wave and the slow progress of vaccination. Residents are likely to continue investing abroad instead of domestically. Low inflation is expected this year and next, with the rate unchanged at 1.1% in 2021 and 1.0% in 2022 (Figure 3.4.41).

Risks to the outlook are more heightened than they were in *ADO 2021*. Significant downside risks are posed by the possibility of further severe COVID-19 outbreaks in the country and more contagious variants. Delays in the schedule for the vaccine rollout could adversely affect domestic mobility, consumption, and tourism. If vaccines are less effective for the more contagious variants, or the vaccine rollout slows, the impacts on the economy from both will be much worse than was expected in *ADO 2021*, and recovery will be more uncertain.

Viet Nam

GDP growth recovered in the first half of 2021, supported largely by an expansion in trade. But a resurgence of the COVID-19 pandemic in April tightened the supply of labor, lowering industrial output and disrupting agriculture value chains. Growth is now projected at 3.8% this year and 6.5% in 2022, both lower than *ADO 2021*'s forecasts. Inflation will be muted in 2021 and 2022, with the rate below earlier projections. The current account is expected to deteriorate, turning to a deficit this year compared with a projected surplus in *ADO 2021* and returning to a surplus in 2022, albeit a lower one than earlier projected.

Updated assessment

The economy gained momentum in the first 6 months of 2021, with GDP growth accelerating to 5.6% from 1.8% in the first half of last year. This was, however, still lower than prepandemic growth of 6.8% in the first half of 2019. Strong export demand drove agriculture, forestry, and fisheries growth up to 3.8% from 1.2% in the first half of 2020 and 2.3% in the same period in 2019. This output contributed 0.4 percentage points to first-half growth. First-half industry growth more than doubled to 8.4% year on year, just below 8.9% in the same period in 2019, contributing 3.0 percentage points to GDP growth. Services rose by 4.0% year on year, but still lower than 6.7% in the first half of 2019 as international tourist arrivals plunged by 97.6% year on year. The contribution of services to GDP growth declined to 1.7 percentage points year on year (Figure 3.4.42).

The spread of COVID-19 and an extended lockdown since June dampened the recovery. The strict lockdown in Viet Nam's southern region and in Ha Noi and surrounding industrial areas, which contribute nearly 50% of the country's GDP,

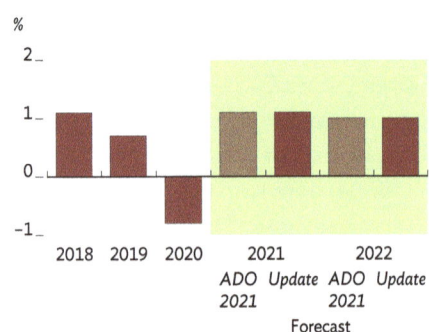

Figure 3.4.41 Inflation

ADO = Asian Development Outlook.
Source: ADO database.

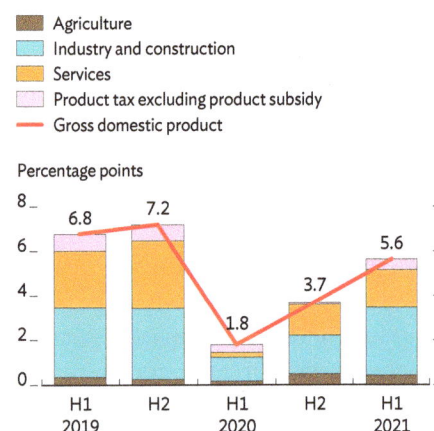

Figure 3.4.42 Supply-side contributions to growth

- Agriculture
- Industry and construction
- Services
- Product tax excluding product subsidy
- Gross domestic product

H = half.
Sources: General Statistics Office of Viet Nam. https://www.gso.gov.vn/en/homepage (accessed 11 September 2021); Asian Development Bank estimates.

dragged down the index of industrial production in August to 4.2% month on month and 7.4% year on year. The index rose 5.6% year on year in the first 8 months of 2021, lower than 9.5% in the same period in 2019.

Viet Nam's fourth wave of the pandemic hit enterprises and the labor market hard. In the first 8 months of 2021, nearly 85,500 enterprises suspended operations, 24% higher than in the same period last year. The lockdown and stringent movement restrictions disrupted labor mobility and hampered production. Consequently, 12.8 million people lost jobs or had their incomes reduced. Rising unemployment and falling incomes dampened private consumption growth to 3.6% in the first half 2021, up only 0.2% from the first half of 2020 and half the level in the same period of 2019. Public consumption growth also halved, to 3.2%, as the government reduced current expenditure.

In August 2021, wholesale and retail trade plunged by 34.9% year on year on the effects of the lockdown (Figure 3.4.43). Factory closures and disrupted labor mobility constrained domestic and foreign investment. For the first half of this year, total investment increased 5.7% year on year from 1.9% in the first half of 2020, but this was still lower than growth of 7.1% in the first half of 2019. Investment growth stalled in August. Investment from the state budget declined by 7.1% month on month, and 24.7% year on year. The disbursement of foreign investment also showed signs of slowing, with year on year growth falling from 6.8% in June to 2.0% in August.

Inflation was 0.25% higher in August than in July as fuel prices increased and disrupted food supply temporarily raised food prices. The inflation rate was 1.5% in the first half and 1.8% in the first 8 months, with impaired incomes, rising unemployment, lower public investment expenditure, and limited mobility depressing demand (Figure 3.4.44). The exchange rate between the dong and the US dollar remained relatively stable during the first 8 months, with the local currency trending slightly higher.

The central bank maintained an accommodative monetary policy stance, with policy rates unchanged since October 2020. Commercial banks extended debt restructuring, waived interest rates for existing loans, reduced interest rates, and provided new soft loans to firms hit by the COVID-19 pandemic. Total liquidity (M2) increased by 13.3% year on year in the first half of 2021, only a marginal increase on 12.8% growth in the same period in 2020. Nevertheless, this boosted credit, which grew by an estimated 14.9 % year on year in August, compared with 7.9% in the same period last year (Figure 3.4.45).

Increased receipts from taxes on trade and land use lifted government revenue by an estimated 13.9% in the first 8 months year on year. Expenditure fell by 5.8% year on year

Figure 3.4.43 Retail sales

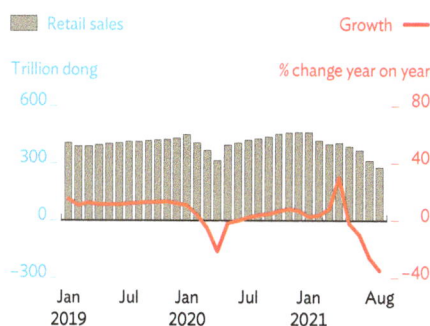

Sources: CEIC Data Company; General Statistics Office. https://www.gso.gov.vn/en/homepage (both accessed 11 September 2021).

Figure 3.4.44 Monthly inflation

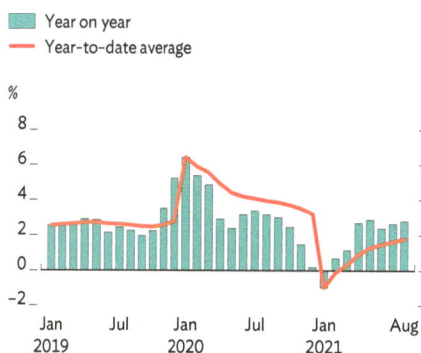

Source: General Statistics Office. https://www.gso.gov.vn/en/homepage (accessed 3 September 2021).

largely due to the slow disbursement of public investment and a cut in current outlays. The budget turned a surplus estimated at the equivalent of 1.3% of 2020 GDP in the first 8 months. However, sharp budgetary pressure emerged in August, as the impacts of increasing insolvency and unemployment, and tax deferrals, dragged down revenue by 9.8% year on year and spending for COVID-19 containment increased by 90%.

Merchandise exports increased by 29.0% in the first half of 2021 and imports by 36.2%, which narrowed the merchandise trade surplus to the equivalent of 3.2% of GDP from 9.3% in the first half of 2020. This, together with lower net receipts from services, turned the current account balance into a deficit equal to 2.3% of GDP from a surplus of 2.5% in the first half of 2020. The deficit widened in the first 8 months as exports declined relative to imports for 4 consecutive months starting in May.

With interest rates still low, net capital inflows were sustained in the first half of 2021, contributing to an overall balance of payments surplus estimated at 2.9% of GDP. Foreign reserves at the end of June were estimated to cover 3.9 months of imports, down from 4.2 months cover at the end of 2020 (Figure 3.4.46).

Prospects

The COVID-19 pandemic is expected to drag down 2021's growth prospects. The labor shortage caused by the lockdown in the Mekong Delta will disrupt agriculture supply chains. Agriculture exports may also suffer from the monsoon in the third and fourth quarters and the quarantine measures imposed on Viet Nam's agriculture exports. On the bright side, improved market access from free trade agreements and recoveries in the European Union, the People's Republic of China, and the United States will boost agricultural exports. Agriculture growth is expected at 2.7% in 2021, the same level as in 2020.

Extended lockdowns in major cities will continue to disrupt the supply of labor, hurting especially labor-intensive manufacturing and lowering output. The purchasing managers' index hovered below 50 from June to August, signaling a deceleration in manufacturing (Figure 3.4.47). Because of this, industry growth is forecast to slow to 5.0% in 2021 from the prepandemic level of 8.9% in 2019.

The increasing need for nonphysical transactions and health care will sustain the growth of financial and health services. But closures of tourist areas and limited mobility will continue to hit tourism, lowering growth in the services sector to a forecast 3.3% this year from of 7.3% in 2019.

As of 15 September, 33% of the population had received a first dose of a COVID-19 vaccine, but less than 6% were fully vaccinated. While the rapid first-dose vaccine rollout will help reduce infections and deaths, the low fully vaccinated

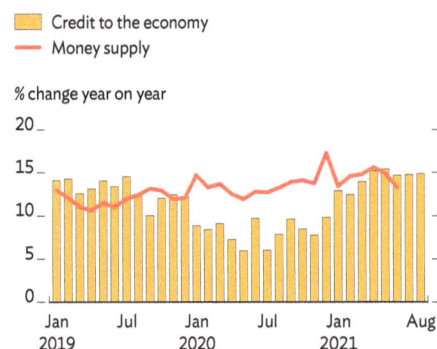

Figure 3.4.45 Credit and money supply growth

Credit to the economy
Money supply

% change year on year

Sources: State Bank of Viet Nam; Asian Development Bank estimates.

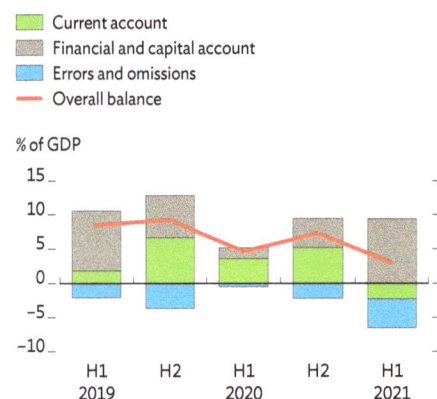

Figure 3.4.46 Balance of payments indicators

Current account
Financial and capital account
Errors and omissions
Overall balance

% of GDP

GDP = gross domestic product, H = half.
Sources: State Bank of Viet Nam; Asian Development Bank estimates.

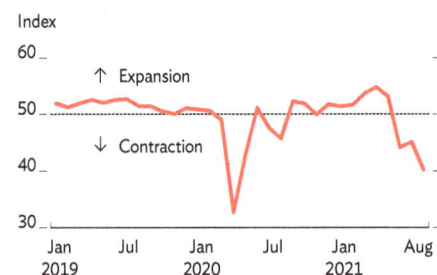

Figure 3.4.47 Purchasing managers' index

Index

↑ Expansion

↓ Contraction

Source: IHS Markit. https://www.markiteconomics.com (accessed 3 September 2021).

rate could prevent a full return to work in 2021, as only fully vaccinated people can go to work. Excessive and paper-based procedures, especially in the issuance of travel certificates, have disrupted labor mobility and the food supply chain, exacerbating the impact of the pandemic on the economy.

A prolonged pandemic and an extended lockdown are expected to weaken consumption and investment in 2021. The labor shortage, slow land acquisition and resettlement procedures, increasing costs of construction materials, and the third and fourth quarter monsoon will slow the disbursement of public investment. The disbursement of the state budget in the first 8 months fell by 46.4% compared with the same period last year. Cumbersome and unclear procedures constrain the disbursement of needed fiscal support for firms and people affected by the COVID-19 pandemic. As of 31 August 2021, only about 32% of a $1 billion social security support program had been disbursed. While fiscal policy may support growth, it is unlikely to significantly raise domestic demand given the modest government spending due to increasing budget constraints, and a deficit equal to 5% of GDP expected in 2021, slightly over the targeted deficit.

Credit demand has remained subdued so far in 2021 due to the pandemic disrupting production and businesses. Credit growth is expected to slow to 10%–11% this year, below the target of 12%. In September, State Bank of Viet Nam, the central bank, instructed credit institutions to extend credit relief measures for affected clients through debt restructuring and retaining debt classifications, waiving or lowering interest rates on existing loans, and providing soft loans until 30 June 2022. Credit demand should improve in 2022, as economic activities begin to return to normal.

The fast recovery of Viet Nam's main overseas markets, particularly the European Union, the People's Republic of China, and the US, will support exports, especially for textiles, garments and footwear, electronics, and mobile phones. But the lockdown of major industrial hubs in the Mekong Delta will constrain production capacity, triggering a shift of orders to other countries, as 18% of European companies doing business in Viet Nam already did in July and August. The small increases in FDI flow and disbursement in July and August are unlikely to continue over the rest of the year because of factory closures and labor shortages (Figure 3.4.48).

Because of all these factors, this *Update* revises down the GDP growth forecast to 3.8% in 2021 from the 6.7% projection in *ADO 2021* (Table 3.4.5). Assuming the COVID-19 pandemic is brought under control by the end of 2021 and full vaccination covers 70% of the population by the second quarter of 2022, the growth forecast for next year is revised to 6.5%, which is still lower than the earlier projection (Figure 3.4.49).

Figure 3.4.48 Foreign direct investment

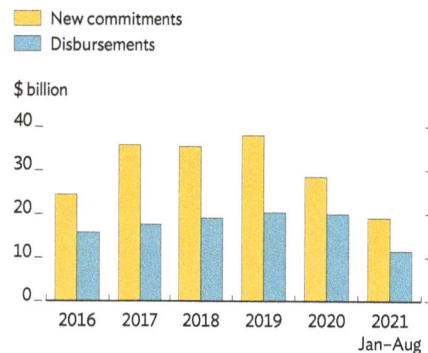

Source: Haver Analytics (accessed 24 August 2021).

Table 3.4.5 Selected economic indicators in Viet Nam, %

	2020	2021		2022	
		ADO 2021	Update	ADO 2021	Update
GDP growth	2.9	6.7	3.8	7.0	6.5
Inflation	3.2	3.8	2.8	4.0	3.5
CAB/GDP	4.6	2.0	–1.0	2.5	1.5

ADO = *Asian Development Outlook*, CAB = current account balance, GDP = gross domestic product.
Source: Asian Development Bank estimates.

Figure 3.4.49 GDP growth

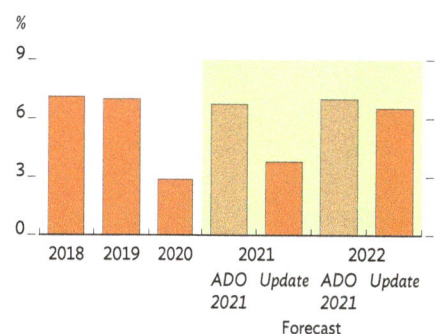

ADO = *Asian Development Outlook*, GDP = gross domestic product.
Source: *ADO* database.

The inflation rate forecast is also revised down, to 2.8% for 2021, as subdued domestic demand has pushed the rate to its lowest level since 2016. The inflation rate is forecast at 3.5% in 2022 as growth accelerates.

The deterioration in the external current account this year and next is expected to be worse than *ADO 2021*'s forecasts. A modest current account deficit equal to 1.0% of GDP is expected in 2021 since the impact of the pandemic on production will slow export growth over the rest of the year. The current account is expected to return to a surplus, at 1.5% of GDP in 2022, as exports increase on a revival in domestic production and external demand.

Viet Nam's economic outlook in the near term is challenging. The main risk to the outlook is a prolonged COVID-19 outbreak if the vaccination rate does not increase substantially. Because vaccines are not reaching Viet Nam fast enough, the government's efforts to start up domestic COVID-19 vaccine manufacturing in 2021, combined with increased procurement from outside sources, will be crucial for the country to avert a health crisis caused by the pandemic. The growth prospects for this year and next will also depend on the timely and sufficient provision of necessities, such as food and cash, to those affected by the outbreak. Nonperforming loans could become a risk in 2022. Cutting unnecessary administrative burdens and digitalizing government procedures will be critical for improving the efficiency of pandemic containment measures and to support recovery this year and next.

Other economies

Brunei Darussalam

Growth in the first quarter of 2021 contracted by 1.4% year on year on declines in government consumption, investments, and exports that more than offset the growth in private consumption. Exports of goods and services decreased by 4.3% by volume, primarily on plunging sales of mineral fuels. Government consumption fell by 9.8%, as measures to contain the COVID-19 pandemic affected some government services. Investment fell by 5.7%, with declines in both private and government capital spending.

The contraction in first-quarter growth was mainly driven by lower oil and gas production (down 3.1%) and manufacturing of natural gas (down 11.4%). Services output recovered slightly. This was a broad recovery, however, spanning wholesale and retail trade, restaurants, business services, information and communication, and real estate and personal services. The recovery in services is an indication that the effects of COVID-19 on the economy are receding.

Table 3.4.6 Selected economic indicators in Brunei Darussalam, %

	2020	2021		2022	
		ADO 2021	Update	*ADO 2021*	Update
GDP growth	1.2	2.5	1.8	3.0	3.5
Inflation	1.9	0.7	1.3	0.7	0.7
CAB/GDP	4.3	8.5	6.5	10.5	10.5

ADO = Asian Development Outlook, CAB = current account balance, GDP = gross domestic product.
Source: Asian Development Bank estimates

Even so, output in several other sectors declined, particularly transport, government services, and hotels.

Because of weaker-than-expected GDP growth in the first quarter, this *Update* revises down its forecast for growth for the full year from the projection in *ADO 2021* (Table 3.4.6). The forecast for 2022 is higher, due largely due to an expected rise in production and investment at Hengyi Industries' refinery project and in state-owned Brunei Fertilizer Industries' ammonia and urea production plan.

The inflation rate in the second quarter was at 1.3%, lower than the peak of 2.5% in June 2020. All components of the consumer price index, except for transport and restaurants and hotels, rose at a softer pace. Inflation is expected to continue moderating in the near term due to the large output gap.

Although exports were slightly down in the first 4 months of this year, it recovered in May and June to post growth of 33.6% in the first half of 2021. They are expected to continue to rise over the rest of 2021. Higher global oil and liquefied natural gas prices this year and next, compared with their levels in 2020, will support growth in goods exports. As exports pick up, imports will also rise—their value was up 169.8% from January to June—on the anticipated strengthening of domestic demand and inputs, such as mineral fuels for Hengyi's refinery. The net result of all this will be a lower current account surplus this year than was forecast in *ADO 2021*, but the surplus will still be higher than 2020's.

Cambodia

This *Update* revises down the forecast for growth in 2021 from the projection in *ADO 2021* due to the prolonged outbreak of COVID-19, which has slowed the recovery in domestic demand. This will result in slightly lower inflation than earlier forecast (Table 3.4.7). A growing trade deficit will widen the current account deficit this year. The rollout of COVID-19 vaccinations is on track for completion by the end of 2021 and will position the economy for stronger growth in 2022.

Lockdowns and temporary factory closures hit production in the garments, travel goods, and footwear sector, and exports were well below prepandemic levels in the first half of 2021, albeit marginally higher than in 2020. Other manufacturing sectors have continued to thrive, and construction has begun to recover, with imports of construction materials rising by 23.5% year on year in the first half. Industry growth is projected at 5.3% in 2021, subject to stronger garments, travel goods, and footwear exports and continuing strength in other manufacturing sectors.

COVID-19 outbreaks caused some disruptions to agricultural supply chains, but the overall impact has been limited. Agricultural exports rose 30.3% year on year in the first half of 2021, with particularly solid growth in non-rice exports. The agriculture sector is expected to grow by 1.5% this year.

Table 3.4.7 Selected economic indicators in Cambodia, %

	2020	2021		2022	
		ADO 2021	Update	ADO 2021	Update
GDP growth	–3.1	4.0	1.9	5.5	5.5
Inflation	2.9	3.1	2.9	3.0	2.7
CAB/GDP	–12.1	–15.6	–15.6	–12.3	–12.9

ADO = *Asian Development Outlook*, CAB = current account balance, GDP = gross domestic product.

Source: Asian Development Bank estimates.

Restrictions on international travel remain, and international visitor arrivals were down by 91.3% year on year in the first half. Domestic demand for food, accommodation, transportation and other in-person services has been severely hit by COVID-19 and its associated lockdowns. Services output is projected to contract 0.6% in 2021.

While inflows of foreign direct investment and other capital continued, a surge in gold imports caused the current account deficit to widen in the first half, leading to a modest decline in international reserves to $20.2 billion in June, cover for 8.8 months of imports. The current account deficit for the full year is projected at the equivalent of 15.6% of GDP, but it will widen significantly if the unbalanced trade in gold continues.

Cambodia's authorities have continued to implement policies to mitigate the pandemic's impact. The loan restructuring program has been extended to the end of 2021, and other regulatory forbearance maintained. These measures enabled banks and microfinance institutions to continue lending, with total private sector credit increasing by 23.3% year on year in the first half.

Vaccine rollout is progressing well and the government is finalizing a medium-term recovery plan. The emergence of new COVID-19 variants is a key risk to the outlook. Other risks include a rapid increase in nonperforming loans when the loan restructuring program is phased out, and a sharp adjustment in the construction and real estate sector.

Lao People's Democratic Republic

An unexpected second wave of COVID-19 delayed economic recovery in the Lao People's Democratic Republic (Lao PDR), with consumption hard hit by the pandemic containment measures implemented since April 2021. This *Update* revises downward the GDP growth forecast for this year from the projection in *ADO 2021*. The global recovery will spur domestic growth in 2022, albeit less than earlier forecast (Table 3.4.8).

Policies to stop the spread of COVID-19 have curbed output in manufacturing and hurt growth in retail trade, transport, and tourism services. Curtailed economic activity has increased joblessness, particularly among women, and reduced incomes, with households whose members have lower skills and education being hardest hit. An outbreak of lumpy skin disease among cattle disrupted livestock trade, dampening agriculture performance.

In a swift COVID-19 vaccine deployment, one in four people were reported to have been fully vaccinated by the end of August. New mining concessions over the rest of this year are expected to bring new investment and strengthen commodity trade. The economy is also set to receive a steady increase in earnings from expansions in electricity production capacity.

Table 3.4.8 Selected economic indicators in the Lao People's Democratic Republic, %

	2020	2021		2022	
		ADO 2021	Update	ADO 2021	Update
GDP growth	−0.5	4.0	2.3	4.5	4.0
Inflation	5.1	4.5	3.7	5.0	4.5
CAB/GDP	−5.8	−7.8	−6.0	−8.0	−6.5

ADO = Asian Development Outlook, CAB = current account balance, GDP = gross domestic product.
Source: Asian Development Bank estimates.

The planned inauguration of the railway linking the Lao PDR with the People's Republic of China in December is expected to support growth in tourism and urban real estate. With warmer temperatures forecast and rainfall on-trend, rice and cash-crop harvests are expected to be sustained.

Commodity exports, particularly food crops, electricity, and gold, remained strong in the first half of 2021, helping to offset continued weakness in manufactured exports and payments for imports and investor dividends. With the growth in exports set to outpace import growth this year and next, the narrowing of the current account deficit is projected to be sharper than *ADO 2021*'s forecast.

With domestic demand softening, inflation was contained at an average of 3.1% in the first 7 months of this year. The kip depreciated against foreign currencies, with the spread between official and parallel rates for the kip and US dollar exceeding 20% during July, reflecting a domestic shortage of currency following large external public debt payments.

At the end of June, government expenditure reached 35.8% of the annual plan. This is on par with disbursements before the COVID-19 pandemic, but with a higher share of spending allocated to capital for completing large infrastructure projects. Revenue reached 40.5% of the annual plan, but had not returned to prepandemic levels. Public finances remain under stress, with public and publicly guaranteed debt reported at equal to 72.0% of GDP in 2020 and total debt service at $1.9 billion in 2021.

Gross international reserves were reported at $1.2 billion in June 2021, cover for 1.5 months of imports and servicing of the government's external debt. Concerns over external liquidity pressures are partially mitigated by projected robust export growth that will provide much needed foreign exchange receipts.

Myanmar

This *Update* forecasts a contraction in the economy in fiscal year 2021 (FY2021, ending 30 September 2021) that is nearly double the contraction projected in *ADO 2021* (Table 3.4.9). Weaker aggregate demand has weighed on the economy, with supply constraints adding to the slowdown.

Agriculture production was dampened by lower farm-gate prices; higher prices of key inputs, such as fertilizers and pesticides; limited access to finance; and reduced cross-border trade. Agriculture is estimated to have grown by 0.8% in FY2021, lower than the forecast of 1.9% in April.

Industry output and employment have declined since the first quarter of FY2021 due to the political turmoil in the country. Measures taken to contain COVID-19 infections and weaker demand caused factory closures. Industry output is forecast declining 20.9% this fiscal year compared with

Table 3.4.9 Selected economic indicators in Myanmar, %

	2020	2021		2022	
		ADO 2021	Update	ADO 2021	Update
GDP growth	3.3	−9.8	−18.4	...	...
Inflation	5.7	6.2	6.2	...	...
CAB/GDP	−2.6	−4.4	−1.5	...	...

ADO = *Asian Development Outlook*, CAB = current account balance, GDP = gross domestic product.

Note: Because of the uncertain situation in Myanmar, no forecasts are provided for fiscal year 2022, ending 30 September of that year.

Source: Asian Development Bank estimates.

the 10.8% decline projected in *ADO 2021*. COVID-19 mobility restrictions and political turmoil disrupted activity in services. Output in this sector is forecast declining by 26.4%, compared with an earlier forecast of a 15.1% drop.

The dollar value of merchandise exports contracted by 15.8% in the first 10 months of FY2021 due mainly to sharp declines in exports of livestock, minerals, and manufactured goods. Delays in approving and implementing investment projects, and contractions in manufacturing industries, caused merchandise imports to decline sharply by 24.8% in the first 10 months of FY2021. Because of this, the current account deficit for the full fiscal year is likely to be narrower at equivalent to 1.5% of GDP, lower than the 4.4% deficit forecast in *ADO 2021*.

Inflation in the first 7 months of FY2021 accelerated to 4.0% (starting out at 1.5% at the beginning of this period), despite slowing aggregate demand. An uptick in prices for fuel and other essential commodities is expected to keep the average inflation rate for the full fiscal year at about *ADO 2021*'s forecast 6.2%.

Myanmar's exchange rate has been highly volatile, with the kyat depreciating by 19.4% against the US dollar between July 2020 and July 2021. This was despite the central bank's interventions to limit the depreciation. Weaker capital inflows and subdued demand will continue to put pressure on the kyat. Foreign direct investment declined by 54% in the first half of FY2021.

This *Update* projects a higher fiscal deficit in FY2021, equivalent to 6.0% of GDP from the earlier projection of 5.2%. Although significant cuts in public services will result in lower expenditure, declines in revenue collection will be steeper than earlier forecast.

Risks to these forecasts are tilted to the downside, with political uncertainties and the effects of the pandemic continuing to weigh heavily on the economy.

Singapore

Propelled by expansions in services and manufacturing, Singapore's economy surged to 14.7% year on year in the second quarter (Q2) of 2021, the highest quarterly expansion in 11 years. The economy also benefitted from effective COVID-19 management, with 35.8% of the population fully vaccinated by the end of Q2. Services rebounded on higher Q2 trade activity and robust business and consumer demand for digital solutions and services. Construction rebounded strongly in the first half of 2021 due to a resumption in public and private construction after a substantial contraction in the same period a year ago. Manufacturing rebounded from a low base on buoyant global demand for electronics. Growth was supported by a rapid rise in exports, a smaller but more targeted stimulus package amounting to the equivalent 2.4% of GDP, and the gradual loosening of social distancing restrictions that boosted consumer and business confidence.

The reintroduction of mobility restrictions following a surge in COVID-19 infections in mid-July, both in Singapore and trading partners, could temporarily disrupt the upturn in trade and tourism services and dampen the growth momentum, but overall prospects remain upbeat. The purchasing managers' index in July 2021 climbed to 56.7, and Q2 business expectation surveys showed more positive responses. Strong growth in public consumption and capital spending should also boost domestic demand. The economic revival in key trading partners, and strong demand for electronic products and financial and insurance services, will continue to support exports. Given these prospects and the better-than-expected performance in the first half of 2021, and that more than 75% of the population will be vaccinated by the end of the year, this *Update* forecasts higher growth in 2021 compared with *ADO 2021*'s projection (Table 3.4.10). The forecast for 2022 is unchanged. COVID-19 uncertainties remain the greatest downside risk to these forecasts.

Rising oil and food prices and accommodation costs, accompanied by pick-ups in consumer spending and an improving job market, caused inflation to accelerate to 2.5% in July 2021, the highest in 7 years, and to 1.7% in the first 7 months of 2021. Based on this trend and the continuing recovery in economic activity, the inflation rates for this year and next are projected to be higher than forecast in *ADO 2021*.

The 20.1% year on year rise in exports in the first half of 2021 caused the trade surplus to widen from $45.8 billion in the first half of last year to $50.9 billion, and the current account surplus to improve from the equivalent of 17.4% of GDP to an estimated 19.8%. This *Update* projects a higher current account surplus than was forecast in *ADO 2021*, while the forecast for 2022 is unchanged.

Timor-Leste

The economy weakened on a surge of COVID-19 cases since March 2021 and the historic flooding caused by cyclone Seroja in April. Stringent COVID-19 lockdown measures were imposed in March, and progress in the country's vaccination program has cushioned some of the pandemic's impacts on the economy. Still, this *Update* revises down the GDP growth forecast for 2021 and 2022 from the projections in *ADO 2021* (Table 3.4.11).

Under the national COVID-19 vaccination plan, 52% of the population had been vaccinated with a first dose of the AstraZeneca or Sinovac vaccines and 26% fully vaccinated as of 31 August. A supplementary budget in April reprioritized $263 million to be spent through the State Budget's Contingency Reserve Fund to tackle COVID-19 in addition to the country's second-largest state budget of $1.9 billion for 2021 to stimulate a postpandemic recovery.

Table 3.4.10 Selected economic indicators in Singapore, %

	2020	2021		2022	
		ADO 2021	Update	ADO 2021	Update
GDP growth	−5.4	6.0	6.5	4.1	4.1
Inflation	−0.2	1.0	1.6	1.2	1.4
CAB/GDP	17.6	17.0	20.0	17.0	17.0

ADO = *Asian Development Outlook*, CAB = current account balance, GDP = gross domestic product.
Source: Asian Development Bank estimates.

Table 3.4.11 Selected economic indicators in Timor-Leste, %

	2020	2021		2022	
		ADO 2021	Update	ADO 2021	Update
GDP growth	−8.5	3.4	2.2	4.3	4.0
Inflation	0.5	2.0	2.3	2.0	2.0
CAB/GDP	−19.6	−26.5	−27.2	−43.0	−44.2

ADO = *Asian Development Outlook*, CAB = current account balance, GDP = gross domestic product.
Source: Asian Development Bank estimates.

Government capital spending fell sharply since March, initially dampened by lockdown measures. Total public spending, however, remained high, with a 24% increase in recurrent spending in the first half of 2021 due to large transfers to support private consumption.

The suspension and deferment of some taxes in early 2021 depressed tax and nontax revenue, which contracted 11% in the first half. Investment returns on the sovereign wealth fund—the Petroleum Fund—reached a record value of $19.4 billion in May. Revenue from petroleum taxes and royalties will, however, continue to decrease this year due to the depletion of Timor-Leste's oil and gas field, although the discovery of additional natural gas and reserves of natural gas liquids could postpone the end of the field to 2023.

The high exposure of services in retail trade, transportation and storage, accommodation, and food to demand shocks hit the real economy hard. April's floods affected about 33,000 households. Damage to households and critical infrastructure was estimated at $225 million. Merchandise exports, after falling in the first quarter of 2021, made a strong recovery in the second quarter, increasing by 12% over the first half and contributing to a slight decline in the current account balance. Coffee exports, the largest non-oil export, rebounded. Tourism, identified by the government as a potentially productive sector, will not recover in 2021 because the local travel industry continues to be badly affected by the closure of international borders due to the COVID-19 pandemic.

Inflation this year is expected to accelerate due to the impact of mobility restrictions and the effect of April's floods on harvests putting upward pressure on food prices, the key determinant of domestic inflation. As a result, the inflation forecast for this year is higher than projected in *ADO 2021*. The forecast for 2022 is unchanged, supported by the economy's medium-term recovery prospects.

The Pacific

The subregional economy is now projected to contract in 2021, with Papua New Guinea and Fiji severely constrained by local COVID-19 infections. Stronger recovery and higher inflation are expected in 2022 as Pacific economies reopen borders. Subregional current account surpluses will likely be higher than projected in *Asian Development Outlook 2021* because of curtailed imports in 2021 and recovery in commodity exports and tourism in 2022.

Subregional assessment and prospects

The aggregate Pacific economy is now forecast to contract by 0.6% in 2021, the projection revised down from growth at 1.4% in *Asian Development Outlook 2021 (ADO 2021)* in April and at 0.3% in the July *ADO Supplement* (Figure 3.5.1). The less favorable outlook arises largely from dimmer prospects in Papua New Guinea (PNG), the predominant economy in the subregion, and Fiji, the second-largest economy. Both countries are working to contain local outbreaks of COVID-19 with restrictions on travel, both across borders and domestic, that have severely constrained economic activity. Further, mineral and petroleum industries in PNG are performing more weakly than anticipated, with a major gold mine now expected to remain closed for most of 2021.

From an *ADO 2021* forecast of growth in Vanuatu in 2021, this *Update* now revises the projection to contraction because of delays in reopening the borders of this tourism-dependent economy. This *Update* also sees deeper contractions in Palau, where recovery in tourism has been delayed by the risk posed by the Delta coronavirus variant, and in the Marshall Islands, where prolonged border closures have depressed fishery output and construction. Border closures have similarly constrained tourism and public infrastructure projects in Samoa and Tonga.

This *Update* sees modest growth in Kiribati and a smaller contraction in the Federated States of Micronesia. In both economies, government stimulus measures have mitigated the economic impacts of the pandemic.

Figure 3.5.1 GDP growth in the Pacific

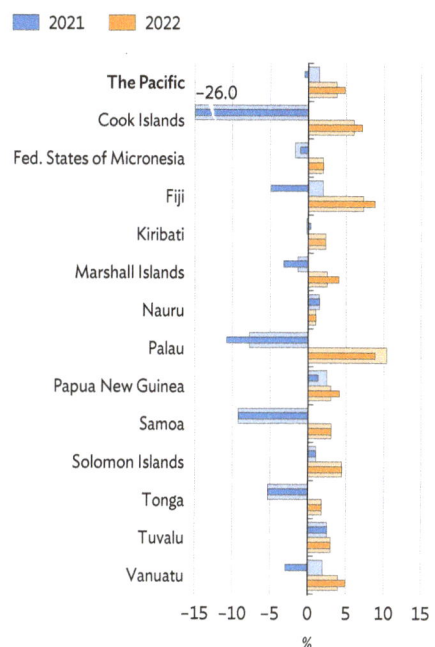

GDP = gross domestic product.
Note: Lighter colored bars are *Asian Development Outlook 2021* forecasts.
Source: *Asian Development Outlook* database.

The write-up on the Pacific economies was prepared by Edward Faber, Lily Anne Homasi, Magdelyn Kuari, Remrick Patagan, Rommel Rabanal, Cara Tinio, Isoa Wainiqolo, and James Webb of the Pacific Department of ADB, and by Prince Cruz and Noel Del Castillo, consultants to the Pacific Department.

The Pacific is projected to achieve somewhat stronger recovery in 2022 than forecast in *ADO 2021* as countries vaccinate more of their populations against COVID-19 and as borders are reopened. In PNG, a boost to GDP is seen from a full year of mineral production after the reopening of Porgera—the country's second largest gold mine—and recovery at the large Ok Tedi gold and copper mine. Growth projections for 2022 are revised up as well for Fiji, where borders are expected to reopen gradually with tourism restarting in earnest in the second half of 2022; the Cook Islands in light of its travel bubble established with New Zealand; and Vanuatu, though a low vaccination rate poses a significant risk to the outlook for this country. However, continuing concerns about progress in tourism recovery temper the outlook for Palau.

This *Update* forecasts slightly lower subregional inflation in 2021 (Figure 3.5.2). Weaker demand is restraining price increases in Fiji, and utility subsidies have contributed to deflation in Palau and Samoa. Higher international commodity prices drive upward revisions to the outlook for PNG, Tonga, and Vanuatu, while duties on unhealthy food products have raised prices in Tuvalu. This *Update* projects faster inflation in 2022 than forecast in *ADO 2021* because commodity prices are now expected to be higher than initially thought and economic recovery is likely to contribute to increased demand.

The consolidated current account surplus of the Pacific is now projected to be 3.2 percentage points higher in 2021 than forecast in *ADO 2021* (Figure 3.5.3). In PNG, higher commodity prices have contributed to increased exports, while lower imports have reflected the impact of COVID-19 on the economy. Declining imports are similarly seen to help narrow the current account deficit in Fiji and push higher the surplus in the Marshall Islands. Meanwhile, continued bleak tourism prospects keep earnings from service exports depressed, causing larger deficits in Palau and Vanuatu.

This *Update* also forecasts a higher current account surplus in 2022 than projected in *ADO 2021*. Commodity exports from PNG are forecast to remain buoyant, though imports are expected to increase in line with economic recovery. Reopened borders and the resumption of tourism brighten service export prospects for Fiji, Tuvalu, and Vanuatu. In Palau, continued slow tourism recovery and more expensive fuel imports point to a deeper current account deficit than forecast in April.

Figure 3.5.2 Inflation in the Pacific

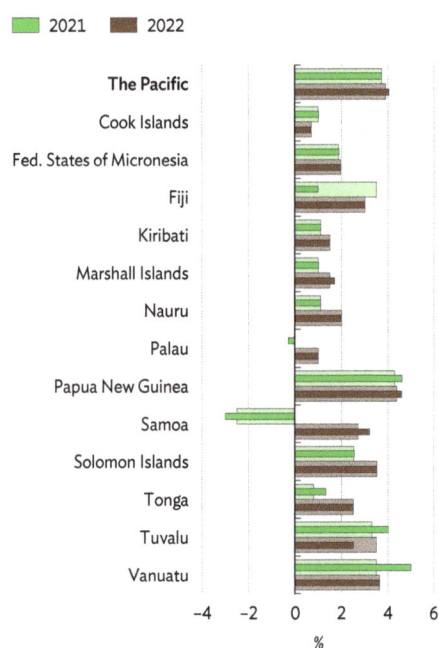

Note: Lighter colored bars are *Asian Development Outlook 2021* forecasts.
Source: *Asian Development Outlook* database.

Figure 3.5.3 Current account balances in the Pacific

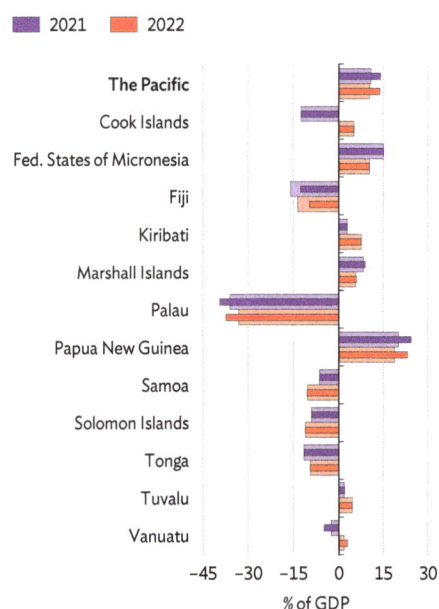

GDP = gross domestic product.
Note: Lighter colored bars are *Asian Development Outlook 2021* forecasts.
Source: *Asian Development Outlook* database.

Fiji

Economic recovery projected for 2021 in *ADO 2021* is now likely postponed to 2022 (Table 3.5.1). A second wave of COVID-19 community transmission that started in April 2021, this time the highly contagious Delta variant, dampened hope of travel resumption in the second half of 2021. The 7-day moving average of confirmed cases recorded in July 2021 exceeded not just earlier peaks in the Pacific subregion but also, weighed against population, surges in Brazil, India, the United Kingdom, and the United States. As economic costs increased under a prolonged lockdown, the government responded with less stringent containment measures than a year earlier. With the virus spreading into new areas, it is unclear when the outbreak will peak. This is likely to inhibit consumer and business confidence in a vaccination-led economic turnaround this year. By mid-August, the recorded number of new cases had dropped significantly, but this reflected a change in strategy under which health authorities focused testing on severe cases.

ADO 2021 assumed that borders would gradually reopen after midyear with pandemic-safe protocols in place and effective rollouts of vaccination programs in both Fiji and its major tourist source markets, Australia and New Zealand. This *Update* now projects that the high number of active cases locally and slow progress in vaccination in traditional tourist markets will likely delay any noteworthy improvement in tourism this year.

Improvements were noted in the primary sector in the first half of 2021, with gold production benefiting from improved efficiency and ore grade, while strong foreign demand underpinned increased exports of pine logs and woodchips. The number of building permits and completion certificates issued in the first quarter, and the value of the buildings, showed construction still on a par with 2020, though it may now be lower as a result of the current Delta outbreak. A higher economic rebound is now projected for 2022.

The impact of the tourism shock on government operating revenue restrained spending in fiscal year 2021 (FY2021, ended 31 July 2021). The fiscal deficit is estimated to equal 11.5% of GDP, lower than 15.5% projected in *ADO 2021* because of low outlays and high nontax revenue from grants and asset sales. The government received $114 million in grants from development partners and $95 million from asset sales, well above the amounts assumed in April. In light of the recently approved national budget—and of the current outbreak necessitating increased social spending and a higher frontline workforce—the fiscal deficit projection for FY2022 is revised up more than threefold from the equivalent of 5.0% of GDP in *ADO 2021* to 16.2%. As a result, outstanding debt is expected to climb from 62.3% of GDP at the end of FY2020 to 91.6% at the end of FY2022.

Table 3.5.1 Selected economic indicators in Fiji, %

	2020	2021 ADO 2021	2021 Update	2022 ADO 2021	2022 Update
GDP growth	–15.7	2.0	–5.0	7.3	8.8
Inflation	–2.6	3.5	1.0	3.0	3.0
CAB/GDP	–13.2	–15.9	–12.8	–13.5	–9.6

ADO = *Asian Development Outlook*, CAB = current account balance, GDP = gross domestic product.

Source: Asian Development Bank estimates.

Low inflation to date reflects weak internal demand and lower prices for some food products. This *Update* now downgrades the inflation forecast for 2021, but the forecast for 2022 is maintained in the expectation that these factors will revert to trend.

The merchandise trade deficit is expected to be lower than projected in *ADO 2021*, more than compensating for a higher service deficit. Lower merchandise imports have been led by mineral fuels, while exports increased. Personal remittances have remained high so far in 2021. The current account deficit is thus expected to be somewhat narrower in 2021, not substantially wider as forecast in *ADO 2021*. Further reduction in the current account deficit is projected for 2022 as payments for merchandise imports are likely to moderate while tourism inflow improves.

Papua New Guinea

The forecast for growth in 2021 is revised down from *ADO 2021* following weaker performances than expected in the large mineral and petroleum industries (Table 3.5.2). Another factor is the persistence of COVID-19, which continues to affect society, business, and the economy. Additionally, the take-up of vaccines in PNG has been very limited, which is affecting the speed of recovery.

Mining and quarrying were expected to show modest recovery in 2021, but production is now seen to fall slightly from 2020 output. The large Porgera gold mine, which operated for about 4 months in 2020 before closing when its operating license was not renewed, is likely to remain closed for much of 2021. The operator and the government have now agreed on terms for the mine to reopen, but the operator has indicated that production will resume toward the end of the year at best because of the time needed to gear up. Similarly, the Ok Tedi gold and copper mine, which was closed for 6 weeks in 2020 after a COVID-19 outbreak at the mine site, no longer appears likely to increase production in 2021 after COVID-19 and a fire in its processing facility further affected operations. Oil and gas production is also likely to contract in 2021, not stall at a plateau as earlier forecast. With the expected decline in mineral and petroleum production in 2021, the anticipated rebound in 2022 as Porgera resumes operations is likely to be greater than earlier forecast because of a base effect.

Growth outside of mining and petroleum is now seen to be weaker than earlier expected in large part because of the effect the Delta coronavirus variant is having on trade and investment partners and travel restrictions PNG is implementing in response. While there have been only a few cases of Delta reported in PNG to August 2021, if the variant were to spread widely, growth could weaken further.

Table 3.5.2 Selected economic indicators in Papua New Guinea, %

	2020	2021		2022	
		ADO 2021	Update	ADO 2021	Update
GDP growth	−3.3	2.5	1.3	3.0	4.1
Inflation	4.9	4.3	4.6	4.4	4.6
CAB/GDP	23.4	20.1	24.2	18.7	23.1

ADO = *Asian Development Outlook*, CAB = current account balance, GDP = gross domestic product.

Source: Asian Development Bank estimates.

The vaccination rate in PNG is among the lowest in the world, with fewer than 2% of adults inoculated by late August. Rates are likely to remain low because of pervasive vaccination hesitancy and the administrative challenges posed by vaccine rollout.

Inflation projections for 2021 and 2022 are revised up from earlier forecasts in *ADO 2021*. Prices increased by 3.0% in the first 6 months of 2021, led by rising outlays for food, fuel, and education. Prices for vegetables increased by 17.5% in the period, for fruit by 6.5%, and for meat by 4.8%. Diesel and petrol prices were 24% higher, reflecting upswings in global commodity prices. Education prices rose on increased school fees. Price pressure is expected to remain as the pandemic continues to affect domestic and international supply chains and other business costs.

Forecasts for current account surpluses in 2021 and 2022 are revised up from *ADO 2021* largely because of higher commodity prices. The forecast for imports of goods and services in 2021 is revised down in line with the weaker growth outlook. In light of difficult business conditions in PNG, dividend payments to investors overseas are now expected to fall below earlier estimates, resulting in a smaller deficit on the income account balance than earlier believed.

With business conditions likely to remain challenging, government revenue probably will not meet projections, which will put additional pressure on the 2021 fiscal deficit. Expenditure cuts may therefore be required if the government is to meet targets outlined in its revised medium-term fiscal strategy of a fiscal deficit equal to 7.3% of GDP and debt equal to 51.5%. Some deficit financing will likely be sourced using an allocation of special drawing rights from the International Monetary Fund.

Solomon Islands

In line with earlier expectations, growth in 2021 is expected to be led by fishing and by construction on the Tina River Hydropower Project and for the Pacific Games in 2023. While the fish catch in the first half of 2021 increased by 18.2% year on year, contraction beset public services and logging, as projected.

A decline in log output by 18.7% year on year in the first half of 2021 has hit government revenue, with customs revenue estimated to have fallen by 7.7% in the period. Further, grants from development partners are expected to be substantially lower, and total revenue is projected to decline by 2.7%. However, cuts in public services in the 2021 budget contribute to a projected 8.7% reduction in expenditure, so the fiscal deficit is seen to fall by almost half from SI$622 million in 2020, equal to 5.1% of GDP, to SI$329 million this year.

Table 3.5.3 Selected economic indicators in Solomon Islands, %

	2020	2021		2022	
		ADO 2021	Update	ADO 2021	Update
GDP growth	−4.5	1.0	1.0	4.5	4.5
Inflation	3.0	2.5	2.5	3.5	3.5
CAB/GDP	−1.7	−9.0	−9.0	−11.0	−11.0

ADO = *Asian Development Outlook*, CAB = current account balance, GDP = gross domestic product.

Source: Asian Development Bank estimates.

Projections for 2021 and 2022 remain critically dependent on the government's ability to prevent the local transmission of the virus. All of the 20 COVID-19 cases to date, now fully recovered, were repatriates, mainly students and athletes. With cases rising in neighboring Pacific economies, the government has extended a state of public emergency to November 2021.

Vaccination rollout has been slow. Despite having enough COVID-19 vaccines for 21% of the targeted adult population, as of 30 July only 8.7% had received at least one dose and 2.5% two doses. To hasten uptake, the government ordered mandatory vaccination for all workers in the public sector, including state-owned enterprises, and for frontline private-sector employees and their families. Workers risk losing their jobs if they are not vaccinated by November 2021. The government aims to fully vaccinate 80% of adults by 28 February 2022.

Despite deflation in the first half of 2021, the earlier projection of positive but low inflation in 2021 as a whole is unchanged from *ADO 2021*, as is the forecast for higher inflation in 2022 (Table 3.5.3). The overall price index declined by 2.4% in the first quarter of 2021 and 1.5% in the second quarter, with lower deflation reflected more in the imported price index. Inflation in the second half of 2021 is expected to be driven mainly by higher international fuel and food prices. With the Central Bank of Solomon Islands maintaining accommodative policies to support economic recovery, the money supply and private sector credit are seen to increase over the rest of this year.

The current account deficit widened to the equivalent of 4.2% of GDP in the first quarter of 2021. Exports fell by 19.2% with logs and timber down by 19.0%, minerals by 65.7%, and crops by 23.5%—and despite exports of fish soaring by 39.5%. Imports rose by 6.2% in the same period with sharp increases for basic manufactured goods and for machinery and transport equipment. With construction expected to accelerate in the second half of 2021, the current account is on track to meet *ADO 2021* forecasts of much wider deficits this year and next. The central bank reported gross foreign reserves rising by 3.3% year on year in June 2021 to SI$5.4 billion, sufficient to cover 13.7 months of imports.

Vanuatu

To counter the continuing threat from COVID-19, the government has extended a state of emergency until the end of 2021. This effectively closes Vanuatu to international visitors, further straining an ailing tourism industry and delaying several large infrastructure projects financed by development partners.

The GDP forecast for 2021 is revised down (Table 3.5.4). After steep contraction in 2020, the *ADO 2021* forecast was for recovery as trade and travel restrictions were lifted. This assumed successful vaccination rollouts in Vanuatu and its main tourist markets in Australia, New Zealand, and New Caledonia in that order, enabling the establishment of travel bubbles.

The growth forecast for 2022 is raised, largely to reflect the lower base in 2021, but its realization will depend on several factors, not least the vaccination rate in Vanuatu. Even with widespread vaccination in the main source markets, reopening may still be difficult for fear of breakthrough infections from the highly contagious Delta coronavirus variant. Any local transmission could quickly overwhelm Vanuatu's health-care system and economy.

Being free of COVID-19 has provided benefits. In August, New Zealand announced that arriving seasonal workers from Samoa, Tonga, and Vanuatu no longer need to quarantine for 2 weeks. Vanuatu has sent 1,000 workers to New Zealand since the resumption of its guestworker scheme in November 2020, and 900 more are expected by November 2021. Remittances from seasonal workers rose by 9.5% in 2020 and are projected to rise further this year. Meanwhile, limited vaccine supply has kept the vaccination rollout since June slower than expected, with only about 11.5% of the population receiving at least one dose by 29 August.

The government launched in March the Tourism Business Support Program of business survival grants, a renewable energy subsidy, and agritourism support. Following Vt5.1 billion in stimulus in 2020, the government launched in May a second stimulus package worth Vt2.1 billion, equal to 2.0% of GDP. In June, a supplementary budget of Vt1.1 billion boosted expenditure this year by 2.5%, mainly for education, infrastructure, and agricultural export assistance. This increase is supported by grants from development partners.

Government spending fell by 6.3% year on year in the first half of 2021, mainly reflecting a 42.9% decline in capital expenditure as major infrastructure projects were further deferred to 2022. Although wages and salaries, and use of goods and services increased; subsidies, grants, and transfers from the national government declined significantly. Revenue fell by 0.9% as a 63.9% increase in grants did not fully compensate for 5.8% lower tax receipts and 19.4% lower nontax revenue, mainly from honorary citizenship programs. Nontax revenues provided more than 40% of revenue in 2020 but suffered due to correspondent banking issues this year. A fiscal deficit equal to 2.0% of GDP is projected.

Inflation remained elevated at 5.5% year on year in the first quarter of 2021—lower than the 6.1% average in the previous 3 quarters but above the 0%–4% target set by the Reserve Bank

Table 3.5.4 Selected economic indicators in Vanuatu, %

	2020	2021		2022	
		ADO 2021	Update	ADO 2021	Update
GDP growth	–8.5	2.0	–3.0	4.0	5.0
Inflation	5.3	3.5	5.0	3.7	3.7
CAB/GDP	1.3	–2.5	–5.0	1.8	3.0

ADO = *Asian Development Outlook*, CAB = current account balance, GDP = gross domestic product.

Source: Asian Development Bank estimates.

of Vanuatu, the central bank. With the lingering impact of Cyclone Harold on food supply, food prices rose by 11.7%, while prices for alcoholic beverages and tobacco increased by 3.8%. The forecast for inflation in 2021 is revised up in light of higher international food and fuel prices but still slightly lower than inflation in 2020. The money supply rose by 4% to June 2021 as the central bank kept monetary policy accommodative. Credit to the private sector continues to fall, down in June by 1.8% from a year earlier.

Lower exports of copra, kava, and beef drove merchandise exports down by 29.7% year on year in the first quarter of 2021, while imports rose by 8.7%, mainly on higher fuel and machinery imports. With lower visitor arrivals, crop exports, and honorary citizen revenue, a wider current account deficit is now projected for 2021, but with a higher surplus restored in 2022. The central bank reported official reserves at $65.7 billion in June 2021, up by 8.3% from a year earlier and providing cover for 12.7 months of imports.

Central Pacific economies

All three island economies in the Central Pacific are projected to expand in 2021. The forecast for Kiribati is upgraded to marginal growth. Meanwhile, GDP growth forecasts for Nauru and Tuvalu are unchanged, as are most other forecasts for primary economic indicators across the Central Pacific. Exceptions are inflation forecasts for Tuvalu, now revised up for 2021 and down for 2022. Forecasts for current account balances in Kiribati and Tuvalu see surpluses narrowing somewhat this year and rebounding in 2022.

Kiribati

Modest GDP growth is now expected in 2021, slightly slower than in 2020 (Table 3.5.5). Higher growth in 2022 remains as projected in *ADO 2021*. Although travel restrictions will continue to constrain construction and disrupt outbound seafarers and seasonal workers, the government's social protection spending, equal to 17.8% of GDP, is expected to increase household income and other domestic consumption. Growth is forecast to accelerate in 2022, supported by pandemic response measures including a COVID-19 vaccination program, as well as by the implementation of high-value infrastructure projects supported by the government and development partners.

The fiscal deficit in 2021 is expected to widen, reflecting the $14.5 million supplementary budget approved at the end of August this year. The deficit will be financed by cash reserves and a drawdown of $28.6 million from the Revenue Equalization Reserve Fund. Tax revenue is expected to equal 18.7% of GDP in 2021, sustaining receipts similar to 2020.

Table 3.5.5 Selected economic indicators in Kiribati, %

	2020	2021		2022	
		ADO 2021	Update	ADO 2021	Update
GDP growth	0.6	−0.2	0.3	2.3	2.3
Inflation	1.0	1.1	1.1	1.5	1.5
CAB/GDP	3.9	2.8	2.8	7.5	7.5

ADO = Asian Development Outlook, CAB = current account balance, GDP = gross domestic product.
Source: Asian Development Bank estimates.

The fiscal forecast for 2022 is unchanged. The lifting of travel restrictions, anticipated in the first quarter of 2022, promises to drive recovery in fishing revenue, which can be used to support the resumption of large infrastructure projects.

Projections for inflation in 2021 and 2022 are unchanged, but risks to these forecasts may arise from upward movement in prices for food and fuel on account of higher shipping costs and other supply disruption.

Kiribati is still projected to post surpluses in its current account, somewhat narrower in 2021 but rebounding sharply in 2022, as forecast in *ADO 2021*.

Nauru

Forecasts for Nauru are unchanged from *ADO 2021*, with economic growth estimated to have accelerated in fiscal year 2021 (FY2021, ended 30 June 2021). Growth is still expected to slow in FY2022 as public spending falls. Forecasts for modest inflation are likewise unchanged (Table 3.5.6).

As operations wind down in the Regional Processing Center, government revenue is projected to decline by 14.3% in FY2022, with tax revenue forecast to fall by 40.8% due to lower income and business tax collection. Nontax revenue, which includes fishing license fees, is projected to increase by 3.9%.

Expenditure is forecast to decline by 11.3% in FY2022 as the government scales down pandemic-related support for households and state-owned enterprises. Public sector compensation is set to rise by 20.8% even as capital expenditure falls by 22.5%. The overall fiscal balance will depend largely on the realization of a loan for aircraft purchases.

Almost all adults in Nauru have been fully vaccinated against COVID-19, and the government hopes to establish travel bubbles with Australia and other tourist markets. However, with 40% of the population below the age of 18 and therefore still unvaccinated, the government is exploring options for acquiring vaccines for this group. To date, Nauru remains free of COVID-19.

Tuvalu

Growth forecasts for Tuvalu in 2021 and 2022 remain unchanged from *ADO 2021* (Table 3.5.7). While geographical isolation and dispersed population remain key constraints on long-term growth, they have shielded the economy from the direct impacts of COVID-19, allowing the government to continue to pursue its development goals.

In its 2021 budget, the government provided for expenditure equivalent to 160.7% of GDP on the long-term development plan, much of it on imports. It targets continued infrastructure spending with capital spending reverting close to its pre-pandemic average equal to 37% of GDP.

Table 3.5.6 Selected economic indicators in Nauru, %

	2020	2021		2022	
		ADO 2021	Update	ADO 2021	Update
GDP growth	0.8	1.5	1.5	1.0	1.0
Inflation	0.9	1.1	1.1	2.0	2.0
CAB/GDP	4.2	...	...	...	...

... = unavailable, ADO = Asian Development Outlook, CAB = current account balance, GDP = gross domestic product.
Source: Asian Development Bank estimates.

Table 3.5.7 Selected economic indicators in Tuvalu, %

	2020	2021		2022	
		ADO 2021	Update	ADO 2021	Update
GDP growth	1.0	2.5	2.5	3.0	3.0
Inflation	1.6	3.3	4.0	3.5	2.5
CAB/GDP	3.8	1.9	1.9	4.5	4.5

ADO = Asian Development Outlook, CAB = current account balance, GDP = gross domestic product.
Source: Asian Development Bank estimates.

A balanced budget is projected for 2021 with higher revenue expected from fishing license fees and grants from development partners. However, Tuvalu is projected to post a fiscal deficit equal to 15.6% of GDP in 2022 as nontax revenue falls by 20.9%.

The inflation projection for 2021 is revised up from *ADO 2021*, reflecting structural increases in duties on unhealthy food products. Meanwhile, the projection for inflation in 2022 is lowered as the one-off impact from these duty changes on consumer prices is expected to wane, as is inflation in trade partners.

The current account is projected to remain in surplus in 2021 and 2022, supported by stable fishing license revenue and budget support from development partners. A higher surplus is expected in 2022 than in 2020 in line with anticipated improvement in tourism income as international travel recovers.

North Pacific economies

The economic outlook over the near term is revised across the North Pacific, reflecting variation in impact from the pandemic and prospects for reopening across the three economies. Although a milder decline is expected for the Federated States of Micronesia (FSM) in fiscal year 2021 (FY2021, ends 30 September 2021), steeper contractions are seen in the Marshall Islands and Palau. Subsequent recovery will be determined by the pace of vaccination and border reopening in the FSM and Marshall Islands, both of which are still preparing to welcome visitors. In Palau, disruption to a phased border reopening suggests a more muted recovery than earlier forecast for this tourism-dependent island economy.

Federated States of Micronesia

Compared with *ADO 2021* estimates in April, this *Update* projects a milder decline in the GDP of the FSM in FY2021 but no change to the forecast for tepid recovery in FY2022 (Table 3.5.8). The economic fallout from the pandemic has been severe, and, consistent with earlier projections, the private sector has borne the brunt of border closures and public health restrictions, with reduced economic activity in hotels and restaurants, transportation and communication, and wholesale and retail trade. However, the government, with assistance from international partners, has responded with a number of pandemic mitigation programs worth $75 million, equal to about a fifth of GDP in the 2-year period of FY2021 and FY2022.

The Tourism Sector Mitigation Relief Fund supported tourism through subsidies for wages and payments of loan interest, taxes, and social security contributions. Workers in the formal sector received unemployment assistance under the US Coronavirus Aid, Relief, and Economic Security Act.

Table 3.5.8 Selected economic indicators in the Federated States of Micronesia, %

	2020	2021 ADO 2021	2021 Update	2022 ADO 2021	2022 Update
GDP growth	-3.9	-1.8	-1.1	2.0	2.0
Inflation	1.6	1.9	1.9	2.0	2.0
CAB/GDP	21.6	15.0	15.0	10.2	10.2

ADO = Asian Development Outlook, CAB = current account balance, GDP = gross domestic product.
Note: Years are fiscal years ending on 30 September of that year.
Source: Asian Development Bank estimates.

Meanwhile, the COVID-19 Pandemic Relief Option of the Asian Development Bank provided concessional financing for businesses and financial assistance to vulnerable households through targeted cash transfers, subsidies, and sector-specific grants. Finally, the country's programs to mitigate health risks under the FSM COVID-19 Response Framework supported public health expenditure, mostly to pay for imports of personal protective equipment, medicines, and ventilators.

The growth forecast for FY2022 remains unchanged. Although restrictions on travel and trade are expected to be maintained throughout this year, a favorable outcome is foreseen for the renewal of economic assistance under the Compact of Free Association with the US. Despite an early COVID-19 vaccination rollout, progress on immunization has been slower than expected, and the authorities maintain a cautious stance on reopening to international travel.

The national government's fiscal position is projected to remain stable in light of steady fishing license royalties, only minor impact from the pandemic on domestic revenue collection, and support from development partners to cover the government's additional spending needs. The fiscal surplus is expected to narrow in FY2022 as the government draws down accumulated reserves and unspent grants.

The outlook for inflation and current account surpluses in FY2021 and FY2022 remains unchanged from *ADO 2021*.

Marshall Islands

Growth forecasts for the Marshall Islands are revised from *ADO 2021*, projecting deeper contraction in FY2021 and faster expansion in FY2022 (Table 3.5.9). Borders are set to remain closed for all of FY2021, which has constrained the availability of inputs for construction. A continued decline in fisheries over the current fiscal year has weighed down related manufacturing and transport services.

Reopening is anticipated to begin in earnest in FY2022, after the population has been immunized against COVID-19. Recovery in fisheries, tourism, and related businesses such as manufacturing, onshore fishery support services, and wholesale and retail trade is now forecast to drive faster growth than was projected in *ADO 2021*. However, construction is expected to continue to shrink as access to inputs remains constrained. The pace of COVID-19 vaccination will significantly influence growth prospects. As of 31 August 2021, 67% of the adult population had been fully inoculated, but this progress is concentrated in the major urban centers of Majuro and Ebeye. The vaccine rollout for the outer islands has been more challenging, with only 24% of the adult population in these areas fully vaccinated so far.

The FY2021 inflation projection is retained from *ADO 2021* as higher international food and fuel prices have offset lower

Table 3.5.9 Selected economic indicators in the Marshall Islands, %

	2020	2021		2022	
		ADO 2021	Update	ADO 2021	Update
GDP growth	-2.6	-1.4	-3.3	2.5	4.0
Inflation	0.3	1.0	1.0	1.5	1.7
CAB/GDP	13.4	8.2	8.7	5.6	6.0

ADO = *Asian Development Outlook*, CAB = current account balance, GDP = gross domestic product.

Note: Years are fiscal years ending on 30 September of that year.

Source: Asian Development Bank estimates.

domestic demand, but the FY2022 forecast is increased in the expectation that domestic demand will rise with economic recovery. This *Update* projects wider current account surpluses for the Marshall Islands than did *ADO 2021*, largely because of lower imports for construction.

Palau

Contraction in FY2021 is now expected to be deeper than projected in April (Table 3.5.10). Nearly the entire adult population has been vaccinated, but a travel bubble established with Taipei,China was less successful than expected and suspended in mid-May. Over its 7 weeks in operation, the bubble brought fewer than 300 tourists into Palau—only 2% of total pre-pandemic arrivals during the months of April and May—with high costs and stringent health surveillance requirements dampening demand.

A subsequent relaxation of restrictions allows entry for fully vaccinated travelers or registered tourists who will receive vaccination on arrival, and the travel bubble with Taipei,China was resumed in mid-August. However, these developments are unlikely to fuel any significant recovery in tourism in the near term, particularly as global risks intensify with the spread of the Delta variant. With tourism recovery now likely to be slower than expected in April, this *Update* downgrades the economic outlook to deeper contraction in FY2021 and more muted recovery in FY2022.

Declining utility costs over the first 3 quarters of FY2021, partly reflecting expanded government subsidies to assist households adversely affected by the economic downturn, motivate a revision to the outlook from zero consumer inflation to slight deflation in FY2021. However, rising import prices, in particular for imported fuel, and a more subdued outlook for tourism receipts translate into forecasts for wider current account deficits in FY2021 and FY2022 than projected in *ADO 2021*, but with the deficit still narrowing somewhat in FY2022.

South Pacific economies

As projected in *ADO 2021*, the Cook Islands economy is estimated to have contracted sharply in fiscal year 2021 (FY2021, ended 30 June 2021). The Cook Islands growth forecast in FY2022 is now revised up from the earlier projection as tourist arrivals gradually recover with the establishment of a travel bubble with New Zealand—though a recent outbreak in New Zealand shows how fragile these arrangements can be. The GDP outlook for Samoa and Tonga remains unchanged. Samoa saw a slightly steeper decline in FY2021 consumer prices than projected, with a corresponding upward adjustment to the FY2022 inflation forecast.

Table 3.5.10 Selected economic indicators in Palau, %

	2020	2021		2022	
		ADO 2021	Update	ADO 2021	Update
GDP growth	-10.3	-7.8	-10.8	10.4	8.8
Inflation	0.7	0.0	-0.3	1.0	1.0
CAB/GDP	-32.6	-36.0	-39.5	-33.0	-37.3

ADO = Asian Development Outlook, CAB = current account balance, GDP = gross domestic product.

Note: Years are fiscal years ending on 30 September of that year.

Source: Asian Development Bank estimates.

Meanwhile in Tonga, inflation was higher than expected for FY2021, and seen to accelerate further in FY2022 on upticks in import prices and construction.

Cook Islands

In the Cook Islands, estimated economic contraction in FY2021 was in line with the *ADO 2021* forecast (Table 3.5.11). The projection for growth in FY2022 is revised up, reflecting gradual recovery in tourist arrivals with the beginning on 17 May 2021 of quarantine-free travel (QFT) between the Cook Islands and New Zealand. Arrivals in May equaled 10.3% of year-earlier numbers, in June 37.9%, and in July 33.3%. However, the recent suspension of QFT in response to COVID-19 community transmission in New Zealand will affect growth forecasts if the suspension is not resolved quickly. Further supporting recovery, 96.8% of the target population aged 16 and older is now fully vaccinated. Vaccination rollout in the Cook Islands is being implemented with assistance from New Zealand, as in Niue (Box 3.5.1). Contact tracing has been operationalized and a polymerase chain reaction laboratory set up to support efforts in the Cook Islands to track, trace, and test in-country, should any infection occur. These measures build tourist confidence and should further increase arrivals in FY2022.

The recent closure of QFT travel between Australia and New Zealand had spurred a dramatic increase in forward bookings for travelers from New Zealand to the Cook Islands, the only international destination available to those looking to escape the New Zealand winter. The main downside risk to forecasts remains the possibility of new local cases in New Zealand or the Cook Islands, which could prolong QFT suspension and rapidly unwind progress made to date. Inflation forecasts remain as reported in *ADO 2021*.

The estimated fiscal deficit in FY2021 equaled 28.5% of GDP, which was less than expected because of slightly lower government spending on wage and business subsidies than anticipated in response to COVID-19, and because a decline of 42.0% in tax revenue was somewhat less than forecast in *ADO 2021*. A fiscal deficit equal to 14.4% of GDP is projected for FY2022 as tax revenue begins to improve and support spending. The estimate of government net debt at the end of June 2020 is revised from 16.3% of GDP to 17.1%, forecast to reach 49.6% by the end of FY2022.

The outlook for the current account remains as reported in *ADO 2021*. Expected tourism recovery in FY2022 should restore the current account to a surplus.

Table 3.5.11 Selected economic indicators in the Cook Islands, %

	2020	2021		2022	
		ADO 2021	*Update*	*ADO 2021*	*Update*
GDP growth	–5.9	–26.0	–26.0	6.0	7.1
Inflation	0.7	1.0	1.0	0.7	0.7
CAB/GDP	–6.0	–12.5	–12.5	5.1	5.1

ADO = *Asian Development Outlook*, CAB = current account balance, GDP = gross domestic product.

Note: Years are fiscal years ending on 30 June of that year.

Source: Asian Development Bank estimates.

Box 3.5.1 Niue's quick path to herd immunity

For Niue, the arrival of COVID-19 vaccines in June 2021 marked a critical milestone that has opened a clear path toward safely reopening and revitalizing this tourism-dependent island economy. Before the pandemic, tourism receipts amounted to about a third of annual GDP. The pause in international tourism has severely depressed business activity, and recent trends in the ongoing downturn point to the potential for business closures that could undermine supply capacity over the long term.

However, the same structural constraints that have limited economic performance in the past facilitated a successful vaccination drive in Niue. A small population of only about 1,700 lent itself to a swift vaccine rollout, especially with low vaccine hesitancy, as evidenced by near-universal immunization against other diseases.

Further, as Niue is one small island, it does not face the logistical challenges that have slowed vaccination progress in other Pacific island countries with more dispersed populations. With assistance from New Zealand in procuring and administering COVID-19 vaccines, Niue inoculated 97% of its population aged 16 and older during about 5 weeks ending in early July, thereby achieving herd immunity.

The completion of the vaccination program will allow Niue to gradually reopen its borders. This will likely begin with the implementation of a quarantine-free travel bubble with New Zealand, reciprocating current arrangements that have permitted one-way travel from Niue to New Zealand since March 2021. Gradual but safe reopening will be the key to restarting tourism in Niue and reviving business activity.

Samoa

Tourism and related services are expected to remain weak for some time, with borders unlikely to open by the end of 2021. Political instability since an election in April stemmed from the delayed appointment of the newly elected government, now all but resolved with Samoa's Court of Appeal ruling on the election result and the outgoing prime minister conceding defeat on 26 July 2021. Despite this political crisis in the final months of the FY2021, GDP is estimated to have performed in line with the *ADO 2021* forecast, albeit with sharp contraction caused by the complete elimination of tourism receipts in the fiscal year and only sluggish implementation of public investment projects (Table 3.5.12). Remittances remained relatively strong, posting growth at 6.7% in FY2021 and partly compensating for steep contraction in economic activity.

The forecast for modest recovery in FY2022 remains as in *ADO 2021*, assuming the relaxation of emergency measures and gradual return of tourists late in the fiscal year. A recent decision by New Zealand to allow in seasonal workers without quarantine provides increased opportunities, but uptake may be hampered in the coming months by limited quarantine capacity for repatriating Samoans under current regulations. Another complication is a recent COVID-19 outbreak in New Zealand.

Deflation in FY2021 was slightly steeper than the *ADO 2021* forecast, which took into account expected food price declines and utility subsidies but not cheaper transportation. This *Update* maintains the forecast for a rebound to positive inflation in FY2022 with the removal of utility subsidies and a return to trend for food and import prices, but with the projection raised to accommodate a lower base.

Table 3.5.12 Selected economic indicators in Samoa, %

	2020	2021		2022	
		ADO 2021	Update	ADO 2021	Update
GDP growth	–3.2	–9.2	–9.2	3.1	3.1
Inflation	1.5	–2.5	–3.0	2.7	3.2
CAB/GDP	1.2	–6.4	–6.4	–10.4	–10.4

ADO = Asian Development Outlook, CAB = current account balance, GDP = gross domestic product.
Note: Years are fiscal years ending on 30 June of that year.
Source: Asian Development Bank estimates.

A fiscal deficit equal to 3.1% of GDP is estimated for FY2021, unchanged from *ADO 2021*. Lower grant commitments from development partners and an increase in government capital spending are expected to widen the fiscal deficit to 8.9% of GDP in FY2022, though this outlook depends on expenditure under the new government. The current account in FY2021 is estimated to have fallen into deficit as forecast in *ADO 2021*, largely because of the loss of tourism receipts. Remittances are still expected to moderate in FY2022 from recent highs, and imports are projected to increase in line with gradual economic recovery, causing the current account deficit to widen in FY2022.

Tonga

This *Update* confirms forecasts of deepening GDP contraction in FY2021 and modest growth in FY2022 (Table 3.5.13). Prolonged border closures are expected to continue to constrain tourism and construction, weighing down growth prospects, but remittances remain high, supporting domestic spending. Seasonal worker programs in Australia and New Zealand have performed better than expected during the pandemic, and the recent decision by New Zealand to allow quarantine-free access for seasonal workers provides additional opportunities. However, as in Samoa, the ability to take them up may be hampered in the coming months by limited quarantine capacity for repatriating Tongans under current border arrangements, and by uncertainty stemming from the recent COVID-19 outbreak in New Zealand.

The inflation estimate for FY2021 is adjusted upward from the *ADO 2021* forecast. This reflects consumer price results in the last quarter of the fiscal year driven unexpectedly high by rising import prices and increases in the indexes for transportation, food and beverages, and housing, utilities, and fuels. The projection for higher inflation in FY2022 is retained, with domestic construction and higher import prices driving inflation.

The estimated fiscal deficit in FY2021 equaled 1.1% of GDP, broadly in line with the earlier forecast. It is still expected to widen to 1.2% of GDP in FY2022 with a slight increase in public expenditure. Meanwhile, the outlook for deep current account deficits in *ADO 2021* is confirmed, the estimated result in FY2021 caused by a complete shutdown in tourism receipts. Slight improvement is still forecast for FY2022 with gradual reopening in the latter half and as remittances level off over the 2-year period.

Table 3.5.13 Selected economic indicators in Tonga, %

	2020	2021		2022	
		ADO 2021	Update	ADO 2021	Update
GDP growth	–0.8	–5.3	–5.3	1.8	1.8
Inflation	0.2	0.8	1.3	2.5	2.5
CAB/GDP	–3.8	–11.5	–11.5	–9.4	–9.4

ADO = *Asian Development Outlook*, CAB = current account balance, GDP = gross domestic product.

Note: Years are fiscal years ending on 30 June of that year.

Source: Asian Development Bank estimates.

4

STATISTICAL APPENDIX

Statistical notes and tables

This statistical appendix presents economic indicators for the 46 developing member economies in the Asian Development Bank (ADB) in three tables: gross domestic product (GDP) growth, inflation, and current account balance as a percentage of GDP. The economies are grouped into five subregions: Central Asia, East Asia, South Asia, Southeast Asia, and the Pacific. The tables contain historical data for 2018–2020 and forecasts for 2021 and 2022.

The data are standardized to the degree possible to allow comparability over time and across economies, but differences in statistical methodology, definitions, coverage, and practice make full comparability impossible. National income accounts are based on the United Nations System of National Accounts, while data on balance of payments use International Monetary Fund accounting standards. Historical data are ADB estimates variously based on official sources, statistical publications and databases, and documents from ADB, the International Monetary Fund, and the World Bank. Projections for 2021 and 2022 are generally ADB estimates based on available quarterly or monthly data, though some projections are from governments.

Most economies report by calendar year. The following report all variables by fiscal year: Afghanistan, Bangladesh, Bhutan, India, Nepal, and Pakistan in South Asia; Myanmar in Southeast Asia; and the Cook Islands, the Federated States of Micronesia, Nauru, Palau, the Republic of Marshall Islands, Samoa, and Tonga in the Pacific.

Regional and subregional averages are provided in the three tables. Averages are computed using weights derived from gross national income (GNI) in current US dollars following the World Bank Atlas method. The GNI data for 2018 are obtained from the World Bank's World Development Indicators Online. Weights for 2019 are carried over to 2022. GNI data for the Cook Islands and Taipei,China are estimated using the Atlas conversion factor.

The following paragraphs discuss the three tables in greater detail.

Table A1: Growth rate of GDP, % per year. The table shows annual growth rates of GDP valued at constant market price, factor cost, or basic price. GDP at market price is the aggregation of value added by all resident producers at producers' prices including taxes less subsidies on imports plus all nondeductible value-added or similar taxes. Constant factor cost measures differ from market price measures in that they exclude taxes on production and include subsidies. Basic price valuation is the factor cost plus some taxes on production, such as those on property and payroll taxes, and less some subsidies such as those related to labor but not to products. Most economies use constant market price valuation. Pakistan uses constant factor costs, and Fiji and Maldives use basic prices.

Table A2: Inflation, % per year. Data on inflation rates are period averages. Inflation rates are based on consumer price indexes. The consumer price indexes of the following economies are for a given city only: Cambodia is for Phnom Penh, the Marshall Islands for Majuro, Sri Lanka for Colombo, and Solomon Islands for Honiara. For Indonesia, there is a series break starting in 2019 because of a change in base year from 2012 to 2018.

Table A3: Current account balance, % of GDP. The current account balance is the sum of the balance of trade in merchandise, net trade in services and factor income, and net transfers. Sums are divided by GDP at current prices in US dollars.

Table A1 Growth rate of GDP, % per year

	2018	2019	2020	2021		2022	
				ADO 2021	Update	ADO 2021	Update
Developing Asia	**6.0**	**5.0**	**-0.1**	**7.3**	**7.1**	**5.3**	**5.4**
Central Asia	**4.5**	**4.9**	**-1.9**	**3.4**	**4.1**	**4.0**	**4.2**
Armenia	5.2	7.6	-7.4	1.8	5.2	3.0	3.5
Azerbaijan	1.5	2.5	-4.3	1.9	2.2	2.5	2.5
Georgia	4.8	5.0	-6.2	3.5	8.5	6.0	6.5
Kazakhstan	4.1	4.5	-2.6	3.2	3.4	3.5	3.7
Kyrgyz Republic	3.8	4.6	-8.6	3.5	3.5	5.0	5.0
Tajikistan	7.3	7.5	4.5	5.0	5.0	5.5	5.5
Turkmenistan	6.2	6.3	1.6	4.8	4.8	4.9	4.9
Uzbekistan	5.4	5.8	1.6	4.0	5.0	5.0	5.5
East Asia	**6.1**	**5.3**	**1.8**	**7.4**	**7.6**	**5.1**	**5.1**
Hong Kong, China	2.8	-1.7	-6.1	4.6	6.2	4.5	3.4
Mongolia	7.2	5.2	-5.3	4.8	4.6	5.7	6.0
People's Republic of China	6.7	6.0	2.3	8.1	8.1	5.5	5.5
Republic of Korea	2.9	2.2	-0.9	3.5	4.0	3.1	3.1
Taipei,China	2.8	3.0	3.1	4.6	6.2	3.0	3.0
South Asia	**6.4**	**4.2**	**-5.6**	**9.5**	**8.8**	**6.6**	**7.0**
Afghanistan	1.2	3.9	-1.9	3.0	...	4.0	...
Bangladesh	7.9	8.2	3.5	6.8	5.5	7.2	6.8
Bhutan	3.8	4.3	0.9	-3.4	-3.4	3.7	3.7
India	6.5	4.0	-7.3	11.0	10.0	7.0	7.5
Maldives	8.1	7.0	-32.0	13.1	18.0	14.0	15.0
Nepal	7.6	6.7	-2.1	3.1	2.3	5.1	4.1
Pakistan	5.5	2.1	-0.5	2.0	3.9	4.0	4.0
Sri Lanka	3.3	2.3	-3.6	4.1	3.4	3.6	3.4
Southeast Asia	**5.1**	**4.5**	**-4.0**	**4.4**	**3.1**	**5.1**	**5.0**
Brunei Darussalam	0.1	3.9	1.2	2.5	1.8	3.0	3.5
Cambodia	7.5	7.1	-3.1	4.0	1.9	5.5	5.5
Indonesia	5.2	5.0	-2.1	4.5	3.5	5.0	4.8
Lao People's Democratic Republic	6.2	4.7	-0.5	4.0	2.3	4.5	4.0
Malaysia	4.8	4.4	-5.6	6.0	4.7	5.7	6.1
Myanmar	6.4	6.8	3.3	-9.8	-18.4	...	...
Philippines	6.3	6.1	-9.6	4.5	4.5	5.5	5.5
Singapore	3.5	1.3	-5.4	6.0	6.5	4.1	4.1
Thailand	4.2	2.3	-6.1	3.0	0.8	4.5	3.9
Timor-Leste	-1.1	1.8	-8.5	3.4	2.2	4.3	4.0
Viet Nam	7.1	7.0	2.9	6.7	3.8	7.0	6.5
The Pacific	**0.8**	**4.3**	**-5.3**	**1.4**	**-0.6**	**3.8**	**4.8**
Cook Islands	8.9	5.3	-5.9	-26.0	-26.0	6.0	7.1
Federated States of Micronesia	0.2	1.2	-3.9	-1.8	-1.1	2.0	2.0
Fiji	3.8	-0.4	-15.7	2.0	-5.0	7.3	8.8
Kiribati	2.3	2.4	0.6	-0.2	0.3	2.3	2.3
Marshall Islands	3.6	0.7	-2.6	-1.4	-3.3	2.5	4.0
Nauru	5.7	1.0	0.8	1.5	1.5	1.0	1.0
Niue	6.5	5.6	...	...	...	...	...
Palau	5.8	-1.8	-10.3	-7.8	-10.8	10.4	8.8
Papua New Guinea	-0.3	5.9	-3.3	2.5	1.3	3.0	4.1
Samoa	-2.1	3.6	-3.2	-9.2	-9.2	3.1	3.1
Solomon Islands	3.0	1.2	-4.5	1.0	1.0	4.5	4.5
Tonga	0.3	0.7	-0.8	-5.3	-5.3	1.8	1.8
Tuvalu	4.3	13.9	1.0	2.5	2.5	3.0	3.0
Vanuatu	2.9	3.5	-8.5	2.0	-3.0	4.0	5.0

... = not available, ADO = Asian Development Outlook, GDP = gross domestic product.

Note: Because of the uncertain situation, no forecasts are provided for 2021 and 2022 in Afghanistan, and for fiscal year 2022 in Myanmar.

Table A2 Inflation, % per year

	2018	2019	2020	2021 ADO 2021	2021 Update	2022 ADO 2021	2022 Update
Developing Asia	**2.5**	**2.9**	**2.8**	**2.3**	**2.2**	**2.7**	**2.7**
Central Asia	**8.2**	**7.2**	**7.5**	**6.8**	**7.7**	**6.3**	**6.7**
Armenia	2.5	1.4	1.2	3.8	5.5	2.5	3.0
Azerbaijan	2.3	2.6	2.8	3.5	4.5	3.0	3.0
Georgia	2.6	4.9	5.2	5.0	9.5	3.5	4.0
Kazakhstan	6.0	5.3	6.8	6.5	6.9	6.2	6.4
Kyrgyz Republic	1.5	1.1	6.3	7.0	10.0	7.0	7.0
Tajikistan	5.4	8.0	9.4	9.0	9.5	8.0	9.0
Turkmenistan	13.2	13.0	10.0	8.0	10.0	8.0	10.0
Uzbekistan	17.5	14.6	12.9	10.0	10.0	9.0	9.0
East Asia	**2.0**	**2.6**	**2.2**	**1.5**	**1.4**	**2.2**	**2.2**
Hong Kong, China	2.4	2.9	0.3	1.3	1.5	2.0	2.0
Mongolia	6.8	7.3	3.7	6.9	6.9	8.5	8.5
People's Republic of China	2.1	2.9	2.5	1.5	1.3	2.3	2.3
Republic of Korea	1.5	0.4	0.5	1.3	2.0	1.5	1.6
Taipei,China	1.3	0.6	−0.2	1.1	1.5	1.1	1.1
South Asia	**3.7**	**5.0**	**6.5**	**5.5**	**5.8**	**5.1**	**5.1**
Afghanistan	0.6	2.3	5.6	5.0	...	4.0	...
Bangladesh	5.8	5.5	5.7	5.8	5.6	5.8	5.8
Bhutan	3.6	2.8	3.0	6.4	8.2	5.3	6.2
India	3.4	4.8	6.2	5.2	5.5	4.8	4.8
Maldives	−0.1	0.2	−1.4	3.0	2.5	2.5	2.0
Nepal	4.2	4.6	6.2	5.0	3.6	6.0	5.2
Pakistan	4.7	6.8	10.7	8.7	8.9	7.5	7.5
Sri Lanka	4.3	4.3	4.6	4.5	5.1	5.0	5.3
Southeast Asia	**2.6**	**2.1**	**1.2**	**2.4**	**2.2**	**2.4**	**2.4**
Brunei Darussalam	1.0	−0.4	1.9	0.7	1.3	0.7	0.7
Cambodia	2.5	1.9	2.9	3.1	2.9	3.0	2.7
Indonesia	3.2	2.8	2.0	2.4	1.7	2.8	2.7
Lao People's Democratic Republic	2.0	3.3	5.1	4.5	3.7	5.0	4.5
Malaysia	1.0	0.7	−1.1	1.8	2.5	2.0	2.3
Myanmar	5.9	8.6	5.7	6.2	6.2	...	...
Philippines	5.2	2.5	2.6	4.1	4.1	3.5	3.5
Singapore	0.4	0.6	−0.2	1.0	1.6	1.2	1.4
Thailand	1.1	0.7	−0.8	1.1	1.1	1.0	1.0
Timor-Leste	2.4	1.0	0.5	2.0	2.3	2.0	2.0
Viet Nam	3.5	2.8	3.2	3.8	2.8	4.0	3.5
The Pacific	**4.3**	**3.0**	**3.4**	**3.7**	**3.6**	**3.9**	**4.1**
Cook Islands	0.1	0.0	0.7	1.0	1.0	0.7	0.7
Federated States of Micronesia	1.7	−1.0	1.6	1.9	1.9	2.0	2.0
Fiji	4.1	1.8	−2.6	3.5	1.0	3.0	3.0
Kiribati	2.1	−1.8	1.0	1.1	1.1	1.5	1.5
Marshall Islands	0.8	0.1	0.3	1.0	1.0	1.5	1.7
Nauru	0.5	4.3	0.9	1.1	1.1	2.0	2.0
Niue	10.1	1.9	2.7	...	...	...	...
Palau	2.0	0.6	0.7	0.0	−0.3	1.0	1.0
Papua New Guinea	4.7	3.6	4.9	4.3	4.6	4.4	4.6
Samoa	3.6	2.2	1.5	−2.5	−3.0	2.7	3.2
Solomon Islands	3.5	1.6	3.0	2.5	2.5	3.5	3.5
Tonga	5.3	4.0	0.2	0.8	1.3	2.5	2.5
Tuvalu	2.2	3.5	1.6	3.3	4.0	3.5	2.5
Vanuatu	2.3	2.8	5.3	3.5	5.0	3.7	3.7

... = not available, ADO = Asian Development Outlook.

Note: Because of the uncertain situation, no forecasts are provided for 2021 and 2022 in Afghanistan, and for fiscal year 2022 in Myanmar.

Table A3 Current account balance, % of GDP

	2018	2019	2020	2021 ADO 2021	2021 Update	2022 ADO 2021	2022 Update
Developing Asia	**0.6**	**1.1**	**2.4**	**2.1**	**1.9**	**1.7**	**1.5**
Central Asia	**-0.2**	**-2.4**	**-3.1**	**-1.2**	**-1.2**	**-1.5**	**-1.6**
Armenia	-7.0	-7.4	-3.8	-5.8	-6.8	-5.5	-6.2
Azerbaijan	12.8	9.1	-0.5	3.9	7.0	5.5	8.1
Georgia	-6.8	-5.5	-12.5	-10.0	-9.0	-7.0	-6.5
Kazakhstan	-0.1	-4.0	-3.7	-0.5	-0.5	-1.7	-1.9
Kyrgyz Republic	-12.1	-12.1	5.2	-8.0	-8.0	-8.0	-8.0
Tajikistan	-4.4	-2.3	4.3	-2.5	-1.5	-2.5	-2.0
Turkmenistan	5.5	1.3	0.5	2.0	0.4	0.5	-0.1
Uzbekistan	-7.1	-5.8	-5.4	-4.5	-6.0	-4.0	-5.5
East Asia	**1.1**	**1.5**	**2.7**	**2.6**	**2.5**	**2.0**	**1.9**
Hong Kong, China	3.7	5.8	6.5	5.5	6.5	5.5	6.5
Mongolia	-16.7	-15.2	-5.1	-8.3	-8.7	-10.7	-10.2
People's Republic of China	0.2	0.7	1.9	1.9	1.7	1.3	1.1
Republic of Korea	4.5	3.6	4.6	4.0	4.5	3.8	4.0
Taipei,China	11.6	10.6	14.2	12.0	14.0	11.0	13.0
South Asia	**-2.6**	**-1.3**	**0.5**	**-1.0**	**-1.2**	**-1.0**	**-1.1**
Afghanistan	12.2	11.7	14.2	10.0	...	8.3	...
Bangladesh	-3.5	-1.5	-1.5	0.7	-1.1	0.8	-0.6
Bhutan	-19.1	-20.5	-12.1	-7.7	-7.7	-10.4	-10.4
India	-2.1	-0.9	1.0	-1.1	-1.1	-1.0	-1.0
Maldives	-28.4	-26.5	-29.8	-23.0	-19.0	-25.0	-20.0
Nepal	-7.1	-6.9	-0.9	-2.5	-8.0	-3.8	-5.0
Pakistan	-6.1	-4.8	-1.7	-1.0	-0.6	-2.0	-1.5
Sri Lanka	-3.2	-2.2	-1.3	-1.1	-2.8	-1.7	-2.3
Southeast Asia	**1.4**	**2.3**	**3.5**	**3.0**	**2.2**	**3.4**	**2.4**
Brunei Darussalam	6.9	6.6	4.3	8.5	6.5	10.5	10.5
Cambodia	-11.8	-15.0	-12.1	-15.6	-15.6	-12.3	-12.9
Indonesia	-2.9	-2.7	-0.4	-0.8	-0.5	-1.3	-0.9
Lao People's Democratic Republic	-13.1	-12.2	-5.8	-7.8	-6.0	-8.0	-6.5
Malaysia	2.2	3.5	4.2	4.4	5.0	4.4	3.4
Myanmar	-4.7	0.4	-2.6	-4.4	-1.5	...	...
Philippines	-2.6	-0.8	3.6	2.5	1.0	1.8	0.8
Singapore	15.4	14.3	17.6	17.0	20.0	17.0	17.0
Thailand	5.6	7.0	3.5	4.0	-1.4	6.5	2.0
Timor-Leste	-12.3	7.9	-19.6	-26.5	-27.2	-43.0	-44.2
Viet Nam	2.4	4.6	4.6	2.0	-1.0	2.5	1.5
The Pacific	**15.1**	**15.2**	**14.3**	**10.7**	**13.9**	**10.2**	**13.9**
Cook Islands	39.3	33.4	-6.0	-12.5	-12.5	5.1	5.1
Federated States of Micronesia	20.4	24.8	21.6	15.0	15.0	10.2	10.2
Fiji	-7.2	-4.8	-13.2	-15.9	-12.8	-13.5	-9.6
Kiribati	13.4	7.5	3.9	2.8	2.8	7.5	7.5
Marshall Islands	6.5	9.4	13.4	8.2	8.7	5.6	6.0
Nauru	-4.5	11.0	4.2	...	...	...	...
Niue	15.7	...	...	...	...	...	...
Palau	-15.5	-26.9	-32.6	-36.0	-39.5	-33.0	-37.3
Papua New Guinea	22.9	22.0	23.4	20.1	24.2	18.7	23.1
Samoa	1.1	3.0	1.2	-6.4	-6.4	-10.4	-10.4
Solomon Islands	-3.1	-9.9	-1.7	-9.0	-9.0	-11.0	-11.0
Tonga	-6.3	-0.8	-3.8	-11.5	-11.5	-9.4	-9.4
Tuvalu	5.0	-6.5	3.8	1.9	1.9	4.5	4.5
Vanuatu	10.2	12.3	1.3	-2.5	-5.0	1.8	3.0

... = not available, ADO = Asian Development Outlook, GDP = gross domestic product.

Note: Because of the uncertain situation, no forecasts are provided for 2021 and 2022 in Afghanistan, and for fiscal year 2022 in Myanmar.

www.ingramcontent.com/pod-product-compliance
Lightning Source LLC
Chambersburg PA
CBHW041428270326
41932CB00031B/3497